Korean-American Relations

Korean–American Relations

DOCUMENTS PERTAINING TO THE FAR
EASTERN DIPLOMACY OF THE UNITED STATES

VOLUME II

The Period of Growing Influence
1887–1895

EDITED, WITH AN INTRODUCTION,
BY SPENCER J. PALMER

UNIVERSITY OF CALIFORNIA PRESS

BERKELEY AND LOS ANGELES, 1963

UNIVERSITY OF CALIFORNIA PRESS
BERKELEY AND LOS ANGELES, CALIFORNIA

CAMBRIDGE UNIVERSITY PRESS
LONDON, ENGLAND

To WOODBRIDGE BINGHAM

Foreword

THE FIRST VOLUME of documents on Korean-American relations was published more than a decade ago. In its Introduction, George McCune and John Harrison wrote that one purpose of this series is "to make more clear the processes of American diplomacy and the record of American representatives in East Asia." Clearly, there are few countries in the world where the recent American commitment has been so substantial.

Even as that first volume was being published, American men were fighting and dying in an effort to prevent the forceful Communization of the Republic of Korea. In the decade that has followed the Korean war, American military assistance and economic aid have flowed into South Korea in extensive degree. Cultural exchange has also represented an important link between our two peoples. Thus, the United States is deeply involved in the complex problems of modernization faced by this troubled nation. And we have been always conscious— as have the Koreans—of the 38th parallel, which divides a people and a world.

When the full story of American involvement in Korea can be set forth, it may prove to be one of the most significant case studies of the strengths and weaknesses of American diplomacy in a so-called "emergent society." The culture and traditions of Korea are both ancient and rich. But in political and socio-economic terms, it must now be considered a young society, faced with the tremendous problem of experimenting to see whether economic development and any degree of political freedom can go together. The answer is not yet clear, but in all likelihood our own position in Asia will hinge in some degree upon the outcome.

Against this setting, the collection of major documents pertaining to American-Korean relations takes on additional importance. This second volume, dealing with the period between 1887 and 1895, covers a chaotic, fascinating era. Reading through these documents, one is able to capture the flavor of late-nineteenth-century Korea: the tragedy of a society that was politically sick, plagued with incompetence, ultra-conservatism, and incessant factionalism; the intrigues of the major powers that surrounded a moribund state; the desperate efforts of a small group of Korean patriots to save their nation from oblivion.

In an official sense, the role of the United States during the unfolding of this drama was little more than that of sympathetic and detached onlooker. Yet, as these documents make clear, individual Americans, especially certain missionaries, had a truly extraordinary impact upon the Korean court. Perhaps it is no exaggeration to say that they were the first Westerners to be trusted, because their respect and love for Korea were apparent. As a result, the ruler of this remote kingdom turned to the United States in his hour of need, in the hope that a young, vigorous republic would help an aged, weak, and threatened monarchy. Our inability to respond is completely understandable, but one cannot avoid wondering whether this could not have been one of those truly extraordinary occasions when a people exceed themselves and seize the future. What might have been the effect upon modern Asia if the United States had answered the call of Korea in this period, and that of Sun Yat-sen a few years later?

Professor Spencer Palmer is to be congratulated for carrying on the work so well started by Professors McCune and Harrison. It is to be noted that this present volume is much larger than Volume I, containing nearly 50 per cent more documents. Each document has been carefully checked, and in all cases the work has been done from the original document so as to avoid errors. This is a work that will be useful to all scholars who wish to trace the American record in modern Asia.

ROBERT A. SCALAPINO

Preface

THIS IS THE second volume of a projected three-volume series on Korean-American relations from 1883 to 1905. Documents appearing in the first volume, *The Initial Period, 1883–1886*, illustrate the problems of that phase of the diplomatic relations.

This volume, *The Period of Growing Influence, 1887–1895*, constitutes a logical extension of the subject matter of Volume I. It completes many of the problems of the initial period yet leads to new issues of great magnitude. To aid in clarifying them, personnel tables have been prepared and are to be found in Appendixes A and B for the period of the first volume as well as of the second. Aside from that feature, this volume is designed as a self-contained unit.

I have viewed my labors as an opportunity to place before scholar and layman alike an accurate and convenient source-book on a crucial period of diplomatic history, in which Korea played a pivotal role. There has been no attempt here at extensive analysis or interpretation. Such work should follow as a natural result of this compilation.

The selection of documents for this volume was based upon the principle that nothing essential to an understanding of the American role in Korea should be omitted. I have relied primarily on microfilms of the Seoul legation archives, kindly made available to me by Mrs. Evelyn B. McCune, and on the United States National Archives films (FM 134 series), "Despatches from the United States Ministers to Korea." The legation films were taken at Seoul in 1938 by the late George M. McCune and the Honorable U. Alexis Johnson. They contain copies of most of the non-routine instructions of the Department of State to the United States ministers in Korea and of the relevant dispatches of the ministers to Washington, for the period 1883–1905. These dispatches are occasionally accompanied by enclosures of private correspondence, maps, and official letters between the U.S. diplomatic representatives in Korea, Japan, China, and Russia. A few of the letters in this collection are partially illegible, owing either to the condition of the original archives or to the photography.

The National Archives films consist of original dispatches received by the Department of State from diplomatic representatives of the United States in Korea. Many of these are accompanied by enclosure copies of exchange by the Presidents of the Korean Foreign Office and the American representatives in Seoul, copies of correspondence between American ministers and consular officials, correspondence with private individuals, and pamphlets, issues of newspapers, and other printed materials.

Other sources of tangential value, and available at the National Archives in Washington, have been Consular Dispatches, Notes from the Korean Legation, and Notes to the Foreign Ministers and Consuls in the United States from the Department of State. I have also had access to *Ku Hanmal Oekyo Munsŏ* 舊韓末外交文書 (Former Late Han Official Dispatches) Seoul: Tonga Ch'ulp'ansa, 1960, a volume of photostatic reproductions of selected letters of American ministers to the Korean Foreign Office during the years 1883–1891, exclusive of 1889. Finally, I have consulted *Foreign Relations of the United States*. A fraction of the documents printed here are available in that distinguished series. But on this point I must offer a word of caution: such documents as appear in *Foreign Relations* for the years 1887–1895 are seldom complete or faithful reproductions of the originals. The editors showed no reluctance to "clean up" the original flamboyant style of the American ministers in Korea, and whole paragraphs from letters have been deleted in their published versions without explanation. On the other hand, Appendix I, 1894, of this series, contains an excellent synopsis of American diplomacy pertaining to the Sino-Japanese war.

Materials in this second volume are both topically and chronologically arranged. That is, documents have been grouped according to their subject but appear chronologically within each subject category. Also, despite the diverse nature of the topics they tend to unfold in chronological sequence starting with 1887.

Some letters have been difficult to classify because of the heterogeneity of their subject matter. This problem underscores the present need in the scholarly community of an integrated index, not merely of the selected materials printed in the compilations of this series, but of the entire corpus of available archives documents.

The documents in this volume are cited verbatim. In the inspection of the handwritten materials, this has meant a careful effort to retain maddening inconsistencies in punctuation, romanization (e.g., Tong Hăk, Ton Hâk, Tŏng Hauk, Ton-hăk, Tonghak, etc.), capitalization, and spelling—much of which prompts me to appreciate the value of the McCune-Reischauer romanization system in a way I had not done before. Victorian salutations and endings have been omitted, as have the great bulk of routine notices from Seoul of contingent expenses, telegram accounts, interpreters' salaries, requests for office supplies, acknowledgments of dispatches received, and reports of minor legation repairs.

My research has been very rewarding. I feel I have explored an epochal period of Asian history in a unique way, observing intimate firsthand accounts of minor episodes, yet encountering as never before the comprehensive subject of the Western impingement upon the old Korean order. For this experience I owe thanks to the Institute of International Studies, University of California, Berkeley, whose research grant made this volume possible; and particularly to Thomas C. Blaisdell, Jr., Executive Secretary, who recognized the value of the project from the start, and to his Administrative Assistant, Mrs. Cleo C. Stoker; to John A. Harrison of the University of Florida, co-editor of Volume I; Evelyn B. McCune, who lent the microfilms already mentioned; John H. Jennings of the University of California Press; Mrs. Isabel Jackson and staff of the University Documents Library; Chong Soon Kim, who checked out the accuracy of Appendix B; and especially to Miss Sheila McDorney, who typed the manuscript and rendered able assistance in seeing the project to completion. I deeply appreciate the support and suggestions of Robert A. Scalapino, and of the members of the project committee: Woodbridge Bingham, chairman; Armin Rappaport; and Michael C. Rogers. Of course, I owe a lasting debt to my family—Shirley, Dwight, and Jennette.

Brigham Young University, Provo, Utah   S. J. P.

Contents

Introduction

AMERICAN POLICY in eastern Asia during the last quarter of the nineteenth century was marked by a desire to maintain a position of impartial neutrality toward the international struggle for control of the Korean peninsula. This policy was never consistently implemented in Korea, as the documents contained in this volume indicate.

The King of Korea looked upon the United States representative in Seoul as the symbol of a friendly and beneficient power capable of protecting his kingdom from multiple external pressures. He encouraged a confidential relationship with American ministers, he sought American drill masters for his armed forces, he employed American teachers to staff Korean schools, he appointed Americans to important government positions, and he stood firm on his decision to establish diplomatic offices in the United States despite determined Chinese opposition.

Furthermore, Americans in Korea frequently ignored the stated policy of home government by embroiling themselves in palace politics, generally resisting Chinese claims of suzerainty over Korea, and by 1895 many who had previously preferred Japan over China became highly critical of Japanese policy.

Korean-American diplomacy between 1887 and 1895 was fundamentally concerned with Chinese claims of a privileged position in Korea and with the use of American good offices in mediating disputes between Korea, Japan, and China. From 1885 to 1893 Japanese political influence in Korea was considerably weakened, leaving the United States as the only barrier to complete Chinese domination of the Korean government. A chain of important circumstances led up to this situation.

The Japanese-Korean treaty of 1876 and the Korean-American treaty of 1882 had recognized Korea as an independent state, giving impetus to the formation of a "progressive" group among Korean officials who, impatient of China and the Chinese system, were impressed by the technical and political advances made by a western-influenced Japan during the early Meiji period. The conservative

[1]

opposition to this reform group was divided between the party of the highly reactionary and Confucianist Taewŏngun, ex-Regent and father of the King, and that of the family of Queen Min, the King's wife. In December of 1884 the reform party, led by Kim Ok-kyun, Sŏ Jae-p'il and Hong Yong-sik, attempted to eliminate the conservative hold over the government through a coup d'etat. They pressed the King into calling upon Japanese soldiers for "protection"; thereupon he was forced to send for heads of governmental departments, who were killed on the spot.

Koreans were outraged by these events. Mobs burned the Japanese legation, and Chinese troops forced the Japanese soldiers to flee to the port of Chemulpo. Foreign representatives feared an imminent clash between China and Japan. The King telegraphed directly to Washington for the use of American good offices, but a settlement was not finally reached until April 3, 1885. This convention at Tientsin, in which Li Hung-chang and Ito Horibumi were the principal participants, provided for an indemnification for injured Japanese subjects; that both countries withdraw their troops from Korea within four months; that neither Chinese nor Japanese instructors were to train Korean soldiers; and that in the case of disorders in Korea so severe as to require the dispatch of troops by either China or Japan, written notice of such intention to dispatch troops would be sent by one to the other.

Commenting upon the results of the abortive pro-Japanese coup, George C. Foulk, American attaché at Seoul, reported to Washington that,

While Japan was formerly highly active in using her influence in the affairs of Korea, since the treaty of last April with China, she has been apparently little more than a passive observer. The new Japanese legation, now being built, is small and insignificant. The representative is a Chargé d'Affaire ad. interim. There is much to indicate that Japan has greatly altered her policy in regard to Korea, yielding much to the Chinese claim of suzerainty.[1]

Japanese willingness to recognize China's pretensions of hegemony over Korea during these years was not shared by Americans in Korea. The lack of explicit instructions from Washington no doubt contributed to the tendency of Americans in Korea to question Chinese claims. Secretary James G. Blaine wrote Minister Augustine Heard in 1889,

---

[1] No. 214, Foulk to Frelinghuysen, August 16, 1885, in George M. McCune and John A. Harrison, *Korean-American Relations: The Initial Period*, 1883–1886, (Berkeley and Los Angeles: University of California Press, 1951), I, 126.

for example, that the King of Korea was under "some form of feudal subjection to the Chinese Crown," that the functions of the Chinese agent in Korea, Yüan Shih-k'ai, "might be considered analogous to those exercised by the French resident in Madagascar or the British representative in the capital of the South African Republic," but that the Department "is not sufficiently advised on these points to instruct you positively in regard thereto."[2]

The Chinese representative bent every effort not only to place Korea under his control but also to curtail American influence in the peninsula. Consequently, George Foulk, as a leader of progressivism among the Koreans, became an early Chinese target. Yüan pressured the Korean Foreign Office into demanding his recall. Foulk was charged with having written a defamatory report "subversive and highly injurious to Korea."[3] When strongly worded protests against Foulk by Foreign Minister Kim Yun-sik failed to accomplish his removal, Yüan threatened to leave Korea altogether. The Chinese representative informed Minister Hugh Dinsmore that he could not tolerate the special treatment the King continued to give the American attaché (among other favors, he built a home for Foulk in Seoul) because Foulk was misrepresenting the nature of the traditional Sino-Korean relationship.[4]

Chinese prestige was also at stake in the "Hsim Hsin Chang" incident. In this case employees of the Chinese Telegraph Company refused to vacate a building owned by American merchant W. D. Townsend. The agent for the company insisted that his men would not leave the premises without an order from the Korean government. Repeated letters from Rockhill to the Korean Foreign Office failed to get action because "the employees in question are all Chinese subjects, and the Foreign Office is apprehensive of offending the Chinese Minister."[5] Finally Rockhill wired for a ship of war and a file of marines to effect a forceful ejection of the occupants of the house. Thereupon the Foreign Minister agreed that the telegraph employees should be removed at once.

American ministers in Korea were constantly irritated by the fact that Yüan Shih-k'ai could ride to audiences with the King in a closed chair, whereas other foreign representatives had to dismount at the

---

[2] No. 112, Blaine to Dinsmore, May 7, 1889.

[3] No. 52, Rockhill to Bayard, January 24, 1887; No. 55, Bayard to Rockhill, March 3, 1887.

[4] Yüan to Dinsmore, May 28, 1887.

[5] No. 53, Rockhill to Bayard, January 24, 1887.

palace gate and walk the 4,000-yard distance to the reception hall. When the problem was presented to the King, he ruled that the American minister be allowed the same privilege as the Chinese minister; but Washington decided that it would be inexpedient for Americans to accept any favor not extended to the diplomatic community at large—especially if in so doing, it would appear to lend to "the provocation of a question concerning the exceptional relation of Korea to China."[6]

On a rainy day in October, 1893, Yüan sent his Secretary to represent him before the King. The other foreign representatives were "all mortified to find themselves wading through mud and rain while the Chinese Consul rode past us right up to the door of the reception room."[7] The sedan-chair problem thereby assumed major proportions. Horace N. Allen, who was then serving as Chargé of the Legation, united with representatives of other Western powers in announcing that they would not attend future audiences with the King unless they were allowed to ride into the palace in sedan chairs. The Korean Foreign Office agreed to a compromise by building a closed gallery from the nearest palace gate to the reception hall.[8] However, this issue was not settled until 1894 when, as the result of Japanese policy, all foreigners were given equal protocol treatment.

The embroglio between the pro-American King and the pro-Chinese Foreign Office over the issue of establishing Korean diplomatic representation in Washington placed a great strain upon Sino-Korean relations. This was the first modern historical instance in which a Korean monarch publicly refused to follow the instructions of a Chinese emperor by sending a representative to a foreign country who functioned independent of China.

The diplomatic mission, of which Pak Chŏng-yang was designated Envoy Extraordinary and Minister Plenipotentiary, no more than reached the city walls before it was stopped "by threats of the Chinese minister."[9] Yüan informed the King that he had received a special telegraphic dispatch from the Emperor of China, through Li Hung-chang at Tientsin, ordering him to detain it. He insisted that the King must abandon his idea of establishing offices in western countries. But the King remained surprisingly steadfast in his decision. The American minister, who had maintained close contact with

---

[6] No. 39, Wharton to Heard, August 25, 1890.
[7] No. 469, Allen to Gresham, October 6, 1893.
[8] Allen to Gresham, November 4, 1893 and Joint Note, November 1, 1893.
[9] No. 53, Dinsmore to Bayard, September 30, 1887.

the King throughout the controversy, interpreted the King's decision as an American triumph.[10]

Pak exchanged his credentials with United States President Grover Cleveland at New York on January 17, 1888. After Pak's return in the spring of 1889, Yüan demanded he be punished for acting independently of the Chinese legation during his tenure in Washington.[11] Although this was never done, a promotion in rank which the King had given Pak upon his return was later withdrawn at the insistence of the Chinese representative.[12] Nevertheless, Korea retained diplomatic officers in Washington until the Japanese assumed control of Korean foreign affairs in 1905.

American missionaries exerted a particularly significant influence upon the course of events in Korea. They were a subject of constant concern for the Korean Foreign Office and American officials in Korea. Before 1891 they operated without the legal sanction of the American government and in defiance of a Korean law which prescribed punishment by death to teachers of Christian religion and slavery to their wives,[13] yet they openly conducted religious meetings, distributed literature, and organized schools, and many of them actively meddled in political affairs. Their western religion instilled subversive ideas among Korean youth in the environs of the capital, and it played an important negative role in the Tonghak movement which figured prominently in bringing on the Sino-Japanese war of 1894.[14]

Ironically no group of foreigners ever enjoyed greater intimacy at the court of an Asian state than did the American missionaries during the last quarter of the nineteenth century. Unlike their counterparts elsewhere in Asia, American missionaries in Korea largely escaped the opprobrium of the "imperialist" label; although they were western intruders they ultimately became identified with the Korean anti-Japanese nationalist movement.

Reports of conspiracy and revolt at the court, of widespread discontent among the peasantry in the countryside, and of the breakdown

---

[10] See Yüan to Dinsmore, September 30, 1887; No. 71, Dinsmore to Bayard, November 11, 1887.

[11] No. 212, Dinsmore to Blaine, December 10, 1889.

[12] No. 212, Dinsmore to Blaine, December 10, 1889; No. 213, Dinsmore to Blaine, December 24, 1889.

[13] No. 357, Heard to Blaine, January 16, 1893.

[14] See No. 381, Heard to Blaine, April 4, 1893; also, Tonghak "edicts" following.

of discipline among Korean soldiers appointed to preserve order[15] were commonplace between 1891 and 1893. It was rumored among the foreign community that an ancient prophecy of the collapse of the dynasty was approaching imminent fulfillment. Apparently Chinese ascendancy had brought nothing better than chaotic political conditions in Korea.

How much the resurgence of a strong Japanese policy in Korea after 1893 derived from the deterioration of conditions in that land, or how much of it was a reflection of the liberal-conservative struggle of the time within Japan itself, the documents do not specifically show. But that Russian advances in Korea during this period aroused the Japanese to the need of a stronger policy on Korea seems clear indeed. Japan began pressing her interests with unusual vigor. For example, the Japanese representative at Seoul in 1893 (Oishi) issued an ultimatum giving the Koreans fourteen days in which to come to terms on a long-standing bean-export case.[16] The United States offered its offices to arbitrate the incident, but it was settled mainly through Chinese mediation. Also, in the fall of 1893 the Japanese entered into a contest with the Chinese for control of the rice-export trade. The Chinese succeeded in causing the defeat of the Japanese effort to bring about the removal of the prohibition of exports on rice revealing, according to Horace Allen, that China still "rules here with a rod of iron when necessary, yet she manages to make the people kiss the hand that smites them. The Japanese on the contrary make themselves positively hated. They will in all probability push this rice export question to an ugly end . . ."[17]

Two spectacular events, the murder of Kim Ok-kyun in Shanghai on March 28, 1894,[18] and the dispatch of Chinese troops to Korea to suppress a rebellion of the Tonghaks on June 6 of the same year, brought on a crisis as a result of which Japan embarked on war with China and on a single-handed effort to force "reform" in Korea. Invoking the provisions of the Tientsin Convention of 1885, the Japanese landed troops at Chemulpo within a fortnight of Chinese troop landings. The Koreans became terribly alarmed. The King begged the Chinese to leave, but they refused to do so as long as the Japanese remained. The American minister blamed the Chinese for

---

[15] See No. 220, Heard to Blaine, December 3, 1891.
[16] See No. 376, Heard to Foster, March 27, 1893; and No. 396, Heard to Foster, May 6, 1893.
[17] No. 504, Allen to Gresham, December 20, 1893.
[18] Details are found in No. 551, Allen to Gresham, April 6, 1894.

the difficulties, but placed primary responsibility on the Korean government for "prostituting the competitive examinations by selling rank openly, and for such high prices, that officials are not only encouraged, but compelled to grind the last cash, or its equivalent, from the people."[19] There would have been no rebellion against the government in the countryside, and hence no *casus belli* between China and Japan, had the Korean government been willing to initiate reform.

Washington instructed Sill to use "every possible effort for the preservation of peaceful conditions." Korean Foreign Minister Cho called upon Sill and the other foreign representatives to prevail upon Japan to withdraw her troops—that China had given assurances she would then follow suit. The representatives of the United States, Russia, France, and England, joined in sending an appeal to Yüan and Ōtori, the Japanese minister, that their troops be simultaneously removed. Ōtori responded by informing the Korean King that radical changes would have to be made in his governmental policy, such changes to be made upon consultation with the Japanese authorities, before Japanese troops would be withdrawn. Sill did not conceal his feeling that the Japanese should be supported in their policy. "She seems only to desire, once for all," he wrote, "to throw off the yoke of Chinese Suzerainty and then to assist her small neighbor in strengthening her position as an independent state, by aiding her in such reforms as shall bring peace, prosperity and enlightenment to her people—a motive which pleases many Korean officials of the more intelligent sort, and one which, I imagine, will not meet with disapproval in America."[20]

By July, 1894, Japan was eager for a showdown with China. Her one policy was to oust the Chinese from Korea by force.

With the signing of the Treaty of Shimonoseki in April, 1895, the fate of the Yi dynasty became tied to the struggle for supremacy in northeast Asia between Russia and her allies on the one hand and Japan and her allies on the other. The predominance of China in Korean affairs was replaced by that of Japan, and nominally independent Korea became a cockleshell on the dips and swells of Japanese power. Her future now depended not so much on the course of her internal development as on the outcome of the contest for military and commercial supremacy in the area between Japan

---

[19] No. 14, Sill to Gresham, June 18, 1894.
[20] No. 16, Sill to Gresham, June 29, 1894.

and Russia. Deprived of the true direction of her own affairs and steadily descending into political and economic chaos, Korea's story becomes tragic, and even shameful.

At the conclusion of the Sino-Japanese war, China recognized the "full and complete independence and autonomy of Korea." The liberation of Korea from Chinese dominion had long been a Japanese desire, but such altruism as might have been behind this is hardly discernible in the subsequent destruction of that independence and autonomy by Japan, ably assisted by other powers. After the war and the retirement of China, the Japanese representative, Ōtori, busied himself in the personal direction of Korean politics. He took possession, figuratively, of the King, who was the focus of nationalism and authority in Korea. He dictated the appointment of pro-Japanese officials to the Cabinet, and he favored the former regent of the Kingdom, Taewŏngun. By promoting the ambitions of this man, the Japanese representative at Seoul incurred the opposition of practically every faction in Korea. Tokyo recognized the danger of this state of affairs and Ōtori was recalled and replaced by Count Inouye Kaoru, one of the great men of the Meiji Restoration. But while Inouye removed all power from the Taewŏngun and his clique, he tended to a course similar to that started by Ōtori. Antagonism against Japan grew in hapless Korea, but no effective intervention was made in her behalf. In two months' time Inouye was replaced by Viscount Miura Gorō, whose initial step was to help eliminate the most powerful anti-Japanese force in the Kingdom—namely, Queen Min. In October, 1895, Japanese gangsters, protected by Japanese regular troops, invaded the Royal Palace and murdered the Queen.[21] The King was placed under what amounted to house arrest and a new Government appointed, completely subservient to the interests of Japan. The American community in Korea, several of whom were serving as palace guards at the time, was "deeply grieved" and felt "the surest support to progressive ideas had been removed." The murder of Queen Min marked the beginning of a new period in American relations with Korea, and the Japanese rise to ultimate supremacy in northeast Asia.

---

[21] A lengthy account of the details of the murder was filed in No. 156, Allen to Olney, October 10, 1895.

1.

THE EQUIVOCAL SINO-KOREAN RELATIONSHIP

Legation of the United States
                                      Söul, Korea, May 27th 1887

Secretary of State

Sir:

To my mind it appears that Korean political affairs are gradually approaching a crisis. China is slowly but surely tightening her grasp upon this government and its King. A spirit of resistance seems almost to have died out of the Koreans and there is an apparent acquiescence on the part of a number of foreign representatives. One at least, H. B. M.'s Consul General is quite outspoken in his declaration that Korea is a vassal state and altogether incapable of self-government. From the tone of the public press of Japan it would seem that even that government has almost decided to allow the absorption of Korea by the Chinese without opposition from her. Nichi Nichi Shinbun of March 7th in a discussion of the Korean status, amongst other things, says: "Should therefore the closeness of the two countries China and Korea lead the Korean authorities to ask for the formal incorporation of Korea into Chinese territory as an outer province, it is probable that no foreign power would object. . . . Leaving Russia's case which is of a special nature aside, in reply to the question as to how such an event would affect Japan, we have no hesitation in saying that whether Korea maintains her independence or becomes a part of China is a matter of comparatively little concern to us. We should of course like best of all to see Korea a strong progressive and independent power, able by virtue of her natural position to hold both Russia and China in check, but as things now are she has the name of an independent country without the reality: She is going down hill with no probability of being able to recover herself and therefore rather than that she should be exposed to the risk of attack by some strong power it is better for her to become an outer province of China."

And concludes by remarking, "If matters in Korea come to a crisis Japanese politicians ought to make up their minds to have nothing more to do with that country." Japan continues her work of fortifying the island of Tsushima but that she would do in any event.

The Japanese representative here so far as I am able to observe regards the increasing encroachments of the Chinese with apparent indifference.

The Koreans do not impress me as having any affection or strong attachment for the Chinese. On the contrary there is among the common people a well-defined dislike for them, but they fear them and it is under the influence of this fear that they are gradually yielding to Chinese supremacy. As you are ~~doubtless~~ aware it is now but a very few years since Chinese intercourse with Korea was limited to the observance of their ancient mutual rites and ceremonies as "brother countries," and no Chinaman was allowed even a temporary residence on Korean soil; now China "the elder Brother" avails himself of the excuse that it is necessary for him to have officials on the ground with a view of protecting his "Younger brother" from the dangers of association with foreign powers, which association he has been largely instrumental in bringing about.

The Chinese representative memorializes, provides, dictates and directs, all under a system of intimidation mixed with affectation of disinterested Kindness.

Whereas the accredited agent of a treaty power under a very proper regulation of eastern etiquette on going to an audience with the King dismounts from his chair without the gates of the palace and is conducted on foot through the numerous inner gates to the audience chamber, "His Imperial Chinese Majesty's Resident" goes in his chair with a retinue of soldiers and coolies to the very threshhold of the audience chamber and into the actual presence of the King. The Koreans at first protested against this but have yielded a sickly acquiescence as I am informed.

By a private letter from Mr. Rockhill at Pekin to Lieutenant Foulk I learn that there is more or less excitement amongst Chinese officials, and a growing fear lest Korea through the influence and moral support of her treaty friends may assert independence, and they are discussing the rumors about Lieutenant Foulk which I have the honor to communicate to you in my dispatches Nos. 14 and 16 of the 3rd and 9th of the present month.

On the 14th instant, Admiral Ting commanding the Pü Yang or Northern squadron of the Chinese Navy arrived in Chemulpo with four ships of war. He called on me on the 16th and in the course of conversation told me that he had left two large iron Clads at Port Hamilton.

He sailed on the 18th and told Commander Miller of the Marion USS on the eve of his departure that he would return to Chefoo picking up his iron Clads by the way. Port Hamilton is on the route from Japan to the Korean capital rather than from China but there may be no significance in his visiting the island. The Chinese lights were sighted in the harbor at Port Hamilton by the Marion as she passed in the night.

While in Söul the Admiral was entertained for a day at the palace, and a dinner was given by Mr. Yuan the Chinese representative to which there were none invited save Korean and Chinese guests, the Tai Wan Kun the King's father being of the former.

On the next evening another dining was given by Mr. Yuan to which all the foreigners of high and low degree were invited excepting Lieutenant Foulk and two or three Missionaries. I having incurred a lameness from a slight accident on the day before did not attend.

The foreign office is absolutely under Chinese control insomuch that the Royal pleasure does not seem to be consulted concerning any of the affairs of state of great importance and I am inclined to believe that at some time they act against his desire. The president in a dispatch to me discloses it to be the will of the King that Lieut Foulk should leave Korea, while I have reliable assurance that his wish is quite the reverse.

Under a sentiment of humanity I cannot but hope that in the fitness of things the time may come when we may see this country free and unrestrained that they make work out their own national establishment, but all in all, at this time the prospect for Korean independence is gloomy.

HUGH A. DINSMORE

NO. 30   *Confidential*   Legation of the United States
Söul, Korea, June 21st, 1887

Secretary of State

Sir:

As mentioned in my despatch No. 29 under date of the 20th instant Prince Min Yong Ik arrived in this city on the 14th instant after an absence for almost a year in China. Upon his coming he was greeted with many honors by his people. Besides the officials sent by the king to receive him it is said that more than a thousand people went from Söul to Chemulpo to welcome his return.

Much interest attaches to this man in Korea beyond that which naturally springs from his being the first Prince of the land after the Crown Prince. The evil fate which has attended him for so long having driven him twice to seek refuge from dangers in other lands, and subjected him to the murderous assault of the conspirators in 1884, and left him long a wanderer, has excited conflicting sentiments in the people, and has told severely upon him.

He seems to have awakened at last to the real dangers that are impending to his country and is greatly concerned.

Since his arrival he has been twice to see me, each time spending a long while in earnest conversation at times accompanied by tears, about the condition of Korea and troubles which oppress the King. The greatest trouble now arises from a fear entertained with what reason I do not know, both by himself and the King that a conspiracy was inaugurated last year, and was failed of the purpose $\wedge$ tempo- rarily, by the adjustment of the affairs of last August, between the Chinese, the Tai Wen Kun and a few other Koreans under their following, notably Kim Yun Sik, to depose the King, destroy the Mins, and place a younger son of the Tai Wen Kun on the throne. Min's belief is that the Koreans suspected to be engaged in this scheme are convinced that it merely means a change from one brother to another as King, hoping to have a regent for the younger brother possibly the Tai Wen Kun again himself, but he is firmly convinced that the Chinese are merely using these people to incite a revolution out of which they may seize the country, and establish here an outer prov- ince of China dominated wholly by Chinese. He has warned me and the Russian representative also that there is danger to foreigners, claiming that if his fears are realized, and the effort made, while the policy of the revolutionists will be to protect foreigners from harm, yet the followers of the Tai Wen Kun knowing his long and great dislike of foreigners, will be disposed to destroy them, as they were taught by him to do in the past, and in the excitement of the time get beyond control.

He begs me to advise him what course to pursue, and asks me if there is no help. I have said to him that I could not take the responsi- bility of offering advice further than to say that he should not become excited, and that their future must depend largely if not entirely upon their own prudence, wisdom and courage. He replied "we are too weak to cope with China and can do nothing without assistance from without."

The situation is sad, absolutely pitiable, for while he talks thus to me, and His Majesty's trusted servants dare to express to one or two of us in whom they confide their sincere opinions, still they keep up, must do so, the outward forms of deference, and Prince Min calls almost daily on Yuan Sü Kwai the Chinese representative; and the king dares not to undertake enforcement of his own authority.

I should not be surprised to see trouble come at any time, it may not do so, but the absorption process go on [sic] gradually, until nothing is left of Korea.

But in any event I cannot feel that at this day there can be any great danger to foreigners, and I have no alarm for our people. Nevertheless a ship should be Kept at Chemulpo all the time until there is a change in the situation favorable to quiet and safety.

HUGH A. DINSMORE

NO. 112

Department of State
Washington May 7, 1889

Hugh A. Dinsmore

Sir:

Your despatches Nos 168 and 169 relate to the efforts made to enlist the active participation of the Diplomatic Body resident at Seoul in a movement for the relief of Sufferers from the famine which has afflicted the Southern Provinces of Corea. Your No 169 reports the attitude of the Chinese Resident, Mr. Yuan Sie Kwai, who declined to join in the meeting of foreign residents which you had called for the purpose in question, on the ground that in the Event of a famine prevailing in Corea, the King would memorialize the Emperor of China for relief, and that this circumstance made it unnecessary for the representative of China to take part in the other proceedings looking to relief of the Sufferers.

The communication which has been made to this government by the Corea Chargé at this capital, of which a copy was sent to you with my No. 109 the 16th ultimo, will have apprised you of the apparent reluctance of the Corean Government to encourage any appeal to foreign charity and in preference for dealing with the famine according to domestic methods. How far this position responds to Chinese influence or direction, it is not necessary or perhaps advisable to question. It is enough to know that the Government of Corea avers that it has resources at command which enable it to take all requisite measures for the succor of the suffering people of that country, without recurrence to foreign aid, however freely and bounteously tendered.

I observe that in your No 169, you Make this incident the occasion of a request for the instructions of this Department as to whether you shall hold relations with the Chinese representative at Seoul as with your other colleagues, and, if so, by what title you shall address him; and, further, what place shall be accorded Mr. Yuan in matters of official precedence.

As you observe, Mr. Yuan styles himself "His Imperial Chinese Majesty's Resident" and states in his note to you of 21st February last, that his presence at Seoul is "under different circumstances" from the foreign representatives. The repeated announcements which have been made to this Government from time to time, touching the relation of Corea to China in regard to internal matters, leave no doubt that the King of Corea is under some form of feudal subjection to the Chinese Crown, except so far as concerns his intercourse with, and responsible relations towards, other powers.

Under such circumstances, the function of a "Resident" is neither unusual Nor anomalous. The office and title are frequently met with in modern diplomatic intercourse. France maintains a Resident at the capital of Madagascar. The British representative at the capital of the South African Republic is understood to discharge functions similar to those of a Resident. The officer so styled necessarily occupies a different position from that of a diplomatic representative of an independent power and the status to be accorded to him is a matter for the consideration of the Government which admits his official residence at its capital. The title of Resident is not to be confounded with that of Minister Resident. He is not necessarily a member of the foreign diplomatic body. The Resident is entitled to be treated by the diplomatic body as the Corean Government itself recognizes him. His precedence and his privileges in respect of audience are to be determined by the Corean Government.

The question of the personal rank of Mr. Yuan's Secretary is, however, Very different. You state that you do not recall an instance of Mr. Yuan's having attended a meeting of the diplomatic body for the discussion of business, but that the Secretary of the Chinese Residency "is permitted to be present that he may report to his chief what has been done." It is presumed that this is a usage of long standing, probably dating from the first institution of the diplomatic body at Seoul. But it appears to be none the less irregular. If Mr. Yuan disclaims connection with the foreign representatives as a diplomatic agent, but assumes such an internal relation to the Corean Government as would imply association in the domestic administration of the kingdom, it is not seen how he can delegate to his Secretary a participation which he himself declines to exercise. Nor is it seen how the Secretary can take part in diplomatic Meetings, even as a mere reporter, any more than a subordinate officer of the Corean Government could attend. There is, of course, nothing to prevent Mr. Yuan's officiating in a dual capacity, by superadding to his intimate function of Resident, which concerns only the relations of Corea to China, the Capacity of a diplomatic officer in connection with the foreign relations of Corea to the independent sovereignties of the world. It is not, however, understood that he claims any such dual character as would require his attendance at stated Meetings of the diplomatic body, or as, in the event of his inability to attend, would permit his designation of his Secretary as his personal representative. The Department is not sufficiently advised on these points to instruct you positively in regard thereto, but it is deemed advisable that the position should be better understood than it appears to be at Seoul.

A copy of your despatch and of this instruction will be sent to Mr. Denby at Peking for such discreet inquiries as he may find it desirable to make touching Mr. Yuan's status in connection with the foreign diplomatic body resident at Seoul.

JAMES G. BLAINE

NO. 22 Department of State
Washington, June 27, 1890

Augustine Heard

Sir:

I transmit for your information, a copy of a dispatch from Mr. Denby, relative to "new regulations issued, controlling imports and exports to and from Corea, which apply Chinese customs' rules to Korean ports"; also, a copy of the reply thereto.

In the absence of any indication that the Chinese regulation invades our commercial treaty-rights with Corea, there is no occasion to make any inquiry touching the views of the Corean Government as to the policy of China,—in respect of the reserved relations of the two Countries.

JAMES G. BLAINE

NO. 1013   Legation of the United States
                                             Pekin, December 9th, 1889

Secretary of State

Sir:

I have the honor to enclose a translation of a communication which
was lately sent by the Customs Taotae at Tientsin to all the Consuls
at that port. In this communication the Consuls are notified that when
foreign merchants ship native produce of Corea to China such ship-
ments shall be accompanied by a certificate issued by the Commissioner of Customs at the Corean port of shipment which certificate
shall be issued after the payment of full export duty. On the entry of
the goods in China they shall be examined and a Coast trade duty of
one half the export duty shall be levied. If there is no evidence that
the export duty has been paid the half, or coast-wise duty, shall be
paid and in addition a certificate of payment of the export duty must
be produced when the goods will be allowed to pass. Chinese Subject's
shipping goods from a Corean port to a Chinese port shall comply
with this regulation.

In short, China, by this regulation has applied to Corea the identical regulations which control the shipment of goods from one treaty
port in China to another treaty port in China.

The result is that for Customs purposes China has incorporated
Corea into itself as one of its provinces.

Another result will be that Corean goods imported into China by
a foreigner and afterwards sent by him into the interior will be
required to pay likin—Under the rules now existing a foreigner who
brings goods from the interior of China to a treaty port takes out a
transit pass, giving bond that he will export the goods and pays one
half the export duty. If he sends foreign goods, imported by him,
into the interior, he in like manner takes out a transit pass. In either
event he escapes the likin, which is levied *enroute* on native goods.

Should this new regulation remain in force, and should Corean
goods be treated as native Chinese goods are treated, the foreigners
must pay likin on the Corean goods imported or exported. The likin
vastly exceeds the cost of the transit pass and the object of China is
to benefit by the increased taxation.

It is likely that the German Minister, either individually as the
Dean of the Diplomatic Body, on behalf of his colleagues and himself,

will take up the question as the first case arising under the new regulation comes to him from a German firm at Tientsin.

As at present advised, I shall cooperate with him on the general question because I regard this action as antagonistic to the treaty of the United States with Corea which recognises Corea as an independent State as far as it has relations with the United States.

It might be well for you to bring the subject to the attention of Mr. Dinsmore, in order to ascertain how the Corean government views the gradual absorption by China of its sovereign rights.

CHARLES DENBY

Chinese Legation
Washington, May 6, 1890

Secretary of State

Sir:

I have the honor to state to you, Mr. Secretary, that it having been brought to the attention of the Imperial Government that it is proposed to seek the negotiation of a foreign loan or loans on behalf of Korea, my Government has instructed me to represent to you, and, through you, to the capitalists or bankers of your country that the Imperial Government regards such a step as unwise and likely to involve those who should participate in such loans in serious trouble and financial losses. It should be borne in mind that Korea is a poor country inclined to be extravagant in its expenditures, and with small resources out of which to repay a foreign loan. This is shown by the fact that it has not been able to repay to the Imperial Government a considerable sum of money, which a number of years ago my Government in view of the tributary condition of Korea and out of a benevolent desire to relieve it from foreign embarrassment, advanced to the King of that country.

It should be made known that the Imperial Chinese government will not guarantee the repayment of loans made in behalf of Korea, nor will it permit the customs revenues of Korea to be seized for liquidating any indebtedness contracted on behalf of that country. In view of the friendly relations China desires to maintain with the United States and their people, it has been deemed advisable that I should bring the foregoing facts to your attention, in order that your countrymen may not be misled respecting the proposed loan.

TSUI KWO YIN

NO. 29   *Confidential*   Legation of the United States
                                             Seoul, Corea, July 10th 1890

Secretary of State

Sir:

I have the honor to acknowledge receipt of your despatch, No. 9, of 8 May 1890 in which is enclosed copy of a communication from the Chinese Minister to the Department of State. This letter is a curious & an amusing one. Its assumption of responsibility for the acts of Corea is strongly in contrast with China's repudiation of all responsibility for Corea proffered so earnestly only a few days ago; & the forwarding of such a document to the Government of the United States, who has so far recognized the independence of Corea as to accredit a minister to its Court, might be characterized as bordering on impertinence.

Corea is in need of money, & she has for some time been seeking a loan, but I have now heard that she is attempting to increase her Security by the offer of China's guarantee. The Customs Service is Corean, & is called the "Royal Corean Customs." It is carried on, it is true, by employees of the Chinese service, & acceptance of them has been one of the bitterest regrets of His Corean Majesty. It was one of the weakest of his many weak acts, & has been one of the strongest links in the chain of awkward circumstances which bind him to China. He has tried frequently, but feebly, to emancipate himself from it, but has never had the resolution. He has offered the post of Chief Inspector to Mr. Denny, to Mr. Dinsmore and others, but of course they had refused to undertake it without the assurance of the formation of a distinct, separate, complete service. This he has not had the brain & the firmness—or the ability—to devise or carry out. The Customs service in Chinese hands has more than any other one thing tended to keep him subservient to Chinese influence, & to make him seem to be so in the estimation of the public.

The Management however, of the Customs by Chinese employe's (foreigners) does not give China the right to assume control of the revenues so received, unless they have been pledged for the Security of her loan to Corea, spoken of in this communication, which I am disinclined to believe. The net income I have been given to understand has always been paid over to the Corean Government, frequently indeed anticipated, and it is to be noted that in most contracts made by Corea with foreigners it is stipulated that their salaries shall be paid from the Customs. This is the case with the contracts made with Colonel Cummins & Major Lee, of which I have spoken in another despatch.

The relations of Mr. Yuan with the Foreign Representatives remain unchanged. My colleagues do not seem disposed to disturb the existing quiet, but they would perhaps be pleased to see me take some step to assert my, & indirectly their, rights to the same consideration at the Palace as is given to him. You are aware that for some time, indeed I believe from the time of his arrival here, he has insisted on entering the Palace Court Yard in his chair, and being carried in it to the door of the Audience Chambers, instead of descending, as all the other Foreign Representatives do, at the Gate. His rank, so far as we know, & is recognized, is Commissioner, which has been defined to be a Consul-General with diplomatic functions, and this, I am told, is the translation of the inscription over the entrance to his Yamen.

There would not seem to be then, looking at ostensible rank, any reason why we should not enjoy the same privileges, but it would be very inexpedient to assert it without a certainty of being able to secure it. I should not wish to order my chair coolies to take me inside the Gate, and be stopped by the Guards; and it is quite possible that it would be necessary to resort to force, as was done, I am informed, by Mr. Yuan himself on the first occasion when he was escorted by a large number of soldiers.

It is, however, within the bounds of possibility that the King should desire to give me (even) that mark of favor with a view perhaps of knowing Chinese pretensions, and ask me (even) to order our chairs taken inside: and I submit the case to the opinion of the Department. It would be necessary, of course, that proper orders should be given in advance at the Gate, in order to avoid any unseemly contention; but the disadvantage of this precaution is that these orders would probably at once be communicated to Mr. Yuan, and he might take measures to neutralize them.

The political situation is tolerably clear. In broad outline, it is this. China bitterly regrets the blunder she made in permitting and encouraging the conclusion of treaties with Western Powers. She sees that America & Europe by sending and receiving diplomatic Representatives, recognize the independence of Corea, and sooner or later may protest against her being relegated to the position of a province; and she is endeavoring by all the measures in her power—by provocation & by threats, and by assumptions like those of the letter addressed to the Department above spoken of, to place her in a position where full recognition would be impossible.

England, always anxious to curtail the influence of Russia, and to secure for herself a useful ally, in view of possible eventualities, supports China. She has no minister here, but only a Consul-General, who is a subordinate of and reports to her minister at Peking.

Russia's policy can only be inferred from her history. She is represented by a Chargé d'Affaires, a man of long experience, who smiles contemptuously when he hears the tales of Russian projects of aggrandizement, with which the Chinese and Japanese Journals (all English) from time to time are filled. Lately the newsmongers have been very active, and one of their recent stories was to the effect that the American Minister was negotiating for the cession of Port Hamilton, which was to be subsequently transferred to Russia. Mr. Waeber was ridiculing this to me a few days ago, as a specimen of what could be said and believed, and took occasion to remark that Russia had absolutely no design on Corea. But the acquisition of Port Lazaref especially was supposed to be coveted, but so far from this being the case, no Russian man of war, with the exception of an accidental visit last year, has touched there since the days of the Crimean War.

The intentions of Russia may be perfectly harmless, for we may believe if we like that Mr. Waeber has not been informed that they are not, but we may be permitted to infer the future from the past, and to imagine that she would not regret the pushing of her boundary line further South. But her time has not yet come. She is not ready yet, & it may not be for many years. When she does move, she will move with effect, & the forces of China, unless better organized than they are now, will be able to offer only feeble resistance. It is a question whether Corea, independent and prosperous, & recognized as such by Western Nations would not be more difficult of conquest, than as a simple province of China.

Meanwhile Russia has here an able Chargé d'Affaires, & is building an expansive legation.

Japan has larger trading interests in Corea than any other nation, and she has always treated the Government with courtesy and consideration. She watches China & Russia with anxious eyes, and I believe would hail with satisfaction any measure, which, by heightening the prosperity of the country, and relieving her political fears, would allow the peaceful development of her commerce.

A league between these three nations, China, Russia, & Japan to guarantee the neutrality and integrity of Corea would conduce enormously to her advancement, politically, financially & Morally; and there would seem to be no insuperable obstacle to it. China's present course, stimulated by England, is no doubt dictated in a large degree by dread of Russia, and may produce exactly the reverse effect of what is intended. Corea—government & people—naturally look to China as a friend and "elder brother," upon whose support she would be glad to rely. Her relations with her socially and commercially are closer than with any other nation, & encouragement from China would be valued, and her advice cherished and followed; but she seems to be getting restive under restraint and threats, and may turn . . .

The treatment of Corea by China suggests the reflection whether after all what used to be called the "English Gunboat Policy" is not the only true one to employ with Eastern nations. China may be supposed to know her own character, and certainly the methods she uses are based on threats and force. All Orientals love and are adept in reasoning, but they yield only to physical arguments. Of this the destiny of China since the Burlingame Mission furnishes a practical example.

In all this, what is America's part? At the present moment, her interests in Corea are Small, but with the development of the country they may become important, and in that View it is my duty under your instruction to contribute to that development in the measure of my power. Corea is naturally a country of resources and under a different Government and a different Social System, might become rich. The Coreans are intelligent & progressive, and, given the opportunity, would become prosperous—but their System degrades labor, and the Multitude are taxed and oppressed, almost beyond endurance, to support in idleness the nobility, who are very numerous. The task
of change seems $\wedge$ almost hopeless, but is not so altogether. The King is kindly and well intentioned and has a tolerably clear idea of what is before him—especially of the difficulties that beset his path. If America could see her way to aid and encourage him without departing from the lines of a conservative neutrality, it would give him strength, and her an increase of influence & power for good.

America opened Japan, and we are today her largest Customer. The aggregate amount of our Purchases & Sales is far in excess of that of any other nation; but our political influence there is almost nil. Germany and England, and even France, are of greater weight.

We have opened Corea, and our position with the King and people is now good. Is it our intention to maintain it, and to advance it? And how?—

I hope I have said nothing which would give the impression that I am hostile to China, or in any way disposed to create unpleasant feelings. Mr. Yuan and I are on the best of terms, and he dined with me a few days ago. I merely indicate my observation of the trend of events, which it is my duty to transmit to you, and I trust I have not done so at wearisome length.

AUGUSTINE HEARD

NO. 75   *Confidential*   Legation of the United States
Seoul, Corea, Oct 21, 1890

Secretary of State

Sir:

Since my despatch, No 29, of July 10, upon the political Situation here, I have Seen no reason to change the opinions therein expressed, and I am induced to return to the subject now by the assumption of the Chinese representative of a right to intervene between me, as Minister of the United States and His Corean Majesty, of which I wrote in my last, No. 74, of Oct. 15

By the mail lately arrived, I received a clipping from the New York "Sun" of Aug. 21, containing a statement said to have been made by Mr. Shing Woon, Chinese Consul in New York, to a reporter of that paper by instructions from the Chinese Minister at Washington. I have seen several similar articles, but, as this is given to the public apparently by Official order, it seemed desirable to call your attention to it in connection with the course pursued by Chinese officials of this country. I have only this copy, & I desire to retain it, or I would send it to you. It may, however, easily be procured in America.

It is filled with wilful misstatements, and, as generally the case with attacks of this nature, much more is insinuated than is positively asserted; and even the assertions are insinuations. China "disclaims every liability." Without this statement, no one would have supposed that she had any liability, & in reality it might as well have been made by the United States as by China; but the insinuation is intended that Corea looks for Security to China—which is not the case.

I have made diligent inquiry, and so far as I can learn, no one in Corea believes that the Custom's revenues are pledged to China in such a way as to entitle her to control them. Among her debts Corea contracted one to the China Merchant's Co. in 1883 for M300000, which with interest may now amount to somewhat over $400000, and it is possible that this loan may have been transferred to the Chinese Government, but no mortgage of the Customs for it is on record, and no special obligation of the Customs for it is believed to exist, while the object of the new loan is to make Corea to pay off this with her other debts. These may be estimated at about a million dollars which would be funded at a lower rate of interest than is now incurred.

Corea is described as a poor country, but she is not a poor country. She is rich. She is poor only in the Sense that she is undeveloped. So California was supposed to be a poor country, fit only for cattle grazing, till her marvelous ore Sources were discovered, & there are many countries, which hold a high position in Europe, whose natural advantages do not equal those of Corea. She has an unusually fertile Soil, capable of yielding in abundance a great Variety of products, and the quality of those products excites the admiration of experts. Her rice is better than the best rice of China in the opinion of China-men themselves, & is equal to, if not better than the best of Japan. And So of wheat, & beans & many other articles. Her admirable climate, combined with her productive Soil, enables the husbandman to harvest two, or more, Crops in a year. She should be a great fruit country, and her mineral resources, though little Known, are un-doubted. She only needs freedom of action with enlightened admin-istration to prove that She possesses wealth; and of the many causes which hold her back one of the most potent is the treatment She receives from China. That the King and a large party desire reform and development is unquestionable, and it is no answer to this desire to Say, as the Chinese do, that they are incapable and would only squander any money that might come into their hands—pointing as examples, to the Mint and other useless purchases. All countries, notably Japan, make mistakes at the beginning of their new life, but there is no reason to Suppose that Corea, like others, would not profit by experience.

It is a curious fact that it is only Since China lost all right to that assumption if she ever had any, that She claims the vassal of of [sic] Corea. Whatever may have been the relations of the two countries in the past, the Signing of the treaty of the United States in 1882 made a new starting point, when the position of Corea was defined, and defined with the consent if not with the initiative of China. As if the treaty were not enough—an equal compact between two independent nations—the King of Corea in a letter addressed to the President of the United States, States that—"hitherto full sovereignty has been exercised by the Kings of Chosen in all matters of internal administration and foreign relations," and the President of the United States in his reply takes act of that declaration and says the United States would only make a treaty with a Sovereign power.

Up to this time China has practically held aloof, and when Summoned to make amends for Corea by France and the United States on well-Known occasions She absolutely repudiated all responsibility. But the ink was hardly dry on these documents, when She began to interfere not only in Foreign affairs, but in Home administration; and from one pretension She has gone on to another, till now She announces to the world that Corea, her "dependent," her "tributary," desiring to contract a loan, She opposes it; and notifies the Minister of the United States to Corea that he must not act in accordance with his own views of the policy of his Government or with the wishes of the King without having submitted his proposed course of action to the criticism of the representative of China. Is it not time that this Should be stopped? and for the treaty Powers to take counsel together and warn the Imperial Government that it goes too far?—

I have no disposition to deny that there may be private relations between China and Corea, involving questions of etiquette & precedence with which the United States has nothing to do. These are explicitly declared to exist, and have been Scrupulously respected by the United States and her Ministers. But it has been declared with equal explicitness and by the same authority that in all matters of national administration and foreign relations the King of Choson are sovereign; and this I maintain that China Should equally respect. She began by opposing the Sending of ministers to America and Europe; She succeeded in delaying the one and in utterly frustrating the Mission of the other. She attempted to cause the Minister of the United States to be punished and degraded on his return, & was only defeated by the intervention of powerful friends—while the King has never dared to renew the project of a European envoy. She has seized upon the Customs; appropriated through the guise of an agreement, the Telegraphy; forbidden the opening of new ports; and conducts herself throughout as Sovereign Mistress.

How far she is supported in this by England, I cannot say, but I do not think that the other Foreign Powers look on with indifference, although the smallness of their interests in Corea, as compared with those in China, is sufficient to induce them to abstain from action.

There is a certain delicacy about the position of Japan and Russia, which holds them quiet. France & Germany hope for contracts in that free future of China, which is always promised and which never comes; but I am not aware that the United States has any interests in China, which would be subserved by Submission to her dictation, and the abandonment of her rights in Corea.

This is hardly the spot for conducting negotiations on the Subject, if negotiations be desirable, for there is no person here of Sufficient Authority to treat; but it is here that the question may at any time be brought up. And in effect it is brought up now by the pretension of Mr. Yuan. I cannot see myself that any "negotiations" are necessary. The United States, or the Treaty Powers, have only to Signify to China their interpretation of the Treaties, and if China have any acceptable plea for a different construction, negotiations may then be considered.

As a friend of China,—and I *am* a friend of China by long intercourse and association—I would urge upon her in her own interests Not to check Corea in her aspirations towards development and reform. There is a strong affinity between the two peoples. Corea looks up to China as a younger brother to an elder, and would be proud of her encouragement & Support. If China, as is supposed by many, is following her present policy of reducing Corea to Subjection from fear of Russia & in the hope & belief that She can give protection, she is making a fearful mistake. No one who Knows what the Chinese Army and Navy are, as at present organized, can participate in any Such delusion, and the instant She comes in contact with Russian troops, She will herself discover her error. The rank & file are good material, but the officers are comparatively worthless, and Russia fully counts, and with reason, on finding when she comes South only another "weak organism," like those She has absorbed in Central Asia. So much for the protection She could give without reference to Corea herself, but Corea is not in this matter a "quantiti negligiable". Which is likely to offer the most resistance to aggression from without, or to be the better ally—a Corea prosperous & quasi-independent, Supported & recognized by Western powers, proud and fond of her connection with China; or a Corea, low & crushed, isolated as China would make her or a dependent province, and detesting a connection that had only been formed and cemented by force? To state the question is to answer it.

But I am being led on beyond proper limits. The subject is an engrossing one, and tends to large extension. The difficulty is to say little, and not to say much. But it Seemed proper as the matter is likely to be brought up in Washington, that I should express my Views.

Briefly, Corea can never become prosperous, So long as She is held down and expansion prohibited by China. With that oppression removed She would have a chance of reform and progress. She is naturally a rich country, and, if She fails, She would fail by her own fault. Her development should be conducted under the benevolent auspices of China, who would find her account in it by the Creation of a prosperous and grateful ally, and thereby add to her own strength. I fear this is too much to hope for, but at all events She has no right to impede it.

Augustine Heard

no. 78   Legation of the United States
Seoul, Corea, October 30th 1890

Secretary of State

Sir:

I desire to add a few remarks to the despatch, No. 75, which I had the honor of addressing to you on the 21st instant.

The original draft of that despatch contained a partial parallel between China & Corea as regards poverty of their resources for contracting foreign obligations. The conditions of the two countries are in this respect much the same. In stating that Corea was a poor country no doubt the chief object of the representative of China was to assert that She had no available resources except for receipt from Customs. For all the purposes of a Foreign Loan this is true; and it is also in a great measure true of China. She has larger receipts, and in So far is capable of offering security for a larger loan, but in a proper proportion the Security offered by Corea is equally good with that of China. The difference is one of degree, not of kind. In both countries the other revenues are in the hands of native officials, where methods are such that no Western banker would regard them as of value for Security to any amount. A loan in China might be raised for a Railway, or for Some Similar purpose, but money would be lent in this case, because of the intrinsic Merits of the Scheme, and not on the security of China, properly socalled; and the Same is true of Corea.

These reflections being obvious to anyone familiar with the two countries, I struck them out of my former despatch for the Sake of briefness, my object then being mainly to bring forward three points.

1. That Corea was worth developing.
2. That China interfered with that development and with the relation of the Powers with her, in contravention of treaty; and
3. That this development should properly be conducted with the aid and support of China, whose best interests would be subserved.

Although I consider that China's interests would be decidedly favored by a creation of a friendly & prosperous Corea, all our experience forbids us to hope that She will herself entertain this View or adopt this plan. The "conservative element", as it is called, has Sway at Peking, and China is little further advanced towards Western civilization than she was twenty years ago. Her inclinations and beliefs are today what they were twenty-five years ago before Mr. Burlingame's Mission, and prosperity in Corea following upon the adoption of Western Methods would be a reproach to her. The opportunity is therefore, in her opinion to be avoided rather than seized; and the same reasoning explains her opposition to all progress here.

The difficulties in the way of carrying out any Scheme of reform are very great, and the boldness of the innovator would probably be in inverse ratio with his Knowledge of the Country. The less he knew the more ready he would be to undertake it. The whole Social and governmental fabric needs remodeling, and the task that confronts the "Confidential adviser" is formidable. Unless he can succeed in impressing his personality on the perceptions of the King & his "entourage" it is indeed hopeless.

Mr. Mollendorf was a Visionary, and it was exceedingly unfortunate for Corea that he should have been the first to take her in hand. He possessed her confidence, and led her into much wild adventure, in which she left her money & her credit and a good deal of her faith in foreign ways.

Mr. Denny succeeded, and I have no doubt that he has often given excellent counsel, but whether from the opposition of Mr. Yuan, or from other causes, it has not been followed, and I do not think he has to his credit the adoption of one good measure.

Gen. Le Gendre is now the man. He is honest and capable, and if he is patient and wiling [sic] to wait his opportunity he may do Some good. As he has had much experience in the East, & knows how important it is not to be hasty and brusque, it is possible that he may be more Successful than his predecessors.

I cannot Say I am Very hopeful, but I think improvement is quite possible, and we have before us the example of Japan to prove it. So long as there is a party of progress, in the true sense of the word, with the King as its head, who really desire reform, it seems to be a duty in my position representing America, as a friend of Corea, to remove when I can, obstacles from her path; and, as we were the first to induce her to join the family of nations; it would be churlish after prevailing upon her to quit her isolation, to refuse to lend her a helping hand—especially when requested—if it can be done without injury to the rights of others.

It was in View of these considerations that I penned my despatch No 75. Since it was written, I find I was misinformed with regard to the telegraph lines. I have procured a copy of the convention between China and Corea, which I enclose. It does not warrant the statement that China had Secured a monopoly.

AUGUSTINE HEARD

NO. 86   Legation of the United States
                                          Seoul, Corea, Nov. 17, 1890

Secretary of State

Sir:

I have the honor to inform you that in accordance with ancient custom, a special Embassy was sent by the King of Corea on the 10″ July last by land route to Pekin to communicate to the Emperor of China intelligence of the death of the Queen Dowager; and that on the morning of the 6″ Instant two vessels of war entered the harbor of Chimulpo bearing the return mission with the Condolences of the Emperor. This is the first time that a Chinese embassy has reached Corea by sea, but the great saving of time and expense, together with the late Season of the year, was sufficient inducement for the choice of this route.

The mission consists of Hsa-chong, First Envoy, President of the Board of Review, member of the Tsung-Le Yamen, and Ch'ung-Li, Vice President of the Board of Review, Second Envoy. They landed on the same day without escort, and with only their private Suite, and took up their residence with the Superintendent of Trade. A high

Corean official was in attendance and the shield Soldiers had been sent to greet them, but with the exception of some decoration of the Chinese quarters of the town there was small display. On the next day, the 7th Inst they left for the capital in chairs with a Corean escort. They reached the river about four miles distant from Seoul in the afternoon and passed the night in a palace which had been prepared for them.

On the morning of the 8th Inst they made their Solemn entry into the city, and the King went outside the West Gate to receive them, a tent having been erected for him in a space opposite the Yamen of the Governor of this Province. It was situated at the angle made by the crossing of the street coming from the river to the West Gate with the Great China Road, which runs to the Great South Gate.

The envoys were preceded by three Small palanquins—first containing the funeral presents: the second Vases for the libation, and the third, which was closed with Yellow curtains, the Imperial decree conferring on the deceased Queen the grade of Wife of the President of the Board of War, or the 1st grade of the Second class, and the Imperial invocation or prayer to be read before the tablet of the deceased and afterwards burned. As the palanquin was borne before the King, the yellow curtains were drawn aside, and he is supposed to have prostrated himself in the interior of his tent.

The procession then followed its course to the South Gate, and the King returning by the West Gate, having a much shorter distance to traverse, was ready to receive the Envoys, arriving by the grand avenue of the Palace and the Court yard of the great Audience Hall, where all the high functionaries, in Court dress of White, were arranged in the order of their rank.

The King was clad in sacrificial garments of Hemp, with hat of the Same, his head girt with a cord, & after a short delay he led the way on foot to the Hall of the Tablets situated in an inner Court of the Palace.

Here the Imperial Scripts were placed on a table before the Tablet, and the King Knelt twice and prostrated himself Eight times before them. The chief Eunuch then read the Imperial invocation or prayer while the King remained on his Knees. After the reading was finished, he rose to his feet, and, all returned Slowly to the Great Audience Hall, where a light collation of fruits, tea, wine and Cake was served.

Shortly afterwards the King conducted the Envoys to without the Court, when they entered their chairs, and proceeded to Nam Pieul

Kong, the palace assigned for their residence while in Seoul, and His Majesty withdrew to his apartments.

According to the established etiquette the King Should have called upon the Envoys on each Succeeding day, but it is customary to dispense with this on the day following the ceremony at the Palace, and consequently on the 10th only it was announced in the Gazette that a visit would take place. Accordingly about 1 o'clock of that day, the King in Costume of White & with a long train of followers was taken in a horse litter to Nam Pieul Kong, and passed about an hour with the Envoys, during which a collation was served.

Of course no foreigner witnessed any part of what took place in the Palace or at this interview, and two Versions are current. The Chinese and their friends represent that everything was done in accordance with ancient usage, and was to them perfectly Satisfactory;—that is to say, that the King went to the extreme of deference and homage and yielded to every demand. On the other hand, it is asserted that, while showing himself courteous & considerate, he provoked irritation by his reserve, by his firmness in declining to commit himself to accepting the Suggestions of the Envoy with regard to his conduct in policy, without consideration and without deliberation and consultation with his Ministers. It is too soon yet to know the truth.

On the 11th the Envoys took their departure. At half past 12 on that day the King went out to the Same Spot—the Palace of the Governor of this Province about a quarter of a mile beyond the West Gate—where on the 8th he had welcomed them, to bid them farewell.

The Envoys left their chairs, and passed with him there from 15 to 30 minutes. They then proceeded on their way to Mapoo, while His Majesty returned to the Palace. Rain fell heavily on the 12", and it was not till the morning of the 13th that the Envoys resumed their journey to Chemulpo, where they arrived in the afternoon, and at once embarked.

Satins, Silks, paper, ginseng and about $15000 in Silver were Sent by the King to the envoy, but were returned with the explanation that the Emperor had forbidden the acceptance of any presents. By ancient usage the table service is of heavy Silver, which the envoys take away as a perquisite, but on this occasion the Vessels Were made so thin as to be almost worthless.

AUGUSTINE HEARD

NO. 87   Legation of the United States
                                                    Seoul, Corea, 18 Nov 1890

Secretary of State

Sir:

In connection with my last despatch No. 86 November 7, I have the honor to enclose a copy of the circular issued by Mr. Yuan the 9th instant. You will perceive that although the body of it reads "the different representatives and foreign residents," it is addressed by name to the Foreign Representatives, and I believe in fact it was seen by no others. It reached me just as I was leaving the house to go to church, and on my return I received the visit of Mr. Waeber and Mr. de Planey who called to ask me my impressions with regard to it. I replied that it was evidently a piece of rudeness which in anyone else would perhaps not be worth notice, but with a Chinaman it was more serious. They were both strongly of opinion that it ought not to pass without reply, and Mr. Waeber, who is generally very restrained in his use of language, characterized it as an "insult."

After some conversation we went to see Mr. Hillier together & I asked him how the circular appeared to him. He replied—"no doubt it was rude"—but he was disposed to think it was not worth noting, though he was quite ready to join with us in any steps we might think it proper to take. To my remark that it was either the result of ignorance or of impertinence, Mr. Hillier stated that "It certainly was not ignorance, for I happened to Meet Mr. Yuan yesterday & told him I was sorry I Could not See Hsu who was an old friend of mine, but I supposed he would make no calls & of course I do not call on him first. To which Mr. Yuan Assented."

We decided to meet at this Legation later in the afternoon, and I sent invitations to Mr. Kondo & Mr. Krien to be present. Mr. Kondo was unable to come owing to ill health, and I enclose a copy of his note, which was received a few moments before we met. It seems that he had already sent his card to the Chinese envoy, who was an old friend.

The result of our interview was the signing by the Representatives of the United States, of Russia and of France, of a letter to Mr. Yuan, in which he was politely informed, that, although they would have been glad to exchange courtesies with the high officials of the Imperial Chinese Government, they had no intention of departing from the usages which govern visits between Representatives of different countries.

Our reasons were: we did not conceive it to be incumbent upon us to make the first call—indeed no official intimation had been given us of the presence of the Envoys in Seoul; and the appearance of the circular made it imperative upon us to say so. Mr. Hillier, Mr. Waeber, Mr. de Planey, are familiar with the Chinese language and Mr. Hillier especially is an Expert. All these gentlemen were of opinion that the words used officially by the Chinese to designate the persons in question were not to be rightly translated "Ambassadors", but something inferior, such as "envoys," "ministers." If they were not Ambassadors, it was their duty to call upon us; if they were, they should have sent in their cards; and, although this may seem a trivial matter, nothing that concerns etiquette is trivial with the Chinese. With them especially it is mandatory to guard against the slightest Concession, as it is invariably made a stepping stone to Something more.

Mr. Hillier agreed entirely in the views we took of our duty in the matter, but being only a consul he was so far doubtful of his position as to think it best not to sign the letter; so did Mr. Krien.

If we had taken no notice of the circulars, we should have rendered ourselves liable to the imputation, and perhaps assertion that we had Strongly desired to show deference to these Envoys by calling, & had been refused permission. I trust my action may be approved—

AUGUSTINE HEARD

NO. 89   (*Confidential*)   Legation of the United States
                                          Seoul, Corea, November 19, 1890

Secretary of State

Sir:

A ceremony of great interest has just taken place. Ever since the death of the Queen Dowager the anticipation of it has occupied men's minds. It is the ancient custom of nations tributary to China to communicate the intelligence of any important event affecting their Royal Families to the Emperor as their head. The King was well aware of the importance of the Step, and hesitated for a long time, but finally persuaded, it is said, against his own convictions, dispatched an embassy on the 10 July only, and this embassy by judicious delay did not reach Peking before the end of September or early in October. It then represented that Corea being a poor country, unable to support the burden of the expenses of a special Chinese mission, it would be an act of wisdom and of courtesy to spare her this infliction, and that it would itself bear back the letter conveying the condolence of the Emperor.

But China was not willing to forego this golden opportunity to affirm to the world her Superiority, and the season being so far advanced that the usual overland journey was difficult, if not impossible, she forthwith despatched her Envoys by sea. They have come & gone as described in my No. 86, Nov 17.

It must be recollected, when perusing the details of the ceremonies that no Foreigner saw anything of the Serious part of them, and that the high Corean Officials who were present are Very reluctant to speak of them, so that most of our information comes from Chinese Sources. There is, however, no reason to suppose that the ancient usages were in any essential particular departed from. No doubt the King prostrated himself before the Emblems of Imperial Dignity, though probably not before the envoys themselves, but it should not be forgotten that the Act was Oriental between Orientals, and must not be judged by the Western standard. There is not an extreme difference between an Eastern prostration and the Spaniard's declaration that his house and everything that is in it are yours, or the familiar ending of our everyday letter, "Your most obedient, humble servant". The feeling of the Corean toward the Emperor of China is not wholly, or mostly, one of political subservience; it is rather one of religious deference. The Head of a family in the East has a far higher position than he has in the West, and the elder brother has a real authority over the younger, a claim for service and devotion, which we can never recognize or understand. It is the result of lifelong education for the individual, intensified by centuries of hereditary practice. The sentiment resembles largely the sentiments with which a devout, ignorant Catholic regards the Pope.

This is the feeling of the ordinary Corean, and it is a feeling with which the King must count. His position is peculiar and very difficult. He knows that compared with China, Corea alone is weak & he is told every day that China, if he resists her will, will not hesitate to use her power. He is surrounded by men, who from one reason or another, are in her interests and who persuade or threaten as the immediate exigency may demand. He recollects the unscrupulousness, with which a few years ago his Palace was taken possession of, members of his own family shot down, and his own father kidnapped & carried off; and he is reminded that the same man is at hand in charge of the same troops. Then there is all the traditional glamor, which surrounds the "Son of Heaven"; if he be tempted at any time to feel a confidence in the power and friendship of Western Nations he is shown their Representatives at Peking, content to wait on the outer circle, and supplicate for a glance from the Imperial throne, which they cannot have. Indeed their humiliation in submitting at the close of the 19th Century to the pretensions of China in refusing an Audience of the Emperor goes very far towards excusing the alleged want of dignity in the King of Corea.

Then, again, he is told, if he emancipates himself from China that he will achieve a quasi-independence only to fall into the hands of Russia, and the desperate consequences of this chance are depicted in glowing colors. He will lose all identity, all individuality; and there is throughout the Kingdom a sentiment of affection, of clanship, for China, and one only of dread for Russia.

There is another point which deserves Serious consideration. You are aware that for a long time a prophecy has been current that this year, the 500th, would be the last of his dynasty. I have in previous despatches alluded to this & to the weight of the fear which it causes him. The Queen, who is said to be an able, strong woman, is still more than he under its influence; and I presume not a day, not an hour, passes when it is not ever present. But in three months, early in February, this year will come to an end, and according to the prophecy, if all be then well with him, he shall go on prospering & to prosper. It is then possible, and even probable, that in yielding now, he has simply thought to tide over the evil day, and that once launched upon a New Year, he will commence a new era of greater self-confidence and independent action.

In the above remarks I have taken for granted that the statements of the Chinese with regard to what has just taken place, are correct; and I take no note of other rumors, which have reached me however, from various Sources to the effect that His Majesty showed himself disinclined to commit himself for the future by accepting unreservedly certain propositions of the Envoys—with reference especially to his relations with Foreigners & Foreign Powers; & his firmness is Said to have caused much irritation. These lack confirmation, and it will only be after some time that we shall know the truth.

The question now naturally arises, in connection with this incident, what is to be his treatment by Western Nations, if he show a disposition to act independently and to introduce reforms? What, if any, encouragement will or can they give him?

A great difficulty in the way at the outset is the fact that no one appreciates Corea. It is generally regarded in Europe and America as a poor country, which cannot stand alone and which is not worth keeping. Even in Japan, which is so near, the common opinion of foreigners is to the same effect, and I am inclined to think equally so in China. When I arrived here I confess I was under the same delusion, but the longer I stay the more I am convinced that I was in error, and the deep interest I have learned to feel in her future is my sole excuse for writing at such length. In my No. 75 I spoke of the development of her material resources, which I considered as valuable, and I would now like to add my testimony to the value of Coreans, as a people. Physically they are strong and handsome; eaters of meat, they are larger and taller than the Japanese and the Southern Chinamen, and men, who have been for years occupied in the education of their youth, tell me they are more intelligent and more studious than either of those races. They Seem to have the quickness of the Japanese with Some of the persistency of the Chinese, and they are capable of strong feeling and of real patriotism.

But while I recognize these qualities and faculties I am not ignorant of, or blind to, their numerous faults and failings which engrafted on, and growing out of a Vicious System of Social Nobility, have conducted Corea to where we find her today. I merely wish here to indicate the resources, material & moral, which She possesses, and which under favorable influence and guidance, may lead her to a higher place in the family of nations.

In an inquiry into the probable action of the Treaty Powers, it is necessary first to consider their various relations and interests, political and commercial. In my No. 75 I spoke of the practical alliance between England & China, growing mainly out of a sympathetic dread of Russia; and I see no reason to change the views therein Expressed.

Germany is equally unlikely to take any Step which would alienate from her the good will of China. She is engaged there in a struggle to wrest from England her Supremacy—struggle which would Seem ridiculous and hopeless to any one who had not watched the enormous advances She has made throughout the East during the last 30 years. Her Young men have come in throngs, well-equipped in education, in economy & carefulness of life, & in determination to succeed; and their efforts have been supported & seconded by able and forceful men in Diplomatic and Consular positions. Not to tarry over details, they have achieved a political influence in Japan Second to none. In the commerce & finance of China they are more than respectable, and they have recently established a Bank of Commanding Capital in order to facilitate the handling of large Contracts for Railways and like Enterprises.

The English Admiral of the Chinese fleet has been compelled to resign; & it is not beyond the range of their hopes that a German may succeed him.

But there is another more lofty goal. The Inspector-General of the Customs occupies a position, unique in the East—indeed in the world. In his own province he is all powerful, but that is comparatively nothing. He is the confidential adviser of the Chinese Government in all matters concerning Foreigners and Sir Robert Hart, G.C.M.Q. Millionaire, beginning with nothing as Simple Employé, declined the post of British Minister to China, which was offered him, in order to remain where he is. He can keep the place no doubt, as long as he chooses but he is old and would be glad to retire. He would have done so before, if he could have named his brother as his successor. But the time will soon come when he must withdraw, whether he can name his successor or not. An able man in his position would be a power for good or evil, and Germany has her eye on it.

With these prizes in China to strive for, it is not likely that Germany will care to keep Corea.

France is more doubtful; her aims in China are of much the same nature as those of Germany, but not so ambitious.

Japan has a larger commerce with Corea than any other country, and she would be glad to increase it, not only by natural growth, but by the opening of new ports, which has been hitherto opposed by China. Mr. Kondo asked me recently to cooperate with him in trying to secure the opening of Ping An, where there is now a large Chinese smuggling trade. She is a friend of the independence of Corea, whose complete subjection to China or Russia, and the possession of whose Southern & Eastern ports by a strong, hostile power would be a standing menace to herself.

Russia too favors Corea's independence. At least the Russian
representative here has no hesitation in expressing himself $\wedge$ in this (to me) Sense, & in doing so favorably expresses the opinion of his Government. Does she take this view because it accords best with her own ulterior plans? Is Corea, independent, more easily absorbed than She would be if she were a province of China? My own feeling is that it makes very little difference. In the fulness of time, Russia may

move Southward & take part or the whole of Corea; and it matters not whether she is alone, or then constitutes a province of China. China can offer no serious resistance; and Russia argues that, independent, Corea will be a much more valuable possession 10 or 20 years hence than She would be if She had remained under the domination of China, who would have prevented all development, and kept her as She is today.

This is taking the most pessimistic View of Russia's intentions. She may be disinterested.

In any event, She favors independence, and I think would join a league to guarantee her integrity, such as I have already spoken of. This would answer certainly her temporary purpose, even if She had ulterior designs. I have no doubt that Japan would do the Same, but I fear there is little hope of the acquiescence of China.

As I have said in previous despatches, if Corea could find free development under the protecting wing of China—preserving her ancient, private relations, but independent as by Treaty in her Governmental administration—I should be the last to seek to withdraw her from it, but the policy China pursues within her own borders, & has pursued ever since we knew her, forbids the entertaining of any such hope. Nothing can be looked for under the present Relations, but a checking of all healthful aspirations and a smothering of the life of the nation.

There is probably little or nothing in these Views which is new or strange to you, and perhaps I should apologize for taking up your time to such an extent. But it seemed to me appropriate that I should sieze this occasion to lay them before you, and to ask for such instructions as Your wisdom may dictate. A knowledge of the general Views entertained by the Department would aid me in Shaping my course in Such a way as not to give offense.

I have expressed myself with great frankness as it was my duty to do, but I trust that all my communications of this nature may be regarded as confidential, as their publicity here would gravely impair my usefulness as Minister of the United States.

AUGUSTINE HEARD

I trust it is unnecessary for me to add that I do not express the above opinions in public. Recent events have of course provoked much discussion, but I have contented myself with saying, when called upon, that they had no political significance. It was purely a family matter.

NO. 124   Legation of the United States
Seoul, Corea, Febry 23, 1891

Secretary of State

Sir:

I have the honor to acknowledge the receipt of your despatch of Janry 2, No. 65. It is gratifying to have your approval of my action under the circumstances detailed.

You will have noticed in my despatch to which this is a reply that I mentioned that Mr. Kondo had sent his cards to the Chinese envoys on the alleged ground that one of them was an old friend. We were at a loss to understand Mr. Kondo's action, as he is a very cautious man, and we were not able to see under what circumstances this friendship could have been formed. I was told afterwards, however, that he had asked his Government for instructions in the matter, and had acted in accordance with those he had received.

The results sufficiently indicates the propriety of the course we pursued.

AUGUSTINE HEARD

NO. 163   Legation of the United States
Seoul, Corea, May 22, 1891

Secretary of State

Sir:

I have the honor to inform you that a ceremonial embassy has been appointed by the Government of Corea, to convey to the Emperor of China the congratulations of the King of Corea on the former having attained to his twentieth year.

The Embassy will be composed of an official of the 1st rank as chief, the 2nd rank as associate, and a lower rank man as Secretary to the Embassy.

The court astrologers are now engaged in the selection of the propitious day for starting.

It is understood that the Embassy will adhere to the ancient custom in going by the circuitous and costly land route; though the more economically disposed officials prefer the route by sea, which was taken by the recent Embassy from China bearing the emperor's condolence on the death of the Dowager Queen.

H. N. ALLEN

Legation of the United States
Seoul, Corea, June 22, 1891

Secretary of State

Sir:

I have the honor to inform you that I arrived here from China late on the afternoon of the 20th Instant, and resumed charge of this Legation on the next day. While in Peking I was with my family the guest of His Excellency, M. von Brandt, the German Minister, who is an old personal friend, and was the recipient of much civility and Kindness from members of the other Legations, and from Sir Robert Hart, Inspector General of Customs, whom also I have known for many years. Col. Denby was especially polite and friendly. You will have heard from him full details of the numerous outbreaks along the Yangtze, which have caused so much excitement and apprehension.

While on my way north I remained in Tientsin only 24 hours, but on my return I thought it proper to pay my respects to the Vice Roy, Li-Hung-Chang, Governor General of Chihli, who is now unquestionably the foremost man in China—indeed one might almost say there is no second. In fact, it would have been a breach of etiquette, to have failed to do so. I wrote him therefore before leaving Peking asking for an interview, and arranged to pass a few days in Tientsin for the purpose. A time was appointed, and I called upon him at his Yamen, where he received me very courteously.

Many Subjects were discussed which it is unnecessary to trouble you with; as was to be expected, he was Very emphatic in his assertion that Corea was a vassal of China, and would have been glad to hear me Express my agreement with that opinion, but I contented myself with Saying that as a Minister accredited to that Country under treaty it was a difficult question for me to discuss, that no one wished to dispute the relations of homage or etiquette that existed between the two Countries and that he himself was chiefly responsible for the treaties and the new obligations which they had created, that in my opinion the feeling of the people in Corea was favorable to China, and that it was China's evident policy to foster this feeling, and do every thing she could to make Corea rich and strong.

His Excellency replied that he had favored opening the country to Foreign Nations, as likely to conduce to her riches and prosperity; (China was anxious for her growth and desirous of promoting it) but that he had never contemplated any change in the relative positions of the two Countries, that he had no desire ever to denounce the treaties; that he was quite willing that Foreign Powers should treat her as if She were independent, but if the King were to attempt to emancipate himself, and to assert his independence, China would interfere. She would never permit it,—never. He was Very emphatic on this point, as I fully expected he would be. I said little in reply, as it was my first interview with him, and it would have been impolite in the Chinese sense to have made disagreeable statements. I wished him to form a favorable opinion of me, and I relied on finding a Suitable opportunity in a Second interview to define with Sufficient exactness my position.

In this I was not disappointed. He returned my call two days later at the American Consulate which had been disposed to receive him. His interpreter was with him as before, Mr. Lo-Seng-Luh who was partly educated in Europe and who speaks English perfectly. No one else was present.

After varied conversation for some time, he spoke of Mr. Yuan, the Chinese representative at Seoul as being an excellent man, frank and open, but young and Sometimes indiscreet. He hoped I would lend him the benefit of my greater Years and Experience in case of need, and expressed his gratification that we had always been on good terms. I replied—Yes, we had always been good friends. Only on one occasion had we had a difference of opinion and that was at the time of the funeral of the Queen Dowager; when in consideration of the importance of the ceremony which had been in preparation for many months and in which the whole country was taking part, I had thought it proper as a mark of respect from a friendly nation to order up a few sailors and marines from one of our men-of-war. Mr. Yuan had written me that before doing so, I ought to have consulted him, and that he had referred the matter to his Government. I replied that I did not agree with him in his estimate of my duties, but as he had referred the matter to his Government, I would not then discuss it. That was the only time when I had had occasion to differ from him, and His Excellency would understand that, as a Minister of the United States, I could not consult any one with regard to what course I should pursue.

The Viceroy said—landing troops was a very Serious matter. China had never done it in such case, and my action might encourage others, the Japanese for instance to do likewise. It might disturb men's minds and lead to complications. These were Serious Considerations, and he hoped I would not do it again.

I replied that I appreciated the gravity of His Excellency's observations, and they would certainly receive due weight. I could not act without reviewing the Situation carefully on all Sides, but it must be in my own mind, and not with the advice and assistance of others. I was aware that by agreement neither the Chinese nor the Japanese could land troops without notice to the other, so that both could act together in the same manner; but no one could suspect the United States of any ulterior object, or misconceive her motives. I was Minister of the United States and responsible to my own Government and to no one else. If I did wrong, I was liable to punishment, but so long as I was charged with her interests I must act by my own opinion, and not by the opinion or advice of others. I wished His Excellency to understand my position.

He said the matter had gone by now, and he did not wish to rèopen it. Yuan had done wrong in writing me. He ought to have come to see me.

We then passed to other subjects. He sat with me nearly an hour and a half, and took leave with many expressions of courtesy.

AUGUSTINE HEARD

2.

CHINESE EFFORTS TO CONTAIN GROWING AMERICAN INFLUENCE

Legation of the United States
                                      Söul, January 28, 1887

Secretary of State

Sir:

   Among the many self-constituted advisers to the King and the government of Korea, none plays so active a part as the Chinese representative here. I have the honor to forward to you herewith a
translation of the greater part of a Memorial which he presented to
the King in September last, and in which after drawing his Majesty's
attention to the present disorganized condition of the realm, the result
of the policy heretofore followed, he makes suggestions on ten urgent
measures of reform. The Memorial contains little or nothing of a
practical nature. While condemning the erection of a Mint, the
opening of a Hospital, the establishment of a model farm, the purchase
of a steamer, etc., he advises the King to develop the resources of
the country, but suggests no means to attain that end. He furthermore
urges the King to rely solely on the help of China which alone can
protect Korea from the insulting treatment of foreign nations.
   Finally, he calls the King's attention to the necessity of treating
with courtesy and good faith the treaty powers and the advantage of
having all questions of State controlled by the Ministers in council.
   Since presenting the above Memorial, Yuan Shih-Kai has made
several other suggestions to the Korean Government as measures of
reform, the most important of which, I have been told, is the suppression of three of the six battalions of troops stationed in Söul, but I do
not Know what are the reasons which he has adduced for his
measure.

                                                    W. W. ROCKHILL

NO. 51   Legation of the United States
                                      Söul Korea August 23" 1887

Secretary of State

Sir:

   I have the honor to inform you that at this time there prevails some
feverish excitement in Söul, growing out of the sudden departure on

the morning of the 20th instant at 3 o'clock of the Chinese minister and his Secretary and a large train of retainers, for Chemulpo, and his since sending to Söul for his family to depart with him on a Chinese gunboat for China.

It is presumed that this course has been induced largely by the action of His Majesty the King of Korea in recently appointing ministers to foreign countries as already reported to you.

But in addition to this I was yesterday informed by a confidential messenger from the King, that Mr. Yuan, the Chinese minister, has within the last few days been urging him to appoint the Tai Wen Kun the King's father to the office of Ussa for the entire Kingdom, which he had persistently declined to do, and that in this Mr. Yuan had found the cause of his departure. Under the laws of this country an Ussa is possessed of most extraordinary power, even having in his hands unrestrained authority to take the lives of His Majesty's subjects, when in his opinion they have been guilty of crimes deserving death. It has attached to it a system of espionage to detect traitors and criminals, and moreover he is (or was formerly, for the office I am informed has not been recognized of late) vested with authority to advise the king and even to rebuke him for supposed errors of conduct.

Apart from this office of general Ussa, there are others of more limited authority in different districts of the Kingdom.

You will observe that this seems to be in the line of policy which Prince Min attributed to the Chinese some time since in an interview with me and which I communicated to you in my No 30 under date of June 21st 1887.

We can only speculate upon what may be the developments of the future.

In this connection I may say that the U.S. steamer Omaha is now at Chemulpo, and will under orders from the Admiral commanding U.S. Navy forces on the Asiatic squadron be relieved by the Essex in a few days.

HUGH A. DINSMORE

Legation of the United States
                                        Söul Korea Feb'y 1st 1890

Secretary of State

Sir:

Referring to my No 169 of Feb'y 28th 1889 and Your instruction
No 112 of May 7th 1889 in reply thereto, I have the honor to communicate that Mr Yuan Sie Kwai the Chinese representative has
continued to withhold his presence from meetings of the diplomatic
body.

On several occasions he has sent in his stead one of his secretaries.
On one of these occasions the secretary upon entering the room said
to me in the presence of the assembled representatives that Mr Yuan
had instructed him to say that he regretted that illness prevented his
coming in person and that he had sent him (the secretary) "in his
stead."

I said to the secretary Mr Loo that with the consent of the representatives present I would make no objection to his remaining in the
room on this occasion as a listener to report to his Chief about what
occurred, although I would not be understood as giving my approval
to the systematic practice of such a course, and that in my opinion
he could not be received in the sense of acting on behalf of Mr. Yuan
or "in his stead."

In this view there was an expressed coincidence on the part of my
colleagues present.

On the 4th ultimo at My request the foreign representatives were
invited by the President to meet him at the Foreign Office to consider
the advisability of reducing the taxes of the Chemulpo foreign
Municipality, it being necessary to an accomplishment of such a
reduction that the Korean Government join in the agreement.

At this meeting Mr S. Y. Tong the Chinese Consul and Chief
Secretary of the "Chinese Residency" appeared on the behalf of
Mr Yuan the latter having written a note to the President saying that
"illness prevented his attending the meeting, and that he had therefore sent Mr Tong to act in his stead."

Mr. J. F. Schounicke a german subject and acting Chief Commissioner of Korean Customs was also present by invitation of the
President that he might have the assistance of Mr. Schounicke's
counsel and advice, he having a conversance with land questions
appertaining to the Chemulpo foreign settlement. Mr Schounicke's

presence was strongly objected to by Mr Krien the German Consul. The President explained that Mr. Schounicke being well advised in the matters about to be discussed, and being also a Korean official under his department, he hoped no objection would be urged by Mr. Krien to his remaining in the meeting for the purpose stated; that no objection had ever been offered by Mr Krien or any of the representatives to the presence of Mr Merrill Mr Schounicke's immediate predecessor in office who had been present repeatedly at such meetings for a similar purpose, for as Mr Krien Knew he (the President) was not well informed in the matter proposed for discussion as to the facts connected therewith. Mr Krien persisted in his objection and finally announced as an ultimatum that either Mr Schounicke must go or he would retire himself. Mr Schounicke with the Presidents consent withdrew.

I availed myself of the occasion to say as apropos of what had occurred that I must express my disapproval of the presence of Mr. Tong as representing the Chinese representative. I disclaimed any other Motive for my position than a desire that public business should be conducted under a proper observance of diplomatic usage and with due respect to the official dignity of the representatives of the treaty powers, and the responsibility of the members of the body participating; and stated that during the whole of my residence near the Korean Court Mr Yuan had observed the practice of sending a subordinate to represent him; that I had on a former occasion announced my disapproval of such a course as a uniform practice. I could not regard Mr Yuan's systematic conduct in this particular with approval but I have the authority of my government to say the presence of a subordinate officer at the stated meetings of the diplomatic body even for the purpose of reporting proceedings to his Chief should be discouraged.

That on this particular occasion I should not make further objection to Mr Tongs presence, but I indulged the hope that Mr Yuan would be able in the future as far as possible to give us the benefit and pleasure of his personal presence at our meetings.

Upon the point raised I invited an expression of opinion from my colleagues, and was sustained by the Russian representative. Mr. Krien having accomplished Mr Schounicke's withdrawal seemed content therewith and offered no suggestion as to the propriety or impropriety of the practice followed by Mr Yuan, nor was any opinion expressed by the Japanese French or British representatives.

Our meeting at the Foreign Office failed of its object and I invited

My Colleagues to meet in the following week in this legation for the purpose of reaching if possible an agreement if possible [sic] which might enable us to obtain the acquiescence of the Korean Government in a Much desired reform of the land regulations of the Chemulpo general foreign settlement, a reduction of the taxes.

Mr Yuan did not attend but sent a uniform personal note to all the representatives saying he "regretted that it would be impossible for him to attend such meetings at any place other than the Korean Foreign Office."

An agreement with the representatives present was reached in a Note prepared for our joint signatures setting forth to the Korean Government the necessity and general desirableness of the reduction of the taxes imposed by the land agreement upon the land holders in the Chemulpo foreign settlement.

It should be borne in mind that the settlement is Composed of American British french, german, Japanese and Chinese residents; and that therefore a concurrence of all the powers signatory to the agreement is essential to a change of its provisions.

The note was sent to Mr Yuan in the english text for his signature. (The British Consul General by agreement was to prepare the Chinese translation to be submitted to all the signers of the note before Transmission to the Foreign Office) but Mr Yuan wrote an informal note to Mr. de Planey the french Commissioner returning our note without his signature, explaining that he could not Correspond with the Korean Government except in Chinese, but that the proposed Change seemed desirable and that he would place in the hands of the President a separate note recommending it.

It is not for me to suggest Motives which may actuate such a Course, but it is certainly not a desirable situation for representatives of treaty powers which demands that in all matters requiring general concurrence, the result of their united labors before they can become effective Must be submitted to the representative of another power separately, subject to the possible necessity of a reformation to suit his peculiar views.

HUGH A. DINSMORE

              Legation of the United States
                           Seoul, Corea, June 3 1890

Secretary of State

Sir:

I had the honor by the last mail of acknowledging receipt of your despatch No. 4 of Mch 20, and it was not my intention so soon to take up the official question of Mr. Yuan's relations with the other Representatives of Foreign Governments which forms its subject. I have not yet had that conference with my Colleagues which it suggests. It seemed to me best, as there was no pressing occasion for haste, to make further acquaintance with the situation here, and above all to establish familiar and friendly relations with the several gentlemen in question. It seemed desirable to know them personally, to know their character and influence and relative position among themselves as well as towards the Corean and Chinese Governments, and to inspire them with friendly confidence in myself before having Conversation on a subject beset with so many delicate complications. And it is only since the 20 May that I have formally assumed charge of the Legation. For this reason during my short stay here, I have devoted myself solely to cultivating the social relations which seem best fitted to conduce to that end. I have dined with several of them; among others, with Mr. Yuan himself, who affects a rather coarse joviality, but who is unquestionably an able man, and, although he speaks no English, even through an interpreter readily impresses one conversing with him of the alertness and quickness of his intellect. I have met him frequently at his own table, at his house and mine in calls, & at the house of our Colleagues, and I have tried directly & indirectly to give him the belief that I have—what indeed I really feel—a sincere admiration for his Country and Countrymen.

But I am induced to allude to the Chinese question now, somewhat prematurely, by a piece of information which was given to me privately this morning and which, if true, will furnish one more proof of the pertinacity and resolution with which China is furthering her claims to dominate Corea.

You are aware that Mr. Denny has ceased to fill the post of adviser to the King. For some time past, His Majesty has been anxiously seeking for someone onto whom he could lean in this capacity and repeatedly solicited Mr. Dinsmore to come to his aid. On the first occasion Mr. Dinsmore referred the question to the Secretary of

State, who was then Mr. Bayard, feeling at the same time himself
that acceptance was impossible. As he expected would be the case,
Mr. Bayard's reply was unfavorable; but the king, unwilling to
receive this answer as final, renewed his request upon two later
occasions, and at the time of our audience he expressed repeatedly
his regret at Mr. Dinsmore's departure, and his hope that he might
return.

Finding Mr. D. impracticable, & yielding to other influences, mainly
Japanese, he named Mr. Le Gendre to fill the post.

On my arrival here, I was made aware by Mr. Dinsmore that
intrigues were in progress looking to the appointment of Mr.
Schounicke, in which Mr. Hillier, the English Consul General, was
playing an active part. Mr. Schounicke is of German birth, but he is
acting Commissioner of Customs in Corea, which you are aware is
simply a branch of the Chinese Service, and is himself an ardent
admirer and follower of Mr. Yuan and entirely devoted to Chinese
interests.

An American, who was formerly in the Consular Service at Kobe
and who is now employed as military instructor by the Corean Govt,
called upon me this morning, and told me confidentially that he had
been informed by a Corean who was present when the demand was
made the day before yesterday—that Mr. Yuan had demanded in the
name of his government that

all military instruction by Foreigners should cease and the Foreign Instruc-
tors dismissed; and that Mr. Schounicke should be appointed Foreign
Adviser to the King, adding that in this demand he was Supported by
England.

The source of my information has precluded me from taking any
steps towards ascertaining its truth, or of discussing it with anyone of
my Colleagues, but probably a few days will develope the facts, and
as the mail leaves tomorrow I bring it to your Knowledge at once,
as an item of intelligence, which may or may not be worthy of
attention.

If Mr. Schounicke is placed in that position it may mean an
accession of strength to the Chinese Cause and a pushing of Chinese
claims by every means possible; and a consequent weakness of the
influence of other powers, including America's. In these matters
England and China are acting together, and their open activity may
have the natural effect of stimulating the hostility of Russia & Japan—
China having the advantage of power in hand.

I am to a certain extent a partisan of China—or rather I should say I recognize the qualities and the ability of her statesmen, but I cannot shut my eyes to the fact that the success of her arms means the extinction of Corea as an independent power, making treaties and sending & receiving embassies.

Since writing the above, I have been told that Mr. Yuan has withdrawn his demand for the immediate dismissal of the Foreign Military Instructors. As several are now under contract he is willing they should serve out their time, but no others must be imported. My informant has heard nothing more regarding the offer to Schounicke. It seems quite possible that what was represented as a "demand" may have been a simple suggestion; but there is no doubt from what I learn from several sources that attempts have been made for some time in that direction.

Of course I shall not Commit myself in any way, and shall watch the game and report the moves.

AUGUSTINE HEARD

8 moon 28 day [Oct 11, 1890]

Augustine Heard

Sir:

I have the honor to address you as follows.

I received your answer today stating that in consequence of the burial of the Dowager Queen, and the friendly relations existing between the United States and Corea, you had on this important occasion, sent an order for naval troops to accompany the procession as a mark of respect and sympathy.

I have given this careful consideration, but find that this sudden peremptory landing of troops by Foreign Ministers is without precedent.

At present, you say, there is no imminent danger; that your bringing naval troops at this time is simply as an escort in token of your respect to a friendly power.

My government very attentively (jealously) watches the attempts of other powers to promote their interests with Korea. If other country's representatives bring troops to Seoul without previously informing my Government, My Government must notice the action and the course of friendship (friendly relations between the two powers) must be impeded.

Your action in bringing these troops to Seoul, I must freely make known to my Government, and it will be a subject for international discussion.

YUAN SHI KWAI

Legation of the United States
Seoul, Corea, Oct 11, 1890

Yuan Tsü Kwai

Sir:

I have the honor to acknowledge the receipt of your communication of this date, stating that you had received a telegram from the Chinese Consul at Chemulpo to the effect that a large number of men, with arms, were being landed from the American ships of war with the intention of proceeding to Seoul; and asking, as this was unusual, whether it was done by my order for protection.

It gives me great pleasure to say in reply that it is from no fear of disturbance that these men have been summoned to Seoul. Your Excellency is aware that the final funeral arrangements in honor of the late Queen Dowager, whose recent death plunged the whole country into mourning, and which are to be conducted with extraordinary pomp, commenced this night; and it seems to me fitting that a nation friendly with Corea like America, should testify to her respect and sympathy by the presence of a small detachment from one of her naval vessels on such an occasion.

I therefore requested Capt. Dawson of the "Monocacy" to send up the men in question, and I expect them this afternoon.

AUGUSTINE HEARD

NO. 114
Legation of the United States
Seoul, Corea, January 22, 1891

Secretary of State

Sir:

I have the honor to enclose copies of recent correspondence between Mr. Yuan and myself, which has had the effect of defining the relations he now assumes to hold towards the Diplomatic Body.

It becoming necessary to call a meeting to deliberate on certain measures of interest to the Foreign Settlement at Chemulpo, I issued notices, as Doyen, to the various representatives, Mr. Yuan among the number. —At first I had not included his name but my attention having been drawn to the omission, it occurred to me that, although he was always in the habit of declining to be present, he might regard the want of an invitation as a discourtesy, especially in view of the correspondence we had had with him at the time of the visit of the Chinese envoys— and I directed one to be sent.

He replied at once in English, the note having been written by his Secretary, who has passed ten years in the United States, and is well acquainted with the language.

The tone of it was rude, and the sense of the meeting was that a short answer should be sent, which was done. Mr. de Planey was of opinion that we should notify Mr. Yuan that we should consider him as no longer forming part of the Diplomatic Body and that we would hold no further communication with him.

On the next day a rejoinder was received from Mr. Yuan, in which he practically assumes that position. He describes himself as occupying a position apart.

In view of the fact that a discussion, involving the point at issue, might be in progress at Washington, as a consequence of Mr. Yuan's statement that he should draw the attention of his Government to my action at the time of the funeral of H.R.H. the late Queen Dowager, and seeing no especial object to be gained by pursuing the correspondence, I did not reply.

AUGUSTINE HEARD

Korean Foreign Office
Sŏul, December 30, 1886

W. W. Rockhill

Sir:

Recently in a Shanghai foreign newspaper, in its issue under date of the 16th and 17th November 1886, your countryman Lieutenant Foulk published three articles discussing affairs of our country in which he tries to establish that traitors to (or conspirators against) our country are loyal subjects, making as true statements untrue ones; and maligning our high nobility in a way to weaken the friendly relations existing between our two countries, and so that our high ministers of state have been filled with amazement on seeing them (i.e. these articles).

Mr. Foulk was formerly Chargé d'Affaires of the United States, and now, though he has been relieved of office, he is still living in your legation and is exercising official functions.

Our government has for Mr. Foulk the highest esteem, and if there be such faults in our government as those he refers to, he should certainly state them to us directly in all loyalty and sincerity— How can it be that such baseless words are circulated broadcast through the press!

who have
Not only ~~have~~ the high ministers of our country ∧ always put great confidence in (Mr Foulk), but also the people ask in surprise how he can have acted in this manner. The good and bad of these articles are but confusedly understood, and cannot but be subversive and highly injurious to the country.

I have therefore to request Your Excellency to carefully and impartially examine the matter, to request the newspaper office to have the erroneous statements in these articles corrected in another issue so as to dispel doubt and to the end that all may be arranged in a sincere spirit of reciprocal friendship.

KIM YUN SIK

Legation of the United States
Sŏul, December 31, 1886

President of the Korean Foreign Office

Your Excellency:

In reply to Y.E.'s despatch in which you inform me that Lieutenant Foulk has published several articles in a Shanghai foreign newspaper bearing on Korean affairs, in which he makes incorrect statements derogatory to the honor of your country, and asking me to have a corrected statement published in the same paper, I have the honor to inform Y.E. that I have never seen the incriminated articles, and I must beg that you will forward them to me for examination. Before seeing them, however, I can assure Y.E. that Mr. Foulk had never published himself any article in any newspaper, for none of the officials of my government are allowed to do so. I feel sure, moreover, that Mr. Foulk's well-Known good feelings towards your King and his country, which he has endeavored to show in all his official acts while serving as Chargé d'Affaires of the United States in Korea, would ever have prevented him doing or saying anything which was detrimental to the honor of Korea.

W. W. Rockhill

Legation of the United States
Soul—Korea
Jany, 2, 1887

W. W. Rockhill

Sir:

You have kindly communicated to me the contents of an official despatch of His Excellency the President of the Office for Korean Affairs of Korea, dated 30th ultimo. In this despatch it is stated that I published three articles in a foreign newspaper of Shanghai of a character false and damaging to the government of Korea; that though Their Excellencies the Ministers of State of Korea have regarded me with trustful feelings, they now, —and not only their Excellencies but the people as well are filled with amazement that I should have published broadcast such articles.

In regard to this despatch of His Excellency the President of the Foreign Office, I beg to submit this official statement and the request that its contents be made known to His Korean Majesty's government, through His Excellency Kim, and as well, to the government of the United States.

His Majesty's Kingdom was fixed in the eyes of nations as a high and honorable sovereign state by a treaty made by the President of the United States and His Majesty the King of Korea. The high Ambassador of His Majesty the King of Korea having visited the United States, the President despatched me to Korea as escort officer to His Majesty's Ambassador, and upon my reaching Korea, ordered me to serve as Naval Attaché to this Legation, with special instructions most friendly to Korea. Knowing well that the President of my country was a good friend of His Majesty the King of Korea, in my service in Korea as Naval Attaché and Chargé d'Affaires ad interim, I have thought only of the dignity and welfare of His Majesty's Kingdom. Is it that I have thought too much so?

I have never published anything whatever in any form, relative to Korea, and it would have been impossible for me to have published articles of the character His Excellency Kim attributes to me.

The articles His Excellency refers to do contain here and there parts of an official letter I sent to our government more than two years ago. As to how the newspaper people obtained these I am in ignorance. There are also parts of the letter of Minister Foote referred to, but the whole article was written and published by some person unknown to me. The letter of mine above referred to was a summary of statements made to me by Korean officers between June 1st and November 1st 1884, and did not in any way treat the events of the deplorable affair of December 1884.

I note, with great surprise, that His Excellency does not ask the question "Did Mr. Foulk publish the articles?", but begins his despatch with the rigid statement that Lieut. Foulk did publish them.

Is it not, may I ask, singular that these articles on events upwards of two years past should now be published?

Is it not singular also that *these* foreign newspapers are brought so energetically to the notice of His Majesty's officers and people that His Excellency Kim, in spite of his trustful feelings for Mr. Foulk, should, without direct inquiry of you, the Chargé d'Affaires ad interim, or myself, assume with positiveness that I published the articles in the Shanghai newspapers?

It is not often that governments lay great stress on newspaper articles. In the case at hand, though the articles are very wrong and much distorted, the harm being done is not so much due to their material, as to those persons who present them in further grossly exaggerated and distorted forms to His Majesty's officers and people.

My feelings towards this country have always been warm and disinterested, and I have been proud of and grateful for the Kindness shown me by its officers and people; you may then understand, Sir, how surprised and regretful I am to observe in His Excellency's despatch that without serious reflection or proper inquiry as to the motives and origins of the newspaper articles in question, they are assumed to be published by me, and that I am responsible for injury done their country, Their Excellencies, the Ministers of State and the people of Korea.

(Sgd) GEORGE C. FOULK
Naval Attaché

NO. 46   Legation of the United States
Söul, January 3, 1887

Secretary of State

Sir:

I have the honor to forward to you herewith a translation of a despatch addressed to me on the 30th ultimo by the President of the Korean Foreign Office in which he states that three articles written by Lieutenant Foulk had appeared in recent issues of a Shanghai foreign newspaper, in which the writer grossly calumniates Korea, and he asks me to devise means of disspelling [sic] the very bad effect which the publication of such articles cannot fail to have on the people, requesting that a correction be published in the Shanghai newspaper which had given the articles.

I replied to the above despatch stating that I had never seen the articles to which he took objection and begged that he would send them to me. I stated at the same time that I can assure him that they could not have been published in the newspapers by Mr. Foulk as officers of our government were strictly forbidden from writing political articles for the press. I felt moreover convinced that the well-Known good feelings of Mr. Foulk for Korea make such a charge against him incredible.

The articles referred to are, I doubt not, those published in the Shanghai "North China daily news" and which are simply transcriptions of the greater part of Mr. Foulk's "Report of information relative to the revolutionary attempt in Seoul, Corea" published in Foreign Relations for 1885 P. 335 *etsqq* as an enclosure to Minister Foote's No. 128 of December 17, 1884 to Mr. Secretary Frelinghuysen.

As I have not as yet received an answer to my despatch to the Foreign Office, I cannot state whether some editorial published at the same time in the "North China Daily News" has not also been attributed to Mr. Foulk.

I deemed it proper to submit the despatch of the President of the Foreign Office to Mr. Foulk requesting him to address me in reply to it; I enclose herewith Mr. Foulk's answer, a copy of which I have also sent to the Foreign Office.

W. W. ROCKHILL

Legation of the United States
Söul, January 8th 1887

President of the Korean Foreign Office

Your Excellency:

In my dispatch of the 31st of December 1886, I had the honor to request your Excellency to forward to me copies of three articles which had been published in a Shanghai foreign newspaper on the 16th and 17th of November 1886 and which you told me had been published by Mr. Foulk. Nine days have elapsed and I have not received the articles you object to—

Your Excellency must see that such a serious charge as that you have made against Mr. Foulk requires a prompt and complete explanation, that I cannot allow this accusation to remain unsettled. I beg therefore that you will communicate to me at once the newspaper articles which have occasioned the charge you have made.

W. W. Rockhill

Legation of the United States
Söul, January 11, 1887

President of the Korean Foreign Office

Your Excellency:

I have the honor to return to you herewith the numbers of the "North China Daily News" of November 15, 16 and 17 which you were so kind as to send me.

It gives me great pleasure to inform you, and I feel sure that Your Excellency will be equally pleased to hear, that the assurances which I gave you in my despatch of Jany 2, that the three articles had not been published in the newspaper by Lieutenant Foulk, are fully confirmed by a careful examination of the newspapers.

The articles are partly made up of extracts from a confidential report made to my government by Mr. Foulk to the month of December 1884.

I do not know how the writer of the newspaper articles obtained Knowledge of Mr. Foulk's report, but Mr. Foulk cannot in any way be made responsible for the publication.

I cannot doubt that under the circumstances, Your Excellency will be pleased to retract what now appears as baseless charges contained in your despatch of December 29th last.

W. W. Rockhill

Legation of the United States
Söul January 24, 1887

Secretary of State

Sir:

As a further reference to my despatch number 46 of the 3rd instant concerning certain charges made against Mr. Foulk by the Korean Foreign Office, I have now the honor to inform you that today during the new year's audience with His Majesty the King at which were present the other foreign representatives and the Korean ministers of state, His Majesty having asked me if my family was in good health, I replied that I was now without family in Korea, that Mr. Foulk had left me today to go to Japan. The King then asked if Mr. Foulk would come back to Korea. I replied that I hoped so, that he was sincerely devoted to His Majesty and had at heart the true interests of the country. The King said that he also hoped Mr. Foulk would come back.

After leaving the King's presence, he called my interpreter back and said to him: "Explain well what I have said to Mr. Rockhill so that he may be able to convey to Mr. Foulk the true expression of the Kindly and friendly feelings I entertain for him."

I have thus dwelt at length on this conversation, because a despatch which I have just addressed to the Foreign Office, asking them to retract the baseless charges made against Mr. Foulk, has remained unanswered. That it will be highly satisfactory I cannot now doubt, after the public expression of the King's feeling on the subject.

W. W. Rockhill

NO. 55 Department of State
Washington, March 3, 1887

W. W. Rockhill

Sir:

I have received your No. 46 of January 3rd, 1887, in regard to the complaint of the Corean Government against Mr. George C. Foulk on account of articles alleged to have been published by him in the "North China Daily News" of Shanghai, reflecting seriously upon Corea.

As Mr. Foulk no longer represents or is under the orders of this Department, there seems to be no occasion for me to take notice of the complaint beyond observing that an Agent's communications to his own Government are privileged, —that they can only be considered in the form in which the Government may publish them, and that we can have nothing to do with publications by unknown parties in the public press, even when they purport to be founded on the published reports of our officers. The many evidences of good will on the part of this Government and its representatives, makes any protestation of friendliness wholly unnecessary and relieve us of any need of considering these unauthorized and probably distorted publications in the press of another country.

T. F. BAYARD

NO. 75 Legation of the United States
Söul, March 31, 1887

Secretary of State

Sir:

I have the honor to forward to you herewith a translation of a despatch which I have received from the President of the Korean Foreign Office in which he requests me to inform Mr. Foulk that he has received such information as enables him to state that the charges made against him in his despatch dated December 29th last—and forwarded to you in my No. 46 of January 3rd, are shown to have been perfectly baseless. The Chinese text of the President's despatch is rather ambiguous, the general meaning is, however, sufficiently plain, and it may be accepted as a tolerably satisfactory though tardy apology.

W. W. ROCKHILL

Korean Foreign Office
Söul, March 28, 1887

W. W. Rockhill

Sir:

In reply to your letters of January in reference to the newspaper articles by Mr. Foulk, I have to state that the matter is now perfectly understood. While Mr. Foulk was in Korea the relations between the two countries were very close, and for this our Ministers are very grateful—while our Ministers had doubts as to Mr. Foulk being the author of the newspaper articles incriminated, the fact of such articles having been published, precluded the possibility of ignoring them. Moreover the articles as published in English contain many inaccuracies. My former despatch (December 29, 1886) was sent before I had come into possession of accurate information. From your last despatch (January 11, 1887) we then first knew that Mr. Foulk did not prompt (the writing of) the articles, and our doubts were all _____ dispelled. Since the receipt (of your despatch of January 11th) stress of business has prevented me, much to my regret, from replying to you.

I hear that Mr. Foulk has returned from Japan, and I have to request that you explicitly state to him _____ that I now Know that he had absolutely nothing to do with the publication of these articles.

(Sgd) KIM YUN-SIK

NO. 19   Legation of the United States
Söul, Korea, May 2" 1887

President of the Korean Foreign Office

Your Excellency:

Replying to your dispatch received yesterday on the subject of certain newspaper publications and the supposed connection therewith of Lieutenant George C. Foulk, naval attaché of this legation, I have the honor to state, that I regret very much that this unpleasant matter should from some unknown cause, or by reason of some unknown agency again disturb the minds of Your Honorable Ministers of State. It is the more to be regretted because the accusation Your Honorable Office makes against Mr. Foulk, reflects upon his conduct

as an official of the United States accredited to the government of
Korea by the government of the United States and while he was
acting under the authority and by the direction of the latter Government.

I must be permitted to express most respectfully my very great
surprise that this matter is again brought to the attention of the
United States through me as its representative, because I find on file
in this office of this legation a formal letter written on the 28th of the
last month to Mr. Rockhill, late Chargé d'Affaires of this legation and
signed by Your Excellency as President of the office for foreign affairs
in which you fully acquit Mr. Foulk of the charge which now you
make, and request of Mr. Rockhill that he assure Mr. Foulk of your
trust and confidence. The publications you complain of appeared in
print many months ago. Your Excellency had seen them before the
retraction of your former accusation against Mr. Foulk was written.
The ink is but little more than dry upon that letter when Your
Excellency renews the charge and offers no reasonable evidence in
support of it.

Mr. Foulk did write a letter to the United States Government in
December 1884 relating certain incidents and historical events immediately preceding the sad and greatly regretted disturbances of public
affairs in Korea which occurred in the winter of that and the succeeding year. That letter the government of the United States has
seen proper to publish in its book of general foreign correspondence
together with many other letters from the various countries of the
world. The volume I refer to was published by authority of the
United States Government in ~~December~~ of the year 1886. For that
letter So published the government of the United States and not
Mr. Foulk is responsible to Korea. But there is nothing in that letter
as published by the government, which tends to show that there has
been any interruption of the uniform good will and respect ever
entertained by the government of the United States and all its officials
for Your Great King's ancient and honorable Dominion and people.
Concerning the matter of the publications and your former complaint
against Mr. Foulk our Secretary of State in a dispatch written to this
legation on the 3rd day of March last uses these words, viz:—"An
agents communication to his own Government are privileged. They
can only be considered in the form in which the Government may
publish them. We have nothing to do with publications by unknown
parties in the public press even when they purport to be founded on
the published reports of our officers. The many evidences of good will

on the part of this Government and its representatives make any protestation of friendliness wholly unnecessary and relieve us of any need of considering these unauthorized and probably distorted publications in the press of another country."

I may be permitted to state such publications as you have described would more naturally proceed from some source unfriendly to Mr. Foulk, and unfriendly to the fraternity between America and Korea, than from Mr. Foulk himself.

Your Excellency speaks of sending a despatch directly from Your Honorable Office for foreign affairs to the Government of the United States. If Your Excellency should determine to do so, I take pleasure in giving assurance that your correspondence will receive the highest consideration at the hands of our high officials, and a courteous response promptly returned; but I can give no assurance that a different course will be pursued than that indicated already in the remarks which I have had the honor to give herein as taken from the late dispatch of our Honorable Secretary of State.

Lieutenant Foulk is an officer of the United States government attached to this legation by its Naval Department, and I have not the authority to send him away, even if there were just cause; and believing as I do that he is a true and loyal citizen and officer of our Government, and a faithful and devoted friend to His Majesty the King of Ta Chosun and to His Majesty's Kingdom and people I have no desire that he should leave.

He will remain in Söul until such time as it shall please the Government of the United States by its properly authorized officers to relieve him from duty here.

HUGH A. DINSMORE

NO. 14   *Confidential*   Legation of the United States
                                                    Söul, Korea, May 3, 1887

Secretary of State

Sir:

Your dispatch No. 55 of March 3rd 1887 to Mr. Rockhill relative to the complaint of the Korean foreign office against Ensign George C. Foulk in connection with certain newspaper publications was received by me on the 18th of last month. Mr. Rockhill having already reported to you in his No. 75 of March 31st a letter from the foreign office retracting the charges against Mr. Foulk, there would have been no necessity for me to make further reference to the subject but for the development of subsequent events which appeared to me to demand additional correspondence.

In the first place perhaps I should state after Mr. Foulk's return to Söul from Japan where he had spent a period intervening between January 24th and March 13th on account of ill health under leave from Mr. Rockhill, His Majesty the King of Korea advised him by messenger as I am informed, that a house was being prepared near to our legation in Söul at the expense of the Korean Government, or of His Majesty, for his (Foulk's) occupancy.

Carpenters have been at work upon this building remodelling and repairing for a time, but fully under Korean supervision and direction. In so far as my Knowledge extends, Mr. Foulk has had nothing to do with it more than to signify some minor preferences as its [sic] arrangement, and he has stated to me repeatedly that he would not occupy the premises, unless he was allowed to take them as a purchaser. The relevancy of this statement will appear later on in the course of this communication.

In view of what had seemed so absolute a settlement of the matter of the publications spoken of, I had not thought that the affair could possibly be revived.

Notwithstanding what has occurred however, on the afternoon of the 31st ultimo I received a call at this legation, from His Excellency Kim Yun Sik, president of the foreign office accompanied by his interpreter, and he soon made Known to me that the object of his visit was to say that "Mr. Foulk had been instrumental in the publication of the newspaper articles previously referred to, that they were prejudicial to Korea and high Korean officials, and that Mr. Foulk ought to retire from Korea."

I expressed to him my utter astonishment at his position and demand and immediately confronted him with his letter of retraction, and asked him if he had received any futher evidences against Mr. Foulk since this letter was written. His only reply to this seemed to me to be pregnant with significance. It was this, "Mr. Foulk did write a letter to his government about Korean officials and according to the translation of this letter by the Chinese, this letter was very detrimental to Korea." Whom he referred to by "the Chinese" he did not explain though I asked him to do so.

I then stated to him that in the text of Mr. Foulk's letter as published by our government there was nothing which reflected dishonor either [sic] his king or his country; that for this letter as thus published Mr. Foulk could not be questioned, and that the government of the United States was alone responsible; that our government could not and would not consider publications nor comments by the public press but for its own official publications it was always responsible.

That in behalf of Mr. Foulk it appeared to me to be absurd to say that he should be responsible for the utterances of newspapers when those very utterances were liable to embarrass him more than any other, and when the papers themselves did not attribute authorship to him and when even His Excellency would not urge that Mr. Foulk had published them or caused them to be published, except indirectly in that he had written a communication to his government which the government had thought proper to publish.

He several times insisted that I should see the papers. I told him that I would read them if he chose to send them to me, but that as a representative of our government it was a matter of total indifference to me as to what might be their contents.

His Excellency then asked to look at my flowers, they being such as the Kindly hand of nature has thrust out from the crumbling ruins of these premises, and after a pleasant walk over the compound he took his departure apparently in an amiable frame of mind.

On the next day however he sent by the hands of his interpreter a formal dispatch as president of the office of foreign affairs, a translation of which I enclose herewith, wherein he insists that the Ministers of State and people in Korea do not trust Mr. Foulk and that he should leave here.

The bearer of the dispatch being the interpreter who had also written it in Chinese was evidently sent to translate it into english for me, though it was not accompanied by a written Translation.

He told me and told my interpreter also in Korean to impress upon me that the meaning of the dispatch was, that I as United States Minister should send Mr. Foulk away; that this would be pleasanter for him than to be sent away by Korean authority. My interpreter however could not make that rendering of it.

I have sent a response to this dispatch setting forth fully what I hope I am not wrong in supposing to be the proper position of our government in the premises, and the proper attitude of Mr. Foulk and on the affair in all respects. I have the honor to enclose a copy of the same herewith and to beg instruction if I have erred in any particular.

It should be borne in mind that Mr. Kim Yun Sik, the president of the foreign office, as you may see by reference to Mr. Foulk's letter in "Foreign Relations of the United States" Volume for 1885 pp. 33f et seq. is the same who was spoken of at some length in that letter as a participant in the events that led up to the troubles of Dec. 1884.

There are several of those persons now holding high positions in Korea, who then belonged and still belong to the pro-Chinese faction, who it is but natural to suppose may for a great while be liable to irritation on the subject of those troubles and the letter in connection with them, and concerning them, and while the matter cannot create distrust, it may cause a jealousy of Americans that may be used as a formidable weapon in the hands of those unfriendly to the success of America's treaty relations with Korea, and will always embarrass to some extent our legation here.

In connection with the foregoing it seems proper that I should communicate some of the recent concurrent circumstances and events which have been brought to my attention in various ways.

On the evening of the 30th of the last month I was informed by Mr. Merrill, an American gentleman who is the Korean Commissioner of Customs, that Mr. Yuan Sui Kai the Chinese minister was on the eve of sailing for China. Supposing this to be on some business of his government I attached no importance to it. On the 1st of May while in the company of Mr. T. Waters H.B.M.'s Acting Consul General I remarked to him what I had heard of Mr. Yuan's contemplated departure and asked him whether he knew if Mr. Yuan had yet sailed.

His reply was "I did not understand that he *was certainly* to go," thus leaving upon my mind that his going depended upon a contingency.

On the following day I heard through a very intelligent Korean of some standing that Mr. Yuan was about to leave Korea because of the presence of Mr. Foulk who he claimed had done him some wrong.

On the 2nd instant I had a visit from Mr. C. Waber the Russian Chargé d'affaires, who told me in confidence "that the Chinese minister was about to leave Korea as he had learned from to him satisfactory evidence; and assigned as a reason, that the King was preparing a house for Mr. Foulk and that Mr. Foulk was in the habit of going in disguise to the palace, and having private audiences with the King." There can be no doubt that he has assisted in giving currency to such a report, which it seems almost needless for me to assure you is without any foundation whatever. Mr. Foulk has not been near His Majesty, nor seen him nor been within the outer walls of the palace since August of last year. I have since heard that Mr. Yuan claims to be acting under instructions from his government and that he has been instructed to await until Mr. Foulk's withdrawal could be demanded.

I do not think he has any intentions whatever of leaving, but am inclined to the opinion that he is performing for political effect.

On the 2nd instant Dr. H. N. Allen, one of our American physicians in charge of the government (Korean) hospital informed me that he had received on that day a message directly from the King saying His Majesty had heard that Judge Denny of the home office and possibly others were endeavoring to bring about a recall of Mr. Foulk by Our Government and requesting him (Allen) to have a petition signed by all the American residents protesting against it. His Majesty is not cognizant I think of the demand of his foreign office for Mr. Foulk's recall.

In conclusion I venture to remark that in my opinion from all that I have seen and heard in the short time I have been in this Capitol, but for Chinese interference all that would go smoothly and well here and the country advance rapidly in prosperity and enterprise. But every step forward is opposed by the Chinese Minister. I call him "Minister" from a lack of Knowledge as to what his true position is. In view of our treaty we cannot concede to him the title of "Resident" in the sense in which he claims it.

My relations with him in a social way are of the pleasantest, and I have not met him otherwise, but his views and ours are so incompatible touching his relations with the Korean Government, that naught but inharmony and confusion can be expected.

As a notable example of his interference I would cite you to his memorial some time since to the king to abolish the hospital established under American auspices, as was reported in Mr. Rockhill's No. 54 of January 28th.

I shall not in any wise attempt to interfere with matters arising between China or any other power with Korea when we are not directly concerned, but the effect upon these people of such presumption as we constantly witness on the part of the Chinese representative, is deplorable, and naturally and I would think unavoidably humiliating to any sovereign power in treaty relations with this unfortunate country.

If Mr. Foulk should be recalled at this time, it will be generally accepted by Koreans, and indeed it would seem to be undeniable that it was forced upon us, and upon His Majesty the King, against his will, and cannot in my belief but prove to be disparaging to the dignity and strength of His Majesty's rule.

HUGH A. DINSMORE

NO. 16   Legation of the United States
Soul Korea May 9th 1887

Secretary of State

Sir:

Referring further to the subject treated of in my dispatch No. 14 of the third instant, viz:—the demand of the Korean foreign office for the retirement of Ensign George C. Foulk from Korea, and which I enclose under cover with this No, I beg to submit some additional facts and features coming to my Knowledge for the most part since the writing of my Number 14, and which it occurs to my mind are proper to be considered in connection with what I have already had the honor to communicate in the last named dispatch. And finally I must inform you that on yesterday the 8th instant, I had the honor to receive from H. E. Kim Yun Sik, the President of the Foreign office, another dispatch of the same tenor of his former dispatch, a translation of which I enclosed in my No. 14, and manifesting a disposition to argue with me with reference to my duty and power, and Mr. Foulk's guiltiness of the imputed charge, and concludes by saying that if I will send Foulk away it will be regarded by the Korean government with great favor, but if I shall not do so it must involve our legation in trouble. I have replied to this dispatch in a courteous way that my position has been clearly defined in my former dispatch that there is nothing further for me to add saving to express my sincere regret that my own conception of my duty differs so widely from His Excellency's.

There is a class of subordinate officials in the Korean government established by the King called Chusa composed in the main of bright and intelligent young men. These have access to the palace and are frequently called before His Majesty and through them he is supposed to receive information touching the transaction of affairs throughout the palace. And occasionally His Majesty makes use of them as confidential messengers.

On Saturday one of them, Mr. Sang, Chusa called on me in a

social way and in the course of conversation asked me if I had heard
that the Chinese Minister was thinking of leaving Söul. I replied
that I had heard rumors of that purport and asked him if he Knew
the cause. He answered "I think it is on account of Mr. Foulk residing here." I said "I am sorry if it be true that Mr. Yuan objects to
the residence in Söul of any citizen of America." He then remarked
I "do not think His Majesty wishes Mr. Foulk to leave." I asked
"When have you seen His Majesty," and he replied "Yesterday."
Very soon he took his departure. Another of this class of officers
on Saturday went directly from the palace to Dr. Allen and informed
him that His Majesty bade him ask if he (Allen) had communicated
his desire with reference to Mr. Foulk to the American minister,
saying he was anxious that it should be done, that His Majesty did
not desire that "high Korean Officers" should know of his communicating any wish upon the subject.

On Monday the 2nd instant, it having been publicly announced
several days before, His Majesty escorted by a number of his generals and other officials and about 3,000 soldiers left the city and
visited the graves of some of his ancestry about sixty ri's (or about
20 english miles) returning on the evening of the same day.

On this day at Chong No, or the place of the great bell the most
public point in the streets of Söul, appeared two public notices as
warnings, one declaring that a conspiracy was on foot in Söul with
design on the life of the King, the other that Pak Yong Hyo, one
of the conspirators of 1884, was en route from Japan where he is
known to have been for a time with five thousand Japanese soldiers.
A rumor was also current on the streets upon that day that four
Japanese men of war had arrived at Chemulpo. Evidently, a con-
centrated effort was made, it is not known by whom, to excite the
Korean people but it seems to have failed of its purpose as the
people seem to understand that it was unworthy of attention. The
announcement or report of the Chinese minister's intended withdrawal from Söul came out a day or two before the incendiary
notices made their appearance.

Having heard as I have heretofore stated to you that H. E. the
Chinese minister's contemplated departure had for its cause something connected directly with Mr. Foulk I felt it my duty in the
fault of his communicating with me upon the subject to call upon
him and express my regret that he should find in the residence here
of an American and of an officer sent hither by the United States
government sufficient cause to bring about so important a state in

the abandonment of his post, and to say that if Mr. Foulk had done aught that would justify such action upon his part it was certainly a matter which in view of our close relations with the Chinese empire it would doubly concern our governments to know. Accordingly I went to his legation but could not get to see him nor his principle interpreter, Mr. Tong, both as I was told being out.

It seems that the president of the foreign office has abandoned the anonymous letters published in the Chinese Times and bases now his whole charge against Mr. Foulk on the letter which is published in our correspondence as enclosure in Mr. Foote's dispatch.

A wretchedly distorted and unfair translation of this has been furnished him, and he is so completely under the influence which controls him in this affair that he is indisposed to accept a fair translation from another source. This translation in Chinese was brought to our legation by a Korean gentleman and officer ~~by consent of H. E. Kim,~~ and it has Mr. Foulk to say, according to my interpreter's rendering, "Kim Ok Yun, and his co-conspirators were good and loyal men," and [word illegible] "other high Korean officers who were not of the conspiracy were traduced" and moreover that his letter detailing the facts which he sent to the government after the Emeute, was written before it actually occurred. It will doubtless seem absurd to you that such a state of affairs can exist, but there being so few interpreters here and such poor ones, it makes the situation truly embarrassing.

The President's position is that Foulk having Known the conspirators intimately, and having been told by them of their purpose, as his translation tells him Mr. Foulk admits, that Mr. Foulk in language of his last dispatch to me "sat quietly by and saw our nobles butchered, our King imposed upon, our people thrown into consternation, our government well nigh overturned, and though he knew it was coming opened not his mouth and is thus as bad and the same as the rebels themselves."

Having been counseled by some capable of advising that Mr. Foulk may be in some personal danger, I on yesterday sent a telegraphic dispatch through our minister at Tokio for a vessel of war, none having been here since the Omaha sailed on April 3rd.

I do not apprehend danger myself, but I think the presence of a man of war at this time would go far toward allaying excitement which seems to be gathering, and toward causing a cessation of the active influences that I believe to be bringing the trouble about.

It seems to me that the affair has assumed an importance that demands the attention of our government.

HUGH A. DINSMORE

NO. 23   Legation of the United States
                   Söul Korea May 30th 1887

Secretary of State

Sir:

Asking your attention again to the subject considered in my two dispatches of the 3rd and 9th instant numbered 14 and 16 respectively, I have to report some further correspondence touching the matter. I had hoped that nothing more would be heard of this troublesome affair for some time at least, but the character of my correspondence has not had the effect to quiet the question and the President of the foreign office seems unshaken in his purpose and the agents behind the scenes untired in their efforts.

On the 21st instant the president sent me a dispatch a copy of which I enclose herewith, in which he indulges in the use of insolent and unwarrantable language to me. In it he makes not only inaccurate but false quotations both from my conversation and my correspondence, and charges me as you will observe with duplicity, and with a desire to protect an enemy of his country and thus assisting him in his treasonable purposes.

To this dispatch I sent no reply, but knowing that outside influence was at most upon his mind I thought it best to call upon him. So on the 28th instant in company with my interpreter I called at the Foreign Office and spent three hours in conversation with him. The interview was in a measure satisfactory as I succeeded in conveying to him ideas which he had failed to get from correspondence. With his last dispatch he sent to me a translation in Chinese of the article published in the North China Herald of Nov. 1–4th, 86, which is merely a partial copy of Lieut Foulks report as published in our Correspondence of foreign relations. He insisted time and again that I should procure the assistance of a good english Chinese scholar and compare the translation with the publication, but I declined saying to him that it could avail nothing for the purpose of having Mr. Foulk sent away, and could be of no benefit whatever since he had repeatedly declared himself to be unyielding in his purpose. It is proper that I should make known to you that the person whom he designated as the proper one to make the comparison with me is a Young Chinaman and intimate friend and associate of the Chinese Minister's Secretary whom I suspect to have made the translation. He insisted that I should send the translation to you and though it seems absurd I promised to do so to conciliate him as much as possible, and therefore send with this dispatch, but under a separate cover.

At his earnest request I promised to refer the whole matter to you again, while I assured him that his former letter had been communicated to you as well as my answer thereto.

I complained to him that he had in his last letter used improper and unauthorized language to me and accused me of a serious offense which was not true.

He begged me not to be offended saying it proceeded not from him but his government, to which I replied that his government had no greater right to accuse me unjustly than he possessed personally. A disposition was manifested by him to talk about China and I encouraged him to do so. He remarked that the relations between China and Korea had been explained when our treaty was made. I said America had no desire to interfere with the relations of other countries any more than she desired they should interfere with hers, but that America had treated Korea as an independent Kingdom and that we so regarded it: but that if the King of Korea and his subjects desired to be ruled by China America could not very well object. Oh, he replied we have no such desire. Korea is truly an independent Kingdom and China is only our elder brother and because we are weak and a small country we ask China to advise and assist us.

I said, "Is the emperor of China Your Emperor?" "Not at all" he answered "Koreans have their King and the Chinese their Emperor." "Then is the emperor of China the emperor of Your King?" "No Our Kings and the Chinese emperor are of equal rank but the emperor is more powerful having a greater country and has ever been regarded as the elder brother of our King."

"Then You do not consider that China has a right to control Your Governmental affairs nor to dictate to you?"

"No, only to give us the benefit of their counsel and aid."

I left him saying that I hoped he would not write to me any further about Lieut Foulk as I would not advise him to leave without orders from his government; that Mr. Foulk had no desire to remain in Korea if the King and the people did not wish it. Nor did our Government have any disposition I was forced to believe to enforce upon them an official who was obnoxious to them, but that I denied the justness of their accusation and the right of their demand. His response was a request that I write to you, and I thought he was a little amused when I told him I would forward a copy of his last dispatch.

Believing that the Chinese minister is causing the whole trouble, and continuing to hear of his covert action with reference to it, I addressed him in a dispatch on the 26th instant, a request to make known to me any cause of grievance he might have against Lieut Foulk that I might advise our government looking to an investigation of it.

I have the honor to enclose herewith a copy of that dispatch as also a copy of one received in reply from him, which must be read to be appreciated.

As you will readily observe he associates himself with the Korean Government, and expresses his hope that the "United States Government will lose no time in taking the proper action to a country in which his own is doubly interested." &c

I have hesitated much as to whether I should say more to him but after careful reflection, I have felt that I could do nothing less in discharge of my duty as it appeared to me than to say as much as is to be found in the enclosed copy of my second dispatch to him to which I have as yet received no response.

I hope I have not exceeded nor misconceived my duty. I am so far away from our seat of government and so long a time is required for correspondence by mail, that I am forced to take responsibility in matters which I would greatly prefer first to submit for your approval.

I will advise Mr. Denby of the situation here by the next mail which departs on the 3rd prox.

                                                    HUGH A. DINSMORE

                                                    H.I.C.M. Residency
                                                    Söul 28th May 1887

Hugh A. Dinsmore

Sir:

I have to acknowledge receipt of your dispatch of the 26th instant in which you informed me that during the past few weeks frequent rumors have come to your ears of great dissatisfaction on my part at the residence in Söul of Lieut Foulk naval attaché to your legation, and even to the extent that at one time I was about to abandon this capital and return to China and that I had declared to do if Lieut

Foulk were not sent away and requests me to communicate to you of any complaints which I had to make against Lieut Foulk so that you may make it Known to your Government, to fairly investigate the matter and proper action taken as in view of the close friendly relations existing between the United States and China, and that Your Government must feel a deep concern in any conduct of one of her citizens and officers which is a proper cause of damage to her friendly ally.

In reply I have to say that when I first read your communication I was greatly astonished, but however I am glad to hear from you and thank you for your assurance of friendship.

I do not doubt for a moment that you are not aware of the relations between my country and that of Corea which were made known to your government before and after the treaty of 1882 in your treaty of friendship and commerce with the latter country. I do not think you have to wait for me to complain of Lieut Foulk as information have reached me that the Corean Government have written to you more than once on the subject, and moreover when you kindly called on me with Mr. Rockhill the former chargé d'affaires of your legation, I asked you if Lieut Foulk was attached to your legation and to which you replied in the negative. And besides I heard about the same time Lieut Foulk was going to be in the employ of the Corean Government, and did not and still not know when he has again joined the service to your legation.

However I must say that when Lieutanant Foulk was in charge of your legation our mutual relations were of a very pleasant one, but I am very sorry to say that I cannot agree with his wrong and self opinion of the relations between my country and Corea which he has made known to the world.

Further, I have to say that my present position here does not permit me to abandon this country and return to China on accout of Lieut Foulk's one single person as you have stated in your communication to me. I am afraid that your information was not correct and that you have not inquired into it.

I am happy to learn of your friendly feelings toward my government and beg to thank you for your sincere desire and readiness to smooth whatever troubles there are existing between the government of the United States and China and I am sure when such can be done the present friendly relations between the two countries will be firmer and stronger, and it is also my sincere hope that such will be the case. You are aware that your government must feel a deep

concern in any conduct of one of her citizens or officers which is a
proper cause of offense to her friendly ally. I therefore hope that
your Government and with your assistance will lose no time in taking
the proper action to a country which My Government feel most
deeply interested in. Again I have to state I have nothing more to
say and only hope that you can agree with me with my requests.

YUAN SIU KWAI

(The dispatch is written in English, a literal copy. H.A.D.)

NO. 21   Department of State
                                          Washington, June 17, 1887

Hugh A. Dinsmore

Sir:

Your despatches Nos. 14 and 16, of the Diplomatic Series, dated
respectively the 3rd and 9th ultimo, in relation to the desire of the
Korean Foreign Office for the recall of Ensign Foulk, were received
at this Department on the 15th instant.

Prior to their receipt, the Chinese Chargé d'Affaires at this Capital,
had made oral and written representations to me that the continued
residence of Mr. Foulk in Korea was a source of peril to the relations
between Korea and China—on the authority of Viceroy Lee it was
even stated that "Foulk, in concert with some evil-disposed persons
of Korea, is planning a rebellion against China—and it was further
stated that The Ministers of the United States in China and Korea,
upon being consulted, suggest that a request be made at the State
Department for his (Mr. Foulk's) immediate recall."

The situation disclosed by your despatches suggests no such
extreme gravity as the statements made here by the Chinese Chargé
d'Affaires would imply, —but, rather, that the motive in certain
quarters to get rid of Mr. Foulk may be stronger than the facts
brought forward to effect his removal.

However this may be, the inexpediency of pressing Mr. Foulk
further upon the Korean Government as a representative of the
United States, is evident. Setting altogether aside, for the present,
the unsubstantiated and probably erroneous charge that Mr. Foulk
is planning a rebellion against China, "international comity is opposed
to any appearance of forcing a government to retain a foreign repre-

sentative required by it to be *persona non grata,* as well as to any discussion of the motives it may allege beyond such controversion of the immediate charges as you have already made in the present instance. The services rendered by Mr. Foulk in his delicate and important mission of Naval Attaché depend moreover, so much upon the friendliness of his relations with the Korean authorities, that his usefulness in that capacity is unquestionably impaired by the hostility exhibited to him by the Government of His Majesty the King of Korea, and his retention upon that official duty could not fail to be personally embarrassing to him.

In view of all this, and after consultation with the Secretary of the Navy, it has been determined to relieve Ensign Foulk as Naval Attaché, and to order him to report for duty, on board the "Marion." These orders were, as I learned, executed by Admiral Chandler on the 15th instant.

I enclose for your information copy of my correspondence on the subject with the Chinese Chargé d'Affaires.

T. F. BAYARD

Enclosure to #21.   Department of State
                                                        Washington, June 16, 1887

Shu Cheon Pon

Sir:

I had the honor to receive on the 8th instant, your note of that date, repeating and amplifying the representations you had previously made to me, orally, respecting the attitude of Ensign George G. Foulk, Naval Attache to the United States Legation at Seoul, Korea, and lately Chargé d'Affaires *ad interim* at that post.

You state on the authority of His Excellency the Viceroy Li, that— "Foulk, in concert with some evil disposed persons of Korea, is planning a rebellion against China; disorders may arise if not checked in time. The Ministers of the United States in China and Corea, upon being consulted, suggest that a request be made at the State Department for his immediate recall."

This statement is so completely at variance with the high character of Ensign Foulk, and so incredible in view of the Department's knowledge of the discretion and uprightness with which Mr. Foulk has rendered important service to this Government and efficiently executed the delicate mission entrusted to him while representing the United States at the Court of His Majesty the King of Korea, under the guarantees of the 2nd Article of the Treaty of 1882 between the United States and Korea, that I cannot but believe that some serious misapprehensions may exist on the part of His Excellency as to his conduct at the present time.

This belief is strengthened by correspondence between Mr. Dinsmore the present United States Minister at Seoul, and the Foreign Office of Korea, which has just been received here from the Legation, which reports coming down as late as the 9th ultimo. The complaint made by the Korean Foreign Office was in continuation of certain objections raised some time since against Mr. Foulk, by reason of the garbled and apparently malevolent misrepresentation, in the public press of a foreign country and otherwise, of despatches written by Mr. Foulk to his own Government in December 1884, narrating the civil disturbances that occurred in Korea, and which despatches were officially published by this Government in 1886. As privileged utterances made to his own Government and so published, Mr. Dinsmore had been instructed to inform the Korean Foreign Office that this Government is alone responsible for them, and there is no need of considering unauthorized and presumably distorted version thereof, originating in another country. This Mr. Dinsmore reports that he had done.

Without prejudice to the consideration of other circumstances, should such hereafter appear, affecting Mr. Foulk's conduct, it is evident to this Government that the position assumed by the Korean Foreign Office in declaring him to be an unacceptable person is such as to seriously impair the utility of his functions as Naval Attache, and to lessen the value of his services to his own government in that capacity.

My colleague, the Secretary of the Navy, with whom I have conferred in the subject has accordingly directed Ensign Foulk to report for duty on the United States Steamer "Marion" and I learn that the necessary orders in the case were given yesterday, the 15th instant, by the Admiral Commanding the United States Squadron in the Asiatic Station.

In thus complying with the expressed wish of the Government of His Majesty the King of Korea, and admitting without comment or discussion, its declaration that Mr. Foulk is not *persona grata,* this government not merely follows the usual rule of international comity in such cases, but is relieved from the necessity of considering whether Mr. Foulk's continued residence in Korea is inimical to the good understanding we are so desirous to maintain between the two Powers, with each of which the United States is gratified to hold relations founded upon treaty and marked by disinterested amity.

That the action of this government has thus incidentally been in the line of satisfaction of the Imperial Government of China is naturally a cause of congratulation.

T. F. BAYARD

Legation of the United States
                                    Soul Korea June 20th 1887

Secretary of State

Sir:

I have the honor to inform you that on the 18th instant Lieutenant
Foulk showed to me a despatch received on that day from him by
telegraph from Admiral Chandler commanding U.S. naval forces on
the Asiatic Station, saying that Lieutenant Foulk has been detached
from the legation and ordering him to report without delay to
Commander Miller commanding U.S.S. Marion now in harbor off
Chemulpo.

Lieutenant Foulk immediately reported in obedience to the telegram and having obtained leave to make preparation for his departure is now in readiness and will join the ship tomorrow. I cannot
but regret the necessity for the order relieving him from duty here
at this time.

There is not an interpreter in this country who can render Chinese
or Korean into english in a fairly intelligible and reliable way, but
through Mr. Foulk's Knowledge of the Korean language, and his
intimate acquaintance with the people and their habits and modes
of thought he has been enabled to be of incalculable assistance to
me and I desire to make proper official acknowledgement of it.

                            a
But the greatest re∧san why, in my opinion, departure is to be
regretted is, that it will most certainly be, and is already recognized,
as an accomplishment of the Chinese minister against my desire and
against the earnest desire of His Majesty The King of Korea and all
his people who are loyal to the sovereignty of their country having
any Knowledge of the state of affairs in the country at the present
time. The King heard of his intended departure on the night of the
18th instant, and sent an officer at 3 o'clock in the morning to enquire
into it and to beg that he would not go. On yesterday the 19th
Prince Min Yon Ik came in person to call upon me and anxiously
ask if the order could not be revoked, and earnestly entreated that
he might be permitted to remain. It should be borne in mind that
Prince Min, who was the ambassador to our country in 1883, is he
who is cited in Mr. Foulk's now celebrated report as being pro-
Chinese, and he is the one mentioned by President Kim Yun Sik
as having been traduced by Mr. Foulk in his report.

Mr. Min who returned from China last week and on the next day came to call upon me and spent several hours, his first official visit. At this visit he met Mr. Foulk, and most cordially. He mentioned the report, saying he had read it and that there were no grounds afforded by it upon which to base a demand for Mr. Foulk's recall.

Moreover during last week I had visits from two of the vice-presidents of the foreign office. Both asked for Mr. Foulk and met him with great Kindness.

One of them just before leaving said to my interpreter in Korean that he was glad I had not mentioned the troublesome matter about Mr. Foulk, that it appeared very silly to him to make so much noise about a letter written so long ago, and that the Chinese minister had forced it upon the president. I mentioned these expressions as giving evidence of the true Korean feeling.

Mr. Yuan having made the demand himself also, and having instigated the course of the Korean Foreign Office will make the best of his advantage thus obtained to carry out his purposes with reference to this country, and to his own government will cite the conduct of the foreign office as a concession of the right of Chinese dictation, and to the Koreans will insist that the United States has recognized that right.

In behalf of and in justice to Mr. Foulk I beg to say without his Knowledge and wholly upon my own motion, that lest it might be suspected that some personal ambition of his own has led on to trouble
the ∧ Mr. Foulk has been most prudent and wise in his course, and while the King has frequently insisted that he should immediately accept service in the Korean Gov't as military instructor, and has prepared a comfortable and commodious home for him and such others as they have long expected and are still anxiously expecting from the United States, he has at all times explained that under no circumstances could he enter upon such service without leave of absence granted by his government, nor until the matter was formally addressed through the foreign office to the legation. This is thoroughly understood. My firm belief is that the Chinese objection grows out of his Knowledge of the Korean language, Character and government, and his successful work here under the auspices of his government.

Mr. Waeber, H.I.R.M's Chargé d'Affaires, has expressed to me his deepest regret at the recall, and thinks it greatly prejudicial to the interests of this government under the present situation.

In conclusion I beg if it shall meet with your favorable consideration that Mr. Foulk may be restored to his position of Naval Attaché, at least for a time, and I do so merely for the purpose of carrying out what I have been instructed to be the policy of our government with reference to this country.

HUGH A. DINSMORE

<table>
<tr><td>NO. 23</td><td align="right">Department of State
Washington, June 23, 1887</td></tr>
</table>

Hugh A. Dinsmore

Sir:

The cipher telegram received from you last night, has been interpreted to read as follows:

"The King (and) Min Yong Ik entreat Foulk will be allowed to stay. I think it is very advisable for at least some time—correspondence *en route*." The following reply was sent to you, in cipher, at *2.40* P.M. to-day—

"Naval Attache's utility impaired by the opposition of the Foreign Office—regret we cannot ratify King's wish." The ground taken in my instruction No. 21, of the 17th instant, with respect to Ensign Foulk's recall from the post of Naval Attaché at Seôul, renders it impracticable to comply with the request presented in your telegram, even when coming from so high a source.

Ensign Foulk's presence in Corea is by reason of his being an officer of the United States Navy, detailed to perform there the duties assigned to him by his own Government. The opposition manifested officially by the Korean Foreign Office to the continued presence of Mr. Foulk must seriously impair his utility in that capacity, and his appointment as Naval Attaché has been accordingly cancelled. To authorize him to remain in Korea, without representative employment, and occupying what your despatches indicate to be an equivocal position as respects to the relation of Corea to China, is believed to be inexpedient.

T. F. BAYARD

NO. 26   Department of State
                                                    Washington, July 12, 1887

Hugh A. Dinsmore

Sir:

I have received your No. 23 of May 30, 1887, concerning the demand of the Korean Foreign Office for the recall of Ensign George C. Foulk, as Naval Attache in Korea, and have to say that your conduct in this matter shows good judgment and meets with the Department's approval.

You have placed the Chinese Representative, Mr. Yuan, on record as having himself no grievance against Ensign Foulk and as not having preferred any demand on behalf of China for his recall, —but as leaving the complaint of the Korean Foreign Office to be dealt with by you as and by the Government of the United States.

My instructions Nos. 21 and 23 of the 17th and 23rd ultimo, respectively, will have acquainted you with the disposition of the matter, by the withdrawal of Ensign Foulk on the position of Naval Attaché on the sole ground that the feelings of the Korean Foreign Office toward him impaired his official services towards his government. Behind this conclusion, which befits the relation of the United States and Korea as independent Treaty-Powers, it seems unnecessary to go.

                                                    T. F. BAYARD

NO. 41   Legation of the United States
                                                Soul Korea July 23rd 1887

Secretary of State

Sir:

I have the honor to inform you that on the 20th instant by decree of His Majesty The King of Korea Mr. Kim Yun Sik was removed from the presidency of the Foreign Office and banished to the province of Chung Chuong Do southeast of the city of Söul and that Mr. So Sang Ou has been appointed president in his stead.

Mr. Kim's offense consisted of his having used the seal of his office in a private and personal transaction in business, and as is said in a fraudulent way, in favor of some personal friend or adherent.

Mr. Penn Wan Ju, one of the vice-presidents of the foreign office, was also at the same time removed and banished for complicity in the same transaction.

The removal of Kim Yun Sik relieves the king of an obstacle in the way of a fulfillment of his desires with reference to this country, but I greatly fear he will have but little less in the occupancy of the new president who is a coarse heavy man with less education and intelligence than his predecessor, and whom I suspect to be strongly pro-Chinese.

Min Yong Ik asked me what I thought of the appointment. I said in reply that I had but a limited personal acquaintance with Mr. So but from his appointment by His Majesty a presumption should arise that he was a loyal subject and a man properly qualified for the duties of this office.

HUGH A. DINSMORE

NO. 27

Department of State
Washington, July 27, 1887

Hugh A. Dinsmore

Sir:

I have received your No. 29 of the 20th ultimo, concerning the recall of Ensign George C. Foulk, U.S.A., and his transfer to the U.S.S. "Marion"; and have attentively considered your observations upon the subject.

The suggestions you make touching upon the probable effects of an unqualified withdrawal of Ensign Foulk, were fully evident to this Department, especially in view of the somewhat notable interference of the Chinese Minister at this capital, in demanding Mr. Foulk's recall under instructions from the Viceroy Li Hung Chang. The explanatory instructions heretofore sent you and the copies, therewith transmitted, of the correspondence had here with the representative of China, show that we have abundantly guarded against the inference that this Government recognized the competency of China in the premises, or acquiesced in its demand. Mr. Foulk's recall has been solely on the ground that the opposition of the Korean Foreign Office (with which, under our treaty, diplomatic relations with the independent Kingdom of Chosun can alone be conducted), deprived Mr. Foulk's functions of that utility to his own Government which prompted his detail as Naval Attache.

Not until it shall be apparent that he can render effective and unimpaired service in that important and useful position to the Government which employs him, can the suggestion of your despatch that Mr. Foulk be restored to his position of Naval Attaché be taken into consideration.

Mr. Denby has already been fully advised by us as to what has been done, and to the end that our Legation in China may be Kept fully informed in the premises, and be in a position to avert any misapprehension of the policy and Motives of this Government in respect of Chinese influence in Corea, a copy of your despatch and of this reply, will be sent to Mr. Denby for his confidential information.

If, contrary to the expectations of this Government, the progress of Chinese interference at Seoul should result in the destruction of the autonomy of Korea as a sovereign state with which the United States maintains independent treaty-relations, it will be time then to consider whether this Government is to look to that of China to enforce treaty obligations for the protection of the person's interests of citizens of the United States, and their commerce, in Korean territory as a dependency of China.

T. F. BAYARD

NO. 53   Legation of the United States
                                                         Söul, January 24, 1887

Secretary of State

Sir:

I have the honor to forward to you herewith certain correspondence between this legation and the Korean Foreign Office arising out of the following circumstances.

The Chinese telegraph company, which is nominally a Korean governmental organization, but in reality a thoroughly Chinese affair, had been allowed by Mr. Townsend, an American citizen, to occupy temporarily a house belonging to him and situated in the general foreign settlement at Chemulp'o. No lease of whatever nature had been made. In October Mr. Townsend notified the telegraph agent that he must vacate the present premises by December 1st, but he refused to do so as long as the Korean government allowed him to reside there. Mr. Townsend then asked this legation to assist him in recovering his property, but notwithstanding the earnest appeals of my predecessor and myself it has been impossible to get the Korean Foreign Office to order its employees to vacate the premises.

Mr. Townsend has presented to the legation a claim for damages which appears both moderate and just, but it cannot be considered a definite statement as the property is still in the hands of the Korean telegraph employes.

The probable explanation of this most flagrant injustice to an American citizen is that the employes in question are all Chinese subjects, and the Foreign Office is apprehensive of offending the Chinese Minister here. No other explanation suggests itself.

In itself but an insignificant affair and one which might lay over for a while, I deem that under the circumstances a prompt settlement is absolutely necessary.

I will wait until tomorrow evening for a reply to my note of yesterday after which I will telegraph for one of the ships of our squadron to come at once to Chemulpo and will ask for your instructions. Chemulpo is still without a municipal organization or police force, and I think that a small force of marines might be used, without creating any trouble, to compel the telegraph employes to leave Mr. Townsend's house, but, of course, I will do nothing without your instructions.

W. W. ROCKHILL

Korean Foreign Office
Söul, December 29, 1886

W. W. Rockhill

Sir:

In reply to your note requesting a prompt removal from the (Hsim hsin Chang house), I have the honor to state that it was obtained from the owners who are Koreans and who decided to let the telegraph people occupy it. These people are now dwelling there quietly and it would be difficult to move in such cold weather; moreover there is no other house which they could occupy. These are the reasons for which I have not replied sooner to your note, for which I am very sorry. I have to request that you will ask for a delay.

KIM YUN-SIK

Söul, January 1st 1887

President of the Korean Foreign Office

Your Excellency:

In reply to your note of the 29th December in which you state that the telegraph employés at Chemulp'o now living in the house called "Hsim hsin chang" belonging to Mr. Townsend, cannot leave the house at present on account of the cold weather, and requesting that time be given for arranging the matter, I have to state that Mr. Townsend insists on having his property returned to him as he has immediate use for it.

While I feel very sorry that the people now living in this building should be put to inconvenience and obliged to leave during the cold weather, Your Excellency must agree with me that these reasons are not sufficient to justify me in approving of any delay in settling this affair.

I have learnt that in the Chinese settlement at Chemulp'o there are many vacant houses, one of which the telegraph employés could occupy, and I must beg Y.E. to order them to remove to one of them and return to Mr. Townsend his property.

Mr. Townsend has refused to accept rent from the telegraph employés during the last month, and if Y.E.'s government should any longer allow him to be deprived of the use of his house, he will enter claim against the government for damages.

(Sgd) W. W. ROCKHILL

Korean Foreign Office
Söul, January 5, 1887

W. W. Rockhill

Sir:

In reply to your note concerning the house (which is Known as the Hsim hsin chang), I have the honor to state that this house was originally the property of a Korean Company and it was Koreans who
                    for [sic]
rented it ~~for~~∧the telegraph office. How later on your Countryman Mr. Townsend bought it I donot Know. He now demands that (the telegraph people) shall move away, but this is difficult in the depth

of winter. I shall inform the telegraph people, as you request in your note, to hurry and procure an empty house to move into. My government got the house from a (Korean) Company and let it (to the telegraph company).

KIM YUN-SIK

Soul, January 5, 1887

President of the Korean Foreign Office

Your Excellency:

In reply to your note of this day in reference to the house in Chemulp'o belonging to Mr. Townsend and now occupied against his will by the telegraph office, I have the honor to state that the house was sold to Mr. Townsend at least a year and half ago with the consent of Y.E. to whom the bill of sale and title were shown by Mr. Foulk.

The house is therefore unquestionably Mr. Townsend's, and I must insist on the immediate removal of the present occupants as I stated to Y.E. in my note of January 1st.

(Sgd) W. W. ROCKHILL

Söul, January 10, 1887

President of the Korean Foreign Office

Your Excellency:

I have the honor to forward to you herewith a translation of a letter received from Mr. Townsend, and his claim for damages amounting to $300, and beg to ask Your Excellency if he Knows of any reason why this claim should not be paid.

(Sgd) W. W. ROCKHILL

Söul, January 23, 1887

President of the Korean Foreign Office

Your Excellency:

I have the honor to request that you will give me an immediate
and definite answer in the business of Mr. Townsend's house called
Hsim hsin chang, failing which I will be obliged to telegraph to my
government for it to decide which measures to adopt in the matter

(Sgd) W. W. ROCKHILL

Telegram   Söul, January 25, 1887

Captain Selfridge—Omaha, Yokohama

A ship of war is needed.

ROCKHILL

NO. 61   Legation of the United States
                                             Söul, February 10, 1887

Secretary of State:

Sir:

As a further reference to my despatch no. 53 of January 24th last
giving the correspondence between this Legation and the Korean
Foreign Office concerning the illegal detention by the Korean government's telegraph employes of a house in general foreign settlement
at Chemulp'o and belonging to an American citizen Mr. W. D.
Townsend, I have the honor to inform you that on the 26th January,
I telegraphed to the Admiral Commanding our squadron through the
Captain Commanding the U.S.S. "Omaha" with whom a cipher had
been arranged for correspondence with this legation, requesting that
a ship be sent to Chemulp'o.

My intention was, in case the Korean government persisted in
retaining the property, to ask you for permission to use a few files
of Marines as a police force to enforce a writ of eviction against the
occupants of the house. This measure I conceive to be within the
attributions of this Legation acting as consular representative at
Chemulpo, whose duty it is, in the absence of any organized municipal police force, to enforce, within the limits of the settlement, such

laws or regulations as may enable our countrymen to enjoy the quiet possession of their property and ensure them in their rights.

At the same time I informed verbally the Korean Foreign Office of my intention, but received the same reply which had been ∧~~given~~ given to all the notes of this Legation on the subject, that winter was an impossible time to move in, when the frost was out of the ground a house would be built for the telegraph office.

On the 29th of January I received a telegram from Admiral Chandler asking me to "mail particulars." This reply disposing_____ [sic] of the possibility of having the tenants evicted for at least a month, there being no mail for Japan before the 16th of this month, I had further enquiries made at Chemulp'o about vacant houses which might be occupied by the telegraph office, and submitted the result in a note to the Foreign Office; and after a long discussion with the President of the Foreign Office on the third instant, he agreed to have the telegraph employes removed at once, and I am glad to say that the necessary steps are being taken. It cannot be doubted, however, that the apprehension of having the tenants evicted was the sole cause of his sudden determination.

This case is one of many which will illustrate the utter ignorance of the Korean government in all which concerns its obligations under the treaties, and the dilatoriousness of its methods, so incompatible with Western customs and ideas of justice. There is no legal means of regress for foreigners for wrongs done them by natives except through their legations and the Foreign Office, and the latter, while recognizing the validity of a claim will put off considering it until absolutely forced to do so. So long as such methods endure so long will foreigners be prevented from entering into any commercial or other relations with this country except at great risk and too frequently considerable loss.

W. W. Rockhill

no. 6   Department of State
                                          Washington, April 8, 1887

Hugh A. Dinsmore

Sir:

I have received Mr. Rockhill's No. 61 of February 10, 1887, in regard to the illegal detention of the Government of Corea of a house at Chemulpo the property of Mr. W. E. Townsend, an American citizen.

The Department is pleased to learn that the Corean Government has taken the requisite steps to restore to Mr. Townsend the possession of his property at that place. At the same time it is proper that he should be indemnified for the loss suffered by him by reason of the unlawful detention in question, and you are instructed to press upon the Government of Corea its obligation to make Mr. Townsend such indemnification.

It is not supposed that a case precisely similar to that of Mr. Townsend's is likely to arise again; but as Mr. Rockhill has stated in his despatches that he contemplated applying to this Department for authority to employ force to evict the Corean tenants from Mr. Townsend's house, the Department thinks it proper to say that in general, diplomatic and consular officers of the United States, in such a position as yourself, are not authorized, without express instructions from the Department, to employ force in aid of private interests and rights, unless to protect them from violent invasion and injury.

T. F. BAYARD

NO. 39   Department of State
                                   Washington, August 25, 1890

Augustine Heard

Sir:

Your despatch No. 29, Diplomatic series of the 10th ultimo has been received, and your narration of the present aspects of the political situation with regard to the reserved relation of Corea to China has been read with much interest.

In respect to your request for instruction as to your course should the King give you, as a mark of favor, the privilege of entry into the Palace court-yard in your chair the same as now enjoyed by the Chinese Commission, Mr. Yuan, I have to observe that you will be expected to assert and obtain the same ceremonial rights as the Diplomatic body in Seoul have secured or may hereafter enjoy; but that it is not deemed expedient to accept any special favor not extended generally to your colleagues of equal grade with yourself—especially if by so doing you should appear to lend yourself to the provocation of a question concerning the exceptional relation of Corea to China, and the special treatment, growing out of that relation, which may be conceded to the Chinese Commissioner. For you to claim the same personal prerogatives as Mr. Yuan would, it is thought, to be quite a different thing from any claim by Mr. Yuan to take general rank, as a foreign envoy among the diplomatic body in Seoul.

I note your statement that Mr. Yuan's title as "Commissioner" has been defined as that of a Consul General with diplomatic functions. This is the meaning generally attached to the title Agent and Consul General, borne by some foreign representatives in states whose suzerain dependence is well-established, as is that of Egypt upon the Ottoman porte. We have not, however, regarded Mr. Yuan's function as so circumscribed, but have supposed it to bear some analogy to that of a "Resident"—such as Great Britain maintains in Burmah, or the French maintain in Madagascar. But this point has never been made clear.

Our treaty relations with Corea unquestionably give us the right to look to that Kingdom, as to a responsible government, for the fulfillment of all obligations of international intercourse, independently of China. The treaty was negotiated to that express end, with the sanction and, indeed, under the initiative of China, which disclaimed responsibility for the acts of Corea toward foreigners. With the reserved relation of Corea to China we cannot properly interfere to raise any question, unless the course of China should be such as to manifestly shift accountability, as regards foreign interests and intercourse, to the shoulders of China. Should such a contingency arise, the view of the Government would remain to be determined.

WILLIAM F. WHARTON

NO. 469

Legation of the United States
Seoul, Korea, Oct. 6, 1893

Secretary of State

Sir:

On September 10th, being the anniversary of the Queens return from pursuit in the revolution of 1882, the Foreign Representatives were accorded an audience. Mr Yuan is usually received by himself at some other time than that named for the other representatives. On this occasion he was ill and sent his consul Mr. Tang, who chanced to arrive with us, and sat at the table with us when we dined after the Audience.

The day was a very rainy one and we were all mortified to find ourselves wading through mud and rain while the Chinese Consul rode past us right up to the door of the reception room. Our Chairs had been, as is the custom, left at the Palace Gates some distance away. We have been informed on several occasions of the fact that Mr. Yuan always rides into the Palace as only the members of the Royal Family can do. But while we all knew of this Custom of his, it had never been forced to our notice as on this occasion, which was made doubly humiliating by the rain, our bedraggled condition, and the fact that even the Consul of China could ride dry, where we walked wet.

The French and Russian Representatives were highly indignant, even the English Acting Consul General said that while he had nothing to say as to Mr Yuans rights, he certainly could not let this matter of the Consul pass unnoticed.

I said nothing, as I know that it is His Majestys desire to accord the same privileges of riding into the Palace to the other Representatives, and only awaited some action on their part to answer the protests of the ultra conservative officials of his Court.

After many days of discussion, the Russian Chargé d'Affaires ad interim, Mr. Dmitrevsky announced that he thought we should all refuse to attend the next audience unless this privilege is accorded us, which he as Dean of the Diplomatic Corps would ask for unofficially at first, and, not succeeding in this way, he would make a formal demand, if we were all agreed. Mr. Otori, who will be our new Dean, readily agreed, and I joined with the others, as per your instructions to Mr. Heard, No. 4, March 20, 1890, and I now give you the required notice and ask that if you disapprove of my joining with my colleagues you will cable me to that effect.

I would say further, that this is no insult or menace to Mr Yuan. He fully approves of the stand taken by the other representatives, and told Mr. Frandin that the Korean Government should long ago have accorded us this privilege as an act of courtesy.

I am quite as positive that the matter is not distasteful to the King, as he has sent to me several times to inquire about such matters in other countries. He may not grant it at once, however, as the opposition certainly of his own officials will be very strong, but I think it is the proper thing to do, and am glad it has come up during the absence of an American minister as, at present, we have only to acquiesce and the Russian and French make the demand, and conduct the agitation.

H. N. ALLEN

NO. 479   *Confidential*   Legation of the United States
Seoul Korea Nov. 4, 1893

Secretary of State

Sir:

I have the honor to inform you that yesterday being the birthday of the Queen, we were received in audience by His Majesty the King.

In my No. 469 of Oct. 6, I intimated that it was probable that more courtesy might be shown the Foreign Representatives, as the result of certain unofficial representations that were being made. I have now to inform you that the courtesy in question was not extended.

The case is as follows. Mr. Yuan the Chinese Representative here, has been in the habit of riding into the Palace grounds in his Chair, —a privilege reserved for princes, prime ministers, and aged officials. The distance from the gates to the reception room is some 4000 yards, over common dirt paths which become muddy in bad weather.

While this practice of Mr. Yuans has been known to the representatives for a long time, so long as it was not forced to their attention, they thought it best not to notice it, and the Koreans were careful to have the Chinese to audience at a time when they would not be seen by the others. However, as I wrote to you in my No. 469, referred to above, on the 10th September, we had a very unpleasant evidence of the practice, by having to wade through the mud and rain while, Mr. Yuans secretary, Mr. Tang, who acts as Chinese Consul here, rode past us in his Chair.

Being requested to unite with the other representatives in a protest against what seemed to them a gross indignity, I carefully reread your instructions to Mr. Heard in your No. 4 of Mch 20 ⟨1890⟩ on the subject and decided that I would be justified in uniting with my colleagues in asking that at least equal privileges with the *Consul* of China, and I agreed finally, to unite with them in asking unofficially, that we be allowed to use our Chairs in going into the Palace grounds, and if our requests were not granted to decline to attend the next audience, unless I should receive instructions to the contrary.

Messrs Dmitrevsky and Frandin, the Representatives of Russia and France, with General Le Gendre as the American adviser to the Government, presented the matter very fully to the proper officials, and I saw some of my friends on the subject. Some officers were favorable to it, others, notably those of pro-Chinese sympathies, were opposed. I was and am, assured that the King favored extending the courtesy to the other Representatives, as it would then look less like vassalage if they all enjoyed equal privileges.

Mr. Yuan assured Messrs Dmitrevsky and Frandin that he was quite in favor of seeing the privilege granted, but I was soon able to assure those gentlemen that he was actively opposing it, a fact that they are also now well acquainted with.

The unofficial representations were not complied with, and we received invitations to the audience on yesterday. It was remarkable that the invitations were received four days in advance, while ordinarily they came the day before. The Court doubtless wished to know if we would decline.

A canvass of the Representatives showed that Messrs Dmitrevsky and Frandin were the only ones wishing to decline to attend, and according to the instructions above referred to, I did not consider it proper for me to go with the minority, without instructions. After much discussion I did, however, agree to join with them, as a compromise, in a joint note to the Home Office to be sent with our acceptances, stating that we regret that our official representations had been disregarded, and that we would inform our Governments of the state of affairs, with the probability that we might have to decline to attend audiences in the future unless the privilege is granted.

The four Representatives who were present at the time of the Tang episode signed this note. Mr. Wilkinson, the English Acting Consul General, added a note to show that he meant no disrespect to Mr. Yuan. In this he was acting under orders from his Chief, Mr. O'Conner of Peking.

Mr. Otori, the Japanese Plenipotentiary, as was expected, was not at liberty to do as he declared he wished to do, and as he had verbally agreed to do. He asked time for consideration and then declined to sign the note, giving extended apologies. It is believed that his relations to the Chinese are such that he had to consult them and do as they wished in the case. I refer you to Mr. Herods No 428 of July 29, as his statement of the case was pretty well borne out by recent events.

Mr Krien the German Consul has not been attending audiences of late, owing to the question of precedence discussed in Mr. Heard's Nos 305, Sept. 21, & 343, Dec. 13, which question has developed into such an unpleasantness between himself and Mr. Frandin, who seems to get all he asks, that the two are under very strained relations. Therefore when Mr. Krien learned that Mr. Frandin had been chiefly instrumental in starting the present question, he declined to have anything to do with it and even wrote the Foreign Office opposing it.

He received an answer from the Home Office stating that our predecessors had not asked that that [sic] this whole ceremonial rule be broken, and he could not present our letter to the King. Of course such letters go at once to the King, but as they were unwilling to grant the request they took this method of suppressing the matter. There it may rest unless the Governments concerned wish it pressed.

We ∧ attended the audience, with the exception of Messrs Frandin and Krien. As usual we were kept waiting some two hours. This delay seemed to be especially annoying to the Japanese Plenipotentiary, as we know that Mr. Yuan is never kept waiting.

England, Japan and Germany are with China on the Korean question. England is represented by a Vice-Consul, who acts as "Acting Consul General." Japan has a Minister Plenipotentiary to China and Korea, who will shortly leave his Consul in charge. Germany has a Consul. In the case of the Governments which recognize the independence of Korea, and have agents who correspond direct with the Home Governments, Russia has a Chargé d'Affaires, and France a Commissaire. Fortunately this episode has occurred while we have but a Chargé d'Affaires here, but a new minister should insist on receiving due courtesy, otherwise we "lose face" and have little influence.

H. N. ALLEN

Joint Note   Seoul, Korea, Nov. 1, 1893

President of the Home Office

Your Excellency:

We sincerely regret that our unofficial communications regarding the question of riding into the Palace in Chairs has not been complied with, and as this matter will have to be referred to our Governments, it is

~~possible~~ probable that in the future we shall not be able to attend an audience unless this privilege is granted.

(Sn) P. A. DMITREVSKY
(Sn) H. N. ALLEN
(Sn) H. FRANDIN
(Sn) W. H. WILKINSON.

(Note by H.P.M.'s Acting Consul General)

Understanding that the unofficial communications referred to the great inconvenience caused to the Foreign Representatives, and the high degree of disrespect shown to His Majesty the King by appearing at audiences in soiled uniforms, I have had the honor to subscribe —the above note.

(Sn) W. H. WILKINSON

November 2, 1893

P. A. Dmitrevsky
H. N. Allen
H. Frandin
W. H. Wilkinson

Sirs:

I am just in receipt of your Joint Note. This ceremonial rule is one that is difficult to change. No such arrangement had been made before and you know that your predecessors did not raise the question.

I beg to inform you that I hardly agree with your desires, and it is inconvenient for me to state the matter to His Majesty.

KIM YUNG SHOO

NO. 527   Legation of the United States
                                    Seoul Korea Feb. 12, 1894

Secretary of State

Sir:

Referring to my No. 469, Oct. 6, and No. 479, Nov. 4, in regard to the matter of riding in the Palace in Chairs, I now have the pleasure of informing you that the question has been satisfactorily settled. Mr. Waeber Russian, united with us, and Mr. Otori—Japanese, then joined in the remonstrance. Mr. Krien, German, still held aloof owing to his personal difficulties with Mr. Frandin, French, but, all the other Representatives excepting of course, the Chinese—decided not to attend the New Year Audience, unless our request was granted. Being sick at the time, and as my condition was well known at the Palace, I fortunately had a good excuse for declining to go. *10 4837*

The result was that the Foreign Office promised in writing that if we would come to this audience, they would, before another such occasion, build a closed gallery from the nearest Palace Gate to the Reception Hall, through which we might walk, protected from the weather. This compromise was accepted by all and seems quite satisfactory.

H. N. ALLEN

NO. 45   Legation of the United States
                                          Seoul Korea Aug 24, 1894

Secretary of State

Sir:

I have the honor to inform you that I am just in receipt of a despatch from Department of Foreign Affairs here, informing me that hereafter Foreign Representatives, in attending an audience at the Palace, will be allowed to ride through the gates to the waiting room.

This is doubtless the result of Japanese dictation. It has been regarded here as a matter of considerable importance. See Mr. Allens, Numbers 469, Oct 6, '93 479 Nov. 4, & 527 Feb 12, '94.

This recent action of the Council endorsed by the King, illustrates forcibly the completeness of the overthrow of Chinese influence in Korea, as well as the present supremacy of the Japanese.

The combined efforts of all the Foreign Representatives except the Chinese, could not secure permission to ride from the outer gates of the palace enclosure to the waiting room. Chinese influence prevailed against all opposition. A Chinese Representative might so ride and so might the Chinese Consul and even the telegraph Superintendent, but not the other Foreign Representatives. Within one year a hint from Japan accomplishes all that was vainly sought in '93.

JOHN M. B. SILL

          Legation of the United States
Soul Korea August 21st 1887

Secretary of State

Sir:

For some time I have suspected that Prince Min Yong Ik, from expressions which he has made to me from time to time, as well as from information I was in possession of that His Majesty the King of Korea was seriously contemplating sending ministers abroad both to America and the European Powers in treaty relations with Korea, would soon leave Korea. For some reason, apparently from a nervous fear, he manifestly intended to go quietly without a public announcement of his purpose. Nearly two months ago on the occasion of a visit to me, he asked if I could not in the event of his leaving send him an an [sic] American Man of War. Thinking it better to disarm his fears as much as possible, and believing that such a service although a mere courtesy would be misconstrued by the Chinese I promptly determined that I would not ask it of the Admiral, so told him that while I would be glad of any opportunity to oblige him, I would say to him frankly, inasmuch as he had asked counsel of me unreservedly that I thought it would be much better for him and less embarrassing for his King, for him to go openly and publicly on a mail steamer when he was ready to leave without mystifying his conduct with any unnecessary secrecy, and that for me to comply with his request might subject my country to unfriendly suspicions.

On or about the first of the present month under the pretext of going to Kang Wha, the river fortress below Söul for the purpose of reviewing troups, he set out for Chemulpo, and on the day after his arrival sailed in the Russian gunboat Seawouch, at the time lying in the harbor, for Chefoo, Mr. Waeber, the Russian Chargé d'Affaires and the captain of the vessel having consented.

The matter created some little sensation and interested parties endeavored to create excitement but with only slight success.

The Seawouch returned immediately and is still off Chemulpo. The king having since appointed a minister to America and another to Russia England France Germany and Italy, I believe it is the intention to have Prince Min go and assist in the establishment of legations, but my belief is founded upon private information. Prince Min's departure in the manner described confused and annoyed the Chinese Minister immeasurably, and I am told that he demanded of the Korean Government an explanation, but that he got little for his pains.

HUGH A. DINSMORE

Legation of the United States
                                    Söul, Korea, September 30th 1887

Secretary of State

Sir:

Today at 3'O'clock p.m. I had the honor to despatch to you a telegraphic message in cipher the true reading of which is as follows,
viz:—

Last Saturday Korean minister Plenipotentiary to the United States and
Suite have taken leave the King Started for Washington, D.C. When outside city was induced to Stay by threats of the Chinese minister. Chinese
minister tells King the viceroy Telegraphs has been ordered by the Chinese
emperor to stop the mission The king alarmed but undecided I have
written last tuesday Chinese Minister respectfully, citing terms Of treaty,
asking why and upon What grounds he has interfered No answer. Telegraph instructions.

                                                    Dinsmore

It was publicly announced in Söul in the official gazette on the
date as reported in my despatch No. 48 under date of August 20th
1887 that Mr. Pak Chun Yong had been appointed by His Majesty
the King of Korea envoy extraordinary and minister plenipotentiary
to the United States. Since that time Mr. Pak and his friends have
been very active making preparation to set out on the mission the
King taking the greatest interest in the matter. The minister's suite
was fully formed, all the secretaries and interpreters being appointed.
At the King's urgent request Dr. H. N. Allen, one of our best and
most useful American residents, was induced to accept the second
place in the mission with the title of American Secretary. Doctor
Allen had disposed of household and other property at a sacrifice and
repaired with his family to Chemuplo there to join the minister and
sail on the 27th instant, and two others members of the mission had
gone overland to Fusan there to attach themselves to the suite, when
on Saturday last the minister had taken formal leave of His Majesty,
retired immediately without the walls as is their custom to leave his
capital city for Washington.
The Chinese minister since his visit to Chemulpo professedly to
leave for China, in August last, as reported in my No. 51 of August
23rd, has been in seclusion almost the whole time. Indeed for several
weeks it was not certainly Known by foreigners in general whether
he had retired to Söul or gone to China. His secretary said to all

inquiries that the minister was quite ill and could see no one yet Doctor H. N. Allen who has long been his only physician was never at any time called to see him, and did not see him though called to the Chinese legation to see other patients. But within the last ten days he has made his presence Known by his efforts to interfere with the mission to America. He importuned the King again and again as I am informed to change his purpose but the King was steadfast and insistent that the minister should go at every hazard even after M. Yuan the Chinese Minister had reported to him a telegram received by him from the viceroy Li Hung Chang.

I have obtained a reliable translation of Mr. Yuan's note communicating this message and have the honor to enclose a copy herein, and a second telegram reported as having been received from the viceroy, by order of the emperor demanding that Korea must first obtain China's consent before she sends the ministers abroad.

A correct translation of Mr. Yuan's note containing a copy of this telegram is also enclosed herewith.

When Mr. Pak had gone out of the city gate he was met by Chinese officers it is said, emissaries of the minister, and either by force or intimidation, I have been unable to learn which and have heard the facts differently stated, was induced to delay his departure. He remained outside of the walls I am informed by Koreans two or three days when he was summoned back by the King who at last is wavering in his purpose. He is extremely anxious to have his minister go and has sent me messages every day that he would send him, but he is frightened and has been led to believe that China will make war on him and he knows that without assistance he could offer but a weak defense. He realizes fully that he is involved in a vital issue, that if he ignores China's expressed objection, and exercises this act of sovereignty in carrying out the provision of the treaty, that he evinces to the powers his independence, while on the other hand if he yields it will give to China an advantage over him she has never before possessed. The situation for him as he views it is certainly a melancholy one. If he would act boldly and promptly and order the minister to proceed at once, my firm conviction is that China would acquiesce quietly, and in all probability to save herself from the effect recall Mr. Yuan for having exceeded the scope of his duties and instructions.

I have advised the King through his trusted servants, that our treaty expressly declares that he may send a Minister to the United States at his own convenience, and that this treaty was largely induced by the viceroy Li Hung Chang himself, with the full Knowledge of its provisions, and that he could not justify before the world a position so inconsistent as the one Mr. Yuan assumes in his name. The steamer on which Mr. Pak intended to sail having departed, I with the consent of the commanding officer tendered to the King the use of the U.S. steamer Essex to convey the minister to Japan. He expressed his grateful thanks for the offer but said he could not go just yet, so I telegraphed the Essex to sail.

Day before yesterday a messenger said the King would like to have me in audience, but enjoined when I came that I must be guarded in my expressions as they would be conveyed to the Chinese minister, I told the messenger, "Say to His Majesty that I will be happy to go before him now and at all times when he is pleased to desire my presence, but that I have no fear of the Chinese Minister having full information concerning the views that I would express to His Majesty, that my country has a treaty with him and has sent me hither as her minister, and in this has proclaimed to China and all the world that His Majesty is the sovereign ruler of an independent state, has the right and the power to send diplomatic representatives to a friendly nation without the consent of any other Power on earth. But I shall address a communication to the Chinese minister asking him by what authority he interferes to prevent a minister from going from Korea to the United States."

On tuesday accordingly I wrote a note to Mr. Yuan in respectful terms expressing my surprise at what I had learned to be his course in the matter of the Korean Mission to the United States, citing the terms of the treaty and the instrumentality of the viceroy in effecting the treaty and his Knowledge of its provisions, and asking why he should discriminate unfavorably against us as between the United States and Japan, but no objection had been urged to a minister going from Korea to the latter country. Enclosed I transmit a copy of my note.

Up to the hour of my telegraphic despatch to you today I had received no reply, but on my return to the legation from the telegraph office, I found an official letter in answer, a true copy of which is herewith enclosed, setting forth what he claims to be the facts, and equivocally denying that he prevented the departure of the minister, but setting up the claim of the suzerainty of China and the necessity of her consent before Korea may send missions abroad. It will be observed that he has either unwittingly or with great temerity made the grossest misrepresentation of the treaty in saying "it distinctly declares that your government acknowledges Korea as a vassal state to China, etc. etc."

In the paragraph reading as follows:—"At the present circumstance Corea sends missions abroad to all foreign courts where she has not complied with such obligations as bind her to China, and that such obligations shall be performed without the slightest interference on the party or government," his meaning is not to be deduced from its language.

Today I learned from a source that I consider reliable that Mr. Yuan has a large number of Koreans employed in his hire to go about amongst the people and say that great troubles will come upon Korea if she sends ministers abroad and involve her in war.

What is to be the result I am unable to forecast, but if China is successful in the assertion of such authority it annihilates the autonomy of the country and it would seem that we have no business here.

I have the honor to enclose copy of a note which I will tomorrow send to Mr. Yuan calling his attention to the inaccuracy of his statement that our treaty expressly recognizes Korea as a vassal state.

HUGH A. DINSMORE

Mr. Yuan Sü Kwai to
    the Korean Government
        Sept 23d

To-day at nine-o-clock I received from His Excellency the Viceroy Li Hung Chang the following telegram.

I have received by telegram through Tsung Li Yamun the following Imperial order:—Korea is sending Ministers to Western Countries. She has certainly first to ask our permission and after getting it to send them. This would be the way for a dependent state to act. Let the Korean Government know this as soon as possible so that it may be able to act in accord with the Imperial Order.

Having received this I feel it my duty to officially inform the Korean Government. Please Kindly take notice of this and carry out the Imperial Order.

H.I.C.M. Residency
Söul 30th September, 1887

Hugh A. Dinsmore

Sir:

I have the honor to acknowledge receipt of your despatch No 28 of the 27th instant, in which the contents have been carefully noted.

In reply I beg to say that I have heard all along about the same that you did, with reference to the official announcement of Mr. Pak Chun Yang having been appointed Minister Plenipotentiary to the United States, and that the Secretaries and Minister's suite were completely formed.

But as to your statement "when at the last moment you learned with surprise that the ministers were not to depart and that the cause was my interference acting under instructions from H.I.C.M. government" I cannot explain your surprise otherwise but that you are not acquainted with its full particulars which I will herewith explain to you. In the year of 1882 and the eighth year of H.I. Majesty the Reign of Kwang Su, my Imperial Government granted special permission to the King of Corea to establish a Treaty of Peace and Friendship with the United States, and wherein it distinctly declares and your government acknowledges Corea as a vassal state to China, that any of her obligations to China shall be carried out without the slightest interference from other treaty Powers, and I presume that you are aware of this, before your arrival in Corea.

At the present circumstance Corea sends missions abroad to all Foreign Courts, when she has nøt complied with such obligations that are binding her to China, and that such obligations shall be performed without the slightest interference on the part of Your Government.

Further permit me to say that when Corea sent the minister to Japan, my government were informed of its proceedings after the mission had left Corea and my government had not but more than received the information, and had not even time to give it a reply, when again we hear that a Minister Plenipotentiary had been appointed to the United States. Therefore my government thinking that Corea had no longer remembered her obligations to China, telegraphically instructed me to inform the government to perform her duties and abide with the ettiquette of a tributary state.

I am not aware that the mission had been prevented and moreover

I am not aware that I prevented the sending of the Minister to the United States.

It is the sincere desire of my government to be on the friendliest of terms with all Powers, and hope that you will be convinced that we make no discrimination between our country and another, and as to your statement that China makes a discrimination between the United States and Japan, it is only because Your Excellency are [sic] not aware of the full details of its proceedings and have been caused to a most unnecessary uneasiness and surprise.

(Signed) YUEN SU KWAI

Telegram　　　　　　　　　　　United States Legation, Söul, Corea:
October 9, 1887.

Bayard, Washington.

Minister Plenipotentiary from Corea to the United States has been detained by Chinese interference. It is officially stated by the Chinese minister that the viceroy telegraphed to him China must be consulted. Chinese minister writes me that in the treaty between the United States and Corea an appended letter from the King to the President of the United States, it is stated that Corea is vassal to China.

Under such circumstances do you desire to encourage the King to send the Minister? It can be easily done.

DINSMORE

NO. 71　　　　　　*Confidential*　　　　　Legation of the United States
Söul Korea Nov 11, 1887

Secretary of State

Sir:

As reported to you in my despatch of October 15th 1887, No. 63, Hono. N. Denny Vice President of the Korean Home Office and foreign adviser to the King left Söul some days before that date for Tien Tsin the place of the viceroy Li Hung Chang's official residence.

He returned after an absence of some two weeks and shortly after his arrival in Söul I was invited with Mr. Waeber the Russian Chargé d'Affaires by Mr. Denny to an interview with him upon the subject of the missions which His Majesty the King of Korea has undertaken to establish in the United States and in Europe. At this interview Mr. Denny Kindly gave us a history of his conference with the viceroy Li at Tien Tsin, upon the subject of the missions already referred to as well as the proposed opening of a port by the Government of Korea at Pyong An in the north of Korea which is greatly needed to develop and enlarge the commerce of the country and prevent the extensive smuggling that is practiced in that part of the Kingdom principally by Chinese.

Mr. Denny had reduced to writing the expressions of opinion interchanged at this conference, with the viceroy, and having read it aloud for the benefit of Mr. Waeber and myself I asked him if he would permit me to transmit a copy of his memorandum to my government. He took the matter under advisement, expressing some reluctance growing out of the fear of the possibility of its becoming publicly or generally Known, and used in some manner to impair his influence for usefulness in his official relation.

On yesterday however I received a note from him, a copy of which I enclose, granting me permission to lay the note before you confidentially and enclosing the memorandum for me to copy and transmit to you. I have the honor to enclose the same copied at length.

It will be observed that the position of the viceroy in behalf of China and of the Tsung Li Yamen as expressed by him is substantially as I have reported to you hitherto: namely, that China's permission should first have been sought and obtained and moreover, that if Korea sends foreign representatives abroad, they must not be of higher grade than Ministers Resident.

Permit me also to direct your attention to the fact that the viceroy himself admits his Knowledge of the existence during the last summer of a conspiracy to overthrow the King of Korea, and the complicity therein of Yuan Sü Kwai the Chinese Representative in Söul, who is retained in his position notwithstanding! Of the conspiracy referred to you had information in my Number 30 of June 21st.

In this connection I have the honor to enclose a translation of a communique made by Yuan Sü Kwai on the 21st ultimo to the Korean foreign office, setting forth the language of the telegram received by him from the viceroy Li Hung Chang reporting the orders telegraphed to him by the Pekin Government, expressing assent to the establishment of legations abroad with Ministers Resident only and upon compliance with certain supposed forms, but arguing against it.

A communication received by me from Hon Charles Denby our minister in China, under date of October 13th informing me of your orders to him touching the mission to the United States, which he had made known to the government of China convinces me, that the withdrawal of the Chinese authorities at Tien Tsin and Söul from their position that under no circumstances, must the minister depart without consent from their government, a consent which has not yet I am sure been asked, has been induced by your action.

I have the pleasure to inform you that the minister will sail for Chemulpo on the 13th instant on the U.S.S. Omaha for Nagasaki at which port he will take passage on mail steamer, via Yokohama, for the United States, and that he will bear credentials from His Majesty the King of Korea as Envoy Extraordinary and Minister Plenipotentiary.

HUGH A. DINSMORE

NO. 73   *Confidential*   Legation of the United States
                                            Söul Korea Nov. 17th 1887

Secretary of State

Sir:

I have the honor to inclose a translation of copy of an extract of a telegraphic message of the viceroy Li Hung Chang to Yuan Su Kwai the Chinese minister in Soul. The paper was furnished to me confidentially by Mr. Kondo Masuki the Japanese Chargé d'Affaires.

It will be seen that in this telegram Mr. Yuan is directed to instruct the Korean Government through the foreign office that that [sic] their representatives abroad must first present themselves to the Chinese minister and be introduced by him at the foreign office; that in all the official and social assemblies, the Korean "representative" shall yield precedence to the Chinese "Minister", and that upon affairs of importance touching the business of the service, the Korean "representative" shall always advise with the Chinese Minister "secretly" before taking action.

In this connection I take occasion to inform You that the Korean Minister to the United States sailed yesterday morning with his suite by U.S.S. Omaha from Nagasaki Enroute to Washington.

HUGH A. DINSMORE

NO. 521
Legation of the United States
Peking, December 9th, 1887

Secretary of State

Sir:

I have the honor to enclose, herewith, a translation of a memorial, presented by the King of Corea to the Emperor of China, which lately appeared in the Shih Pao, a Chinese newspaper published at Tientsin. In substance it is a complete recognition of the vassalage of Corea to China.

It Prays that as "an extra act of grace" the Emperor will allow envoys to be sent abroad.

Any remarks offered by me on the relation of Corea to the society of nations must be construed as bearing only on my own country and the country to which I am accredited. I have nothing officially to do with Corea.

Vattel discusses at page 2, the status of dependent states with reference to foreign powers. This discussion furnishes little information applicable to the peculiar relations existing between China and her dependent States. The text has little application to countries which, in their history, antedate international law, of which, also, they never had any knowledge. What unwritten law of tradition controls the relations of China with her dependencies remains unknown.

I assume that the position of the United States with reference to Corea is contained in Mr. Freylinghuysen's declaration that "the independence of Corea of China is to be regarded by the United States as now established." 1 Wharton's Digest, Sec. 64.

Your own despatch, No. 27 of date July 27, 1887, to Mr. Dinsmore, contains this statement: "If contrary to the expectations of this Government, the progress of Chinese interference at Seoul should result in the destruction of the autonomy of Corea as a sovereign State with which the United States maintain independent treaty relations, it will be time then to consider whether this Government is to look to that of China to enforce treaty obligations for the protection of the persons and interests of citizens of the United States."

The co-equality of Corea with the United States being thus considered it would seem that no questions but those of expediency remain.

In the solution of such questions, the geographical locality of Corea, its distracted condition internally, its possible relation to Japan,

Russia, England, and China, if complete independence be assured, are all to be looked at.

It is apparent that citizens of the United States have attained great prominence in the agitation of the subject of Corean independence. Is such prominence desirable? Will it be beneficial to us? Will it compensate us for the loss of the good will of China? As the sending of an envoy from Corea to the United States is now assured, this would be a favorable time to bring about the cessation of agitation of ulterior questions, if such policy is desired.

I make these suggestions with great deference and simply as matters of information.

CHARLES DENBY

Enclosure.

Draft of Memorial presented to His Majesty, the Emperor of China by the King of Corea in the matter of sending Envoy's abroad.

Li-hsi, King of Cho-sen (Corea) reverently presents a memorial upon the subject of sending Envoys to western countries, requesting that permission be first granted by the issuance of Your Majesty's mandate to the end that officers may be deputed hence.

Upon the 7th day of the 8th moon (23rd of September, 1887), Shen-wu-tse, a councillor (Ling-I-cheng) of the Council of State, memorialized the Throne that he had, on the same day, received a communication from Yuen Shih Kai, Chief Commissioner representing the Government of China, Stating that he had received a telegraphic message from the Grand Secretary, Li Hung Chang, to the effect that the Tsung-li Yamen had sent the following edict issued by the Emperor of China, to wit:

"In the matter of Corea's sending diplomatic officers to Western countries it is necessary first to ask our sanction when such officers can be sent, thus acting in accordance with the rules and usages of dependent states. Respect this."

The Grand Secretary instructed me to make this known to the Council of State without delay so that His Majesty's injunction may be observed.

Having received the above instructions, as in duty bound, the Chief Commissioner addresses a communication to the Council of State and begged that they will peruse the same and that a memorial be presented (by the King) asking permission (to send Envoy's abroad) in due observance of Imperial instructions.

The King is mindful that the small state over which he presides has for generations been the recipient of favors from the Heavenly Court—favors as high as the sky and thick as the earth, as exalted as the mountains and as deep as the sea; that Your Majesty perceives and understands all things and he that asks shall receive.

But in the matter of intercourse with foreign nations your memorialist has been the special recipient of Your Majesty's regard and kindly thoughts toward his dependent State, using your power and strength to elevate and assist her, and permit her to enter into commercial and friendly relations, first with the United States and dispatched an officer to assist in negotiation of a Treaty. Further a despatch was sent to the United States authorities before the negotiations of the treaty clearly setting forth that Corea was a State tributary to China, but that, hitherto, full sovereignty has been exercised by the Kings of Cho-sen in all matters of international administration and foreign relations.

As a dependent State Corea reverently maintains and observes the proper rules of courtesy and respect but as regards equality and reciprocity with foreign nations, governmental prestige and international relations, each has full powers.

Later other Western nations negotiated treaties with Corea-all after the terms in general with the United States treaty, and after their provisions were agreed upon by the negotiators a memorial was presented to Your Majesty asking your sanction and approval. After the United States Treaty was ratified the United States Government, in accordance with the treaty, sent a Minister Plenipotentiary to reside at Seoul. Your memorialist in turn sent an embassy of congratulation to the President of the United States which in due time returned to Corea. But no mission has ever been sent to other treaty powers. These powers, in consequence, have frequently represented to the Government of Corea that, as they are represented by accredited agents at Seoul, they invited Corea to send Ministers to their Courts. Your Majesty's dependent state was not unmindful of the urgency of the times at the same time it was desirous of carrying out the provisions of the treaties.

Your Memorialist has now appointed his Minister Pu Ting Yang, as Envoy Extraordinary and Minister Plenipotentiary, and proposes to send him to the United States, also his Minister Chao Chen hsi, as Envoy Extraordinary and Minister Plenipotentiary and proposes to depute him to represent Corea at the Courts of Great Britain, France, Germany, Italy, and Russia—to be clothed with power to attend to international questions arising in those countries.

Your memorialist, in presenting the foregoing facts, begs that as an extra act of grace, Your Majesty will condescend to give your sanction and approval to the sending abroad of the Ministers named, to the end that the question regarding envoys may be settled in conformity with the stipulations of treaty.

Under the existing laws governing Corea, in the matter of tribute and ceremonial, all memorials have been presented to Your Majesty by the

Board of Rites, but all questions of an international nature (with foreign countries) have been presented to Your Majesty in behalf of Corea either by the Prince and Ministers of the Tsung-li Yamen or by the Minister Superintendent for Northern Trade, Li Hung Chang. Unless in matters of the utmost importance Your memorialist would not venture to memorialize Your Majesty.

Your Majesty's mandate which has just been communicated by telegram, has been received by your memorialist on bended knees and he finds it impossible to express his feelings of gratitude as well as those of fear.

Your Memorialist instead of withdrawing from troubling Your Majesty ventures to present this memorial and is sincerely quaking with emotions of fear and alarm for Your Majesty's injunctions.

NO. 59   Department of State
                                                    Washington, Dec. 27, 1887

Hugh A. Dinsmore

Sir:

I have to acknowledge the receipt of your No. 71 of November 11, 1887, marked Confidential, concerning Chinese interference in Seoul, Korea, and to express to you the Department's thanks for the information contained therein.

In this connection, I take pleasure in saying that by a despatch from the Consul General at Kanagawa, Japan, No. 76 of the 29th ultimo, the Department is advised of the arrival in Yokohama of the Corean Embassy en route to the United States and that the Secretary of the Treasury will be requested to accord the Embassy every proper courtesy and facility for the speedy passage of the personal baggage of its members upon arrival in this country.

                                                            G. L. Rives

Korean Minister's Address to the President of the United States, on the occasion of presenting his credentials, January 17, 1888

I, Pak Chung Yang, the appointed Minister Plenipotentiary of Great Chosen (Korea), now, for the first time see, face to face, the ruler of The Great United States, and deliver to him in person, the credentials which I bring by order of my King, after which I hope to reside at this capital to promote friendly and commercial relations.

I hope that our two people may come closer together in everlasting friendship and enduring peace.

All this I present to the great ruler of the United States and wishing him prosperity and ever increasing greatness, I vow.

Pak Chung Yang

Reply of the U.S. President to the address of Pak Chŏng-yang.

Mr. Minister:

It gives me pleasure to receive the credentials you bear from His Majesty the King of Great Cho-sen, as the Corean Minister Plenipoentiary near the Government of the United States.

As the first among Governments organized under modern representation systems to enter into treaty relations with Corea, the Government of the United States is gratified to see the friendly intercourse desired by both now fully confirmed by the establishment of the mutual diplomatic intercourse provided for by the Treaty. Our efforts will not be wanting, Mr. Minister, to strengthen the ties of friendship and to develop relations beneficial to both countries.

As the worthy representative of a friendly nation I bid you, Mr. Minister, a cordial welcome to this capital, where I trust you may find health and comfort in your residence, and be enabled to render lasting service to both countries.

Grover Cleveland

Letter of the Korean King to the President of the United States

The King of Great Cho-sen makes a communication to the President of Great America:

As I concluded the first Treaty with your Honorable Country with which the friendship has ever since been close, and as it is some years since an embassy was sent to America, now to keep the intimacy, and to strengthen and increase our commercial relations between the two countries permanent and without defect, I especially appoint the favorite and confidential official Pak Chung Yang, who is Vice President of the Home Office and of Second Rank, to be accredited Plenipotentiary to your honorable country, to reside at the Capital to manage diplomatic affairs. I know that this official is loyal, careful and discreet and to be entrusted with disposition. In view of this, I have entrusted this communication to the Envoy to be presented in person.

Sincerely hoping the President will treat him with cordiality, and give full faith and credit to what he may say in behalf of this Court, and also permit him on occasion to have interviews in order to deliver my assurances of true friendship, thereby insuring mutual happiness.

Hoping endless bliss for the President.

Beginning of the present dynasty of Cho-sun 496 years, and of the Present Reign 24th year 8th moon, 7th day.

(Signed)

At the palace of Kung Pak in Seoul
Seal

Countersigned by the President of the Foreign Office (Cho Piung-Sik)
With Seal

NO. 212   Legation of the United States
                                       Söul Korea Dec 10th 1889

Secretary of State

Sir:

When Mr. Pak Chun Yang the late Korean Minister to the United States had reached Japan on his return from Washington last year he sojourned at Tokyo for several months. I had the pleasure of meeting him twice in that city in last January during my leave of absence. His appearance indicated ill health and he informed me that illness was the cause of his delay in Japan.

At that time I did not suspect that he remained away from Korea because of action of the Chinese authorities looking to punishment of Mr Pak which it appears had been taken even at that date. In the spring of the present year however he returned to Korea but did not enter the capital for about two months. This was also on account of the Chinese demand for his punishment. The only reason given for such a demand seems to be that the Minister while on duty in Washington in his official relations with the Government of the United States, acted independently of the Chinese legation. During the summer Mr Pak came into the city and was received at the Palace by his sovereign. A few days afterward in an audience with the King I met him together with a number of other officials. I exchanged greetings with him and some pleasant remarks were made by the

King upon the manner in which his Minister had been received and treated by our government during his stay in Washington, and his regret expressed that ill health had necessitated the Minister's return to his own country.

On a subsequent occasion I met Mr Pak under similar circumstances but he has never called upon me and I am informed has not gone out at all in a social way, but has kept in retirement. His reception by the King afforded ground for a renewal of the demands of the Chinese representation that he should receive some Kind of punishment for the alledged illegality or wrong of his conduct already stated. An official note was at that time written by Mr Yuan the Chinese representative to the Foreign Office setting forth the tenor of his or his government's position and requirement. In so far as I can learn no answer was ever made to that note. Two weeks ago the King conferred a promotion in rank upon Mr Pak which was duly gazetted in the daily official paper. Since the promotion Mr Yuan has given expression. I hear that he has repeatedly but unsuccessfully asked to be received by the King to Make his protest, that he has repeated his demand for the punishment of Mr Pak and insisted that the Foreign Office should answer his despatch and make confession that Mr. Pak is deserving of punishment.

Yesterday I was informed by an influential Korean that four days ago Mr Yuan sent two of his secretaries or attachés to the residence of the Prime Minister (not minister for foreign affairs) to insist that *he* should send to Mr Yuan the official note required, and that upon the Prime Ministers declining to accede to this demand, these two attachés under instructions from their Chief have alternated with each other in remaining with the Prime Minister so that he is constantly accompanied by one of them.

The information herein communicated has been received by me from partly unofficial sources and I cannot vouch for its entire correctness but believe the statement is substantially true. The matter has caused much excitement and anxiety in the minds of the native officials. I have been told by the Koreans that a story is being circulated and Mr Yuan has asked for an army or military force to compel a compliance with his government's demand, but this I entirely discredit.

HUGH A. DINSMORE

NO. 213   Legation of the United States
Seoul Korea Dec 24th 1889

Secretary of State

Sir:

Referring to my No 212 of the instant touching of a demand by the Chinese representative in Söul for the punishment the late Korean Minister to the United States Mr Pak Chun Yang, I have the honor to communicate that the attachés sent by the Chinese representative to remain with the Korean Prime Minister have been withdrawn, and that since their withdrawal by order of the King Mr Pak has been reduced to the rank which he held prior to his late promotion, of which you were informed in the despatch referred to.

HUGH A. DINSMORE

NO. 541   Legation of the United States
Seoul Korea Mch 19, 1894

Secretary of State

Sir:

Referring to my No. 528 Feb 14, in which I informed you of the appointment of Mr. Ye Sung Soo, Korean Chargé in Washington, as Minister Resident, I have now to inform you that I am told on good authority, that, owing to Chinese interference Mr. Ye's credentials, as Minister Resident have not yet been sent to him.

H. N. ALLEN

NO. 180   Legation of the United States
Seoul Korea Dec. 16, 1895

Secretary of State

Sir:

I have the honor to hand you enclosed a copy of a letter, with translation, received by me from the Korean Minister for Foreign Affairs, announcing the resignation of Mr. Min Yong Whan as Envoy Extraordinary and Minister Plenipotentiary from this Court to Washington—see Mr. Allens No. 152, Oct. 3, and the appointment in his stead of Mr. Soh Kwan Pom.

This gentleman SOH KWAN POM, was one of the embassy that went to The United States in 1883 to ratify the treaty; he was with Kim Ok Kiun and Pak Yong Hio in the conspiracy and *èmeute* of 1884, because of which he fled to America where he remained for ten years. He was brought back with Pak Yong Hio, by the Japanese last year and by them forced into office. He has been quiet and conservative. He signed the obnoxious decrees degrading the late decrees [sic. No doubt "Queen" was intended] but he declares that he did it under compulsion, and he seems very anxious to get away from the present Government.

JOHN M. B. SILL

3.

AMERICAN POLICY AND THE KOREAN COURT

Legation of the United States
                              Soul Korea April 13th 1887

Secretary of State

Sir:

I have the honor to inform you that on yesterday I received both from the foreign and the home offices a communication informing me that His Majesty the King had ordered them officially to notify me that I would be granted an audience today at 10 o'clock A.M. Accordingly I was at the palace gate promptly upon the hour accompanied only by Mr. Wo In Tak my interpreter. Outside the palace grounds I was met by a deputation of the officials who conducted me through the numerous gates leading to the interior until I was brought to a reception room adjacent to the audience chamber. The approach to the palace and to the Royal Person is effected by three parallel paved walkways, a broad central one flanked on either side by a narrower one, and at each wall and entrance there are three gates corresponding with the walks in size and position.

In recognition of the letter I bore from the President of the United States the central way was assigned to me and the central gates all thrown open at my approach, I alone going in this way.

While being entertained by several distinguished officials in the reception hall, members of the home and foreign offices, and generals of the Army, it was presently announced that His Majesty was in waiting, and I immediately proceeded into the Royal Presence, advancing in the prescribed ceremonial way. Stopping respectfully a few paces in front of His Majesty who stood meanwhile facing me and surrounded by his courtiers, I spoke a brief address, a copy of which I have the honor to enclose herewith. At the conclusion of my remarks I advanced, placed in the royal hands my letter of credence. The seal having been broken by his order His Majesty removed the cover and opened the letter examining it with much apparent interest. Placing his finger upon the signature of the Secretary of State, he asked me if that was the signature of the President. When I directed him to the proper signature of the President he eyed it intently for a moment then looked up and smiling said, "I think your President is a great man, he is honest, sensible, and good." I thanked him and said that it pleased me much as an American to know that

His Majesty so esteemed him. He further said, "I like Americans very much, they have been Kind to me and my people." And again, "I believe the United States Govt is more generally popular than any other power." I replied that "if our people as a nation could lay claim to the especial esteem of other powers it was perhaps attributable in a measure to our well-known Pacific inclination and lack of coveteousness of foreign territory." After a colloquy of some length in which I was asked particularly as to the health and happiness of the President, and ex-Ministers Foote and Parker and Ensign Foulk, I was dismissed by His Majesty, with the assurance that I was cordially welcome to Korea, and an expressed wish that I might long reside in His Majesty's capital.

The personal appearance of the King has been described to you I believe repeatedly, but I may be allowed to say that I was most favorably impressed. He is manifestly a man of quick intelligence and generous amiable disposition.

At the end of my audience I was conducted to another part of the palace and into the presence of His Royal Highness the Crown Prince. After the interchange of a few commonplace expressions I retired. At the request of His Majesty coming to me by one of his officers I went in company with a number of gentlemen through the palace grounds and visited many places of interest.

HUGH A. DINSMORE

NO. 97   Legation of the U. States
Seoûl Corea, March 31st 1888

Secretary of State

Sir:

I have the honor to receive your despatch of Feby 9th 1888 No 64 closing correspondence with Minister Denby touching the policy of the government of the United States with reference to Korea.

I am not apprised of the foundation of Mr. Denby's statement that "it is apparent that citizens of the United States have attained great prominence in the agitation of the subject of Korean independence" unless he may have given credit to publications which have appeared from time to time in the English Press of China and Japan purporting to be correspondence from Korea in which have occurred many perversions of fact, and statements without any foundation whatever of truth. My own course has been strictly within the bounds of the policy outlined in your instructions, and in your note to Mr Denby, and has in all particulars been reported to you.

The American residents here I am happy to say are devoting themselves with commendable energy and Singleness of purpose to the duties they have assumed and have manifested no disposition within my knowledge to interfere in political affairs. Mr. Denny as foreign and legal adviser, I presume, has asked in accordance with his convictions of official duty. It was he who furnised Senator Mitchell with information which induced his resolution in the Senate of the United States calling for correspondence from this legation, as I learned after seeing the resolution as published in the American press My first information concerning it. Mr. Mitchell could only suppose the existence of correspondence from me reporting to the Department of State matters in connection with the subject of his resolution.

HUGH A. DINSMORE

NO. 122   Department of State
Washington, Sept. 16, 1889

Hugh A. Dinsmore

Sir:

I have to acknowledge the receipt of your despatch No. 194 of the Diplomatic Series, concerning the proposal of the French Commissioner for the joint action of the foreign diplomatic body in Korea as assertion of the inviolability of legation servants, as reported your views and course in regard thereto.

The Department is gratified that the incident which gave rise to the French Commissioner's proposal was adjusted without resort to joint action. The circumstances of the case, and the unfortunate complications which appear to have been imported into it, might have made such action embarrassing as a precedent.

While the doctrine that the household affairs and representative business operations of a foreign minister are not to be invaded or interfered with by a local government, the abstract right of an envoy to withdraw natives for the country from their original subjection, by temporary employment as menial dependents of his legation, is not well defined. It is, indeed, difficult at precise definition, but its unlimited exercise by the envoy might lead to such a stretch of the privilege as to amount on the other hand to interference on his part with the jurisdictional prerogatives of the State in which he resides. This is especially the case in Oriental countries, where extraterritorial jurisdiction pertains to diplomatic residents and where the assertion of a claim to protect natives might be added that of judging them as well, civilly or criminally. No case is before the Department which would make it proper to say that it would claim for our envoys in extraterritorial countries a right to judge such natives as the minister may take into his personal services.

Even the employment of natives by our agents abroad, while often rendered necessary through the impossibility of obtaining other service, is qualified by the attitude of this Department on several occasions, where it has refused to sanction claims that a native was by such employment, withdrawn from obligations existing or contracted before he was so employed.

Your views in the premises, and having regard to the peculiar features of the incident reported, meet with the Department's approval.

ALVEY A. ADEE

NO. 13   Legation of the United States
                                          Seoul, Corea, June 7 1890

Secretary of State

Sir:

I have the honor to inform you that I yesterday forwarded to you the following despatch in cyphers: "Queen Dowager died fourth. The King fearing outbreak urged landing men for the protection of American interests telegraphed "Swatara", Captain Cooper fifty five men now at the Legation. All is tranquil."

As stated in the telegram the Queen Dowager died on the 4th Instant about 2 PM. Between half past four and five, a Corean gentleman of the family of the Queen, who, as he speaks English, is frequently employed in missions of this Kind, called upon me, and said he came from the King upon the matter of the highest importance. His Majesty was aware that I had received instructions in case of trouble, or anticipated trouble in the Palace to land forces for his protection & that as the case had presented itself now in the death of the Queen Dowager, which afforded to Evil-intentioned people an opportunity for outbreak, he wished me to telegraph at once for men.

I replied that His Majesty was laboring under a great error; that I had no such instructions & that I was only authorized to call for men in case they were needed for the protection of American lives or property.

He seemed much taken aback by this, but besought me to comply with the request he brought me. His Majesty had always looked upon an American as a true friend, on whom he could rely in an emergency, that this was a very grave crisis in his life, and that he felt himself in great danger.

I told him that His Majesty was right in thinking that the United States had a sincere friendship for him, and that personally I should be very glad to be of Service, but that it was utterly impossible for me to send troops to the Palace. At the same time, I recollected the telegraphic communications which had passed between the King & Washington, and, although I did not Know what answers had been made by the Department to his representatives, the sense in which he construed it was evident from the fact that at my audience he asked me to thank the President, as his friend, for the heed that had been shown to his request. I had in mind also the concluding phrase of your telegraphic message of 17" May. The "United States is friendly to Seoul Government"—which seemed to indicate a desire to show this friendship in any way not detrimental to American interests & to have had in contemplation the very case which now presented itself.

He continued to press the matter and finally, reflecting that trouble beginning in the Palace, would almost inevitably extend to the city and might put in jeopardy the lives of Foreigners, chiefly Americans, among whom were many women and children, while I was the only one who could effectively intervene,—there being no English, or German, or French or Russian Ship in port; reflecting also, that it was easier to prevent disturbance than to quell it, & that the Known presence of foreign troops had always acted as a powerful calmant; and that, although the King was perhaps unnecessarily nervous, and exaggerated the dangers of the situation, I could never forgive myself if an outbreak should occur & lives were lost by my neglect to act while a warning so urgently pressed—I told him that I would take upon my self to order up men from the "Swatara", who would be for the protection of the Legation, and the King would benefit by the moral effect which their presence would produce.

It may not be out of place here to remark that the number of

Western
Americans in Seoul far exceeds that of any other∧nationality,—it
being about forty, while of no other nation, except the French, are
there more than three or four.

I then telegraphed Captain Cooper of the "Swatara" which had just
arrived at Chemulpo: "Queen Dowager died, King fears trouble;
please send up at once as many men as you can, fifty if possible.
Come yourself if you can. Reply."

For obvious reasons I thought it best that the demonstration should
be a Serious one. A boat's crew might have answered the purpose,
but it was not a question of exactly how many, or how few men
were needed to suppress an existing Known disturbance, but of a
moral effect, in order to prevent one.

Early the next morning (5th June) before I was dressed, the same
Corean gentleman called upon me to ask if I had received any reply,
and how many men were coming. I had not at that time received
any reply, & so told him. But I was astonished to find he still believed,
or pretended to believe, that I was going to send the men to the
Palace. He said they were not expected to fight, but only to Show
themselves as being there, and that would be sufficient. I replied—
"that is all very well, but things that are not expected, take place,
and if they are attacked they must defend themselves. Go back to
the King and tell him that unless he is satisfied to have the men at
the Legation, they will not come."

And I immediately telegraphed Capt. Cooper "If men not left, let
them wait, but be ready"—

About half an hour after this despatch had been sent I received
from him—"Self and fifty men early tomorrow". As it was about
9 oclk A.M. when I received it, I presumed it referred to the next
day, and that the men would make a night march to arrive early,
but it afterwards turned out that the message had been sent to the
telegraph office on the night of the 4th and had not been forwarded
till next morning. About two o'clock I heard again from the King
that he would be glad to have the men at the Legation, & begged
me to order them up at once.

It is a very Serious matter to take care of 50 men & officers—
Suddenly in a place like Seoul & I did not wish to give the alert
unnecessarily; but getting no answer to my second despatch I had
sent a third asking for a reply, and commenced making my preparations, when a little before 3 I was greatly relieved by having Capt.
Cooper's card put into my hands. I saw him at once. He reported

the main body near the river about 5 miles distant, & desired me to send some one to pilot them through the streets of the City. My interpreter went to meet them, and a little before six they marched into the Legation, dusty and weary, but none the worse for their long tramp about 25 miles. Only one man suffered seriously, & this from imprudently drinking a good deal of water, against orders, at the Half way house. He has since recovered.

Capt. Cooper and I had had time to go the rounds of the buildings & decide upon the allotment of the men & officers. Water & refreshments were speedily at hand & in a very short time they were made comfortable. The march was most creditable for men from on shipboard, entirely unaccustomed to such exercise. They were under 12 hours from the wharf at Chemulpo to within the walls of the Legation. The detachment consists of Lieut. Reynolds, Ensign Chase, Dr. Fried, 25 men with two petty officers, Lieut. Biddle with 25 marines and three or four non-combatants.

The King is no blood relation of the Queen Dowager, who just deceased at the age of 83 years but he is by Corean custom her child by adoption, and owes her his present position. She was the wife of an heir apparent, who died before coming to the throne, leaving a son, who became King. He died without heirs, and without naming a Successor, but having ∧ Royal honors to his father, the Queen

_{decreed}

Dowager, as his widow, took possession of the Seals of State, which she held for three days. During this time, She Selected the present King, then a lad, to inherit the throne, and made his father the Tai-Wan-Koon, regent till he reached his majority. The Taiwonkoon ruled as regent for 10 years, or until the King was 22 years old, instead of relinquishing the reins of power when the King became of age, or 21 years old. His Majesty has an older brother, whose Son, about 19 years of age, the last revolution had for object to place on the throne under the regency of the Tai-Wan-Koon, in the place of the present King; and what is feared now is a repetition of that experiment.

Perhaps you are not aware that a prediction has been current for some time that the end of the present Dynasty & of the life of the King would occur within 18 months, & two revolts have already been attempted to prove its truth. The King lives in constant dread, & it is generally believed that his fears are well founded. The Tai-wan-Koon is a bold, ambitious man, & reported to have been the moving spirit of the late uprisings. He is said to be hostile to Foreigners.

I should have said above that on the arrival of the detachment I immediately sent a messenger to apprise His Majesty of the fact. In a short time an official came from the Palace to bring the thanks of the King, & an offer to provide food, bedding, & anything that might be desired. I declined, with Capt. Cooper's approval, all these offers with the exception of blankets, of which 53 were sent, & His Majesty hoped I would allow him to pay the expenses of the Expedition. I replied that as the men were here to protect Americans & American interests, he could not be expected to do this, but thanked him at the same time for his civility.

The next day a General of the Royal Forces came with a large retinue to repeat his thanks. His Majesty regretted that I would not allow him to provide for the men, but he must accept my decision & would write a letter to the President to express his sense of obligation. Gen. Lee said the King was anxious the men should be well cared for, & had instructed him to see himself that they were Comfortable. I conducted him over the quarters, which he thought very restricted, & wished at least to be allowed to send them every day beer & cigars. Not to give offense, I consented for that day to receive a few cigars, which were distributed among the men to their great delight.

I have wished to lose no time in giving you the facts of the case as they have occured without comment. I am entirely without instructions applicable to present exigencies. It has been impossible to consult the Department, or to frame such an exposé of the situation by telegraph in an intelligible manner at sufficient length to allow of a proper opinion to be formed, and I have been compelled to take the responsibility of immediate action.

AUGUSTINE HEARD

NO. 80

Department of State
Washington, February 26, 1891

Augustine Heard

Sir:

I have received your number 112, of the 10th of January, ultimo, relating to the question of the ownership of the reclaimed land fronting the Japanese Settlement at Chemulpo and enclosing copies of an agreement between the Governments of Korea and Japan; of correspondence between the British minister and the Korean Foreign Office, and of a plan of the foreign settlement at Chemulpo.

Without entering at length into a discussion of the merits of the question, clearly presented by you, I will not omit to say that the views of the Department on the subject are in accord with those which you express.

The British minister, Sir Harry Parkes, in his note of May 7th, 1884, to the Korean Foreign Office, reviewing a former note in the same relation, writes that he had urged upon the Government of Korea the desirability of an extension of the provision for building-ground for European and American residents at Chemulpo, and had recommended that a part of such extension be made to the south of the Japanese settlement on the foreshore fronting that quarter. The effect of the adoption of this plan would be the closing in of the Japanese settlement in apparent contravention of the agreement between Japan and Korea, and in derogation of the priority rights of the Japanese residents.

You inform me that at a meeting of the foreign representatives held at your legation on the 29th of December last, to consider the matter, the Chargé d'Affaires of Japan did not disguise the belief that his Government was convinced of the righteousness of its claim (to the fore-shore fronting its settlement) and would be firm in maintaining it.

While, as I have alredy [sic] said, the opinion you express of the merits of the case is approved, it is contrary to the practice of this Government to direct or sanction the participation of its representatives abroad by vote or voice, in any conference of their colleagues the result of which might tend to restrain or impair the free exercise of the rights of an independent State, except where the circumstances are such as to demand or warrant the intervention of the United States in behalf of its own citizens and their rights and privileges.

You will therefore, at the next meeting of the diplomatic body in Korea, held to consider the present subject, announce to your colleagues, should the occasion be proper, that while it is your duty and purpose to secure and maintain the same rights, immunities, and privileges for American residents at Chemulpo as those enjoyed by citizens or subjects of any other nationality, you are not authorized by Your Government to take part in any movement looking to that object at the expense of Japanese rights.

You also invite my intention to the desirability of conserving a right-of-way for other foreign residents between the western and eastern portions of their settlement through the Japanese settlement, in the event of the success of the Japanese Chargé's contention.

An examination of the plan enclosed in your despatch discloses the importance of such a thoroughfare by the present main street of the Japanese settlement to enable the two portions of the general foreign settlement to communicate with each other; and, in view of the con-templated extensions, such a way through the bund or street to be constructed on the Japanese water front, in the contingency men-tioned, would appear to be indispensable to convenient access from the eastern part of the foreign settlement to the custom-house and Korean offices at the western end.

In consideration of the assurance given on this subject by Mr. Kondo, the Chargé D'Affaires of Japan, the Department does not doubt such a privilege will be secured by adequate means in any adjustment of the question that may be determined upon.

James G. Blaine

<table>
<tr><td>NO. 197</td><td style="text-align:right;">Legation of the United States
Seoul, Corea, August 31, 1891</td></tr>
</table>

Secretary of State

Sir:

I have the honor to inform you that having been unwell for several weeks, I was urged by my physician to take a sea-voyage, and that on the 20th Instant, I left Chemulpo for Chefoo. I returned by the same steamer on the 28th instant, having been absent eight days, during which time Mr. Allen had charge of the Legation.

The 29th was the King's birth-day, and as it was the most important of all birthdays up to this age, in Corean estimation the 40th, I was desirous of being present to offer my congratulations. (The day on each successive 10th year afterwards has peculiar significance, the 50th, 60th, 70th, and 80th, birthdays, but most important of all is the 61st). I was unable to leave Chemulpo in time to reach the City Gates before sundown, the hour of closing, but spent the night at Oricol, the halfway station, and leaving there before 5 in the morning, arrived at Seoul shortly after eight, to learn that that hour, 8 had been named for the audience. Knowing that punctuality was not a Korean virtue, I made my preparations as soon as I could and hurried to the Palace. As I was going up the broad street leading to the gate, I was disappointed at meeting the other ministers coming away. The audience had already taken place. My remarks on the long waiting and delay at New Year's seemed to have produced an effect. I went on however—found the usual officials, the President of the Home and Foreign Office in the Reception Room and explained to them the efforts I had made to be present and my regrets about not having arrived in time.

His Majesty was pleased to receive me at once, keeping the Consuls and others waiting, and I had a very satisfactory interview with him of some length. He had heard the telegraphic report in the newspapers that an American Squadron had been ordered to these seas and wished to know if it was in consequence of the troubles in China. How many ships were coming and where would they go? Would they come here? For some months there had been no American Man-of-War in Korea, and he hoped one would be sent. I gave him what information I possessed about the ships that were expected and told him they would go first to Yokohama where the admiral was stationed, and be distributed according to his orders. I had no doubt that a ship would shortly be sent here, but of late the squadron had been very much reduced, and that the disturbances in China had made their presence on that Coast indispensable.

All of which he appeared to recognize.

He has lately received some arms from America, and he wished me to express his thanks to the Government for selecting them and permitting them to come.

The King was exceedingly gracious, but the interview was important only so far as it was an expression of his feeling of friendship for America. Her Majesty, The Queen, has recently been quite unwell, and I was able to offer at the same time with my congratulations on his birthday, my congratulations on her recovery. He said that she was much better and that he hoped, as soon as this excessive heat was over, to receive my wife and daughter. With the exception of the audience accorded to Madame Pausa, wife of the Italian minister and Mrs. Allen, while we were in Peking, no foreign ladies have been received at the Palace since the death of the Queen Dowager.

In this connection (friendship for America) I may say that the Instructors of the Royal School, Mr. Bunker and Mr. Hulbert, Americans, have recently had their contracts renewed for three years; and that the Royal Hospital has been maintained under an American physician, both, especially the latter, due to a very large degree to the influence directly asserted, of this legation. The Hospital owing to the imprudence of a Doctor newly arrived from the United States was very nearly passing under English control, but after some correspondence and one or two interviews with the President of the Foreign Office, I was able to retain it as before. You are aware that this Hospital was originally established in 1884 with Dr. H. N. Allen, at its head.

The Foreign Advisers of the Government, General Le Gendre and Mr. Greathouse, are Americans, and by the exercise of suitable prudence and with directness and honesty in our dealings there seems no reason why we should not retain the influence we now appear to hold in Korea.

The dinner was given in the evening to the Foreign Representatives at the Foreign Office, but I was not well enough to attend.

AUGUSTINE HEARD

NO. 45

U. S. S. "Alert" (3rd rate)
Cheltos, Ping Yang Inlet, Korea
22nd June, 1892

Rear Admiral D. B. Harmony
Commander in Chief, U.S. Naval Force
Nagasaki, Japan

Sir:

I have the honor to submit the following report upon Korea, which I will preface with the statement that I was there with the first United States Embassy in 1883, when Korea was formally opened to foreigners, and when we lived in Seoul nearly a week as guests of the Korean Government, and remained several weeks at Chemulpo, taking from there to Nagasaki the first Korean Embassy that proceeded to the United States, headed by Min Yon Ik.

So far as the United States is concerned she has, at present, no particular interest in Korea, further than the protection of about 50 of her citizens who have momentarily taken up their residence in the country. The most of these are Missionaries, although the Legation claims 7 and there are several others holding prominent positions under the Government, such as the Government Electrician, Chief of Police and two Advisers to the King, although I believe that one of the latter now resides near Tokio, Japan.

The Missionaries, mostly of the Presbyterian and Methodist Boards, are undoubtedly doing good work and should receive encouragement. There are also in Seoul, some Military Instructors, and teachers, from the United States, who are in the employ of the Korean Government.

There is but one American firm in Korea, that of Morse, Townsend & Co., at Chemulpo, and I am of the opinion that the "Co.," of this firm is far reaching. Of the two "American Advisors of the King," who are registered at the Legation in Seoul as "Vice Presidents of Korean Home Affairs," and who each receive a salary of $12,000 a year (one of them now living near Tokio) I am of opinion that their real influence upon the Home Affairs is quite limited, and I will illustrate it by fact. The Japanese who have by far the largest trade interests in the country, offered to make themselves a good wagon road connecting Chemulpo with Seoul, a distance of nearly 30 miles, to replace the bridle road crossing some bad cuts which at present exist, which compels either a walk, a chair, or a pony, a matter in either case of 8 hours to make the distance and very exhausting. The King declined to allow it to be done. I think that China is the "Advisor to the King of Korea" and that the King of Korea is much afraid of his Advisor. Again there is a Conservative party in Korea that wishes everything to remain in the old way. This I think results in a great measure from their form of life which keeps the majority of the men about the house all day only depending upon the water and the cultivation of the land to a sufficient degree that will clothe them and give them the bare necessaries. In fact they are very lazy. China favors this party and for the present things must go on in the old primeval way. But there is a race growing up that will change things. Some of them are already grown. The King may amuse himself in his Palaces covering several acres with his women of whom it was said when we were there in '83 that there were 700 official concubines inside the palace gates, with its electric lights. Anyway, in fact, that is but personal to himself, but for real advancement, the Dragon blocks the way.

Every where and wherever you go, you will find the Koreans most agreeable and hospitable to all foreigners, especially, as my observation has led me, to Americans from whom the Koreans have received so much, and there is no more need of a "Gunboat" continuously at Chemulpo, than there is at any town in Japan.

There are now 56 citizens of the United States who reside in the Kingdom of Korea, or rather who are registered as residing there, which is 22 more than the British who come next with 34.

(Signed) R. D. HITCHCOCK

NO. 413   Legation of the United States
                                                Seoul Korea, June 28, 1893

Secretary of State

Sir:

I have the honor to inform you that His Majesty granted me a special audience yesterday in which I presented my letter of recall with a few remarks of which a copy is enclosed.

His Majesty's reply was marked by much Cordiality and warmth of feeling which was evidently sincere. He had always looked on America as a disinterested friend on whom he Could rely in times of emergency, and he thanked me explicitly for my action in acceding to his request to have some men up from the Men of war on the two occasions,—at the time of the death and burial of the Queen Dowager in 1890. He regretted that so little had been seen of the American Navy for the last two years, and when I pointed out that the exigencies of the service called for the presence of the ships in China during a great part of the time he said that he understood this perfectly, but that now he hoped there would be a change and asked me to represent the matter to my Government. He wished to thank the President of the Government for all the marks of Kindness that had been shown him and his officers in America, and to ask that these should be continued in the future. I told him that no action of this nature was needed on my part, that the interest felt by the United States in Korea was sincere and deep.

The interview lasted half an hour, and, making all allowances for Korean politeness, His Majesty was definitely desirous of creating the impression of extreme consideration and friendliness. He reverted two or three times to the question of the presence of the Navy in these waters and only desisted on my promise to speak of it. Of course there were profound expressions of personal regard and regret at my departure.

Mr. Herod accompanied me.

As bearer of a letter from the President, I passed through the Central Gates and there were the usual honors of presenting arms, etc.

                                                AUGUSTINE HEARD

NO. 482
Legation of the United States
Seoul Korea Nov. 12, 1893

Secretary of State

Sir:

I have the honor to inform you that on yesterday Their Majesties The King and Queen of Korea, with the attendant officers, made the ceremonial visit to the Mortuary Temple, nearly adjoining this Legation, referred to in my No. 468, Oct. 6th. They were attended by thousands of soldiers and banner men, making in all a rare display.

As the procession was to pass along the street lined by American residences, and in front of this Legation, we Americans arranged for a suitable display of decorations. We also united in sending a message of greeting to Their Majesties.

The Royal Family were immensely pleased with these evidences of good will, and The King at once sent several of his highest officials to return thanks. The Queen also sent the Chief Eunuch to Mrs. Allen with kind messages, and to express Her Majestys regret that custom forbade her coming in person to see her (Mrs. Allen).

In the case of the other, European, Legations nearby, which were also decorated, His Majesty sent only interpreters to express his thanks for the attention shown.

H. N. ALLEN

NO. 60
Department of State
Washington, February 26, 1895

John M. B. Sill

Sir:

I enclose herewith copies of two communications which were received with a letter of the 21st instant from the Secretary of the Navy, they being the correspondence between the Commander-in-Chief of the naval forces on the Asiatic Station and yourself in relation to the permission granted to the King of Korea to store valuable packages in your Legation.

You have not hitherto reported the incident, and it is now brought to your attention inasmuch as the permission given by you to the King "to place certain sealed packages of treasure in the Legation" seems to have been outside of your representative functions or pre-rogatives.

The Department is gratified to learn from your letter of January 18 to Admiral Carpenter that the privilege you incautiously granted was not made use of.

EDWIN F. UHL

NO. 86

Department of State
Washington, July 8, 1895

John M. B. Sill

Sir:

I have to inform you that this Department has received a communication from the Secretary of the Navy in which he expresses regret that his Department has no funds available for the erection of quarters for the officers and men of the Navy who may be detailed to protect our Legation at Seoul.

On several occasions since the establishment of our Legation in Korea the presence at Seoul of an armed United States force to protect our Legation and the American citizens at that place, has been considered necessary, and while the Department does not wish to in any way forbid you calling on the Commander of the United States naval force on the Asiatic station for protection, when in your judgment such is imperatively demanded, it does wish to discourage, so far as possible, such practice, and you should insist on the Korean Government affording at all times, that full protection from all insult and injury of any sort, not only to our diplomatic and consular representatives in the kingdom, but to all our citizens, which it has promised to extend to them in Article IV of our treaty of 1882. You are directed, before the departure of the guard now on duty at the Legation, to inform the Korean Foreign Office of the purpose of the present instruction.

I enclose for your information a copy of a letter this day sent to the Secretary of the Navy on the subject.

ALVEY A. ADEE

Telegram   Seoul, Korea
                                     Dec. 1, 1895

Olney

  Washington

    Three days ago Loyalists made a fruitless attempt to Capture Royal Palace, In consequence of which usurpers are very bold, arresting and killing Loyalists. I have eight refugees. See my despatch No. 159. No charge made against them, but if caught they will be tortured and killed by the Kings Father. The demands may all soon be made for them for some reason or other. It is desirable for them to leave. Yorktown will shortly leave for Shanghai. Will you authorize Commander in Chief to grant them passage.

                                             SILL

NO. 177   Legation of the United States
                              Seoul Korea Dec. 3, 1895

Secretary of State

Sir:

    Continuing the subject of the recent attempt to Capture the Palace, explained in my No. 175 of yesterday, I have now the honor to inform you that I have today heard reports to the effect that Americans were mixed up in that affair, of Nov. 28.

    The alleged reasons for these reports are, that three Americans went into the Palace that evening and remained with the King, being armed with revolvers; that Gen'l Dye, of the Palace guards is said to have attempted to aid the intruders, and that I with my Secretary of Legation and the Russian Representative went towards the Palace in the night. Also American missionaries are accused of having expressed themselves as favorable to the attempt and some of their native teachers have been arrested for complicity in the plot.

    As nearly as I can ascertain the facts are as follows:

    We heard first of this plot at 5-30 P.M. of the 27th Nov. the night of the attack. I had a consultation with my Russian and British colleagues who came to see me as they had also just heard reports of the same nature. The attack being somewhat serious, we at once wrote a letter to the Japanese Minister asking him if he had heard the same and if he could give us any light on the subject. see enclosure. He was absent at the Palace as we shortly learned, and his reply did not reach me till noon the next day. His having gone to the Palace tended to strengthen the rumor of coming trouble.

As I have been allowing one or two of our missionaries to sleep in Gen'l Dyes quarters at the Palace at the urgent request of the King, as a sort of moral support; and as the British physician to the Government Hospital (who by the way is employed by the American Presbyterian Society) was going in upon a summons from His Majesty to see him professionally, I allowed two American missionaries to accompany him, giving them my card and one of the Legation runners to gain admission. During the night these men, hearing shots, made their way to the King's door and announced their presence, when His Majesty eagerly asked them in and held the hand of one or the other of them during the remainder of the night. These men do not deny that they had revolvers in their pockets.

General Dye, according to his own story, collaborated by other good testimony, posted the guard in a proper way to prevent the intrusion, and I have no reason for suspecting that he did not do his whole duty in the defense of the Palace, which defense was quite successful.

Our guards having been given especial instructions to keep a sharp lookout during the night, awakened us at 12-30, because they had heard 3 pistol shots, and again at 3 A.M. because of the noise of great shooting at the Palace.

Messrs. Waeber, Hillier and myself, as our places adjoin each other, met in the lane at the back of our compounds, and decided we had better go over towards the Palace with our Secretaries and see what the disturbance meant. Mr Waeber proposed taking a guard, but Mr Hillier and myself objecting the guard was not taken.

Just as we were starting a letter was handed in to the servants of each of our Legations, purporting to come from the attacking party, but as we had no interpreters and the paper was in a Chinese and a Korean mixture, we could only make out that there was trouble on and we were not to be alarmed. I enclose a copy of this letter with translation. The same was sent to each Legation except that the one received by the Japanese was much fuller and more alarming. I send you a Japanese translation into English of this, not having seen the original.

As we were leaving, Mr Yun Chi Ho, Vice Minister of Foreign Affairs appeared and urged us to do all in our power to avert danger to His Majestys life. We had already decided to go, but this emphasized what we had already heard and we hoped to prevent any such disturbance, or at least by our presence to preserve the Kings life.

Approaching the rear gate of the Palace, with Mr. Yun Chi Ho, we learned that the intruders had not gained access to the inside of the Palace, so the King's life was not in danger. We sent word to the insurgents through a follower of Mr Yun Chi Ho, that they were in danger of committing a grievous wrong and that they ought to disburse at once. We immediately returned to our homes.

In the reports above referred to, Mr. Hilliers and Mr Komuras names do not seem to be mentioned, but each of these gentlemen went to the Palace, Mr Hillier with us, and Mr Komura who lives at the opposite side of the city, by himself.

I fear our missionaries may have been indiscreet in their expressions of sympathy and interest. I am quite sure that none of them had a guilty knowledge of this attempt, though doubtless some of their native instructors in the Korean language had and the latter may have counted unduly upon the sympathy of the foreigners.

Our refugees did not know of this attempt until just before I heard of it myself, but one of the refugees at the Russian Legation seems to have had a knowledge of this or some other plot, and to have carried on a correspondence with an officer in the present Palace guard, who, we have since learned, was supposed to be in full sympathy with the plot, but who, either for fear, or with malice oforethought [sic], gave up the correspondence and did not aid the attacking party.

Mr Waeber is reported to have sent his refugees to Chemulpo under an escort of Russian soldiers, and they were received at Chemulpo on board a Russian man-of-war which shortly put to sea. Mr Waeber has since given me to understand that his refugees are still at his place. He did send off two Koreans, but I do not know who they were.

The unsuccessful attack has tremendously strengthened this usurping Government and made them bolder as I have already mentioned in the despatch above cited.

The reports involving Americans, however over-drawn they may be, render the situation exceedingly critical for the 80 men, women, and children resident in Seoul. The Japanese seem to be making the utmost of any suspicions that can by any means be interpreted to the disadvantage of Americans and other foreigners in order apparently to call away attention from the horrors of the 8th October, which they have never yet seriously investigated.

We are now experiencing the reign of terror which I Plainly foresaw and foretold, whenever I ventured to urge the Representatives of Japan to do at least something to avert the danger which has overtaken us. There has been no time since my return from Japan when a word, firmly uttered by Japan would not, in all probability, have been sufficient. Of course there was a possibility that a show of force might have been required, but Mr. Komura himself thought such possibility most remote and so expressed himself. The old order of things has been broken up and nothing has been supplied to replace it.

JOHN M. B. SILL

Telegram

Department of State
Washington, December 2, 1895

Sill, Minister, Seoul

Refugees cannot be sheltered by you against officers of *de facto* government charged with apprehending them as violators of the laws of their country. Use of Yorktown in manner suggested is wholly inadmissable. The Department sees with disfavor your disposition to forget that you are not to interfere with local concerns and politics of Korea but are to limit yourself strictly to the care of American interests.

OLNEY

Telegram

Washington
January 11, 1896

Sill

Seoul

Your despatches Nos 175 and 176 Your course in continued intermeddling with Korean political affairs in violation of repeated instructions noted with astonishment and emphatic disapproval. Cable briefly any explanation you have to make also answer whether you intend to comply with instructions given.

OLNEY

Telegram   Seoul, Korea
                                                          January 13, 1896

Olney

Washington

Telegram received. I did err unintentionally in certain points recited
in my 175 and 176. No harm has resulted in Korea. There will not
be henceforth any cause for criticism. I will act according to instructions scrupulously. Affairs here quiet. Legation guard leaves on
Wednesday. I will write you fully.

                                                                    SILL

NO. 63   Legation of the United States
                                              Söul, February 13, 1887

Secretary of State

Sir:

As a further acknowledgement of your despatch No. 42, December
16, 1886, touching the question of the American military officers for
Korea, I have the honor to forward to you herewith a translation of
a note which I received from the Korean Foreign Office on the 3rd
instant.

This note being very vague, I called the President of the Foreign
Office to try and reach some understanding on the subject which
might facilitate an arrangement.

I explained to the President that although this question had been
pending for over two years, the President of the United States and
the Department of State had shown throughout their sincere and
earnest desire to comply with the request of His Majesty. The difficulty in the way was the necessity of a law being enacted by Congress, which alone could enable officers now holding commissions in
the Army and Navy accepting temporary service in Korea. If the
Government of Korea would be willing to accept the services of
resigned officers or of men who, having graduated at the Military
Academy, had not received commissions in the Army, it appeared
to me that the difficulty of obtaining such instructors would be greatly
diminished and, I added, although speaking in a personal way only,
I feel sure that the government of the United States will insist on
having competent men chosen for the work.

Three days later an official was sent by His Majesty to tell me that he in no wise insisted on the Army instructors being officers in active service, that so [sic] they were competent to teach soldiers, their present occupation was of no consequence. The Korean Government would make a contract with the instructors for a period of two years which might be extended later on. The chief instructor would receive $4000 (Mexican) per annum, and the subordinates $1950. A sum of $500 (Mex) would be allowed each of them to cover the expenses of their voyage to this country, and they would be lodged while here. His Majesty requests that two subordinate drill masters be sent. These, I think, might easily be found among men who have received an honorable discharge as non-commissioned officers from our Army.

Although the above conditions of the contract have only been made known to me verbally, both the President of the Foreign Office and the official sent here by His Majesty, requested that I would lose no time in making them Known to you that they would embody them in a despatch to be sent me in a short time.

W. W. ROCKHILL

NO. 11   Legation of the United States
                                    Soul Korea April 25th 1887

Secretary of State

Sir:

Referring to Mr. Rockhill's despatch No. 63 of Feby 13th 1887 treating of a request of the Korean government for military instructors, I have the honor to transmit herewith, translation of a note received at this legation on the first of the present month, making a definite proposal in writing of salaries to be paid to military instructors in case they come in accordance with request of His Majesty's government.

I beg to impress upon you the great persistent anxiety of the Koreans upon this subject. I have been spoken to on the subject several times already since my arrival. They urge that the American Secretary of State promised assistance of this Kind to their embassy three years ago. When the Russian government offered to furnish instructors they declined on the ground that the United States government had been requested to furnish them, and they continued to hold the Russians off hoping to get them from our government.

If the instructors should be selected and sent, though unofficially, bearing the endorsement of the Dept of State, as were the teachers who have been so successful, it would be highly gratifying to the King and those of his officials who are in sympathy with his policy, and would give to the work of instruction and to those engaged in it, a support here that would be of great value.

HUGH A. DINSMORE

Telegram   U. S. Legation
                                              Seöul, Korea, June 29, 1887

Bayard

Washington

The king is very anxious for military teachers. Will they come?
DINSMORE

NO. 67   Legation of the United States
                                          Söul, Korea, October 24, 1887

Secretary of State

Sir:

On the 18th instant I had the honour to receive from you a telegraphic message in the following words.

Dinsmore Minister Seoul Korea Send definite proposals guaranteeing army instructors liberal monthly pay from departure. Allowances transportation prepaid return for Chief and two assistants. Bayard

Immediately upon recept of this despatch I communicated its contents to the Korean Foreign Office. Yesterday I received a despatch from the President of the foreign office bearing the office seal offering the following terms to such military instructors as may come to Korea and enter the service of His Majesty the King through the Kind offices of the government of the United States, viz.:—

Five Thousand Dollars per annum to be paid in Mexicans, as salary to a Chief Instructor, and a salary of three thousand dollars, Mexicans, to be paid to each of two assistant instructors. Five Hundred Mexicans to be paid to each of the three upon his arrival in Söul in addition to salary, in lieu of expenses of coming from the United

States to Korea, a compound including its houses granted by the King for their use during their service as instructors free from rent.

I have stipulated that their salaries must be paid monthly or quarterly in advance, and that a sum of five hundred Mexicans must be paid to each upon his retiring from service toward defraying expenses of return to the United States. These last two items are features of the agreement not expressed in the despatch from the foreign office, it having been written before my demands for them was communicated to the King, but he sent an officer immediately to say to me that he acceded to the items Cheerfully and that though it was not written in the despatch I would certainly accept the King's assurance.

Of course I replied that such assurance was satisfactory, that a despatch was but the means of conveying His Majesty's word, and that it is always respected and trusted in whatever form it came.

The King is extremely anxious for their early arrival and at his request and expense I sent to Nagasaki a telegraphic message to be despatched to you from there, so that it may not pass through the hands of the Chinese.

I may remark that the house offered for the occupancy of the instructors will be unfurnished and they will have to furnish it themselves. It is a compound which the King had fitted out for Mr. Foulk and the place is fresh and clean having never been occupied since it was finished. Its capacity is not ample for three gentlemen but the King offers to make it comfortable for them.

The terms seem to me to be reasonable. His Majesty would have offered more with my encouragement but I did not feel at liberty to offer it even if I had not believed the terms liberal enough.

The despatch received by me from the foreign office specifies that salary is to begin on entering service, and the King preferred to give a specific sum in lieu of expenses going and coming.

HUGH A. DINSMORE

NO. 113   Legation of the U. States
                                               Seoûl, Corea, June 11th 1888

Secretary of State

Sir:

I have the honor to inform you that General McE. Dye, Colonel Cummins and Major Lee in pursuance of the request of His Majesty the King of Corea communicated through this legation to the Department of State arrived in Seoûl about two months ago. A contract was executed with the Corean Government a little more than a month since in accordance with the terms proposed in my correspondence to the Department and now after some delay quarters have been provided and the officers have entered actively into the performance of their duties.

In addition to the three gentlemen mentioned the Government has engaged the services of Mr. F. J. H. Nienstead, an American formerly connected with the U. S. Navy and more recently the U.S. Consulate at Kobe Japan to assist in the work for which these officers have been employed.

A class of about forty young men have already been chosen and uniformed and are now receiving daily instruction to prepare them for drill officers. Their zealous interest and aptitude gives much encouragement to the instructors.

It is proposed soon to add to this number and eventually to take the regular troops in hand.

Shortly after the arrival of the instructors at the invitation of His Majesty the King I introduced them at the palace to His Majesty and the Crown Prince both of whom expressed great satisfaction at their arrival and a hope for good results.

I am pleased to say that these gentlemen have met with a cordial reception by all the foreign representatives and residents.

HUGH A. DINSMORE

NO. 70 F.O.   Legation of the United States
                                         Seoul, June 15th 1888

President of the Korean Foreign Office

Your Excellency:

It is with much regret that I so soon have to make complaint of the treatment of the Military instructors by the Corean officials.

From the time when I first arrived in Corea I received repeated and urgent applications from your Government to secure military instructors to come from the United States to teach your young men and drill your soldiers owing to the great friendship of my country for His Majesty the King and for your Great Country. Able men with large military experience were chosen and left their families and homes and came so far away in answer to that request.

These instructors are men who have commanded Soldiers in the United States. General Dye has Served in our army as a General and has had thousands of men under his command. They are willing and anxious to discharge the duties which they have undertaken for your country. But they are not rich men and have families at home which they must support. Your government made a contract with these gentlemen in which it promised to pay their salaries every month in advance.

I am very sorry to know that your government has not complied with this contract and three months salary is now due, no part of which has been paid.

The house which was given to General Dye and Col Cummins to live in has no water and they have not been able to induce your honorable officials to have a well made. No Kissus nor soldiers have been furnished them, and it pains me to see that the interest taken by my country in assisting your honorable country is so little appreciated and meets with such poor reward. May I beg that Your Excellency will give this matter Your official attention and communicate it to His Majesty Your Great King. I am sure His Gracious Majesty cannot wish that it should be so.

HUGH A. DINSMORE

NO. 203   Legation of the United States
                                 Söul Korea Sept 25th 1889

Secretary of State

Sir:

On the 21st instant I was addressed by Col E H. Cummins and Major John G. Lee two of the three gentlemen who came out to Korea from the United States in the beginning of the year 1888 to enter upon service as military instructors under His Korean Majestys government, advising me that they had received notice through their colleague General Dye that the Korean authorities had ordered that their services be dispensed with on the 18th instant, and their salary paid up to that date. A copy of General Dye's note to Major Lee was enclosed, and I enclose a copy with this despatch.

These gentlemen invoke my official assistance in protesting against this action of the Korean Government as in violation of the contracts entered into at the beginning of their term of service in which the

Government undertook to give them employment for two years from the 9th day of May 1888, and to pay them for their service under such employment three thousand silver or Mexican dollars per annum in Monthly payments in advance.

A copy of the contract made with Major Lee is enclosed, which is uniform with that made with Col Cummins.

No charges of any nature whatsoever appear to have been made against the two officers of inefficiency, unfaithfulness, or violation of duty or contract.

Impelled by a conviction of duty therefore, in behalf of two American citizens, I wrote a Note to the Foreign Office in respectful terms referring to the Contract and insisting that unless the two officers have been guilty of such conduct as would absolve the Government from the obligation of its conduct, in the case of their being relieved of duty the Government should pay them for the full term of the contract, and provision being made therefor in the contract to pay $500.00 to each to defray expense of return to the United States. I have the honor to enclose a copy of my note which bears the date of the 23rd instant.

Though no reasons have been given for the discharge of the two officers, I have heard unofficially of complaints against both. Of Col Cummins that he has been neglectful of his duties which if true is just cause doubtless for the Government action. Major Lee appears to have been attentive to his professional duties and to have given satisfaction in that respect but a strong feeling has been engendered against him at the Palace and in official circles growing out of objectionable utterances attributed to him in correspondence with the public press in the United States.

The Government has not reserved to itself the right of terminating the service at its pleasure in the contracts, and I should be pleased
    have
to ∧ the views of the Department as to the course proper for me to pursue in case charges of the Character described are urged as a reason for Major Lee's dismissal.

Both of the gentlemen have declined to leave Korea until payment has been made according to the terms of the contract.

No answer has been received by me from the Foreign Office, and it is probable that as is usually the case it will be long delayed. Meanwhile I await the Department's instructions.

HUGH A. DINSMORE

NO. 130   Department of State
                                        Washington, Nov. 21, 1889

Hugh A. Dinsmore

Sir:

Your despatch No. 203, Dip. Series, of the 25th September last, has been received. You therein inform the Department that Col. E. H. Cummins and Major John G. Lee, two of the gentlemen who went to Corea from the United States in the beginning of the year 1888 to enter upon service as Military instructors under His Corean Majesty's Government, had been notified that the Government would dispense with their services in that capacity on the 18th of September, and that they would be paid to that date. You further state that both these gentlemen refuse to leave Corea until payment is made them according to the terms of the contract entered into at the beginning of their term of service by which the Corean Government stipulated to give them employment for two years from the 9th day of May, 1888, and that they had invoked your assistance in the matter. You therefore request the view of the Department as to the proper course for you to pursue.

In reply I have to say that if any satisfactory charges of incompetence or malfeasance are preferred against the gentlemen recommended by this Government at the earliest solicitation of Corea, no objection can be intraposed to the abrogation of the contract on the ground of non-fulfillment by the parties contracting to perform a definite service; but even in such a case—of which, however, no evidence ever is tendered—the payment of the return expenses of the officers is confidently expected as an act of equity, and must be earnestly urged.

JAMES G. BLAINE

NO. 220   Legation of the United States
                                        Söul Korea Jan'y 27th 1890

Secretary of State

Sir:

I have the honor to acknowledge receipt of your instruction No. 130 of November 21st 1889 directing me to urge equitable treatment of the two American citizens Col E. H. Cummins and Major John G.

Lee with reference to their dismissal from the service of the Korean Government, and in connexion therewith to inform you of correspondence between this legation and the Korean Government's foreign office.

In reply to my note of Sept 23rd" 1889 to the President of the Foreign Office, which was communicated to you in my No 203 of September 25th 1889, treating of this subject, he wrote me on November 27th, claiming that the dismissal of the two officers was within the proper authority of the Korean Government, and intimating as I construed the note, a copy of which is enclosed, that his Gov't is not under obligation to make explanation of its conduct on the premises, but setting out a vague and general accusation of noncompliance with his contract on the part of Mr Cummins, and equally indefinite charges against Mr Lee of drunkenness and incompetence, and using objectionable language; (probably about the Korean Government, the Chinese text is vague). It is proper to state at this point that in the first rendering of the Chinese furnished by My writer and interpreter the accusation of drunkenness was overlooked therefore no reference was made to it in my reply of Nov 30th a copy of which is herewith enclosed.

This reply as will be seen by reference to the copy insists that the Charges shall be made specific, and offers my respectful dissent from the President's view of the right of the Korean Government to ignore the contract.

No further communication has been received from the Korean Government upon the subject.

The President gave me a personal interview in which the subject was discussed and I received respectful consideration from him but he would not promise me enough.

On the 21st instant I informed the Foreign Office of the receipt of your instruction above acknowledged, and urged payment of the sums due.

It may not be amiss to advise you that the Korean Government is giving like trouble to all of its foreign employes, excepting only the two American teachers employed in the Government school.

Some have been dismissed, including two miners, Americans, of which I will write a separate despatch later. All have difficulty in collecting their salaries.

Mr. Denny the foreign adviser has not received a third of the salary due him for four years service.

I have the honor to enclose a copy of my note of the 21st instant to the foreign office.

A demand was made some weeks ago upon Major Lee to yield possession of the house assigned to him by the Government for the residence. He declined to do so.

My belief is that the government of Korea cannot justly complain of either of these two officers, on grounds sufficient to excuse itself from compliance with its contract.

None of the four military teachers have received consideration they deserved, nor all the benefits Pledged in their Contracts.

HUGH A. DINSMORE

NO. 137   Department of State
                                        Washington, Mar. 4, 1890

Hugh A. Dinsmore

Sir:

Your No. 220 of the 27th January last, in relation to the unwarranted dismissal of Col. E. H. Cummins and Major John G. Lee, American citizens, from the post they occupied as instructors under the Corean Government is received. Your dissent from the Corean Claims as to the propriety of dismissing these officers summarily and without due formulation of charges is approved.

You will use your best endeavors to prevent any injustice being done to these citizens of the United States, who were selected for their competency and left their homes for the distant posts where their services were required, under the good faith of the Corean Government.

JAMES G. BLAINE

NO. 227   Legation of the United States
                                        Söul Korea March 24th 1890

Secretary of State

Sir:

Referring to my No. 203 of September 25th 1889 and 220 of January 27th 1890 touching the dismissal of Messrs Cummins and Lee from the service of the Korean Government, and their claim to compensation, I regret to have to report that I have been unable to move the Korean Government to a settlement admitting any further sum due either of these gentlemen other than has been paid.

There has been no correspondence in writing between the legation and the Government since I reported to the Department in the last despatch above referred to. The Foreign Office has failed to reply to either of my last two notes in relation to the matter.

However I have at times seen the President and urged upon him the importance of an amicable settlement, and called his attention to the injustice of the action of the Government, not to say discourtesy in dealing so arbitrarily in the matter, when the service of the two gentlemen had at the pressing solicitation of the Korean Government been secured by selection of the United States government authorities.

The President insists that the matter is entirely out of his hands and that the disposal of it has been committed to General Han Kin Sul, the Military official having charge of the instruction department. I have visited General Han and have spent hours with him endeavoring to impress upon him the injustice of his course, but without avail. He always hears me respectfully but is unyielding in his assertion that the Korean Government should not be expected to pay anything more to the two gentlemen, who he insists are incompetent.

He is bitter in his feeling against Mr. Lee who, is he insists in gross violation of duty, and a certain loyalty he owed to the Government employing him, used the public press for utterance of criticisms and reflections upon the Government's political policy, and to denounce its officials.

He has given me No evidence of this beyond his own statement and has shown to me none of the alleged publications.

I am ignorant of what they are, but have heard unofficially and I cannot say how reliably that they were communicated to the Government from its legation in Washington.

Mr Lee's conduct since his dismissal has been such as to render a settlement of his Claim much more difficult, if not to make it impossible.

He has indulged in the most indiscreet denunciation of the Korean Government and its officers, of Mr. Denny the foreign adviser, of General Dye the Chief Military instructor, and of Captain Nienstead his associate, to say nothing of a general tirade against the American Missionary community. In an interview published some weeks ago in the "Hong Kong Telegraph" he was represented as using many offensive expressions with reference to the Government and very many of the Söul residents.

The writer whose name was I believe signed to the article was at the time of the writing spending a week as Mr. Lees guest. I am unable to enclose a copy, but I enclose for the Department's information, as tending in a measure to account for the native Governments hostile attitude, clippings from The Shanghai Mercury a daily newspaper published in China, from a Söul correspondent which is unquestionably Mr Lee though the articles are not signed by him in his name.

The most damaging and offensive portions are indicated by red lines on the enclosure.

It will be seen that both General Han and General Dye are accused of dishonesty, a specific charge being made against the latter which is wholly unfounded. General Dye commands universal confidence and esteem and is a zealous and faithful servant of the Korean Government. The publications mentioned as they have appeared have been brought to the attention of the Koreans by some one unKnown to me and naturally provoke indignation.

I have been unremitting in my efforts to induce payment, and have insisted that the contract should govern: that it binds all the parties, and that the government should not ask to be excused from its obligation; since during five months it has been unable to offer any evidence to show the propriety of its actions.

If Mr Lee had been a more prudent and well disposed person, neither he nor Col Cummins would in my opinion have been placed in so embarrassing a position.

HUGH A. DINSMORE

NO. 5   Department of State
                                         Washington, March 25, 1890

Augustine Heard

Sir:

With reference to the Department's instructions No. 130 of November 21st, 1889, and No. 137 of March 4th to Mr. Dinsmore, your attention is called to the subject matter of the controversy between the Corean Government on the one part and Colonel Cummins and Major Lee on the other, now for some time protracted; I desire to impress upon you the importance of a thorough acquaintance with the merits of the case.

Colonel Cummins and Major Lee went to Corea at the request of the Corean authorities and under contract to serve the Government there as military instructors, each at a stipulated salary and a stated allowance for the expenses of their return to the United States.

It is not contended by this Government that the Government of Corea is not at liberty to terminate the contract with their officers for good and sufficient reasons; but it is distinctly insisted upon that the contracts shall not be terminated arbitrarily—that is to say, without good and sufficient reasons—nor the payment of salary and expenses be withheld, when actually due, under any circumstances.

The simple assertion of the Corean Government that Colonel Cummins and Major Lee are, by reason of any alleged facts, incompetent to perform the duties required of them or are misusing their offices, does not determine the contract, and that Government does not appear to have supported by proof its charges against these gentlemen. Moreover, the retention by Corea of the salaries due Colonel Cummins and Major Lee, and the sum for travelling expenses to the United States, is in the nature of a penalty on the contract for which no provision is made therein, and which, even in the event of such provision, would seem on the facts of the case to be unwarranted.

You will, therefore, if the merits of the controversy in your opinion justify such a course, ask of the Government of Corea payment of all arrears of salary due Col. Cummins and Major Lee, as well as payment of their expenses to the United States as secured by their contract, and insist upon a reasonably prompt compliance with that request, or a reasonably prompt and full explanation of the position of the Corean Government in the premises.

It is my wish and it is the intention of this Government that exact justice shall be done these two American citizens in Corea, and that there shall be no misunderstanding of the contention that the Corean government is not empowered either to terminate its contract with them at will, or to visit upon them any penalty, whether by retaining their salaries or otherwise—for the alleged breach of a civil undertaking.

JAMES G. BLAINE

Legation of the United States
                                        Söul Korea April 15th 1890

Secretary of State

Sir:

On the 6th instant I had the honor to receive from the Korean Foreign Office a brief note enclosing both in Chinese and english a statement declared in the note to have been prepared by General W. E. McDye the principal American Military instructor, referred to in the notice containing the grounds, and the evidence in support thereof, upon which Col. Cummins and Major Lee were dismissed from the Korean service. An immediate reply was made to the Foreign Office, communicating your instruction No.   , [sic] upon the subject which I had just then had the honor to receive, and stating that since I had to from the beginning and frequently urgently requested that I might be furnished with the specific Charges and such evidence as might tend to support them, and that until that should be done, the two officers should remain in Korea, as I Should insist receiving pay according to their contracts; and as no evidence of any Kind had been offered until the statement Mentioned was communicated, being received only three or four days before the expiration of the contracts, I declined respectfully to comment upon the statement further than to call attention to the fact that no official provision had been made to subordinate the two officers to General Dyes authority, and that I must urge the payment of salary for the whole term of employment specified in the contracts together with the amounts agreed to be paid to defray expense of return to the United States.

The statement has not been communicated to the two officers as yet, nor submitted for their inspection, because in my opinion it was Not important to their rights or interests in view of the course I have felt it my duty to pursue with reference to the Matter. I may mention also that I have been influenced to some degree by the disposition which Major Lee has, and which apparently he cannot control, to make every thing which concerns him, and Many which do not, the subject of newspaper correspondence.

                                        HUGH A. DINSMORE

Legation of the United States
Seoul, Corea, July 1, 1890

Secretary of State

Sir:

With reference to your instruction No. 5 of 25 March 1890 regarding a controversy between Col. Cummins and Major Lee on the one part, and the Corean Government on the other, I have the honor to inform you that I assumed charge of this legation on the 26th May. On the next day Col. Cummins called upon me & said that he & Major Lee would like to state their case, & wished to Know on what day they might come for the purpose. I replied that I was tolerably familiar with the facts through the perusal of the Correspondence on the Subject, but I should be happy to see them on any day that would suit them to call. They came on the morning of the 4th inst, a short time before the closing of the mail (12 o'clock), & as I was busy with my letters I asked them to return on the next day. This they did; and after Col. Cummins had given me the official facts of the case, Major Lee dwelt on the personal influences which had been brought to bear against them. I told them I would do what I could, but, as the Queen Dowager had died only the day before, I doubted whether any communication from me would be received by the Foreign Office, or replied to for some time, probably several weeks.

On the 18" I addressed a note to the President of the Foreign Office, of which a copy is enclosed, & yesterday, I received his answer, copy enclosed. I had not expected any answer before the 5" of this month, which I believe ends the period of strict mourning, & so far it is satisfactory. No reply has been received from Mr. Dinsmore's last despatch on this subject, dated 15 April, and I wished to make my note as curt and imperative as I could without being in any way threatening. I preferred to hint at ulterior measures.

Your instructions are peremptory, & I trust I may be able to bring the Corean authorities to a sense of their duties peacefully, but if I should not, & if they persist in delay, am I to resort to harsh measures? I do not wish to threaten, unless I can enforce; and it may be necessary to resort to the seizure of property; such for instance, as of the customs in the hands of the foreign employees.

I do not think it will be necessary to resort to any such extreme measures, but it may be, and I would desire to have the Views of the Department on the subject.

AUGUSTINE HEARD

Corean Foreign Office
Augustine Heard   12th day 5th moon
[June 28, 1890]

Sir:

In reply to the above despatch [June of 18, 1890], that the reasons for the dismissal of those two officers has been discussed in our correspondence with Mr. Dinsmore, you will see when you examine the record.

As regards their salaries and the expense of the return Voyage they ought to be settled according to the agreement, but unfortunately our Government is in great mourning now, and it is no time to decide. We shall not be able to take it up for discussion, before the end of the period of deep mourning (27 days) I am sorry to say.

MIN CHONG MOK

NO. 11 F.O.   Legation of the United States
Seoul Corea Aug. 6, 1890

President of the Corean Foreign Office

Your Excellency:

The views of Your Excellency as detailed at our interview at the Foreign Office last week upon the discharge of Col. Cummins and Major Lee from the military service in Corea, differs so widely from those of my government that I cannot but believe there must be some misconception of the facts, and I feel constrained in the hope of preventing serious consequences to recapitulate the main features of the case. My Government feels that it has not received the consideration, and that the action of the Corean government, in its treatment of these officers has not been dictated by that spirit of courtesy and justice which it had a right to expect. A reference to the files of correspondence between this Legation and the foreign office will show that as long ago as 1884, application was made by the Corean government to the American minister to procure for it, military instructors, and I would especially call your attention to the correspondent interviews in October 1886 and February 1887.

The American government was very reluctant to undertake the responsibility of choosing men for the purpose and it was only after repeated and continued solicitation by letter and telegraph that it finally authorized the general of the American army, General Sheridan, a most distinguished officer, to make the necessary selection. He chose as two of them, Col. Cummins and Major Lee, and identical contracts were signed, each stipulating that the salary of $3000. per annum should be paid monthly in advance, out of the receipts of the Corean Customs, commencing April 7th 1888 and that $500 further should be allowed to defray the expenses of the trip outward and the same amount for the homeward voyage. To these contracts were affixed the seals of first the President of the Foreign Office, His Excellency Cho Piong Sik, and, secondly of General Han Kin Sul, as representing the Corean Government. The contracts were for two years, and contained no clause allowing either party to terminate them, except by mutual accord, at any time before the expiration of the period.

Often when it is suspected that there may be a desire to anticipate the termination of a contract, an especial clause is introduced stating that by giving six months—or some agreed upon—notice, or pay for that time, the contract may be abrogated, but in this instance no such provision was made. And in September last, some seven months before the termination of the contract, these gentlemen were abruptly notified that their services were no longer required, and that their pay would cease at the end of the current month. Even the commonest servant, a cook or a coolie, though without any written notice, could not be so discharged in Europe or America; but here are gentlemen of position and character, selected by the highest military officer in America, with the approval of the American Government, and sent out of under contract at the especial and repeated request of His Majesty, suddenly turned off without a word. No previous notice was given, no complaint of any kind was made, no reason was then assigned or afterwards, though repeatedly asked for by my predecessor, until in the early days of last April, when the contracts were about expiring by limitation, a long statement purporting to be written by General Dye, was forwarded to Mr. Dinsmore. If every word in that statement were upon examination verified, it would be of no avail, for it came too late;—It should have preceded the discharge, instead of following it at nearly seven months' distance,—and so far from it being undisputed, the officers in question deny every one of the hostile allegations, and assert that they are made in consequence of personal antagonism.

If their contracts had been made with private individuals, they would have the undoubted right to demand an open trial in Court, where accusations could be properly investigated, and either refuted or confirmed.

They contend moreover that if it were true, which they deny, that they had failed in attention to their duties, they were fully justified in so doing in that the Corean government had failed to pay their salaries regularly monthly as had been stipulated in their contracts.

It is far from my wish to say anything that should reflect in any way upon Your Excellencys colleagues; since my arrival in this country, it has been my strong desire to show in all I have done and in all I do, my strong friendship, and the friendship which animates my country for Corea; but can Your Excellency be surprised if in view of facts, my government should feel that its citizens have been treated without equitable consideration, and itself with scant courtesy?

I urgently request Your Excellency to again review the circumstances, as my Government is peremptory in its late instructions. I am loth to see disagreement growing up between us and for so trivial a cause, and I am confident that if Your Excellency will once thoroughly look into the case with impartial eyes, Your Excellencys sense of Justice and equity and Courtesy will bring us into perfect accord.

AUGUSTINE HEARD

NO. 35   Department of State
                                    Washington, August 9, 1890

Augustine Heard

Sir:

I have received your No. 24 of the 1st ultimo, concerning the cases of Colonel Cummins and Major Lee.

The announcement, in the acknowledgement of the Korean Foreign Office, that the question of salaries and expenses of the return voyage of these gentlemen "ought to be settled according to the agreement" indicates a disposition to adjust the matter on an equitable basis and with due regard to the just representations of this government. It is premature to suggest any minatory tone on your part, still less any hint of resort to forcible reprisals. It is assumed that the Corean Government must be fully impressed with our friendliness and that it must realize that our requests in regard to Messrs. Cummins and Lee are prompted solely by a conviction of the equities of the case, and that they rest on the assurance that the Corean Government will heed them in the same friendly spirit with which they are presented.

I enclose copies of Department's Nos. 136 of Feby 25th and 137 of March 4th last, relating to this matter, which you state are not on the Legations files.

WILLIAM F. WHARTON

NO. 53 [Enclosure]   Legation of the United States
                                      Seoul Corea September 5th 1890

Augustine Heard

Sir:

I have the honor to enclose a copy of an article published in the "Hong Kong Telegraph" of Aug. 20th 1890, containing a copy of a letter purporting to have been written by me to General Dye. As the article further contains some reflections on certain high officials I have thought it best to lay the matter before you.

I have addressed General Dye on the subject, copy enclosed, as to how a private letter from myself to him could get into print. I enclose his reply, in which he shows that only by Malicious purloining could the letter have been obtained. I also enclose copies of his letters to the Editor on this subject.

Allow me to say in explanation that the letter of which a portion is published in this article, was written by me when in Korean service, to Gen'l Dye, when, during the absence of Mr. Denny, he was acting as adviser to the Korean Government and living in Mr. Dennys house. The letter further was in answer to a request from the King, transmitted by Dye, for information concerning rumored reductions in the grade of the representative at Seoul, from the United States. What I wrote was strictly private, sent in a sealed cover, and entirely in the line of my then official duty.

As to any "ring" at the State Department, or of New York capitalists, that of course is too absurd an accusation to need comment. I sincerely regret however the names of the Vice-President and the Secretary of State should be used in this connection.

I wrote to Mr Dinsmore and to General Dye, at one time, that Mr. Bliss of the firm of Morton and Bliss and Company was with others, somewhat interested in Korea. And it must have been from such private advice as this that Mr. Mortons name became connected with this country.

I have unfortunately no proof [nor] any reason for such conduct, unless it may be that he is a disappointed candidate for the position I now hold.

Regretting very much that I should be mixed up in the political asperities of this remarkable foreign settlement, and trusting that it may give you no annoyance, since everyone who is liable to read the article will doubtless know both its author and myself.

H. N. ALLEN

NO. 53
Department of State
Washington, October 27, 1890

Augustine Heard

Sir:

With reference to so much of my instructions of this date, No. 54 in regard to the repeated representations of this government respecting the settlement of the claim of Col. Cummins and Major Lee for salary and homeward transit, I now transmit copies of a letter addressed to this Department by Mr. Charles Fry, of Boston, in behalf of Major Lee, and of my reply.

You will note what I say touching the resolve of this Department to wholly dissociate the equities of this claim, under all the circumstances, from the personal acts whereby one of the parties interested has weakened his title to the sympathy of those from whom he seeks redress and those through whose mediation it must be obtained, if at all. The relations of Major Lee to the members of your legation or to others in Seoul, and his unfortunate indiscretions, should not be allowed to impair your just treatment of a claim which in itself appears to be equitable.

ALVEY A. ADEE

NO. 54

Department of State
Washington, 27th October, 1890

Augustine Heard

Sir:

I have to acknowledge the receipt of your despatch No. 54 of the 9th ultimo, enclosing copies of correspondence between yourself and General Dye. It appears therefrom that he applied to you to issue a warrant to search the premises of Major John G. Lee for certain private papers which General Dye alleges to have been wrongfully extracted from his premises, and which he believes to be in the former's possession. Your action in the matter, especially in view of the incompleteness of the application as a basis for such action, is commended as wise and discreet.

Your letter, however, to General Dye, as well as your request to the Department for instruction, renders it proper that you should be more fully informed with reference to the nature and extent of your judicial authority. It is true that Article 4 of our treaty with Corea of May 22, 1882, only provides specifically for cognizance by the agents of the United States of offenses or controversies in which an American is respondent or defendant. But later in the same Article there is a provision that in the event of a certain contingency "the right of extraterritorial jurisdiction over United States citizens in Chosun shall be abandoned, and, therefore, United States citizens, when within the limits of the Kingdom of Chosun, shall be subject to the jurisdiction of the native authorities."

In the judgment of this Department extraterritorial rights in Corea are clearly enough conceded to this Government, as well as with respect to controversies between its own citizens as in regard to those between citizens and natives.

This view of the extent of your jurisdiction is borne out by the case of Japan. By Article 6 of our treaty with that country of July 29, 1858, explicit provision is only made for jurisdiction over Americans committing offenses against Japanese or answerable to them as defendents in Civil Cases. In the execution of that treaty, however, the statutes have given jurisdiction, both civil and criminal, over controversies between citizens, and such jurisdiction has always been exercised since then. It may be observed, also, that Article 2 of the treaty of May 29, 1856 with Siam, only confers jurisdiction over disputes in controversies between American Citizens by implication.

The exercise of this right in non-Christian countries is so sanctioned by ancient customs as to almost amount to a principle of International Law. Its admission is a much smaller concession on the part of the local government, than to permit our intervention in civil and criminal matters in which a native of the country is a party; and it could not have been intended to concede the greater and withhold the lesser privilege.

The statutory authority for the exercise of extraterritorial jurisdiction in Corea is found in § 4129 of the Revised Statutes and § 4127 as amended by the Act of June 14, 1878 (20 Stat. 131).

With respect to Marshals or other officers to execute the decrees of your Consular Court as well as the other means for performing your duties or functions, the Act of July 14, 1890 only makes specific appropriation for Marshals in China, Japan and Turkey. But the creation by Congress of juridical authority in foreign countries must include the means of exercising it, or otherwise justice which it is sought to secure would fail; and so in countries where no marshal is provided for by law, it is usual for the consuls, in case of necessity, to designate someone to act as a special constable or marshal, reporting the expense to the Department, which is allowable out of the Contingent funds. In extraordinary cases, also, the course of Consuls has been approved in applying to local authorities to assist them. In some treaties this is secured as a right, and in any case it would probably be granted as a favor. It is impossible to dictate any exact course of procedure which would apply to particular cases; but it is believed that in the exercise of your wise discretion, you will find no difficulty in carrying out the judicial authority which the statutes impose upon you.

The incident reported in your despatch impresses upon the Department the great desirability of the early settlement of the claim of Messrs. Cummins and Lee against the Corean Government for the balance of their salaries and return passage home.

Recurring to your Number 24 of July 1, it appears that the Corean Foreign Office has acknowledged that their claim "ought to be settled according to the agreement"; but asks a delay of twenty-seven days, until the expiration of the period of deep mourning. I have not yet been informed that such a settlement has been made, and if it has not been effected before the receipt of this instruction, you will urge its settlement at once. In the interest of all parties it is desirable that it should be adjusted without any further delay.

ALVEY A. ADEE

Legation of the United States
Seoul, Corea, Mch 2 1891

Secretary of State

Sir:

Referring to my No. 113, Jany, 19, I have now the honor to inform you that the Corean Government has finally recognized the expediency of settling the claims of Col. Cummins and Major Lee, and have paid Me (on Saturday, February 28) the sum of $4333.34 for their account.

This represents for each of them,

> Balance of salary for unpaid term of contract, Viz, from
> Sept. 18, 1889 to Apl 7, 1890.................$1666.67
> Return voyage 500.00
> $2166.67

The money has been delivered to them, and I enclose duplicates of the receipts which were forwarded to the Foreign Office. As I was not asked for a release in full, I did not insist on that point with the recipients. I also enclose copy of the letter written in acknowledgement. You will notice that I say I do not consider their claims as fully covered by this payment. In this remark I alluded to interest from the date of discharge, at which time their pay became properly due, & which I have included in the statement, which I handed to the President in January last.

I may say that I have not informed Mess Lee & Cummins that I had made any claim for interest, and it is not my intention to press it further, unless I am instructed to do so by you. The clause in my letter is sufficiently elastic to cover, á la requerir, any other item you may decide to introduce, if you should at a later period wish to entertain the question of damages. My own opinion on that point has been sufficiently indicated, and I trust it may be in accordance with that of the Department, but I should have less reluctance in insisting on the recognition of interest. It is urged, however, by the Government, that it has never paid interest on overdue claims, and that to do so would establish an inconvenient precedent. In this I certainly have the support of the practice of many Governments of the West, including in a great proportion of cases, I believe, our own.

After forwarding my despatch to the President of Jany 15, I waited for Several days in the expectation of receiving a reply from Genl le Gendre to whom I presumed the claim had been referred, but on learning from him at the Commencement of the holy days that he had received no instructions on the subject, & hearing nothing from the Foreign Office, I took the opportunity of my New Year's call to ask for an interview as soon as possible, and was assigned the first day after the resumption of business. I went to it with my Secretary & Interpreter, and, as soon as the usual introductory compliments had been exchanged, I said to the President, very seriously—"We have been making to each other congratulations and calls, and have always been punctual in the usual outward Manifestations of friendship, but I wish to ask Your Excellency if we are really friends or enemies."

"Friends, of course," he replied, "What do you mean?"

"Friends," I said, "do not have important despatches unanswered, and you have not deigned to notice several that I have addressed to you."

"Lee & Cummins—" he cried —"yes and others."

"Whenever there is any disagreeable subject, it is dropped."

He then began to enter upon the usual arguments against the Military Instructors, charging incompetence, newspaper writing &c. &c., but I interrupted him by saying that I would not listen to any discussion; for me the matter was closed; my Government was no longer to be trifled with, and I insisted on a categorical reply, warning him that if it were in the negative, the consequences would be unpleasant. I pointed out to him the many instances in which the American Government and Minister had shown their friendly feeling, not only in Corea but in Washington, and if their just demands were to be simply put aside unnoticed, there would speedily be a perceptible change.

Our conversation lasted an hour and a half, and at the end of it he promised to see the King and endeavor to gain his consent to a settlement. He gave me to understand that he hopes to get an order for the payment without interest—which he could not accept for the reasons assigned above that they could not afford to make such a precedent.

The interview was Satisfactory, not only for the moment, but its influence will I think have some duration, —and on the next day I heard from him that he had received His Majesty's order to pay the sum without interest, but he had not the full amount in hand, and wished me to wait for a few days—which I did.

Major Lee informed me again today that he intended to push the question of damages in Washington. I told him if he had not brought that question forward before, he could have been paid last October. Of course he could do what he thought was right, but in my opinion he had no claim for greater damages than he had received, that his remaining in Corea did not constitute any claim on the Corean Government; that the acceptance of his case by his own Government terminated his active connection with it, and his remaining here or his leaving were equally indifferent. He stated that he had remained by the advice of Mr. Dinsmore, & considered him as responsible for it.

In this connection I may say—with reference to the remark in my No. 61 of Sept. 22 "that I could find no trace of any such claim"— that I overlooked the following words in Mr. Dinsmore's despatch No. 233 of April 15 last, as did also My Secretary who went over the correspondence after I had done so myself, by my desire, in order to make sure I was right— "I had requested that I might be furnished with the Specific charges and such evidence as might tend to Support them, & that until Such Should be done the two officers would remain in Corea as I should insist receiving pay according to their contracts." It did not occur to me that this meant anything more than a true execution of the contract would be insisted on, and I do not think now that anything more was intended. Indeed Mr. Dinsmore has since written me in a private letter—"it came to my Knowledge that Major Lee was claiming that the Government would have to pay his Salary as long as he remained in the country waiting for settlement, but I never gave it a serious thought, nor for a moment intended to give my support to such a claim."

For the full presentation of the subject I also enclose a copy of Mr. Dinsmore's note to the President of the Foreign Office, dated April 15, which may *possibly* be construed as favoring Major Lee's contention, but in all probability it was never intended as anything more than a vague threat, if even so much. Col. Cummins made no allusion to any proposed further action. The subject was not raised by either of us, & he was not present during my conversation with Major Lee.

I took the opportunity to urge that the claims of Mess. Scott & Harvey, which have also been paid, and about which I shall address you separately, but probably not by this mail.

AUGUSTINE HEARD

NO. 92   Department of State
                                      Washington, April 18, 1891

Augustine Heard

Sir:

I have to acknowledge the receipt of your No. 130, of the 2nd ultimo, in regard to the payment made by the Government of Corea in the matter of the claims of Major J. G. Lee and J. H. Cummins.

Your action in this matter is cordially approved. Your note of the 2nd of March to the President of the Corean Foreign Office sufficiently reserves the rights of Messrs. Lee and Cummins, if it should be decided later that they are entitled to have any further claim pressed in their behalf. In the meantime, the matter may well remain as it is.

                                      WILLIAM F. WHARTON

NO. 171   Legation of the United States
                                  Seoul Corea June 5, 1891

Secretary of State

Sir:

I have the honor to inform you that since the recent settlement of the claim to the Americans, Lee, Cummins, Scott, and Harvey, against the Corean Government, the latter has been active in making further settlements.

In the case of the German subject, A. H. Maertins, who came here in 1883 at the request of von Mullendorf—then in charge of the new developments—to reorganize the silk industry, there was an indefinite claim of between $40,000 and $50,000 (Yen) $25,000 of this was for damages. He received in all $15,000.

An English subject, A. B. Stripling former Commissioner of Customs under von Mullendorf, received $1,000 for a claim of some $4,000. He held no contract however.

The more extensive claim of E. Meyer & Co. of Hamburg is now in process of settlement. This firm has a vast money to the Corean Government, to whom they have also sold steam-ships, arms, etc., on terms arranged by themselves.

These claims have been attended to entirely by messengers and Messrs le Gendre and Greyhouse, the advisers of the Government. The action of these gentlemen regarding these claims has been highly commended.

The above mentioned American claims however were settled by Mr. Heard without being referred to the Foreign Advisers.

H. N. Allen

NO. 49　　　　　*Confidential*　　　　　Legation of the United States
Sôul, January 22, 1887

Secretary of State

Sir:

I have the honor to inform you that I have learnt from a generally trustworthy source that Mr. O. N. Denny, Foreign Adviser to the Korean Foreign Office, etc., has been requested by the King to resign the offices he holds under this government, or, to use the words of my informant "to leave the country."

The peculiar circumstances under which Mr. Denny came here, have prevented him ever gaining the confidence of the Koreans or of ever taking a prominent role in the affairs of the country, and the large salary paid him (Tls. 12,000 *per annum*) is, under the circumstances, an expenditure but little to the taste of Korea.

I have also been informed that Li Hung Chang has recently addressed a memorial to the King of Korea in which he offers to send a special ambassador to Korea to help it settle the question of its relations with Russia and also to advise means of settling the financial questions which are becoming more and more embarrassing here. In other words Li offers a new adviser for Korea. This latter report and that of Mr. Denny's resignation being called for appear to corroborate each other so strongly that I entertain but small doubt of their truth.

Mr. Denny, it appears, has not yet sent in his resignation, and the King evinces much anxiety concerning the outcome of his own unwanted energy.

W. W. Rockhill

NO. 68 F.O.   Legation of the U. States
                           Seoul, Corea, June 13th 1888

President of the Korean Foreign Office

Your Excellency:

Some time ago in answer to an inquiry from me as to whether it was the intention of His Korean Majesty's government to retain the service of the three American teachers who are engaged in the government school, Your Excellency informed me that it was not yet decided.

I trust Your Excellency will pardon my again troubling you about the same matter. A child of Mr. Gilmore one of the teachers is ill, and under the advice of the physician must be removed from Seoul as early as possible. Mr. Gilmore is therefore extremely anxious to Know whether terms will be made for his retention or whether he will be discharged so that he may make necessary arrangements for his family and sick child.

At the request of the teachers, I am induced to call Your Excellency's attention to the extremely small salary the gentlemen have received for their labor. So small indeed that Mr. Gilmore assures me that having had a family to support, he has not been able to save enough money to defray the expense of his return to the United States without the assistance of the Korean government.

The teachers also state that it was their intention and desire to have provision made in their contracts for expenses of return to the United States, but that they were assured by Mr. Foulk then in charge of this legation that the Korean Government would deal liberally and generously with them. They beg me to call attention to the custom which prevails in the service in Korea of giving pay for a term beyond the date of the discharge of the person employed in the service of the King when a discharge is made, and hope that in case it is His Majesty's royal pleasure that they shall no longer remain in His Majesty's service, that they may not be made an exception to the rule, as without assistance of that kind they will be greatly embarrassed in effecting a return to their homes.

I hope that these gentlemen who are worthy Citizens of the United States, and have rendered faithful service to the Korean people, may meet with a generous and fair consideration.

                             HUGH A. DINSMORE

NO. 159   Legation of the U. States
                                   Seoul, Corea, December 31st 1888

Secretary of State

Sir:

I have the honor to submit for your information that shortly after my return from my expedition to Quelpaert Island, the Minister Resident and myself were invited to a private audience with His Majesty the King of Corea.

His Majesty seemed greatly concerned as to the result of the recent elections in America and expressed the hope that the *Entente Cordiale* existing between America and Corea could be continued. Reassured upon the point, His Majesty manifested great interest in my recent journey to a possession over which his authority is more nominal than real, and about which, the history of the country is silent, or contained only in a few fragments of Chinese history, and the myths and legends of the people of Corea.

His Majesty earnestly requests me to submit to him, the result of my observation in the Mysterious Island of Quelpaert: its resources, etc., and referring in a flattering way to my past military experience, urged me to advise him as of the possible defenses at Quelpaert, (having in mind perhaps the fear of a recurrence of some such incident as that at Port Hamilton). I promised the King to accede to his request at a future day.

On the 17th instant I received an urgent invitation to again meet His Majesty in private audience. Having in mind the substance of your despatch No. 63 dated August 19th 1885 to Mr. Foulk, I also was careful not to commit myself to any action which might be interpreted as entering the lists of intrigue, or which might incite jealousies in any circle whatever. No such motive however could possibly be impuned to me, for it is a matter of public notoriety that on two occasions during the past year His Majesty (to my own surprise) tendered to me, Chief Command in his Army. And it is also Known in public that I respectfully but positively declined His Majesty's flattering offer. This fact alone could place any action of mine beyond the circle of criticism. On the 18th instant as appointed, I went to the Palace and in an interview which lasted quite three hours, I gave His Majesty a full account of my expedition as detailed in my enclosure with my No. 158 of this date. Referring to the defenses at Quelpaert and the Coast Defense of Corea, I took occasion to point out to His Majesty that in view of his financial difficulties it would be impossible to proceed to the construction of costly fortifications or the purchase of heavy guns, I counselled rather, a reliance upon a good infantry organization; the selection of one gun with the same calibre, (and discarding all others,) as its arm, and as to the Coast Defenses the organization of a simple and economical torpedo service, having more than this will seriously embarrass if not bankrupt the country.

In conclusion I refer to the Military Instructors whom he has employed in his service and advised His Majesty to consult with them freely.

His Majesty seemed greatly relieved with the results of the audience and with many expressions of thanks and great esteem and regard for my telling him, the audience was announced as ended, and I withdrew.

CH' CHAILLE' LONG

NO. 101   Department of State
                                        Washington, 15 March 1889

C. Chaillé Long

Sir:

Your No. 159 (Diplomatic) of the 31st of December last is received. I notice that in it you report that the King of Corea in his two audiences after your expedition to Quelpaert Island interrogated and consulted you as to the resources and possible defenses of that Island and that you gave His Excellency an account of your trip essentially the same as in your No. 158 and suggested certain means of defense as being the most economical and practicable under the circumstances.

As regards the latter point I cannot too urgently caution you against any remarks or suggestions which might have the appearance of advice regarding the military defences or operations of Corea. The position of our Legation must be distinguished as much for its impartiality, as for its friendly desire to promote good relations between Corea and the United States.

JAMES G. BLAINE

NO. 111   Department of State
                                             Washington, May 1, 1889

Hugh A. Dinsmore

Sir:

I have to acknowledge the receipt of Mr. Long's despatch No. 160 of January 21, 1889, relative to the desire of the King of Corea to obtain plans and descriptions of torpedos with a view of Establishing a torpedo Service in his Kingdom.

Upon application to the Secretary of Navy it appears that the Department has not formally adopted any torpedo of its own, for use in the naval service, but has recently contracted with a private firm for a supply of Howell Torpedos. While the Secretary of the Navy does not therefore feel at liberty to furnish a description of the said torpedo, yet he suggests that the Government of Corea communicate with the manufacturers of the Howell Torpedo, the "Hotchkiss Ordinance Company, No. 1503 Pennsylvania Avenue, Washington, D. C., from whom all necessary information can be obtained.

JAMES G. BLAINE

NO. 219   Legation of the United States
                                          Söul, Korea, Jan'y 14th 1890

Secretary of State

Sir:

On the 12th instant His Majesty the King sent one of his officers to me with a request that I should telegraph to the Department asking for the appointment of Dr. H. N. Allen, recently arrived in Korea from Washington where he attached to the Korean legation as secretary, as secretary of this late legation.

I made reply expressing my regret that I could not with propriety offer any suggestions to the Department of that nature especially in view of the fact that I expect to very soon give over the legation to a successor in office.

On the following morning the same officer, a relative of the royal family, returned to ask me on the King's behalf if there would be any

impropriety in His Majesty's making a request for Dr. Allen's appointment, and if such a request from him would be unusual.

To this I answered that I knew of no precedent for such an action,
but that I could not presume to advise His Majesty as to matters of
propriety. In the afternoon he came once again saying that the King
had directed him to request of me that I would send a message by
wire to the Department, stating for him that he would be gratified
if Dr. Allen would be appointed explaining that he made the request
with diffidence, but that he had great confidence in Dr. Allen's
integrity and intelligence as well as his loyalty to America and good
will to Korea and that he believed the interests of both countries
would be promoted by having him made secretary of our legation.

I yielded to this request and accordingly had the honor today to
despatch to you a telegraphic message in cipher being as follows in
the true reading:— "The King has requested me to communicate by
telegraph that he will be gratified if Allen should be appointed secretary of the legation here. Is minister appointed?"

The last sentence I added for my own information as I will require
some time to make my preparation for departure, having to dispose
of my household effects.

                                                    HUGH A. DINSMORE

NO. 165   Legation of the United States
                                              Seoul, Corea, May 28, 1891

Secretary of State

Sir:

I have the honor to inform you, that in an interview with Min,
President of the Foreign Office, at my house yesterday, he brought
up the subject of the American Teachers of the Government School.

Of the three young men selected by the Secretary of the Interior,
who arrived here four years ago as teachers, two remain,—Messrs.
Bunker and Hulbert. Mr. Gilmore left upon the expiration of his
two years contract.

The gentlemen teach, at present, from 25 to 30 pupils, four hours
daily, for five days in the week, excluding the numerous holidays.
They receive, without irregularity, a monthly salary of $225.00 silver,
and separate houses. They would be very glad to have more scholars.
Their second contract expires next month, and the government is

considering the advisability of retaining but one man hereafter. The President dared to ask my opinion on the subject, but aside from speaking in high terms of the school, and showing how it might be made more useful, I declined to advise him.

He stated that they were desirous of employing only such foreign assistants as they could use to advantage, and pay adequately and regularly; in which connection he assured me that the balance now due the present military instructors, Dye and Nienstead—would soon be cancelled and proper arrangements made for the avoidance of any irregularity in the future.

H. N. ALLEN

NO. 222 Legation of the United States
Seoul, Korea, Dec 17, 1891

Secretary of State

Sir:

In my No. 197 of Aug 1891, I spoke of the renewal of the contracts between the Korean Government and Mr. Bunker & Mr. Hulbert, Instructors in the Royal School; and I have now to inform you that the latter of the two has been terminated by mutual consent.

You are aware that these gentlemen with Mr. Gilmore came to Korea during 1886 under contract for two years at $125 gold, which was converted into $100. Mexican, monthly, each. At the end of this term Mr. Gilmore being a married man, found his salary insufficient, and, the Koreans not being willing to accord the advance demanded to $300, he left for America. The others renewed their contracts for three years for $225. per month. At the expiration of these contracts last August, the Korean Government, having lost much of their interest in the School, were not disposed to continue the same disbursements and intended to retain only one teacher, Mr. Bunker, but owing to my representations they finally consented to renew both contracts for a further term of three years at the same salary.

The school has hitherto been situated on a lot of ground in close proximity to this Legation in the midst of Foreign residences, but this ground has been recently exchanged for the Site of the German Consulate (Pak Tong) which is much nearer the Palace, and which from a Korean point is more eligible, though much less agreeable to a foreigner. Mr. Hulbert was told of the Exchange, & he agreed before signing his contract to remove his residence. The day of the transfer was to be 9 December.

On my return to Seoul, 23 Nov, after a month's absence, Mr. Hulbert called on me, &, telling me that Mr. Reinsdorf, the German Consul, occupied two small houses, very near together, one of 17 Kang as an office, and one of 14 Kang, or say 35 x 22 ft. one story, as a bedroom, etc. and Said he had reason to think it was intended to force him to occupy the smaller of the two, and he hoped I would see that he was properly treated. He had no objection to going to Pak Tong, but he had a right to Expect Suitable accommodations, & it was impossible for him and his family to find room in this house.

On the next day the President of the Foreign Office sent me word that he was coming to see me on the subject, but he did not do so till the 5 Dec. He then stated that he wished to put Mr. Hulbert into the small house, as Mr. H. feared, but would also give 4 Kang, (about 250 square feet) of the office house, the remainder of which he must reserve for School rooms. I deferred any reply till I could see the premises which I promised to look at as soon as possible. I went that afternoon, & was at once satisfied that the proposition was inadmissible. Mr. Reinsdorf who was present, was also of opinion that neither of the two houses would alone suffice, and that Mr. Hulbert ought to have both. I communicated my impressions to the President, who however persisted in his declaration that he must have part of one of them for school rooms.

After consultation with Mr. Hulbert, who said that as the interest of the Government in the school seemed to be becoming weaker, he did not care to remain. I was authorized by him to submit the following propositions any one of which the President was at liberty to choose.

1st, that he should give Mr. H. the two houses occupied by Mr. Reinsdorf.

2nd, or $25 per month, and Mr. H. would find his own house.

3rd, or Mr. H. would cancel his contract at the end of this or next month on being paid his expenses home, which he estimated at $600—

The President who had only retained Mr. Hulbert in consequence of My urging him to do so, at once selected the 3rd proposition. He would close the contract at once paying Mr. H.'s Salary to the end of this month and the passage money, and had already given orders for the payment of $825. This was afterwards increased at my request to $900, and Mr. Hulbert leaves I believe by the next mail. I may mention that if he had left at the end of his previous contract, he would have received nothing for the Expense of his home journey.

The school now remains in charge of Mr. Bunker, who has hopes of its future. Since its transfer to Pak Tong the numbers of pupils present daily has been 25 to 30. It bears about 50 on its books, but the daily attendance has ranged from 50 to 10; generally the past year about 25 and of late, since the transfer has been agitated, only 10 or 12; perhaps in the afternoon not one of those who had come in the morning, would be present. All may live on the premises if they choose. Sleeping apartments and food are provided free of charge, most of them live at their own homes, taking lunch or supper, at the school. Only 10 or 12 sleep there. The average age of the scholar is 23 or 24. They are intelligent, quiet and gentlemanly: have wonderful memories and a clear enunciation of English. They are appointed by the King, and belong to noble and well to do families. Occasionally by outside influence, one of the poorer class is named (though always a noble) and from these, as they have only their own exertions to depend upon, the best scholars are recruited. Over the others it is difficult, indeed impossible, to establish discipline or secure regularity of attendance. They Know that their families will take care of them. The great want of the School is an intelligent, active President, who would take an interest in its progress, and to whom reports of the good or bad conduct of the Scholars could be made with the assurance that reports would be noticed and acted upon. The President at this moment is His Excellency Min Chung Mook, President of the Foreign Office, who takes little interest in it, and whose other occupations are so engrossing that he has no time or thought to give to it.

Mr. Bunker proposes to pay more attention in the future to the teaching of colloquial English. It has been a reproach among the Coreans that it has turned out few, if any, good interpreters; and he feels that this is in some degree just. English is taught of course, and all instruction is given in English, but the teachers came from America with the idea of founding a University, & proceeded to educate their pupils in Political Economy and International Law, when a knowledge of conversational English would have been far more highly appreciated. The King is thought still to feel a strong interest in the School, and with a change in the President, who might keep him informed of its actual condition and through his authority establish a more wholesome discipline, Mr. Bunker has good hope of success.

AUGUSTINE HEARD

NO. 289   Legation of the United States
Seoul Korea July 28, 1892

Secretary of State

Sir:

In reply to No. 137, June 9, from the Department of State, requesting "detailed information concerning the postal system of the Government of Korea," I have the honor to inform you that this Government has no postal system, letters for the interior are carried by private messengers explicitly. The ports however are served by the Imperial Japanese Postal Department, which supports branch offices at the ports and at this Capital. The postage between Korea and Japan being the same as the internal postage rates of Japan.

In 1884 a postal system was organized in Korea, a postal department was formed and the office at Seoul was opened with a dinner, in which the American Minister Gen'l Foote was present. The *emeute* of 1884 began that night, and guests at the official dinner were disbursed—some were assassinated,—the first and only mail was lost, and the postal project was fully abandoned.

H. N. ALLEN

NO. 456   *Confidential*   Legation of the United States
Seoul Korea Sept. 28, 1893

Secretary of State

Sir:

I have the honor to hand you enclosed, copy of a translation of a letter received by me the day before yesterday, from the Foreign Office, announcing that His Majesty has created a Postal Department in connection with the present Telegraph Department. The whole to be known as The Department of Electrical and Postal Affairs, with Mr. Chyo Pyung Chik, Minister of Justice, and late President of the Foreign Office, as President of the new department; Mr. Ye Yong Chik as director of Domestic Mails, and Mr. C. R. Greathouse as Superintendent of Foreign Mails.

The letter further states that His Majesty is desirous of making the first Postal Treaty with the United States, and asked that I be empowered to negotiate the treaty with Mr. Chyo.

I am given to understand that this step will not be a surprise to yourself, as Mr. Ye Cha Yun, late of Washington, assures me that he discussed the matter fully with you, and the Postmaster General, while in Washington. In fact I may say that it is due to Mr. Ye Cha Yun that the step has been taken, though he has been greatly aided by Min Sang Ho, a bright young man who was educated in Washington, through whom the powerful Min family and Queen became actively interested.

I have carefully gone over the Postal Treaty between the United States and Japan, which could I presume will be used as a basis for the Treaty in question. I may say that I suggested that negotiations be conducted in Washington, but it was carefully impressed upon me that His Majesty was very anxious to have the *first* treaty completed as soon as possible, lest opposition should arise from China or Japan. If, however, you desire negotiations should be conducted in Washington, and will cable me to that effect, I think it can be satisfactorily arranged.

The establishment of the Department, and the appointment of the officials, was duly announced in yesterdays Gazette, and has caused much adverse criticism. Foreigners fear that under a Korean administration they may have poorer postal facilities than they now enjoy; notwithstanding the fact that the Japanese Branch Post Office at the consulate here, is the cause of continual complaint, owing to the unaccountable disappearance of letters—even though registered. But this fault is so common that this Legation, in common with others here, sends its mail by special courier to Chemulpo, where in our case, the American firm of Morse Townsend & Co. despatches and receives our mail, entailing an extra expense for special couriers service.

If what Mr. Ye Cha Yun tells me regarding the counsel he received from yourself is true, I have, of course, nothing to say. If, however, he has construed remarks dropped in a mere friendly conversation as advice, I would like to point out a certain difficulty that I fear may arise.

Korea has no steamship plying between her ports and those of Japan. If the new arrangement is distasteful to the Japanese, Their ship companies that now carry the mail, may exact an exorbitant sum from the Koreans for a similar service. But even if they are fairly reasonable in their demands, the chronic state of exhaustion of the Korean Treasury would doubtless lead to continual delay in payments, in this as in every other case, —resulting probably in a series of temporary delays in the mail service. In such case the United States would come in for much of the blame, for having aided them at the start.

I fear that a failure to carry through this treaty may result in great injury to Ye Cha Yun, who bids fair to be of great service to his Government.

H. N. ALLEN

NO. 464   *Confidential*   Legation of the United States
Seoul, Korea, Oct 4, 1893

Secretary of State

Sir:

Referring to my No. 456, Sept. 28, I would like to say that I have consulted with the Foreign Representatives here, in regard to the announcement of the establishment of the Postal Department, and find that the English, Chinese, and Japanese laugh at the idea. The Russians and French favor it warmly as a mark of progress, the German is indifferent.

There is no question that it is the earnest desire of the King to make a Postal Treaty with us at once lest Korea be included in Chinas postal arrangement.

As the establishment of offices for foreign mail, need not at once follow the ratification of the treaty, but be delayed until Korea is better able to pay for the service; it may be wise to let them have the treaty.

Mr. C. R. Greathouse, formerly our Consul General at Yokohama, whose legal ability is well known, will aid the Koreans in the negotiations if they are carried on here, and he asks me to secure copies of our Postal Conventions.

H. N. ALLEN

NO. 516   Legation of the United States
                                         Seoul Korea Jan. 5, 1894

Secretary of State

Sir:

I have the honor to inform you that todays Official Gazette announces the appointment of Mr. Ye Cha Yun, late Korean Chargé d'Affaires at Washington as one of the Vice Presidents of the Postal Department. This shows His Majestys entire satisfaction with the answer to His request for a Postal Treaty with America.

H. N. ALLEN

NO. 539   Legation of the United States
                                         Seoul Korea Mch. 19, 1894

Secretary of State

Sir:

Replying to your No. 224, Feb. 5th, in relation to the admission of Korea to the Universal Postal Union, I have now to inform you that at the last moment, those having the matter in charge, decided to send Korea's application for admission to the Union, to the Korean Legation, Washington, to be by them handed to the Swiss Representative in Washington, to be forwarded.

I am informed that there were two reasons for adopting this course. In the first place, their advisers were unable to learn the name of the Swiss Secretary of State; and in the second place, they did not wish to forward the letter through the open mail, as it would then have to bear a Japanese stamp.

H. N. ALLEN

NO. 471   Legation of the United States
                                         Seoul Korea Oct. 16, 1893

Secretary of State

Sir:

I have the honor to inform you that soon after my arrival here, I was waited upon by Messrs. Dye, Nienstead, and Bunker, American teachers in the employ of the Korean Government, whose salaries had not been paid for periods of from 12 to 20 months. Mr. Power, the government electrician, also came later. He wished to have his contract renewed, otherwise he would leave, without completing the installation of a $50,000 electrical plant he had brought for them from America.

Without going beyond my province, I obtained a partial payment of salaries, and Mr. Power's contract was signed before me to his satisfaction.

It is apparently impossible to secure the regular payment of these salaries, and it is a question whether it pays to have this Legation continually pressing the Government for money when we gain so little by it.

The question of the renewal of contracts for these gentlemen will come out in a few months, and it is rumored that new contracts will not be made. In fact, the school for English has no immediate prospect of being open, though two months of the school year have nearly elapsed, and Mr. Bunker's contract runs till July. The military Instructors are also discouraged with the prospects of their work.

These three men are all that is left of an original seven,—three teachers recommended by the Department of the Interior, were sent here in 1886, and three military instructors recommended by General Sheridan and sent out in 1888. Col. Nienstead came from Kobe independently.

The men from America were only recommended after repeated, urgent requests from this Government to the Department of State. Two of the teachers left voluntarily after two and three years respectively, and two of the military men, Messrs. Lee and Cummins, were dismissed for gross misconduct. They quarreled among themselves and began airing their troubles in the Press, but as their contracts were binding, as made by Judge Denny—the then adviser—the full amounts named in the contracts were finally obtained for them, after repeated and very strong instructions from the Department. At the time the Koreans bitterly resented being compelled to pay these men for the months of idleness, on a contract made by another American.

The experiment having been well tried and not found altogether satisfactory, it seems to be the desire of their Gov'mt to try instead the education of young men in our own Naval Military Schools, where, away from the restrictions that depressed them they may become increasingly enthusiastic and efficient students.

Mr. Heard in his Nos. 372, Mch 21, and 374, Mch 22, has fully discussed the subject of the new Naval School, to which I informed the British government is sending a regular, and a warrant officer; while Mr. Hutchison, an Englishman here, is about to be engaged at less than half the price of Mr. Bunker, as teacher of English for this school. Mr. Hutchison has a headmaster's certificate. The Chinese are aiding in this matter.

If it is the desire of the Department "to keep the American element up to its full strength," as mentioned in Mr. Heard's No. 372, Mch 21, I think sufficient pressure at the proper time will induce the Koreans to renew these contracts, but we will have to collect the salaries.

Personally, I should say that American influence would be increased, rather than lessened, if we were to content ourselves with keeping in American hands, the one position of Government Adviser, which this Government would not wish to have go to any other power.

The U. S. Representative, whoever he may be at the time, would hardly care to burden his office with the collection of these salaries, and, asside [sic] from its being beyond his province to urge contracts, I think he would be inclined to let matters take their natural course, unless he was assured that it was the desire of the Department to keep the "element up to its fullest strength."

H. N. ALLEN

NO. 203   Department of State
                                        Washington, Nov. 21, 1893

H. N. Allen

Sir:

I have received your No. 471 of 10th ultimo, relating generally to the contracts made by Korea with American instructors and others, and the difficulties encountered in the collection of the salaries due them.

Under all the circumstances, it is not deemed expedient to exhibit solicitude for the appointment of Americans to official positions in Korea.

EDWIN F. UHL

NO. 526   Legation of the United States
                                          Seoul Korea Feb. 12, 1894

Secretary of State

Sir:

I have the pleasure of informing you that I have succeeded in settling the claims upon the Korean Government of Messrs. Nienstead and Bunker, American employes.

Col Niensteads contract expired Dec. 7th and he was informed that his services were no longer needed. Yet he could not obtain a settlement. I finally secured a payment in full, with passage home, and full pay for the time he was kept waiting.

In the case of Mr. Bunker, he had received a more favorable proposition, as a teacher, from one of the mission societies, and as his contract did not expire till July, he proposed to surrender the remainder for a consideration. His proposition was finally accepted, and he has left for a tour of Europe and the Holy Land before taking up his new work.

Both gentlemen seemed exceedingly grateful for what I had done.

The King has asked me to secure a new American teacher, and I have offered it to the Mission societies here, as the delay in salary will not affect them.

                                                    H. N. ALLEN

NO. 192   Legation of the United States
                                          Seoul, Korea, Feb. 5, 1896

Secretary of State

Sir:

Having seen the article enclosed herewith and others of similar tenor republished from Eastern newspapers by the press of the United States, I have thought it advisable to say, that, so far as this or other statements in any way implicating anyone in this Legation with the events of November 28th are concerned they are utterly and absolutely untrue, and no one residing here, so far as I know, gives them the least credence.

                                                    JOHN M. B. SILL

King of Korea Attempt Made to Drive Him from the Palace

Object of the conspirators was to bring strong diplomatic pressure upon the Korean Government to remove Tai Won Kun and several ministers of State.

Yokohoma, Dec. 6.—via San Francisco, Dec. 24, per Steamship China.—The sole correspondent of the Chuo Shimbun describes the disturbances of November 28 [1895]. When an attempt was made to remove the King of Corea and the Crown Prince from the Palace, according to the correspondent, there was a conspiracy among the Russian party, the American missionaries and a few Coreans. A Corean spy, who had the confidence of the conspirators, reported that meetings were held at the Russian legation, which were attended by the Russian minister, Dr. H. N. Allen, Secretary of the American Legation; General W. McE. Dye, General Le Gendre and a few Coreans. The object of the conspirators was to bring strong diplomatic pressure upon the Korean Government to remove the Tai Won Kun and several ministers of State who had been connected with the attack on the Queen last October. An attack on the Palace was arranged for the night of November 27th. A mob of armed ruffs engaged the attention of the police, while a body of disbanded guards marched to the Palace expecting to effect a surprise and an easy entrance. The garrison, however, had been warned and the attacking party itself was surprised and disbursed. The object of the American missionaries who were implicated, it is said, was personal, not political. They wished to avenge the death of the Queen, who was an ardent Christian. The Japan Mail reprints the above story "with all reserve."

The Japanese papers charged that the latest outbreak in Seoul is directly due to Russian influence. The Chuo Shimbun says:

The Corean Government, yielding to pressure, exercised by the Minister of a certain country, has decided to place the Tai Won Kun in confinement, to restore the late Queen to her rank, to give her a public funeral, and to arrest and punish certain fugitives in Japan.

The telegram adds that there are seven Russian men-of-war in Corean waters. Other Japanese papers assert that three foreigners were actually seen leaving the mob in the attack on the Palace, and that American citizens and the Russian legation were implicated; also an American missionary named Underwood.

Legation of the United States
                                         Söul, Korea, Nov 14th 1887

President of the Korean Foreign Office

Your Excellency:

I have had the honor to receive your dispatch of the [   ]
[sic] concerning the removal of foreign merchants and tradesmen
from Söul.

In answer I have to inform you that on the 14th of March 1887,
in reply to a dispatch from Mr. Rockhill then in charge of this legation, written to the Department of state upon this subject, and enclosing a copy of His Excellency Kim Yun-sik's note to him, The Secretary of State, by a dispatch to this legation, made substantially the
following observations, viz:—

The rights of citizens of the United States with respect to residence
and the pursuit of commerce in Söul were first derived from the
British and German Treaties through the favored nation clause in
our own Treaty, and that these rights had been further secured by
the Treaty with Russia. But by their Treaties the British, the Ger-
mans, and the Russians agree that they shall exercise the rights of
commerce in Söul dependent upon the continued exercise of the
same by the Chinese. So it appears that the commercial privileges
of citizens of the United States must depend in Söul, upon the con-
tinuance or abandonment of commerce by the Treaty powers above
mentioned.

But as Your Excellency is aware there are at this time no citizens
of the United States engaged in commercial pursuits in Söul.

Referring however to the residence in Söul of those citizens of the
United States who have under the gracious encouragement, and
assistance of His Majesty the King of Korea, acquired a residence
and property in Söul, in furtherance of the highly creditable and
benevolent work they have undertaken for the benefit of His Majesty's
subjects and which the Secretary has been pleased to observe has
met with the full appreciation of His Majesty The Secretary observes
that the Department of State cannot believe that it is intended that
these American citizens shall be disturbed, and that the United
States must dubly regret any interference with the enlightened and
charitable enterprises of the Americans now residing in Söul, and
that the Government of the United States could not view without

the property or rights of

grave concern any invasion of ∧ these persons who impelled by benevolent and unselfish motives have taken up the residence in Söul.

HUGH A. DINSMORE

NO. 75 F.O.

Legation of the U. States
Seoul Corea July 13 1888

President of the Corean Foreign Office

Your Excellency:

I regret that I am forced to call Your Excellency's attention to an unfortunate incident on the part of the Superintendent of trade at Chemulpo with legitimate trade being conducted by the American firm of Morse Townsend & Co. doing business in Korea. It appears that a few days ago the agent of this American firm To Tang Chib a Corean employed two Corean boats for the purpose of transporting merchandise on the coast and placed upon the boats the flag of the firm; The boats were hired for the use of the firm, when it was learned at the Yaman of the superintendent of trade that the boats were so employed being in the hands of the owners, they were seized by the servants of the Superintendent the owners imprisoned and it is said, beaten, and the flags the property of the firm, taken away and a demand for their delivery refused.

Foreigners have heretofore cherished the privilege of hiring Korean boats for the transport of produce and merchandise on the Corean coast without hindrance or interference the privilege being authoized it seems in section 6 of article 4 of the treaty between Corea and Great Britain.

Article 14 of the treaty between the government of the United States and Corea provides as follows viz.:

"Should at any time the King of Choson grant to any nation or to the merchants or citizens of any nation any right, privilege or favor connected either with navigation commercial political or other intercourse which is not conferred by this treaty such right privilege and favor shall freely enure to the benefit of the United States, its public officers merchants and citizens ec etc.

In as much as the privilege of hiring Korean boats for the transport of merchandise between the different ports of Corea, has been hitherto accorded to foreigners of all the treaty powers when so desired by them without objection by the Corean government and in view of the treaty provisions I have cited I cannot believe that Your Excellency can approve the conduct of the Superintendent of Trade in the matter. I have herein referred to and I respectfully beg that Your Excellency will take the necessary steps to cause the boatmen to be set at liberty, their boats restored to them to be used by the American firm according to the agreement reached between the firm and the boatmen and all property belonging to said firm restored to them.

Hugh A. Dinsmore

NO. 76 F.O.

Legation of the U. States
Seoul Corea July 18th 1888

President of the Corean Foreign Office

Your Excellency:

Referring to my note of the 13th instant communicating the action of the Superintendent of Trade at Chemulpo with regard to the employment of Corean boats by American citizens, I regret to inform Your Excellency that I have received information that there has been a repetition of the conduct complained of in my note. Another boat employed by the firm of Morse Townsend & Company has been seized and the boatmen beaten and compelled to go away from Chemulpo without receiving the wages due them from the American firm.

This conduct seems to be directed Solely against this one firm as I am informed there is no interference with other persons employing boats in the same way. The matter has been carried so far now that Messrs. Morse Townsend & Company find it almost impossible to secure a boat. Why is it Your Excellency that our citizens are thus discriminated against?

I would thank Your Excellency to investigate this matter and inform me or I shall have to report it to my Government.

Hugh A. Dinsmore

NO. 196 Legation of the United States
Söul Korea August 16th 1889

Secretary of State

Sir:

In January of the present year Mr. Aillerd I. Pierce a professional mining engineer arrived in Korea coming from the United States under a contract made through the Korean legation, for the purpose of prospecting and reporting upon the gold mines in Korea and if deemed proper by the government to superintend any mining enterprises that might be inaugurated as a result of his investigations. Having spent a portion of the spring and summer in the mining district of Pyong An Do, he returned to Söul and prepared and submitted his report, of which I am unable to furnish a copy.

Under order from the Government the legation at Washington purchased from the Union Iron Works of San Francisco a quartz mill which was promptly shipped and arrived in Korea about the 1st of July, accompanied by a machinist and four practical miners employed under direction of the Korean legation. The machinery has been sent to the Pyong An mines with Mr. Pierce and the machinist and one miner.

There seems to have been a misunderstanding as to the number of men desired, three of the miners are left unemployed, and are awaiting the decision of the Govt as to whether they will be given employment or be allowed to return to the United States with proper compensation for loss of time and expense in coming from and returning to the United States.

There has been a lack of concerted action, and agreement among the different officials claiming their right to be consulted in matters of mining, I have serious fears that no good results will be derived from the enterprise in hand.

In this connection it may be proper to inform you that Mr. Payne representing the firm of Frazar & Co of New York and Yokohama and Mr. English of the Baldwin Locomotive Works of Philadelphia have spent nearly the whole of the present summer in Söul.

Upon their arrival at the capital there being no comfortable public house of entertainment, and Mr. Payne having shown me some polite attention in Yokohama in the past I invited them to stay at the legation as my guest. Mr. Payne had informed me that they were en route to China, and that their intention was to remain only a fortnight and I was ignorant of the fact that they were here with a view to entering into important business contracts with the native government. These circumstances are detailed because considerable embarrassment was occasioned to me by their protracted stay and negotiations being guests of the legation. While I was pleased to entertain them as American citizens, tourists, and while I am always glad of an opportunity to assist in a proper way the promotion of business with our country and her citizens, circumstances recited were annoying to me, and were allowed to continue because of repeated assurances of departure by "next steamer." The two gentlemen left for Japan on the 6th instant having as I have been informed from other sources secured *promises* of large business in the way of mining franchise and the building of a railway from Söul to Chemulpo: promises which it would gratify me to see fulfilled.

It is hardly probable that the Koreans will before a long while be able to work their mines successfully under their own management. The only plan at all practicable to derive a revenue from that source would seem to be that of making concessions to foreigners with capital.

HUGH A. DINSMORE

NO. 20 Consular Series   Seoul, Korea
                                                      August 15, 1895

Secretary of State

Sir:

I take pleasure in informing you that His Korean Majesty has granted a limited mining franchise to Mr. James R. Morse, an American citizen. There have been many attempts at mining and the obtaining of mining franchises here by people of various nationalities. This is the first instance in which the right has been formally given over the proper seal.

The mines in question are the richest (by Korean report) in the country, and are in the gold mine district of Uhnsan, which belongs to the Royal Family. The district is very mountainous and is from 15 to 20 English miles broad and long, situated in Peng Yang province.

The agreement with Mr. Morse, associates him with His Majesty's Department of the Royal Household for the prosecution of this mining work.

Mr. Morse well deserves the mark of confidence thus received. He has long been associated with Korea in a business way, much to his credit, and for some years he has acted as Korean Commercial agent in New York City. He is president of the American Trading Company of New York, with houses in London, San Francisco, Yokohama, Kobe, and Shanghai, with branches in Chemulpo, Korea, and other places.

I don't think any similar agreements will be entered into until this one is well tried. It is an experiment upon which depends to a certain extent the development of Korea, and of an enlarged commercial interest between Korea and America.

JOHN M. B. SILL

NO. 137 F.O.
Legation of the United States
Söul, Korea Jany 13th 1890

President of the Korean Foreign Office

Your Excellency:

Mr. Townsend, the American merchant at Chemulpo, has informed me that the superintendent of trade has made a demand through his subordinates upon his firm for a large amount of cash as taxes to the Korean government.

I have the honor to call Your Excellency's attention the matter [sic] and the fact that such a demand is in contravention of the treaties, and to beg Your Excellency to make an order to the Superintendent to desist from such demand.

HUGH A. DINSMORE

NO. 232
Legation of the United States
Söul Korea April 10th 1890

Secretary of State

Sir:

About the first of January last I was advised by Morse Townsend & Co., an American firm at Chemulpo, that an organization of merchants and traders existed at that port, claiming to act by authorized privilege from the Korean Government, who were assuming control of trade with the nations letting commissions and fees upon goods bought and sold in the ordinary course of trade; and that a demand had been made upon native employes in the service of the firm to pay assessments upon purchase made previously by the firm, the demand being made by subordinate officials under direction of the superintendent of trade. The firm refused to accede to the demand and reported the matter to the legation as above stated.

It appearing to me that such a demand was in contravention of treaty rights, I addressed the Foreign Office, asking that the Government would take the necessary action to cause a discontinuance of such an unauthorized annoyance of Americans engaged in trade.

A threat has been made that the native employe of the firm should be punished if the refusal to accede to the demand made should be persisted in.

The Foreign Office replied to my note saying that orders had been given that the demand should not be enforced against the American firm.

Only a few weeks afterward I received a communication signed by the above named firm and E. Mayer & Co., a wealthy German firm, addressed to me as the senior representative making request that I should lay before the representatives of the treaty powers, the existence of the organization already referred to which is as they claimed vested with privileges by the Government contrary to trade provisions and greatly injurious to trade.

Upon investigation I ascertained that a monopoly of the trade of the port had been given to an organization of 25 brokers, and that all articles of native production as well as some imported merchandise are required to pass through the hands of the privileged organization under pretense of ascertaining correct weights and measures, and that excessive weighing and measuring charges in addition to large commissions are imposed. To illustrate the system and the oppressiveness to commerce of the system I give a table of the charges imposed upon four leading articles of commerce as I have ascertained them to be established:

		Commission to Broker		Weighing Com'n		Return Commission, Buyer	
Rice	per bag.	150	Cash	90	Cash	75	Cash
Beans	" "	100	"	90	"	75	"
Gold	" tael	400	"	100	"	100	"
Hides	" picul	300	"	100	"	800/1000	",

On shirting and piece goods & etc. bought from importing houses, the buyer is required to pay a commission to the brokers of one per cent, and the seller a return commission also to the brokers. The value of native coin (cash) has for the last four months ranged from 1500 to 750 per dollar (Mexican or yen).

In Article V of the treaty between the United States and Korea is the following provision:—

. . . "and it is further agreed That the duty upon foreign imports Shall be paid one for all At the port of entry, and That no other duties fees an taxes or charges of any sort Shall be levied upon such Imports either in the interior of Chosen or at the ports."

Section I of Article v of the treaty between Great Britain and Korea provides:—

"At each of the ports or places open to foreign trade British subjects shall be at full liberty to import from any foreign port or from any Corean open port, sell to or to buy from any Corean subject or others, and to export to any foreign or Corean open port all Kinds of merchandise not Prohibited by this treaty are paying The duties of the tariff annexed Thereto. They may freely transact Their business with Corean subjects Or others without the intervention Of Corean officials or other persons And they may freely engage Any industrial occupation."

Section 4 of the same Article provides that:— "All goods imported into Corea by British subjects and on which the duty of the Tariff annexed to the treaty shall have been paid may be conveyed to any Corean open port free of duty, and when transported into the interior, shall not be subject to any additional tax, excise or transit duty whatever in any part of the country.

In like manner full freedom shall be allowed for the transport to the open ports of all Corean commodities intended for exportation and such commodities shall not either at the place of production, or when being conveyed from any part of Corea to any of the open ports, be subject to the payment of any tax, excise or transit duty whatsoever."

On the 14th of March there was a meeting of the representatives of the treaty powers at this legation at which the subject of this despatch was considered, and it was agreed that a joint protest should be made to the Korean Government against the practice herein described, and complained of by the two above named firms, as in contravention of the treaty. I have the honor to enclose a copy of our joint note.

It should have been stated above that similar provisions to those quoted from the British and Korean treaty are contained in the treaties of Korea with Russia and France.

On the 15th instant a uniform note was sent to each of the representatives signatory to the first note of March 14th in which the President of the Foreign Office amongst other matters some of which are entirely irrelevant, insists that the organization complained of in carrying on their business under license from the government, are beneficial to trade rather than otherwise and that trade with foreigners is not in any wise affected, and that therefore it cannot be said to exist in violation of the treaty provisions. It is our purpose to send a joint reply to this note of which I have the honor to enclose a copy.

HUGH A. DINSMORE

Telegram   Department of State
                                          Washington, May 17, 1890

Augustine Heard

If disturbance against the Seoul Government threatens American rights call for protection on Naval Vessel which will be at hand. The United States is friendly to Seoul Government.

BLAINE

NO. 116 F.O.   Legation of the United States
                                          Seoul Korea Dec. 24, 1891.

President of the Korean Foreign Office

Your Excellency:

I have the honor to acknowledge the receipt of Your Excellencys despatch of Oct. 8, in which you declare your intention to collect full taxes from the landholders of Chemulpo for the ensuing year.

It is Customary at the last meeting of the Municipal Council to pass in review the disbursements of the year that is past, and to form an estimate of the amount which will be needed for the expenses of the year which is to come, and I deferred replying to Your Excellencys dispatch till I could take cognizance of these disbursements and this estimate. The meeting took place on the 11th instant, and I was present at it.

The accounts of the treasurer were not complete, but it was understood that a considerable balance remained unexpended from the appropriation of this year, which was equivalent to half taxes. I myself drew up a sketch for 1892 which amounted to $1996. This sum appeared to all the council to be amply sufficient, and it was adopted. It is very nearly the same as the product of half taxes—say $2200, and there remains as I have said a balance at hand from the old account.

There would seem then to be no reason for exacting from the landholders any larger amount, but Your Excellency without waiting to know these facts, and heedless of the opinion of those more capable of judging and most affected by the results, prefers to enforce the extreme limit of the law. Your Excellency is aware that in taking this course he is acting in opposition to the deliberate opinion of all the governments having treaties with Korea. When their judgment was invoked on the principle contained in the amendment to the land regulations proposed last year they were unanimous in the expression of the belief that the taxes were too high. They preferred in the place of a fixed sum, a sliding scale which might be adapted to the exigencies of each year. Your Excellency rejected this amendment, but it will become necessary to revert to the subject at an early day.

At the time when the taxes were fixed at a stated sum it was supposed that the engagement entered into by your Government as per art. 3 of the Land Regulations that "The streets and roads of the settlement shall be laid out and graded at the expense of the Korean Government" in accordance with the plan, would be faithfully carried out and the repairs on a large system of roads would involve expenditure on a large scale. This scale fixed the measure of the taxation, but as these streets and roads have never been laid out and graded by the Korean Government, the right of the latter to continue to levy the full tax rate may well be disputed.

Of course the land tax due the Korean Government is not in question under any system of taxation. That must always be paid in full and there has never been any design on the part of anyone to evade it.

During my absence at Chemulpo Your Excellency did me the honor of addressing to me another despatch under date of the 10th instant, in which the intention to collect full taxes is repeated, and I am requested to notify Americans that they must pay them to the authorized agent of the Korean government, Mr. Johnston. In reply I have to state that, if Your Excellency insists upon it, the letter of the law leaves me no alternative but to comply with your request; and I shall expect the Korean Government to exact the same compliance from the other Treaty Powers. I shall bring the whole subject to the notice of my Government and suggest that it asks for a revision of the Land Regulations, and meanwhile I trust that Your Excellency will see reason to withdraw the despatch under reply.

I cannot close this note without again calling your attention to my despatch of October 7th in which I urge the importance of the Kamli himself occupying a seat on the municipal council and to which I have never been favored with a reply. It is evident that Your Excellency is misinformed on many points connected with the Settlement and we are never likely to be in harmony till your knowledge of facts is derived from an authoritative source. I can see little to add to the arguments I have already adduced, but if no other end were subserved than to avoid these constant bickerings, which I believe to be unnecessary, it would be worth a great effort to achieve it, and no great effort is required. All that is needed is a word from Your Excellency and I earnestly trust it may be speedily spoken.

The Foreign representatives will each address you separately on this subject. H.I. Russian Chargé d'Affaires however desires me to express his approval of this letter.

Since writing the forgoing I have had the honor of receiving Your Excellency's despatch under date of the 23rd instant on the same subject.

AUGUSTINE HEARD

NO. 237   Legation of the United States
                                Seoul Korea Jany 24, 1892

Secretary of State

Sir:

I have the honor to transmit with this despatch a Report upon my voyage to Korean ports last Oct–Nov. on board the U.S.S. "Alliance." It has been delayed by the non-arrival of the photographs from Japan.

I did not insist on determining the limits of the Foreign Settlements at Wŏnsan & Fusan, as an understanding on the subject between the Representatives of the different Treaty Powers was properly first necessary, and the local officials had no authority to conclude any definite arrangements. The English Consul-General is about shortly to make a Similar tour, and on his return the subject may be seriously undertaken. On certain accounts it is desirable that limits should be defined, but in the absence of consular authorities there are also objections to the establishment of regular settlements with municipal Governments, etc., which have been brought forcibly to our notice by the bickerings and disputes at Chemulpo, and probably it will be advisable to Stop Short of the complete organization expected there.

There are at present no Foreign merchants or officials at Fusan or Wönson. There is no English merchant in Korea, but a large proportion (57%) of the imports being of English origin, English interest in the country is sufficiently indicated.

There is but one American merchant, but there are many American missionaries, and the Army & school instructors as well as a few Royal advisers are Americans, so that we also have a distinct interest, which may be increased, if the development of the country, in the opening up of its mineral resources and the improvement of its roads, should be placed, as is not unlikely, in American hands. Our mercantile interests, measured by imports, are comparatively small, only about 3% being of American origin.

It is the custom of the English as you are no doubt well aware, whenever new settlement of foreign occupation is laid out in the East to select the choicest sight in it for a Consulate, and in this way without cost or small cash, except for yearly taxes, their Consulates, if not in places most convenient for business—and they generally are—are always conspicuous and most desirable residences. This has been the case in Korea and the English Consulate at Chemulpo unites all these advantages, & it is in a most commanding situation. A similar hill has already been selected in Fusan.

Our own policy has been directly the reverse. Instead of hastening to seize the best lot in the settlement, the American Government has often refused to accept a suitable site when offered to it, as has been the case in Japan & China. Instead of taking without payment, or buying at a very small sum the land it might require at the outset, it has preferred to rent, and, as the importance of the Settlement has increased with their growth, it has been compelled to increase its payments year by year, or content itself with inferior situations at the same rents, moving from the better to the worse, as the years roll on. If the effect of this were felt merely in the Consuls convenience or comfort, it would be of comparatively small importance, but unfortunately an effect is produced on the minds of the natives, and Eastern nations are peculiarly susceptible to Such influences, —which cannot be regarded as favorable.

I have no wish as it would be useless, to comment on this policy, and I speak of it now only to ask in connection with the new settlements, which will be marked out in Korea whether I am to make application for any Consular Sites. They would be accorded probably without payment, but would be liable to a small tax. I should not have hesitated to do so, but for the fact that the Chemulpo site which had been set apart for a Consulate, was declined.

In my Report I have alluded to the desirability of making a new survey of the approaches to Ping Yang Inlet, and I will only add here that it seems to be especially desirable that the "Shenandoah" chart being faulty, should be replaced by a more creditable evidence of American nautical skill. If we are to make any survey in these waters, let us do it in a thorough and workmanlike manner.

I have spoken of the policy of the Government with regard to the opening of Ping Yang. I believe it fully recognizes the advantages to be derived from it, but it wishes, to hold it in reserve as a makeweight in any Diplomatic controversy it may have with a Foreign Power; & I have been confidentially informed that it may possibly make use of it in the negotiation it is now carrying on with Japan for the settlement of her various pending claims.

In an audience of His Majesty shortly after my return, I expressed my thanks to him for the polite treatment I had everywhere received, from his officials and especially for the handsome reception of the Governor of Ping Yang. I spoke of the Coal Mine as likely to prove of value, and requested him to direct that a time should be reserved for a trip to be made by the next United States man of war, arriving in Korea. I also repeated the caution I had given the governor to disregard any unfavorable representation, pending this test, which I was confident would prove satisfactory.

His Majesty seemed to appreciate the importance of the subject, and was most gracious in his replies.

AUGUSTINE HEARD

Legation of the United States
                                        Seoul Korea Feby 22, 1892

Secretary of State

Sir:

In my No. 237, handing a Report upon my visit to certain ports in
Korea I spoke of the interest that was generally felt in regard to
the opening of *Ping Yang* to foreign trade. I am informed that in
the last few days the Japanese minister has applied for a Kwang Ja
for a man of war and government officer to visit that port. The ship
is shortly expected at Chemulpo. A Kwang Ja is a species of letter
or credit issued by the Foreign Office to the officials of any place
authorizing them to furnish money or supplies, as may be called for:
repayment is made at Seoul. As money in the form of cash, which
alone is current, is exceedingly cumbersome, and an arrangement of
this kind is very convenient, it is almost necessary, when traveling in
the interior, and is generally availed of.

It will be recollected that when remitting money in satisfaction
of the claim of Mr. (Pierce) [Scott]* on the Korean Government, I
requested you to require him before receiving payment to furnish
another plan of certain mill machinery which has been destroyed.
Mr. (Pierce) [Scott] denied having destroyed it, but furnished the plan
which has become useful. The machinery is lying about 30 miles
North of Ping Yang, and a Korean engineer who has been educated
at the School of Mines at Columbia College, Washington, & recently
returned to this country has gone to erect it and put it in operation
on as a gold mine in that vicinity.

In the line of progress I may also mention that an American engineer who had recently arrived from the United States to prepare and
Superintend the Electrical machinery at the Palace was sent home
by the last mail to buy a larger plant.

                                        AUGUSTINE HEARD

---

* No. 246, Heard to Blaine, dated March 9, 1892, explains that Scott is here
confused with Pierce. Ed.

Legation of the United States
                                                    Seoul, Korea, Oct. 7, 1892

Secretary of State

Sir:

I have the honor to inform you that early in March I received a
letter from Mr. Edward Rogers, manager at Nagasaki of the China
and Japan Trading Company, a company registered under the laws
of the State of New York, and doing business in China, Japan, England, and America, in which he requested me to assist him in procuring a lot of land for business purposes at Fusan. He stated that he
desired having 300 feet along the waterfront north of the Japanese
settlement, and extending from low water mark to the road running
at the back of the town, but the local authorities to whom he had
applied refused to listen to him, as this lot had been reserved for
the use of the Customs Department of the Government.

It will be recollected that in my report upon Fusan last December,
I alluded to the unnecessary extent of land which had been set aside
for the Customs and expressed the opinion that the greater part, if
not the whole of it should be given up, if required for business estab-
lishments.

I at once therefore made application to His Excellency, the President of the Foreign Office, for the lot indicated, stating that the
applicant was willing to pay the price and subscribe to the Conditions
which might be imposed by agreement between the Foreign Representatives and the Korean Government, and notified the Chief Commissioner of Customs, by whose orders the reservation in question
had been made. No objection was raised. His Excellency immediately
replied, accepting the application, and suggested that lots should be
put up at auction. He added that he would notify the Kamni (local
authority of Fusan) and requested me to give the proper information to the China & Japan Trading Co.

In communicating with Mr. Rogers, who was anxious to commence
building at once, I wrote him that I thought in consideration of the
extremely limited frontage available for all nations, 300 feet would
be too much to assign to any one purchaser, and the lots would not
properly exceed 150 or 200 feet, but that his interests would be cared
for as much as possible.

At the same time that the application was made to me on behalf
of the China and Japan Trading Co. an American concern, Mr.

Rogers, who is an Englishman, applied to Mr. Hillier, the English Consul-General, for a lot for his private account.

Mr. Hillier and I had subsequently several conversations with regard to the size of the lots, the mode of disposing of them and the various conditions to be attached to this sale. It was understood between us in a general way that upon the settlement of the conditions between the Foreign Representatives and the Korean Government the lots should be offered at auction, and disposed of to the highest bidder; we awaited the arrival of a plan of the proposed settlement, which Mr. Hunt, the Commission of Customs had requested to prepare, before laying the matter formally between the Diplomatic Body. The circumstances however had been mentioned at one or two meetings, and now, I thought, generally understood.

It appears however that a Russian Steamship Company whose vessels were to ply between Japan, China and Vladivostock, had applied some time ago for a site for office and Godowon, but had been put off upon the plea that the place for a settlement had yet been designated. The steamers of this company are now running, and the agent, coming to Seoul last summer, urged immediate action upon the Russian Chargé d'Affaires, who insisted that an allotment should be made at once. The President finally yielded to his demands, and the Secretary of the Legation was sent to Pusan with orders to secure and make out a suitable site.

On my return to Seoul early in September I heard of this, but presumed that Mr. Hunt, with the local authorities, would prevent the whole execution of the project. The return of Mr. de Kehrburg soon after however, with title deeds of the land assigned to men Sheveleff & Co. proved my mistake and at the same time showed me the necessity of immediate action if I wished to secure for my countrymen their rights as the first applicants for a waterfront. Although the President had recognized in writing my application it was very doubtful to me whether he had actually respected the Kamni on the subject, and whether he would hold to his agreement, if someone else were strenuously to insist on having the lot which had been promised to me.

I consequently sent Mr. Allen down by the next mail steamer to telegraph Mr. Rogers at Nagasaki to meet him. I also caused the President of the Foreign Office to telegraph to the Kamni Mr. Allen's intended arrival with instructions to receive him properly, and assign to him the land which I had applied for, describing it. He added that Mr. Allen must have the same facilities and privileges as had been granted to the Russians. The despatch was shown to me for my satisfaction.

Mr. Dmitrevsky had communicated to me a plan for a portion of the waterfront, which had been brought up by Mr. de Kehrburg, and I enclose a copy for a clear understanding of this situation. The first 700 feet north of the Japanese settlement had been divided into four lots, the first two of 200 feet each & the second two of 150 feet—the second two being looked upon as equal in value to the first two owing to their greater width and easier slope. These are the lots colored red in the plan taken by Men Sheveleff & Co.

My directions to Mr. Allen were to secure of course the 300 feet originally applied for; and, if Mr. Rogers wished to take the two lots of 400 feet, to insist on his right to do so, they were of no greater value or extent than the lots granted Men Sheveleft & Co.

Mr. Allen returned to Seoul last evening bringing with him for registration the title deeds of the two lots in question, having been entirely successful in his mission. The local authorities advised by telegraph of what was expected of them were exceedingly civil and attentive, and the Kamni, though detained by illness at a town 30 li (10 miles) distant, gave no suitable orders to his subordinates— including the preparation of an entertainment. Mr. Rogers arrived at the same time as Mr. Allen: all the business was speedily settled and the title deeds were forwarded to the Kamni for his signature and seal. They were received back on the following morning, and Mr. Allen, being able to return on that day, was absent from Seoul for only 6 days.

I was reluctant to incur the expense of sending him to Fusan, and had requested Mr. Hunt, the Commissioner of Customs, to act as American Consul for the occasion. The President however was desirous that someone should go from this Legation, and as Mr. Hunt is an employee of the Korean Govt., then the President with perfect propriety might have forbidden him to act, and as he might have found himself awkwardly placed under the circumstances, I thought it best to take the course which was ultimately adopted.

It was fortunate that I did so. Mr. Hunt no doubt would have done all that he could, but the results would have been doubtful, and he informed Mr. Allen upon his arrival that he could not hope to get the matter through before a fortnight at least. The positive telegram from the President however, and the fact that the Kamni was the same officer I had received on board the "Alliance" when visiting the port on November last, contributed to the prompt despatch of the business.

The only hitch arose from the hesitation of Mr. Rogers to take both lots from me, as he had applied for one to Mr. Hillier. Mr. Allen, however, advised him to profit by the fact that the authorities were now willing to grant them to me, and it was doubtful whether later he would succeed in getting it through Mr. Hillier. Mr. Rogers finally saw the wisdom of this advice.

It was well that he did so, as Mr. Hillier informs me that he doubts whether, in view of the understanding that he had with the President, he should have made an extra claim: and he described the question as settled. He had no other British claimant, and there are no others.

I may say, that, like Mr. Hillier, I do not altogether approve of the course that has been followed. I have no understanding of the President, such as Mr. Hillier, but I do not see it the most proper way to open a settlement, and I am quite willing to reinstate matters as they were, and have all lots disposed of at auction, if Mr. Dmitrevsky will consent. Inasmuch as those privileges have been accorded to the Russians, I would not think it right or prudent to leave American interests undecided. It is well known that the arrangement was made by Sir Harry Parkes with the Korean Government for a site for the English Consulate at Chemulpo was disregarded, and the site included in the Japanese Settlement: and it appeared improbable that a private claim would receive more serious recognition in the face of a determined opposition—if any such were made. It has been simply an application of the old rule—"first come, first served."

I trust that what has been done will meet with your approval.

The whole question of the Fusan settlement will shortly be brought before the Foreign representatives. Nothing has yet been decided with regard to the price of purchase, the annual rents to be paid, or any other matter connected with the disposal of lots or the government of this settlement.

AUGUSTINE HEARD

Secretary of State

Sir:

Referring to my No. 481, Nov. 7, and my No. 483, Nov. 20,—Pages 6 & 7, I have now the honor to inform you that under the plea of the prohibition of the rice export, the country officials have been levying such taxes of all produce as to practically suppress trade. This is in direct violation of the British Treaty, Art. V, Sec. 4, which distinctly forbids any such likin taxation.

While the Japanese are chiefly interested in this, our one firm in Korea—Morse Townsend & Co.—is also greatly affected. Mr. Townsend tells me that he has 20,000 pieces of sheetings on hand, which, owing to the fall in silver must be sold at a loss, but that he is unable to sell one at all, owing to the fact that the Koreans have nothing to give in exchange, as the country officials will not allow produce to move without the payment of a tax that virtually amounts to prohibition.

As Mr. Townsend showed me that his condition was decidedly critical, I took the matter up at once. I could get no definite action from the Foreign Office, as the President has really no independent powers, and is said always to consult the wishes of the Chinese Representative, before presenting matters to the King.

I therefore decided that the case was sufficiently urgent to warrant my speaking to the King, and after my interview mentioned in my No. 488 of today, I said to His Majesty, that I had another matter of great interest which I would like to mention, unofficially, if he was disposed to listen. He smiled and said he would not listen to anyone else, but he had perfect confidence in me and asked me to proceed.

I then explained how, the prohibition of exports being in conformity to treaty stipulations, I had been one of the first to agree to it; how the conditions had since changed; how, while a matter of rice was in itself of small consequence, the unjust interference of country officials was killing trade; keeping up the price of rice in Seoul, and that the only American firm in Korea was in danger of utter failure through this unwise interference with trade.

His Majesty was immensely interested, saw at once and demonstrated with his hands how produce should be allowed to move freely from place to place. He was alarmed at the prospect of losing the only business connection his country has with America, and said he would immediately give orders that all interference with trade should be stopped at once on penalty.

He bestowed many kind attentions which had no especial bearing on the subject, except to show that I did right in bringing the matter to his personal attention. I trust my action may not meet with the disapproval of the Department.

I visited the Foreign Office the next day and found the President busy issuing orders as per His Majestys instructions. The President further assured me that I might tell Mr. Townsend to go ahead and buy any kind of produce, at any place in the country, and if he met with any interference I should report the case at once to him for punishment. He also said that the prohibition of the export of rice would be withdrawn soon.

I trust that this relief may be sufficient for Morse Townsend & Co., but a surplus of bad debts, and the depression itself, has so cripled [sic] them that they cannot stand any more losses.

H. N. ALLEN

NO. 549   Legation of the United States
Seoul Korea April 5, 1894

Secretary of State

Sir:

Replying to your No. 202 of Nov. 20, I regret to say that it is impossible to make clear to the Koreans, the matter of electrical measurements.

A considerable course in electrical education will be necessary before the matter can be apprehended.

H. N. ALLEN

NO. 8   Legation of the United States
Seoul Korea May 28, 1894

Secretary of State

Sir:

I have the honor to acknowledge the receipt of your Circular Letter dated Mch. 21, in which you request a report on Tides for the United States Coast and Geodetic Survey.

I regret that I am unble to furnish you the required information. The Korean Government keeps no record of such matters. We have no United States Counselor or other officers at the ports to collect such data and I am not warranted in making the necessary expenditure to have such information collected.

I would suggest that our naval officers might easily collect the facts in this case.

John M. B. Sill

NO. 135   Legation of the United States
                                           Seoul, Korea, Aug. 15, 1895

Secretary of State

Sir:

I have the honor to inform you that the confidence of His Majesty the King of Korea in America and Americans has just been unmistakably manifested, in the granting of a very valuable mining right to an honorable American—James R. Morse, President of the American Trading Co. of New York.

The right is for the mining of gold, for 25 years, in the Uhnsan District of Peng Yang Province, which district is said to be the richest in Korea and belongs to His Majesty personally, having been set apart for his use by the Cabinet.

Mr. Morse is no newcomer here. He has long been associated with Korea in ways usually to the benefit of the latter. In 1892, he came here from New York at the request of the King, to arrange for the building of a rail-road and the development of mines. He did his part most satisfactorily but the King was so handicapped at that time by the Chinese that the plan was easily frustrated by the disaffected persons.

In this case, being free to act, His Majesty has made the agreement as strong as possible and Mr. Morse cannot well be disturbed in his rights.

While Korea is well known for her poverty, her gold mines are known to be rich. It is to be hoped that this new venture may lead to the proper development of these mineral resources, and to the permanent relief of Korea's financial distress.

John M. B. Sill

Legation of the United States
Söul, February 5, 1887

Secretary of State

Sir:

Previous despatches from this legation have informed the department of the opening in Söul, by a number of American missionaries, of schools, an orphanage, an hospital, and of other useful undertaking [sic] due to them. In all these they have received the hearty support of this Legation. But while doing so much good work, the missionaries have had always in view the main object of their coming to Korea, the evangelization of the natives. The example of the Catholic missionaries who, though working in secret, have, it is said, a large following, to which they are quietly adding day by day, appears to have been more than their fervour could stand, for I am led to believe that our countrymen have commenced baptizing the heathen Korean.

I have taken occasion, whenever the opportunity presented itself, of telling the American missionaries here that I considered any evangelizing work here at least premature and as endangering their position and their popularity with the people.

There is in this country a large influential party strongly opposed to Christianity, and, although no persecutions of Christians have occurred of late years, still their enmity cannot be lost sight of, and, in the absence of any treaty provision allowing missionaries to pursue their work among the people, it would appear desirable that our countrymen should restrain their ardour and await the day when religious freedom is granted the Koreans.

The Catholic missionaries live as Koreans, they recognize Korean law and submit to the penalties imposed by Korean justice. They have no protections, they can seek for no outside help. The history of protestant missionary work in China shows that the same course is not adopted by the protestant missionaries; they would appeal for help for themselves and for their neophytes.

In the absence of any express directions as to the course I should pursue in regard to such of our people as are engaged in missionary work in Korea, I respectfully request that I be instructed on this important question.

W. W. ROCKHILL

                Legation of the U. States
Seoûl, Corea, April 21st 1888

Secretary of State

Sir:

Mr. Rockhill in his Number 58 of Feby 5th 1887 called the attention of the Department of State to a restless disposition on the part of the Missionaries in Corea to exceed the bounds of prudence in the prosecution of evangelical work. The matter is of growing importance and I respectfully ask that I may have the benefit of instructions as to the course I shall pursue.

At various times I have greatly remonstrated against imprudence and called attention to the danger of injury to the cause they seek to promote from an exhibition of premature zeal, as well as to a liability of engendering prejudice against Americans, and to more serious possible results.

My admonitions have been kindly and respectfully received by very worthy people, but it appears that under a conception of authority "higher than man" their zeal gets beyond restraint.

Whereas in the beginning assemblies for religious worship were only held for the foreign residents, but attended more or less by Coreans without exciting objection from the authorities, now prayer meetings are held for the natives and as I infer the services conducted in the Corean language.

Moreover occasional journeys are made into remote parts of the country upon passports with a view as is now confessed of religious teaching and administering baptism and other rites. Mr. Appenzeller of the Methodist Mission and Mr. Underwood of the Presbyterian have just left Seoûl for the north of Corea, and even desire if possible to go beyond the border into Manchuria, upon an expedition of this kind. Having learned of their purpose I had an interview with Mr. Appenzeller and kindly but in very positive terms expressed my disapprobation. He intimated a purpose to observe my advice but he is gone notwithstanding.

As was stated by Mr. Rockhill in the despatch cited there is a very strong feeling against Christian work, one which will be intensified by aggressiveness, but I doubt not can in time be wholly dispelled by good example, teaching in the schools which has public and governmental recognition, and work in the hospitals.

The natives show a high appreciation of the benefits resulting from these institutions and with the exercise of patience and regard for the laws and wishes of the people on the part of those engaged in them, I think they will furnish a sure avenue to religious freedom.

The Methodist Mission have [sic] a school which is doing excellent work. Although a mission school and entirely independent of government patronage, it has had a name bestowed upon it by the government in token of its recognition.

For the purposes of this school a large and handsome building, occupying a sightly eminence and built after the western style of architecture has been erected at an expenditure of several thousand dollars. The Coreans watched its progress of construction with great interest and with anxiety. I was frequently asked if the building was intended for a church.

I have been approached to know if the foreign residents would be authorized in erecting a building purely for a house of worship avowedly for the use only of foreigners. If our people have a right to build churches it must be derived by virtue of the "most favored nation" clause of our treaty from provision in the English treaty and perhaps the German and Russian granting "free exercise of religion". Inasmuch as the nationals of neither of these powers have as yet undertaken the building of houses of public worship and the opening of Seoûl (Han-Yang) to foreign commerce being liable, upon the happening of a future contingency, to be suspended or rendered inoperative, I have discouraged the building of a church and counselled against it.

The matters herein presented will doubtless have discussion very soon between the Corean and French authorities. The French Missionaries having been long in the country and perhaps smarting from former persecutions have purchased elevated ground overlooking the Palace, and in close proximity to an old temple and are proceeding to erect a building it is said for school and religious uses. Because of the two facts mentioned in connection with the location, the Coreans are greatly exercised and have protested against the occupation of the grounds. For two months the matter has been under discussion and the King in the exercise of great forebearance has offered if the Missionaries will recede from their purpose that he will refund the money they have paid for the lots and present them with ground to be selected by themselves in the city, without price. All overtures however have been repulsed thus far and the work is still in progress.

The Coreans look anxiously to the arrival of Monsieur Colin de Planey the French representative who is expected to arrive in June next, for an amicable settlement of the affair.

HUGH A. DINSMORE

NO. 63 F.O.   Legation of the United States
Seoul, Corea, April 25, 1888

President of the Korean Foreign Office

Your Excellency:

I have the honor to acknowledge receipt of Your Excellency's dispatch concerning the teaching of the Christian religion by Americans in Corea, and I have carefully considered its contents.

Before receiving your dispatch I have at different times talked with our people and have enjoined upon them a respectful consideration of the wishes of His Majesty, the King, and of the laws and established customs of His Majesty's country.

I beg Your Excellency to be assured that I will exercise my fullest influence and authority to affect upon the part of American residents a careful observance of the rights of the Corean Government under the treaty and to restrict their conduct to the exercise of privileges and rights granted by its provisions.

I have referred the subject treated in Your Excellency's dispatch to the consideration of my Government.

HUGH A. DINSMORE

NO. 106   Legation of the U. States
Seôul Corea April 28th 1888

Secretary of State

Sir:

I have the honor to transmit herewith with translation a copy of the note received from the Foreign Office on the 25th instant informing me of the Knowledge of the Corean government that Americans employed as teachers in the schools are engaged in evangelical work not only in the schools but amongst the peoples of the country as well, protesting against it and requesting my official interference to prevent it. It is claimed that schools and religious teaching are not authorized by the treaty and the government claims the right to restrict schools to such as may be sanctioned by it.

It is my opinion that there is no desire to interfere with the schools already established other than to prevent the inculcation of the Christian religion.

In this connection I would respectfully call attention to the French Corean Treaty in which the right to study and teach laws arts and sciences is accorded by the latter Government, (I have not a copy of the treaty in the Legation.)

In my reply to the note from the Corean Foreign Office I wrote that I would exercise my fullest influence and authority to effect an observance of the rights of the Corean government on the part of our nationals and to inspire them with respectful consideration of its wishes. (A copy of my note is enclosed).

Mr. Appenzeller and Mr. Underwood of the Methodist and Presbyterian Missions respectively having left Seoûl some days before for the north of Corea with the purpose of evangelical work as reported in my No. 105 dated April the 21st instant. I sent them a note advising them of the correspondence herein reported and requested that they would accede to the Corean Government's demand at least until such time as their right to engage in the work of Christianizing the natives shall appear established. My note was accompanied by requests from their respective boards for their return to Seoûl.

Hugh A. Dinsmore

no. 71   Department of State
                                    Washington, June 15, 1888

Hugh A. Dinsmore

Sir:

Your dispatches Nos. 105 and 106, Diplomatic Series, dated the 21st and 28th of April, respectively, have been received and your statements concerning the tendency of foreign missionary organizations in Corea to extend their operations into the interior and to claim increasing privileges in the way of public worship and teaching, have been read with much interest.

I am generally disposed to approve your cautious intimations to the missionaries discouraging any aggressive attempt to enlarge the boundaries of their privileges.

In dealing with a country like Corea, where the traditional policy for centuries has been the exclusion of all foreign intercourse and influence, the change which has taken place within the last few years, and the entrance of Corea into the family of modern nations, necessarily involves large consequences. And while those who are engaged in the effort to implant new principles there are naturally animated with the desire to accomplish much for the cause they represent, yet it should be remembered that the attempt on their part to extend their privileges by acts of aggression, without due regard to treaty limitations and the feelings of the people, might tend to defeat their efforts and to raise opposition to their labors.

Since you state in your No. 106 that you have no copy of the Franco-Corean Treaty, a copy in the possession of the Department has been examined for your information; and in relation to the holding of property and the exercise of religious and kindred privileges, the following passages may be quoted:

Article IV, Section 2, reads as follows:

In the localities above named Frenchmen shall have the rights to lease or buy grounds and houses, to erect buildings thereon, and to establish warehouses and manufactories. They shall have the liberty to practice their religion. All arrangements relative to the choice of boundaries and the regulation of the foreign concessions, as well as the sale of lands in the different ports or cities open to foreign commerce, shall be concerted between the Corean authorities and the competent French authorities.

Section 4 of the same article reads:

Frenchmen may lease or buy grounds and houses outside of the limits of the foreign concessions and within a zone of ten lis beyond those limits; but the grounds so occupied shall be subject to local regulations and fiscal taxes under such conditions as the Corean authorities may deem proper to fix.

Article IX, Section 2, reads as follows:

Frenchmen resorting to Corea for the purpose of there studying or teaching the written or spoken language, sciences, laws or arts, shall, in testimony of the sentiments of good friendship which animate the high contracting parties always receive aid and assistance. The Coreans resorting to France shall there enjoy the same advantages.

In the absence of knowledge of the construction by France and Corea on these treaty stipulations and of any explicit grant therein of such rights, the Department would not be warranted in instructing you to claim as derivative from the French treaty the extended privileges of religious teaching among the natives which are sought to be exercised and against which, as indicated by its protest enclosed in your No. 106, the animosities of the Corean Government appear to be roused.

It would certainly be unfortunate for the cause which the worthy and zealous men to whom you refer seek to promote, if by indiscretion and the assertion of privileges not accorded by the treaty, and in opposition to the distinct protests of the Corean Government, they should render their well-met efforts a ground of hostility on the part of the natives.

T. F. BAYARD

NO. 115   Legation of the U. States
                                    Seoûl, Corea, June 25th 1888

Secretary of State

Sir:

I have the honor to report the occurrence within the past ten days of serious disturbance in Seoul which has given rise to great apprehensions and alarm to the foreign residents. The disturbance had its beginning some weeks ago when it was rumored among the common class of natives that young children were being stolen from their parents. The excitement continued to grow, until last week it reached a point of intensity that culminated in the killing on the streets by the populace of native men at different times and places upon a charge of being engaged in the stealing of children. The accusation took form also involving foreigners it being declared by the people that children were being stolen and sold to foreigners to be eaten by them and converted into medicine and materials to be used in the making of photographs. In all it is said seven men have been Killed. We Know of some certainty, at least one was seen by reliable foreigners lying on the street mutilated and dead where he had been slain by the mob. Among the Killed there were doubtless innocent persons as it has been definitely ascertained that innocent people were attacked carrying their own children in their arms.

The most absurd and unreasonable stories were circulated, supported it seems by persons who claim to be eye witnesses of the boiling of children in the houses of foreigners. It was declared that the schools of the American Missionaries were mere agencies for procuring children for the purpose above mentioned. The accusations seem to be chiefly against the American Missionaries and the Japanese generally. On Monday last week I learned from various sources apparently reliable that threats were being made of an attack on "Chong Tong" the locality in which the Americans reside and the legation is situated. The natives employed by our residents seemed greatly alarmed in some instances refusing to go upon the streets and in others declaring their intention to quit their service as it was said that employers and servants were to be Killed alike. Feeling that the circumstances were of sufficiently Serious character to justify decided action I telegraphed Commander T. F. Jewell commanding the U. S. Ship "Essex" then in port at Chemulpo, on Tuesday, to send a detachment of twenty men for the protection of our people, at the same time sending by courier an explanation in writing to reach him before the departure of the troops. On Wednesday morning, at 10 o'clock in compliance with my request a company consisting of three officers, twelve men, and thirteen marines, Lieutenant C. D. Galloway commanding, arrived quietly at the legation having made a night march from Chemulpo in twelve hours. Similar detachments were sent from the Russian Corvette "Sabre" and the French gunboat "Aspie" upon requests of Mr. Waeber and Monsieur Colin de Planey respectively.

As was anticipated by me the arrival of the forces has had the most salutary effect, the excitement having begun immediately to subside until at this time comparative quiet prevails.

The coming of the troops seems to have met with the full approval of the Corean Government. His Majesty the King sent a messenger to me to commend my action as timely and judicious.

At present there is a public examination of students gathered in the city from all parts of the country contesting for degrees, and I think it best to retain the guard until these people have returned to their homes, when Lieut. Galloway will return with his command to his vessel.

During the disturbance I was in constant communication with the Foreign Office and with my colleagues. Not having time to make a full report by the present mail I reserve a detailed account to be forwarded hereafter.

At present there seems to be no ground for further alarm.

HUGH A. DINSMORE

Legation of the U. States
Seoul Corea July 1st 1888

Secretary of State

Sir:

For further information with regard to the recent critical disturbances in Seoul reported in my No 115 dated June 25th I have the honor to state that on Friday the 29th instant at 4 o'clock Lieutenant C. D. Galloway U.S. Navy left this legation with the force under his command to return to the U. S. Steamer "Essex" at Chemulpo there appearing to Exist no further necessity for their presence. The forces sent from the French and Russian Vessels have also returned.

I beg to make favorable mention of the Cheerful and energetic promptness with which Commander Jewell and the officers of his command responded to the request of the legation for necessary assistance, of the perfect deportment of the men during the whole period of their landing.

I am aware of the Departments objections to the landing of a naval force ordinarily, and was reluctant to ask it without prior permission but the emergency in the situation I had reported seemed to fully justify it and not to admit of the delay necessary to receive instructions by cable.

No objection has been made by the Korean Government and I am firmly convinced that much good has resulted which will extend beyond the present time. Having been informed of portenteous threats against our people made by the populace I addressed the communication on the 18th ulto to the President of the Foreign Office of which I enclose a copy, urging the necessity of action on the part of the government to allay the excitement and remove the unjust suspicions against foreigners and suggested the publication of a proclamation assuring the falsity of the rumors.

On the following night at twelve o'clock I received a short note in reply submitting a proclamation proposed for publication. As will be seen by reference to the English translation of it which I enclose with a copy of the original its terms used were such as would tend to increase rather than cause a subsidence of the disorder. Therefore I sent my interpreter immediately to the residence of the President to arouse him from his bed and point out the objection to the paper. He withheld the publication and returned a message that he would prepare another on the following day.

On the 19th by common consent all the foreign representatives except Mr. Yuan Sie Kwai the representative of China who had been ill since the beginning of the excitement met at this legation and formulated such a proclamation as seemed to be required by the situation and a joint note to the Foreign Office respectfully submitting it for publication if approved. On that night it was posted on the city gates and in the public places. It was first read by the people on Wednesday morning the date of the arrival of the different naval detachments, and doubtless produced a good effect. A copy of the proclamation with English translation is enclosed.

His Majesty the King also caused to be published over the royal seal a very practical and effective proclamation denying that foreigners had any participancy in the taking of children, and offering liberal rewards for the capture and conviction by satisfactory evidence of the Kidnappers, upon the condition that he would impose a fine equal in amount to the reward offered against any person causing an arrest without evidence.

It is generally believed that innocent persons were Killed by the mob and that if the abduction of children was practiced at all the facts were greatly exaggerated. There are some indications that the whole disorder in its details was conceived and planned with premeditated design perhaps for political purposes but if so we cannot point out the guilty principals or agents. It may possibly be accidental.

The incidents of the affair are identical with those precedent to the massacre of foreigners at Tientsin, China in June 1870, in which the French Consul and more than twenty foreign residents were murdered. Thursday the 21st ultimo was the anniversary of the Tientsin massacre. On tuesday the 19th the excitement reached its highest point accompanied by threats of attack on foreigners and a disposition of panic on the part of natives in the service of our residents. The marines left Chemulpo in the evening of this day arriving here the next morning as heretofore reported.

The general disposition of the native masses towards foreigners as manifested by their universal respect and Kindness in the past is wholly inconsistent with the recent events. Our people have travelled in the interior of the Kingdom singly and in small parties and have been invariably treated with Kindness and hospitality. We go through this city at all hours of the day or night frequently undisturbed and without hesitation.

I have myself many a time frequently gone on foot without an

attendant in the remotest and unfrequented quarters of the city, and have never received the slightest indignity but on the contrary Kindness and cheerful respect. There is still a feeling∧against the Japa-
of ancient origin
nese, and the inhabitants of the interior unfamiliar with Western people sometimes mistake them for Japanese. It was that confusion which caused the attack upon and pursuit of Lt. Foulk in 1884. In that affair only the Coreans, Chinese and Japanese were involved. There were no accusations against Americans or Europeans.

At the beginning of the late disorders and before they had assumed an alarming aspect I was informed by one of my colleagues with whom I have entire confidence that he had received information from his interpreter whom he trusts implicitly that Mr. Yuan the Chinese representative had native emissaries receiving money from him to go amongst the common people and engender prejudice and hatred of foreigners, that (the interpreter) had conversed with one at least of these individuals and had heard his confession to such employment.

Quiet seems now to be fully restored. The U.S.S. Essex sails today from Chemulpo leaving the U.S.S. "Juniata" on duty there.

HUGH A. DINSMORE

NO. 71 F.O.   Legation of the U. States
                                              Seoul, Korea June 18, 1888

President of the Korean Foreign Office

Your Excellency:

I would respectfully call your attention to the necessity for the Corean Government to take some prompt action to quiet the excite-
ment that is constantly growing in Seoul based upon irresponsible and false rumors about the Kidnapping of children by foreigners. The lives of our people are endangered by these false reports and great trouble may ensue both to foreigners and to the Corean Government.

Your Excellency and all intelligent Coreans must certainly know that there is no truth in the rumors so far as they relate to foreigners. Therefore I would respectfully suggest that a proclamation should be issued by the Government of Corea, Sealed with the seal of the highest office and posted in the public places throughout the city telling the people that the rumours are false.

If Your Excellency will attend to this matter much trouble will be prevented.

Hugh A. Dinsmore

The Office of Foreign Affairs makes proclamation

Of late certain ill disposed persons have, to serve their own base purposes been circulating rumors to the effect that Corean children are being stolen and sold to foreigners to be eaten by them.

These rumors are false and absurd in the extreme. Foreigners have now been living in our midst for five years and have always been on friendly terms with our people. How is it that now we first hear then charge with wicked practices?

In consequence of these rumors being believed by ignorant people, several persons have been Killed on the streets on suspicion of being kidnappers. This place of taking upon yourselves to attack people in the streets is foolish and wicked. It endangers the lives of the innocent. If children are stolen the Government will punish the Kidnappers who (when caught) should be brought before this office (or the Board of Punishments) for examination. Now this proclamation is issued to warn people against believing or repeating these false reports and also to let them know that should there be any further cases of attacking persons on the streets on these baseless suspicions those implicated in such attacks will be immediately seized and severely dealt with in a summary manner. As also will any persons heretofore found spreading such false and baseless rumors.

no. 86 f.o.   Legation of the United States
                                     Söul, Korea, Sept 8th 1888

President of the Korean Foreign Office

Your Excellency:

I have the honor to request that you will make Known to His Majesty the King that Dr. Heron and Mr. Underwood, American citizens acting for the Presbyterian board of foreign Missions desire to erect a building on land which they now own, and for which they have received title deeds, which have been placed before the authorities of His Majesty for proper authentication, for strictly school purposes. It is the design of these gentlemen to establish a college for the instruction and education of the Youths of Korea, similar to colleges in the United States. If their undertaking shall prove successful great benefits will be conferred upon His Majesty's subjects, by the education of the young men of the country, in english and other modern languages, and in all the branches of science.

After reporting the matter to His Majesty the King will Your Excellency favor me with an early reply.

Hugh A. Dinsmore

NO. 88 F.O.   Legation of the United States
Söul Oct 3" 1888

President of the Korean Foreign Office

Your Excellency:

I have the honor to say in reply to your note asking me to destroy a deed which was given by one Cho, a Korean subject, to Mr. Hulbert, an American citizen, and which bears authentication under seal of the Foreign Office, that I am sorry to be under the necessity of declining to comply with Your Excellency's request.

Under the laws of my country I would not be authorized to do as you request. Moreover, as shown by the deeds in Mr. Hulbert's possession, bearing the seal of your honorable and high office, it would seem that Mr. Hulbert has a good title to the property in question and that he should be placed in possession of it. That question should be fairly tried by a court of competent Jurisdiction and the right of the question ascertained without prejudice to either of the parties. If Mr. Pyon has been unjustly defrauded of his house it should be restored to him and I would not wish to have one of our citizens to get property which rightfully belongs to another.

But it should not be forgotten that our citizen has paid his money for a house to a Korean subject, who claimed to be the owner, and that the Korean government acting through the office of which you are at this time the honorable President, declared to the world by its seal that the house is the property of Mr. Hulbert.

Mr. Hulbert should not be deprived of his property on the mere statement of Mr. Pyon that the house belongs to him.

Let justice be done, let suffer who must for justice's sake.

Hugh A. Dinsmore

Legation of the United States
                                                    Söul Oct 30, 1888

President of the Korean Foreign Office

Your Excellency:

Before Your Excellency assumed control of the Foreign Office as acting President, I received a note from His Excellency Yi Ching Phil, then acting President, stating to me that he had been informed that the American citizen Mr. Appenzeller had closed a street of the city, and asking me to have the same opened, and to write upon the subject to the honorable Acting Consul General for His Imperial Majesty the German Emperor.

I have the honor to communicate to Your Excellency that I have thoroughly investigated the question referred to me and have found the following facts to exist.

Mr. Appenzeller and Dr. Scranton, acting for the Methodist Mission Board, purchased from the Korean owners a number of houses and lots contiguous to each other lying next to the city wall and west of the "little west gate," and these lots they have inclosed by wall and fence. The way in the rear of the lots next to the city wall is open and unobstructed, as is also the street in front leading to the little west gate, and the street on the north leading from Chong Dong to the city wall. So the streets on all sides are open. The inclosed ground all belongs to the citizens of the United States above mentioned. There is no market nor public well in the inclosed ground to which people have a right of access.

Formerly when the land and houses inclosed belonged to and were occupied by the Korean owners, there was a narrow crooked way, about the one hundred and fifty Korean feet in length, leading from the city wall in the west to the street which is still open, and leading to the little west gate. This narrow way was only for the use of the Koreans who then lived in the grounds now inclosed by Mr. Appenzeller, in getting from their houses into the streets of the city, and now since they have all moved and and sold their houses to Mr. Appenzeller, there is no further need for the enclosed way being open.

I therefore must respectfully represent to Your Excellency that to require this way to be opened would only cause unnecessary and unjust expense to our citizens, and would confer no benefit upon any other person. I can see no propriety whatever in my addressing the Honorable German Consul General on the subject.

                                                    HUGH A. DINSMORE

NO. 168
Legation of the U. States
Seoul Corea February 28 1889

Secretary of State

Sir:

I have the honor to report that in consequence of severe draught in Southern Corea during the last summer cutting short the rice crops, a famine now prevails in the provinces of Chul La Do, and a portion of Chung Chong Do and the natives are reported to be in great distress. Rev. F. Ohlinger of the American Methodist Mission here but recently returned from the stricken district informs us that there is great suffering and a prospect of worse conditions. Though there is some rice offered for sale, it is at such a price that the poorer classes cannot buy, and these are driven to dire extremities. A large proportion of the cattle with which the fields are cultivated, and which as beasts of burden furnish to many the means of existence have been converted into food, and money with which to buy rice. Mr. Ohlinger reports that he saw people in the fields pulling up the growing barley to procure the seed Kernels for food.

The government has under orders from His Majesty the King twice recently sent relief in the money of the country, but it is supposed that the greater portion of it was absorbed by the officials through whom it passed.

Officials in this country receive only nominal salaries and are expected to derive their means from the people after the custom which is said to prevail in China.

The foreign residents in Seoul have felt that the situation demands of them such limited help as is in their power and are generally united in an effort now being made to send a relief party with rice.

A fund of something more than a thousand dollars will be thus raised which will be but a small assistance.

I permitted my name to be used by the American Missionaries who have shown a considerable and humane zeal in this matter in a telegraph despatch to the Associated Press in New York asking for contributions from our people at home.

If prudent and practicable measures were adopted by the Corean Government the necessary aid for the subsistence of the people until they can again support themselves, could be furnished by it, but unfortunately for the starving it is not done.

HUGH A. DINSMORE

NO. 169   Legation of the U. States
                                           Seoul Corea February 28th 1889

Secretary of State

Sir:

I beg to bring to your attention an incident growing out of the matters reported in the number 168 which will be interesting if it is not deemed of sufficient importance to provoke any notice from the Department of State.

It has been suggested that an effort should be made to unite the foreign community in Seoul as far as possible in an endeavor to send assistance to the sufferers from famine in the south of Corea, and it being desired by the movers, the American Missionaries to bring to the enterprise such moral support as would be derived from the cooperation of the persons representing the treaty powers here; acting under the counsel and advice of two of my colleagues, I sent out a circular a copy of which is herewith enclosed, on the 20th instant, informing my colleagues of those measures and stating that if the plan met with their approval a meeting of the foreign residents would take place at this legation on a day named to consider plans of relief. The proposal received the cordial cooperation of all the gentlemen excepting Mr. Yuan Sie Kwai the Chinese representative. From him on the day of the meeting I received an official note a copy of which is enclosed declining to participate on the grounds set forth in the following quotation from his note, viz:—

I beg to state that whenever famine prevails upon the people of this Kingdom, H.M. the King of Corea will memorialize Our August Sovereign the Emperor for necessary aid, and when on the receipt of such memorials the necessary measures will be at once adopted by our Government at Peking.

I have already reported to our Government the suffering of the people of the Southern provinces and measure that your foreign powers can adopt in the meantime will be greatly appreciated by our government and the people of this Kingdom. I therefore being under different circumstances from your representatives will be prevented from joining the meeting which will be held at your legation this afternoon.

My only reply to this communication was a personal note directing Mr. Yuans attention to the fact that the whole matter was personal and unofficial, that a meeting of "foreign residents" and not of "foreign representatives" was proposed. Being the senior of the Diplomatic Corps at this Court I would be gratified in this connection to have instructions from the Department as to whether I shall hold relations with Mr. Yuan as with my other colleagues at Seoul, by what title I shall address him, and in questions of precedence what place shall be accorded to him.

He calls himself H.I.C.M.'s Resident and as may be seen by reference to the note quoted from asserts that he is here "under different circumstances" from other foreign representatives.

He but seldom attends a meeting of the representatives for discussion of business. Indeed I do not now recall a single instance in which he has done so since my assuming charge of this legation. He sends his secretary however who is permitted to be present that he may report to his chief what has been done. I have thought that such a course was prompted by a desire to impress the Foreign Office and other native officials that his Secretary and not himself was on terms of equality with us. On one occasion a memorandum of proceedings of a meeting of the diplomatic body at the Foreign Office ~~prompted by~~ prepared by Mr. Watters H.B. Majesty's Consul General Acting as Secretary was sent to me by him for signature. Observing that Mr. Tong, Mr. Yuans secretary was mentioned as one of the parties present on the same terms as myself and my colleagues, I declined to sign it for that reason and did not do so until it was erased.

Mr Yuan persists on visits to the palace in going inside the grounds in his chair attended by a large party of retainers, a privilege which is not accorded to other representatives but which has not been insisted upon by them because it was known to be objectionable to the King and his officials.

In view of Mr. Yuan's extraordinary conduct and the vagueness and uncertainty of his official quality, I would respectfully suggest that such instructions as the Department may deem appropriate be outlined for future guidance.

HUGH A. DINSMORE

NO. 175

Legation of the U. States
Seoul, Korea, April 1st 1889

Secretary of State

Sir:

About a year ago a number of deeds were placed in my possession by the American Missions here to parcels of land some of which have had valuable improvements placed upon them by the present holders (the Missionaries) with the consent and expression of approval of the Corean Government. The deeds were furnished to me for the purpose of having them authenticated in the usual way in this city by the proper authorities.

Accordingly I transmitted them through the Foreign Office to the Mayoralty for that purpose with a request that after they had been properly endorsed they might be returned to me.

After waiting a reasonable time for the return of the deeds I called the attention of the Foreign Office to the fact that they had not been returned. My note was not honored with a reply and I wrote several other notes upon the same subject and with similar results. I then called upon the President and requested an explanation and insisted that the deeds should be returned at once. His Excellency stated that the deeds of our people were all right and that they would be safely returned but that he was instructed by His Majesty the King to say that he begged we might wait particularly for a time until a dispute with the French Missionaries about lots in the city might be settled.

Returning to the legation I addressed a note to the Foreign Office protesting against the rights of our citizens being confused with or in any sense made dependent upon claims of French citizens, but willingly accepting His Majesty's assurance that the deeds should be ultimately delivered to me for our people.

Having allowed six months or more to elapse since the interview reported and the French having gone steadily on with improvements of the land in question, at the instance of the owners of the lots Mr. Long recently while in charge in my absence wrote a note reviewing the requests for the return of our deeds. This note having elicited no reply I wrote saying that unless the matter received prompt attention from the government I should be compelled to report it to my government. I have received no response to my note though written two weeks ago. I respectfully beg that the Department may express its wishes in the matter.

HUGH A. DINSMORE

New York
Oct. 28, 1889

Secretary of State

My respected Sir:

May I call your attention to a sentence in the letter received from my friend Mrs. Heron in Corea? You recall it was she of whom there was some anxiety during the summer.

"Through the U.S. Minister about a year ago, the American Missionaries were absolutely forbidden to teach religion; but we long for the time when our treaty shall be revised and freedom of religion allowed."

Mrs. Heron is a schoolmate friend of mine; of New England parents, who during the Rebellion in Tennessee suffered for their fidelity to the Union. Lieut. Kelly of P.O. Dept. Washington, is her uncle.

My respect for your sincere desire to properly sustain the interest of our Government and our Lord lead me with boldness to write to you.

JOHN G. WILDS.
Pastor, 7th Presbyterian Church.

Department of State
Washington, Nov. 1, 1889.

Rev. John G. Wilds,

Sir:

The Department has received your letter of the 28th ultimo, relative to the labors of American Missionaries in Corea.

It is not understood that Minister Dinsmore has "forbidden" missionary work as intimated in your letter.

You are aware that the Corean people in general look with little favor on the propagation of foreign religious views in that country and that the Government there, in concluding the treaty of 1882, refrained from conferring any special privileges in this regard.

In a period of serious popular excitement during the summer of 1888, threatening even the lives of our citizens, Mr. Dinsmore advised a course on the part of our missionaries that would not provoke hostility and result in injury to their course.

You will doubtless agree with the Department in considering such advice judicious.

JAMES G. BLAINE

NO. 27

Legation of the United States
Seoul, Corea, July 9, 1890

Secretary of State

Sir:

I have the honor to inform you that by the last mail I received a letter from Mr. Pom Kwang Soh (known here as So-Kwang-Pom) dated Washington, May 20, of which I enclose a copy, in which he informs me that he intends to visit Corea, and describes himself as an "American citizen"—having been "in this country five years."

I immediately replied as per Copy enclosed, in the hope that my letter might be in time to prevent him from committing so a egregious a piece of folly. Mr. So Kwang Pom is a well-known rebel, implicated in the affairs of the 1884, and since that time in hiding. He figures prominently in the "Report relative to the Revolutionary attempt in Seoul," written by Ensign Foulk, and published in year & vol. 1885 of "Foreign Relations of the U.S." He has also written, as he says in his intention, to Corean officials, and I yesterday had a visit from the President of the Foreign Office, with reference to him. He had also received a letter to the same effect as mine, and he came to say that So. Kwang. Pom was a very bad man, who had caused the death of a great many Coreans; that feeling was very bitter against him, and that if he but put his foot in Corea, he would be Seized and put to death. He was very anxious to avoid anything like trouble with America, & wished to know if it were possible that the rebel was as he assured himself to be, an American citizen. Anyway, it would be necessary to kill him if he came here, & he wanted me to write and prevent any complications.

I told him in reply that I did not believe So was an American citizen—that simply living five years in the Country was not enough, & that certain prescribed formalities were necessary to constitute naturalization, which I doubted if he had fulfilled. It was not enough that he should assert his citizenship, but he must prove it; moreover

America & Corea were friends, and America could not protect anyone conspiring against the peace of Corea. I would write to prevent his coming, but if he carried out his avowed intention of leaving within a month he was already on his way. I was disposed however, to look upon the whole matter, as pure bravado, and doubted if he should hear anything more of him.

I did not say what I believe to be the case, that, as one of the Mongolian race, So Kwang Pom could not under our present laws be naturalized; for I am aware that in many instances Chinamen have been made citizens, & have even received passports from the Department of State. This was before the feeling against the race was as strong as it is now, & it is hardly likely that he could today procure his papers. It is possible, however, that some out-of-the-way county Court may have conferred them upon him.

Neither did I say that I could not protect him from the consequences of any act, he might have performed before his naturaliza-
                                or to be more precise, before leaving his native country,
tion∧ —as it did not seem necessary. But I believe nothing is more fixed in international law than this principle.

I am not aware that I can add anything further of importance; and as he may arrive at any time I should be glad to receive any instructions you may wish to give me with regard to my treatment of him.

AUGUSTINE HEARD

Washington, D. C.
May 20, '90

Hon. Augustine Heard

Dear Sir:

I am a native of Corea and in exile, but now a citizen of the United States. I have been in this County for five years.

I am intending to go to Corea very soon. I am obliged to let Know that before my arrival there.

You Please explain to the President of Foreign Affairs in Corea about that Corean law cannot be exercised upon me anymore.

I never beg of your favorism, yet I hope you will do your official duty according to the International Law.

That my going to Corea is simply my family visit, and I will be back to my new country (the U.S.) after short stoping [sic] at Seoul.

Please tell the Government & people of Corea not be surprised with my case, but "be quiet." I say this because Know the character of people there. I have written many high officials, too, by the same time I write you.

(Signed) Pom Kwang Soh

NO. 141   Legation of the United States
                                              Seoul, Corea, Apl 2, 1891

Secretary of State

Sir:

An event of some importance has recently taken place. You are aware that Catholic Missionaries are living in various parts of Corea, propagating their doctrine, and that they have succeeded in making a large number of converts, estimated by themselves at 20,000. It is not many years Since they were subject to vigorous persecution, and at this day they find it expedient in the country to adopt the Corean costume, and to draw upon themselves as little notice as possible. The disposition of the people is said to be friendly, but that of the official class is decidedly the reverse.

One of these missionaries in the month of September last passed a few days in the village of Tjyouk-pot-Kol in the province of Kyong-Syang-do (in which Fusan is situated) not far from the popular city of Taikou, and afterwards went on his customary tour through the province. During his absence, the proprieter of the house where he lived was much disturbed by men from the neighboring city; and upon his return they came back threatening to burn the house, and Kill the occupants. On the 25 Febry Mr. Robert went, accompanied by an interpreter, to the Lieut. Governor to make complaint and ask protection, but he was refused admission. The interpreter was called in and explained why he had come, and the Lieut. Governor replied that it was not his (the official's) business and referred the missionary to the Governor. He accordingly proceeded to the Governor's Yamen, followed by a large crowd of persons who had collected, shouting and crying; and sent in his card & passport. The Governor tore up the passport, & refused to receive him, but sent for the interpreter whom he questioned with regard to what had taken place. He appeared to think that what had been done had been well done, and asked, "Are you a Christian?" and in receiving an affirmative reply ordered him to be beaten and cast out. He then commanded the Missionary to leave his premises, which were then surrounded by a howling mob; this the latter refused to do, and said if he were to be Killed, he would be Killed there in the Court of the Yamen. The Governor, apparently reflecting that such an event might be very serious, then placed him under the escort of two Soldiers; who conducted him Safely through the crowd. After proceeding some miles he told them that he would dispense with their further assistance, but he found that he was their prisoner, and they would not let him go; neither would they give him anything to eat, nor any money to buy food; nor would they allow him to return to his house—which meanwhile had been sacked so that a visit to it would have been useless—for necessary clothing, and kept him as prisoner till the night. Then, while the guards were Sleeping, he made his escape, taking refuge at the house of a native Christian about 100 li (30 miles) distant, and finally reached Seoul on the 8th March.

The French Commissioner, Monsieur V. Collin de Planey, under the instructions of his Government, immediately represented the matter to the President of the Foreign Office, and demanded the punishment of the Governor and of all the persons implicated in the affair. He also insisted that a proclamation detailing the facts and denouncing them Should be Sent to all the Governors, and published in all the Provinces, stating the punishments that had been inflicted and enjoining upon the respect for passports and the necessity of protecting foreigners. Indemnity was to be made for material losses. The President immediately accepted all the conditions excepting the first, the punishment of the Governor. This was the most important of all, but the Governor was the near relative of the Queen, and the President hesitated to take any steps against him. Her Majesty was determined to support him, and indeed was of opinion that he had acted rightly, and that no concession should be made to the French.

Affairs were at a dead lock. Meanwhile a French gunboat arrived, and it was intimated by the Commandant that he had been sent to report to the admiral, who would at once appear on the Spot if satisfaction were not speedily accorded.

At this juncture, most reluctantly, the President had recourse to the French Bishop, Monsieur Mutel and begged his kind intervention to induce Monsieur de Planey to modify his demands. It was finally arranged that a strong letter of blame should be addressed to the Governor in the place of the infliction of punishment; and Monsieur de Planey in his acceptance stated that he consented solely at the request of the Bishop—a statement which must have been especially objectionable to the Corean officials.

The affair was finally settled on the following basis:

1st A despatch to be sent to the Governor "by order of the King" reprimanding him. This despatch was drawn up by Monsieur de Planey and forwarded by him on the 31 March.

2nd A circular to be sent to all the other Governors to notify them of what has taken place, to enjoin upon them the strict observance of the treaty.

3rd The Governor to write the French Commissioner a letter to express his regrets.

4th All persons, soldiers or other, implicated in the affair to be punished by imprisonment or banishment in accordance with the gravity of their offense.

5th An escort to be furnished by the Governor to reconduct Mr. Robert to his domicile.

6th A proclamation to be published in Kyong Syang Do to calm the people and to impress upon them the necessity of treating Foreigners with respect.

All the papers referred to in the above conditions were submitted to Mr. de Planey, who found them satisfactory.

The occurrence of this incident induces me to seek for instructions as to the course I am to pursue with regard to our own missionaries. The ground assumed by the French is clear and precise, and far in advance of anything which other nationalities have so far ascribed. They claim that their Missionaries have the right to preach and teach their faith throughout the interior, and in the recent discussions with the President of the Foreign Office this doctrine has been distinctly laid down by Monsieur de Planey. He derives this right from the fact that it was not prohibited by the Treaty. Certain things, such for instance as trading in Ginsing and the introduction of opium, were especially prohibited, and if the propogation of the Christian religion were objectionable, he contends that it should have been distinctly so expressed. The British Treaty allows "British subjects to travel in Corea for pleasure or for purposes of trade to transport and Sell goods of all Kinds, except books and other printed matter disapproved by the Corean Government, and to purchase native produce in all parts of the country under passports, etc.". The French in their treaty omitted the words "for pleasure or for purposes of trade" ∧with the View of covering the action of their Missionaries. They do not consider themselves as called upon to furnish any reason for wishing to travel; and the Representative of the French Government has assured me that without this liberty no treaty would have been made. The Corean Government objected to the building of churches in the interior, and this was not insisted on.

It will be recollected that in April 1888 the Foreign Office addressed a remonstrance to Mr. Dinsmore against proselytizing by American Missionaries in the interior, as being contrary to treaty stipulations— or rather as not being permitted by treaty. A similar letter was addressed to Mr. Waeber who was then charged with French interests. I am informed that Mr. Waeber did not reply, but Mr. Dinsmore seems to have accepted the remonstrance as just, and since that time our Missionaries have received passports only on condition of observing the Treaties—which have been construed as not to allow the preaching and teaching to natives of the Christian Religion. The subject was treated by Mr. Dinsmore in his No. 106, of April 28, 1888, and Mr. Bayard in his reply, No 71, of June 15, while apparently and conditionally approving of Mr. Dinsmore's course, does not seem to be aware of the nature of the French claim. He makes no allusion to the clause regarding passports through which the French derive their authority. His quotations from the Treaty apply solely to the Open Ports unto the 10 li radius; and in no way to the interior of the country, with which we have to do.

The practice of the English has conformed to our own. They do not consider their missionaries as entitled to teach the Christian religion to natives, and they warn all travelers in the interior Not to attempt it.

But, without entering here into the question how far the French are justified in claiming this privilege as a right, if it is accorded to or practiced by them, our own Missionaries may Soon ask under the favored nation clause that the same privilege should be extended to them, or may claim protection under its exercise. And it is desirable therefore that I should be made acquainted with the Views of the Department on the subject.

The practice in China presents a like anomaly. The French by their Treaty of 1860 Art. VI give the right to their "Missionaries to rent and purchase land in all the provinces, & to erect buildings thereon at pleasure", but the English and American Governments have never under the favored nation clause asserted for their own countrymen the same privilege. It is true that the clause in question does not exist in the French text, and the French text is authoritative *in case of any difference of interpretation.* There was never, however, any doubt regarding it in the Mind of the Chinese, but in order to prevent any misconception later it was deliberately reestablished by an Exchange of despatches between Mr. Berthémy and the Tsungli Yamen in 1865.

I am aware that Col. Denby in his despatch, No. 595 of March 19, 1888 states that "it has never been adopted by France or as an intrinsic part of the Treaty," but I am at a loss to understand where he obtains authority for this statement, as in all the passports issued to French Missionaries—which must be Visé by the Chinese Authorities—this clause is quoted at length.

I presume it has been thought advisable not to claim this as a right in China, and to rely Solely upon the toleration and good will of the local authorities; and this reliance has usually been justified by events. The situation in Corea is not widely different, but perhaps rather more delicate.

AUGUSTINE HEARD

NO. 159   Legation of the United States
                                              Seoul Corea May 8, 1891

Secretary of State

Sir:

Referring to Mr. Heard's No. 141 of Apl 2nd, concerning the settlement of a difficulty between the French Missionaries and the Corean Government, by the publication of certain proclamations concerning the treatment of foreigners in the interior; I have the honor to inform you that an American Missionary, just returned from one of his long trips through the country, states that he met with unusually kind treatment from the officials with whom he came in contact; and that, while he has never had serious complaints to make, he thinks this particularly kind treatment to be due largely to the proclamations mentioned in the above cited despatch.

H. N. ALLEN

NO. 95   Department of State
                                            Washington, May 19, 1891

Augustine Heard

Sir:

Your 141, diplomatic Series, in relation to recent correspondence
between the French Commissioner at Seoul and the Korean Government upon the subject of the rights of French missionaries in Korea,
and with special reference to the case of Mr. Robert, a French priest,
has been received.

The Department has heretofore deemed itself precluded by the
terms of our treaty with Korea from initiative action looking to
Extended or additional privileges for American missionaries in that
country; but the measures adopted by the Korean Government as
the resultant of the correspondence between M. de Planey and the
President of the Foreign Office are of a character to warrant the invocation of the provisions of the forthwith article of our treaty with
Korea—the most favored nation clause—in behalf of our Missionaries
whenever the occasion shall arise, and you are accordingly instructed
in that Sense.

ALVEY A. ADEE

NO. 357   Legation of the United States
                                            Seoul, Korea, Jany 16, 1893

Secretary of State

Sir:

I have the honor to enclose for your information copy & translation
of an Extract from the laws of Korea. It was passed 27 years ago in
the early part of the Regency of the Tai Wan Kuhn, and imposes the
punishment of death upon teachers of the Christian religion and of
slavery upon their wives. It was brought to my notice by Mr. Frandin,
representative of France, to ask if I would unite with him in an effort
to have the statute repealed. He thought the present was a favorable
time to make the attempt, as there was no apparent feeling against
the missionaries, and the relations of foreigners with Korea were in
every way cordial. It was well ~~to take advantage~~ to take advantage
of the existing tranquility to abrogate a law, in which a possible change

of sentiment might find in it support for violence. The French priests had requested him to take steps in the matter, as they believe that many, desirous of becoming converts, were deterred by fear of these penalties.

I replied that I should like to think a little further of it before consulting. No doubt the existence of the statutes was a relic of barbarism, and Korea would do well to remove it from her code. But it was a dead letter, and so far as I was aware, entirely without practical effect. Was it wise to raise discussion on the point, & perhaps change indifference to active interest, which might become hostility?

My reflection only confirms me in the prudence of leaving well alone. Our own missionaries tell me that they find in it no obstacle to their labors. They say that there is unquestionably at first a certain fear of receiving their instructions among the natives, but that as soon as they know it is not the Catholic religion, but the "new" faith which is taught, they listen willingly. They were not aware till I told them that such a law existed. It was an act of many years before any of them came to this country. There is apparently in many quarters a strong feeling against the Roman Catholic religion on the ground that converts were encouraged to resist their own officials, & to transfer their allegiance to the priest. Their number increases rapidly amounting to, I am told, fully 1200 a year.

I should be pleased to receive your instructions on the subject.

AUGUSTINE HEARD

NO. 365   Legation of the United States
                                          Seoul, Korea, February 10th 1893

Secretary of State

Sir:

Referring to my No. 357, January 16th I have the honor to inform you that I had a visit yesterday from Mr. Frandin when he stated that he had transmitted the quoted extract from the Korean code against teachers of the Christian religion to his government, with the suggestion that it should consult with the other Treaty Powers with a view to concerted measures for the abolition of these penalties and for the insertion in the treaties of a clause authorizing the free practice and preaching of Christianity.

This was in the course of a conversation upon an outrage a few weeks ago upon a priest at Kamsan, a town in the Southwest; not far from Taku where the affair of Perè Robert occurred in 1890. The Missionary was passing through Kamsan during a fair and was pulled off his horse and severely beaten by the mob. The district is well known to be a bad one, by far the worst in Korea, and Mr. Frandin was very bitter in his denunciation of the want of common discretion in the missionary in passing through the town on such an occasion and in stopping to reply to the insults of the crowd.

He said many of the priests were excellent men but all were carried away by zeal for their calling. Some of them thought themselves above the magistrates and put on great airs, which were entirely out of place. He had felt compelled to ask his Government through their ambassador at Rome to instruct them to moderate their pretensions and to conduct themselves with greater prudence. It was his duty to protect them and he would and did so, but they made his task more difficult than it ought to be.

The present case was not grave. The Korean Government had given ample satisfaction (probably in obedience to threats, as was the case in 1890), and now everything was quiet.

AUGUSTINE HEARD

NO. 164   Department of State
                                        Washington, Feb. 24, 1893

Augustine Heard

Sir:

I have received your No. 357 D.S. of 10th ultimo in which you state that the Representative of France has asked you to join with him in an effort to have a law of Korea, passed about 1866, and directed against missionaries, repealed. In view of the fact that this law,—which provides for the decapitation of foreigners who teach the Christian doctrines, and other similar punishments,— is a dead letter,—you have thought it inexpedient to make the proposed attempt; and your view seems to be discreet. The Department's previous dispatches—No. 71 of June 15, 1888, and No. 95 of May 19, 1891, may be consulted in this relation.

The absence of treaty-immunities for the propagandists of an alien faith and the doubtfulness of the extent to which favored-nation treatment may be invoked under the Franco-Korean Treaty, for the extension of the missionary work of Americans, are additional reasons for not provoking a distinct issue, which,—although it is not for a moment supposable that it could lead to the revival of the edict in question, might lead to curtailment or formal regulation of existing privileges as respects teaching and worship.

The fullest liberty in those regards is to be encouraged and developed, as much by the friendly attitude of this Government in abstaining from aggressive controversy, as by the conduct of the missionaries themselves, in adapting their labors to the needs of the primitive communities in which they dwell, and winning the respect and confidence of the Korean people, by avoiding conflict with traditional prejudices against strangers and demonstrating the conciliatory and benevolent character of their endeavors.

WILLIAM F. WHARTON

NO. 169
Department of State
Washington, Apr. 1, 1893

Augustine Heard

Sir:

Your No. 368 of 10th February, 1893, in which you refer to the provisions of a Korean law of 1866, or thereabout, —mentioned more specifically in your No. 357 of 10th January last,— as declaring decapitation the penalty for dissemination of Christian tenets by foreigners, is received.

Although this provision is apparently a dead letter, the French Representative, out of abundant caution, has made its terms Known to his Government, you say, and suggested consultation with other Treaty Powers, in order to concert "measures for the abolition of these penalties and for the insertion in the treaties of a clause authorizing the practice and preaching of Christianity."

The general views of this Department on the subject are stated in Instruction No. 164 of Feb. 24, 1893, and, —unless some new developments should present the matter in a more pressing phase,— meet the suggestion of Mr. Frandin touching the expediency of moving in concert for a formal repeal of the obsolete law against aliens who teach Christian doctrines.

W. A. GRESHAM

NO. 389 Legation of the United States
Seoul, Korea, April 7, 1893

Secretary of State

Sir:

I have the honor to acknowledge the receipt of your No. 164, Febry 24, with regard to a proposed effort to procure the repeal of an existing law against missionaries in Korea. No steps have been taken in the matter since my No. 365, Feby 10, and in view of recent occurrences detailed in my despatches Nos. 381, 382, & 383, relating to the Tong Hâk, it is improbable that anything will be attempted at present. If there should be, I shall be governed by the instructions before me.

AUGUSTINE HEARD

NO. 468   *Confidential*   Legation of the United States
Seoul Korea Oct. 6, 1893

Secretary of State

Sir:

I have the honor to inform you that it is now formally announced that His Majesty will make his first visit to this Foreign Settlement on November 11th.

His ostensible reason is to make a visit of ceremony to a burial place in front of the British Consulate General, where, 150 years ago, a royal concubine was buried; the remains were afterward taken outside the walls but the place is still kept up, and recently extensive new buildings have been erected there.

The real reasons for this visit are, the gratification of a desire to see the Foreign Settlement with its new modern houses; to cause the roads to be cleaned up and broadened so that we may have better approaches, and to accustom the people to the presence of His Majesty at this quarter. In case of serious trouble I am quite sure the King will come to this temple to gain the protection of foreigners, for he recently asked me to induce American missionaries to live all around this place. He knows that we will protect our own people.

H. N. ALLEN

Korean Foreign Office
Seoul, August 22, 1895

John M. B. Sill

Sir:

I have the honor to say that my Government is deeply grateful to Dr. H. G. Underwood and his friends who have spent a great deal of money for medicines and labor in the management of cholera, resulting in the cure of many sick people. I trust Your Excellency will kindly convey an expression of thanks to them on behalf of my Government.

KIM YUN-SIK

4.

BRITISH INTERESTS

Secretary of State

Sir:

The question of the evacuation of Port Hamilton by Great Britain, or as it is frequently called, its cession to China, has of late taken some definite form, and it is generally believed in China, Japan, and Korea that the present occupation of the island will shortly cease.

It has been frequently stated of late in the english press, with what authority I know not, that England would ceade Port Hamilton to China if that power would guarantee its neutrality. My knowledge of the policy adopted by Great Britain in China in regard to Korea, tends to convince me that, as a matter of fact, Great Britain would be pleased to dispose of the question in this manner. But on the other hand, it is equally well known that Japan cannot admit of a new settlement of the question which would give China a naval station on her very coast, or which, admitting that the latter power did not make a permanent establishment on the island, would give it a vantage ground in case of warlike operations against Japan. I gather from a recent number of the Japanese newspaper that the mere rumor of such a settlement has been deemed sufficient ground for the Japanese government to order the immediate return to Japan of General Saigo, the Minister of the Navy, who is now on a voyage around the world.

This mode of settlement appears therefore impracticable, and a simple evacuation of the islands by Great Britain and their return to Korea either directly or through China, is the solution which is naturally forced upon us as the only feasible one.

The Korean Government, which is well aware of the present state of the question, has not, however, any definite plan as to the course it will pursue in the event of the evacuation of Port Hamilton. It is its intention to send an official to reside there, but it feels that his presence or even that of a body of Korean troops cannot guarantee the future inviolability of the islands, and that the reoccupation of the group by some power, in case it deems it necessary, is a step beyond its power to prevent.

China on its side, while it cannot, as I have stated, occupy the islands without gravely offending Japan, fears, in case they are abandoned, their occupation by some power which would constitute a grave menace against its northern coast.

The question is therefore reduced to this, Great Britain for reasons of her own will no longer hold the islands, China cannot take them and Korea would not be able to Keep them.

There appears another solution to the question which would, I think, unquestionably meet not only with the consent but with the approval of all the powers interested in the question, and that is, as soon as the group is returned to Korea, for that power to lease it to a power at once friendly and entirely disinterested in the questions which make occupation by China, Great Britain, Japan or Korea impossible.

The attention of the Department of State and of the Navy has frequently been called to the desirability of the United States leasing Port Hamilton as a coaling station for our fleet on this station, and the Secretary of the Navy in his Annual Report for 1884 (P.41) strongly recommended such a measure.

I believe that the Korean Government could without much difficulty be prevailed upon to lease these islands for the purpose above mentioned for any length of time which might be thought advisable, and thus dispose of a most troublesome question in a dignified and advantageous way. $6,000 a year (the amount which our Government has until recently paid for the naval depot at Nagasaki) would be gladly accepted by Korea.

I have deemed it my duty to submit the above suggestions to your consideration, and I have no doubt that the negotiations could be successfully conducted to this end should the plan meet with your approval.

W. W. ROCKHILL

NO. 50   *Confidential*   Legation of the United States
                                            Söul, January 22, 1887

Secretary of State

Sir:

I have the honor to inform you that yesterday Mr. Watters, H.B.M.'s Acting Consul General at Söul, handed to the President of the Foreign Office a despatch from Sir John Walsham, H.M.'s Minister at Peking, the substance of which is as follows: In a former despatch from this legation, it was stated that annexation was not (as Your Excellency had implied) intended when a naval force was stationed at Port Hamilton, but that the action of H.B.M.'s government was simply to guard these islands when they were exposed to seizure at a critical time. It was also stated that when the necessity of keeping guard should have passed, the temporary occupation would cease. This time would appear to have been reached, and the British forces will be withdrawn from the islands. To effect this, an agreement has been made by which the government of China guarantees the security of the islands from seizure by any other power. British forces will be withdrawn in the spring and when the evacuation takes place, Your Excellency will be informed of it by the Admiral Commanding our naval forces through the Consul General at Söul. It was my intention, adds Sir John, to visit Korea a short time ago to inform you of these facts in person, but circumstances having prevented it, I have addressed you this communication.

I have been informed from another source that the Chinese government has offered Korea three of its ships of war, manned of course with Chinese crews, to assist in protecting these islands. The Korean government has also appointed an official to reside on the islands which will also be garrisoned with troops.

It will be I think a most unfortunate circumstance if Korea is obliged to accept China's profered aid in this affair, as each step of such a nature greatly decreases what little liberty of action is left this country in its relations with China.

W. W. ROCKHILL

NO. 301   Legation of the United States
Seoul, Korea, Sept. 12, 1892

Secretary of State

Sir:

In my Consular Reports I have had occasion to draw attention to the great increase of Japanese Commerce and influence in Korea. For the past few months the course to be pursued by Japan in Korea has been discussed with much animation by the Native Japanese press, and while some argue in favor of an alliance with England, and others with Russia, the general sentiment would seem to be in favor of an aggressive, independent policy. Those in favor of this policy regard

the present minister as not sufficiently energetic and urge the appointment of a Minister Plenipotentiary, not only on account of the greater
influence, which he might directly exert, but chiefly because such an
appointment would be regarded as a compliment to the King, and
give him a decided Diplomatic advantage over the Representatives
of other nations. I may say that His Majesty is peculiarly susceptible
to attentions of this Kind. He frequently urged Mr. Hillier and Mr.
Krien to have the grade of their posts advanced.

The American Minister has always been looked upon from his
Superiority of Rank as the Head of the Diplomatic Body in Seoul, the
appointment of a Minister Plenipotentiary would naturally deprive
him of that position. The Doyen is indicated either by Superiority
of rank, or, where the rank is the same, by priority of recognition. In
the present case the Japanese minister is of the same rank as myself,
minister resident (recently created) but came after me. He would
take precedence of my successor.

I have been asked by one of my Colleagues what I should do if a
Minister Plenipotentiary were named by Japan. The inquiry was
prompted by the report that when Japan appointed, or proposed to
appoint, some years ago, an Ambassador to China, the other ministers
at Peking, none of them being of that rank, decided to retain their
old doyen, giving as a reason that they could not be represented by
a person who did not speak English.

I replied that I saw no reason why I should retain the position in
the case supposed. A Minister Plenipotentiary would outrank me,
and, coming from a regular Treaty Power, should, it seemed to me,
be rightfully considered as Doyen of the Corps. And, unless I am
otherwise instructed by you, I propose to act in this sense.

Other nations also have shown an mercenary interest in Korea. The
English Consul General has succeeded finally, aided by a letter from
Lord Salisbury to the President of the Foreign Office, in being received in audience of His Majesty at the same time as Diplomatic
Representatives, when presenting their congratulations on New Year's
day and on like occasions. Previously he had been received as Consul
with Mr. Krien the Consul for Germany and this had always been a
subject of vexation to him. Mr. Hillier is subordinate to the English
Minister at Peking, and has therefore been obliged to yield precedence
to the French Commissaire, who, though of Consular rank, claims that
his post is diplomatic, & independent. The building of the new Consulate General a fine, large European structure of two stories, is a
guarantee of permanent interest in the country, and it was especially

gratifying to the King, who made many inquiries about it, and asked for photographs during its progress.

The arrival of Bishop Coope [?] with his corps of missionaries in the summer of 1890 was looked on by many as possessing a political significance, and their number has been considerably increased by subsequent arrivals. Five or six others are shortly expected. They have churches in Chemulpo & Seoul; they have a hospital at Chemulpo, and Dr. Wiles, who is attached to the mission,—an excellent man—would have been named Head of the Royal Hospital in Seoul last year, if I had not taken steps to prevent it. Allusion was made to this circumstance in my No. 197, Aug. 31, 1891. This hospital was originally established by Dr. Allen, & has always been in American hands.

Some of the larger of the English men of war have recently visited Chemulpo—in April last the "Pallas" of 2575 tons & 7500 Horse Power & previously the "Severn" of 4050 tons & 6000 H.P. When Capt. Hall & some of his officers were received by the King. Before the arrival of the "Severn", we had only at rare intervals an occasional gunboat. The Admiral himself is expected on the 25th instant.

The German Admiral whom I saw in Chefoo last month told me he should be here in October. His flagship the "Leipsie", 4060 tons, has already been in these waters,—many years ago. The "Alexandrine" of his squadron, a fine modern cruiser of about 2000 tons has just left. Capt. Wm. Franzius was received by His Majesty.

I am informed that the French Admiral will visit Chemulpo & Seoul in a month or two.

Shortly after Admiral Harmony succeeded Admiral Belknap on this station I invited him to pay me a visit, but he was unable to do so at that time. I am ignorant of his present intentions.

The new Russian Legation is now finished, and presents a commanding appearance. The entertainment was given there on the 11th Instant, H. M. the Emperor's ~~birthday~~ name day.

AUGUSTINE HEARD

Secretary of State

Sir:

I have the honor to inform you that I had a conversation with Mr. Hillier yesterday afternoon, after mailing my No. 372, with reference to the creation of a navy Department for Korea. He declared that the whole thing was absurd; the Koreans had no money or means to make a navy and no English instructor had been engaged. It was true that one had been applied for, and he had passed on the application with his comments. But he did not believe that an English officer would come out because, in the first place, the whole thing was a farce, and in the next the English Government would not permit an officer to come here and wait a year or two for his pay, and be put off with a few copper cash from time to time. It was only one of those ideas of the King, which would cost him a lot of money, and finally be given up in disgust like so many others.

I entirely agree with Mr. Hillier that the whole scheme is absurd, and for that reason did not report it when it was mentioned to me some weeks ago; for when a decree is inserted in the Official Gazette and the President of the Foreign Office himself assures me that an English Instructor has been engaged, it assumes a different aspect.

I think it very likely that Mr. Hillier is sincere in the opinion he expresses, and yet he may not be unwilling to have a hand in anything which the King happens for the moment to favor. It will be very easy with the experience before him of the fate of our Instructors to make his contracts in a way that will hold; and the Chief Commissioner of Customs in Korea is an Englishman who will find no difficulty in retaining money enough for English purposes. The Chinese probably favor it, as they have lent the money recently to buy two ships, and I am inclined to think that an attempt will be made to carry out the scheme.

As pointed out in my No. 301, September 12, there has been of late a decided increase of interest in Korea on the part of England. Mr. O'Conner is a very different man from Sir John Walsham, and has a reputation for being pushing and energetic, which he will try to justify. He is to be here in May, and I have little doubt the Admiral will come with him, when there will be a great display and an advance in the English position. The recent attentions of the fleet have been very grateful to the King, and he will attach much importance to the visit. "There is more joy in heaven over one sinner that repenteth than over ninety and nine that went not astray." And I fear that America being the "constant friend" will lose by the comparison.

His Majesty is much disappointed that so little has been seen of the American navy in these waters the last two years.

I would request that the latter part of my No. 372 from "In view of these circumstances", where I speak of Col. Nienstead, to the end, with the exception of the few lines regarding Mr. Allen may be considered as confidential and so marked.

Augustine Heard

Telegram Seoul
July 17, 1894

Gresham

    Washington

British Consul reports unprovoked outrageous personal violence on public street to him, wife, Secretary of Legation, and friend, by Japanese soldiers. Has ordered British navy guard.

Sill

5.

RUSSIAN CONCESSIONS

Legation of the United States
                                   Söul, Korea, September 14th 1888

Secretary of State

Sir:

As you are already aware negotiations have been pending for more than two years hitherto between the governments of Russia and Korea with reference to the establishment of a trading post on their common frontier.

I have now the honor to inform you that they were brought to a conclusion on the 20th ultimo by the signing of a treaty by the Honorable C. Waeber, H.I.R. Majesty's Chargé d'Affaires and His Excellency Cho Pyong Sik and Honorable O. N. Denny, President and Vice President of H.K.Majesty's Foreign and Home Offices respectively acting by special appointment on behalf of their respective governments. As yet I am not able to communicate to you a copy of the treaty but will do so as early as it can be obtained.

From the memoranda Kindly furnished to me by Hon. Mr. Waeber, however, I am able to report the following is the principal features, viz:— The town of Kiong Hong situated on the Tumen river about fourteen miles from its mouth in Korea is opened for trade between the two countries with privileges granted to Russian subjects of purchase and tenure of land, erection of houses, and exercise of religion similar to those provided in the treaties of Russia and Great Britain with Korea, to obtain at the open ports.

Russia may be represented at Kiong Hong by a Consul or a Vice Consul who after due appointment by the Russian Govt and being authorized by the Korean Government may exercise their official functions. A frontier commissioner or other Russian official may temporarily perform consular duties with the consent first obtained of the Korean Government.

Diplomatic and consular officers and frontier officials shall have unrestricted privilege of travel under passport, and shall be entitled to the benefits of whatsoever postal institutions may exist in Korea hereafter, and in cases of necessity may send correspondence and papers to all parts of the Korean dominion by courier of Russian or any other nationality, who shall have safe-conduct from the Korean authorities, and be allowed to travel without hindrance.

A municipality may be organized at Kiong Hong.

The Korean Government shall set apart at a distance of not more than five li (about one and two thirds English miles) from Kiong Hong suitable ground for the pasturage of live stock belonging to Russian subjects, whether for uses of burden or food.

Personal baggage, domestic birds, agricultural implements gold and silver "refined", gold and silver coins, scientific instruments books maps and charts, fruit vegetables plants trees and shrubs, fire models of inventions
engines ∧ fish, packing bags and matting shall be allowed to enter at Kyong Hong free of duty. All other articles whether imported or exported to pay a tax of five per cent ad valorem to the Korean Government.

The treaty is to remain in force for five years and thereafter until notice having been given by either of the High Contracting Powers changes have been made by agreement, or the treaty abrogated.

HUGH A. DINSMORE

NO. 168   *Confidential*   Legation of the United States
                                         Seoul Corea June 3, 1891

Secretary of State

Sir:

I have the honor to inform you, that in order to insure the autonomy of Corea, His Majesty is desirous of forming a compact between the Great Powers interested, something like that which they are told prevents Switzerland from being divided.

It is thought that Russia, Japan and the United States, could be easily induced to take the lead in joining this combination, and that Italy, France, Germany, England and China might then be induced to join it. When approached on the subject however, I referred them to their advisers Messrs le Gendre and Greathouse.

I have learned that Mr. Kim Ka Chin, referred to in my No. 162, of May 18, who is now enroute for Japan, overland, to negotiate the Austrian treaty, but whose appointment has not yet been duly announced in the Gazette, has been instructed to confer with the Japanese Government on the subject of the above mentioned compact. And I am also informed that Gen'l le Gendre has the matter in hand though as yet the negotiations must necessarily be kept very secret.

In this connection perhaps I should state that the recent attack upon the Czarenitch in Japan caused great excitement here, and a war was feared between Russia and Japan, in which Corea would be the probable battle ground. Many people are said to have left the city in consequence of this alarm.

Trouble is also feared with China, who is reported to be massing troops on the Northern Frontier. The anxiety in this case is so great that His Majesty has caused a new general-ship to be created, to which General Min Yung-Chun, late Minister to Japan, has been appointed, with especial control of the Royal Retreat—Pouk Han—a few miles north of this city, a full description of which may be found in Mr. Foulks No. 229 of Oct. 10, 1884. This place is being refitted and re-garrisoned, while I also am told, on what may be considered reliable authority, that an order for arms amounting to some $60,000 has been sent to New York.

H. N. ALLEN

NO. 364   *Confidential*   Legation of the United States
                                    Seoul, Korea, February 10th 1893

Secretary of State

Sir:

I have the honor to inform you that Mr. Dmitrevsky called on me yesterday morning, and after having asked if I had any news for him, said that he had a piece of news for me. On the steamer which arrived two days ago he had received a letter from his colleague in Peking stating that he had been informed semi-officially that the Japanese had sollicited [sic] the Chinese Government to unite with them in a policy which should drive all Western foreigners out of Korea, and keep it for themselves; the Chinese had refused and as a mark of friendship had informed the Russian Minister. I asked if the Japanese supposed for a moment they could be successful in any such scheme, and Mr. Dmitrevsky replied: "They and more particularly Mr. Oishi are mad with dread and hatred of Russia. This story as it comes now, really originates with me. When Mr. Oishi visited Korea last year he had an interview with the Tai-Won-Kun and an extraordinary conversation upon this subject, which was reported to me. I transmitted it to Peking with the request that it should be borne in mind and looked into. Many of the very expressions said to have been used by Mr. Oishi have come back to me through the Chinese now. The report to me was wonderfully exact."

I said; "You are lucky to be so well served'; and he went on: "The Chinese do not like the Japanese you know, and they have lost all fear of us;" at which I laughed, and he continued, "But, I assure you, we have not the slightest intention to seize any part of Korea. We are perfectly satisfied as we are." "Yes," I replied "no doubt you are at present; but there is what we call 'manifest destiny', and you must come south." "Oh no! If we wanted to do that we should not have spent thousands of dollars on making Vladivostock a first-class fortified port, and we have an ice-breaking steamer to keep it open all winter." "Bah," said I, "Vladivostock is very well in its way and it can't put off taking care of it for an unknown and uncertain future. But do you mean to tell me if Russia saw a suitable opportunity one of these days she would not swoop down on the north of Korea? She wants southern harbors in the East as well as in the West." To which of course he smilingly demurred.

I may say that I have been told on very good authority that Russia has offered $3,000,000 for the North-east province, and been refused. She would give much more. Mr. Dmitrevsky is now occupied in translating, from the Japanese, a book lately published, on Korea, by Mr. Oishi, in which he gives freely his opinion on leading men. According to him the Tai-Won-Kun is the only statesman in the country. Min Yong Chun, the royal favorite and a most powerful noble, is stupid and ignorant. Mr. Dmitrevsky has promised to show me his notes. They should be interesting as emanating from an actual minister, and if possible I will send you a copy.

AUGUSTINE HEARD

6.

THE JAPANESE COMPETITION FOR ASCENDANCY

NO. 436   Legation of the United States
                        Seoul, Korea, August 21, 1893

Secretary of State

Sir:

Referring to my confidential despatch No. 428 D. S. July 29th relative to the rumored change in Japan's policy towards this country, I
have the honor to inform you that I am in receipt of a note on this
subject from Mr. Edwin Dun, United States Minister to Japan, in
which he says: "I attach no special significance to this appointment
[the appointment of Mr. Otori to represent Japan in both China and
Korea] further than the fact that Mr. Otori's long residence in China
and Knowledge of the complicated political relations existing between
that Government, Korea and Japan fit him peculiarly, to represent
Japan, at this time in Korea.

"I am inclined to believe that Japan does recognize China's over-
shadowing influence, and even rights, in connection with Korean
affairs, but I doubt very much her recognition of China's Sovereignty
—tacitly or otherwise in that Country.

"That there may be an understanding between Japan and China to
unite in opposing the encroachments of any other Power upon Korean
territory is very possible."

A strong impression still prevails in this capital that some arrangement has been made by Japan and China, with perhaps the advice
and assistance of Great Britain in regard to policy to be hereafter
pursued in their dealings with Korea.

The Korean Government is devoid of all positive information as are
the Foreign Representatives, is naturally very much exercised by the
rumors afloat, and awaits with interest the arrival of Mr. Otori that
it may ascertain the nature of his credentials and whether or not he
intends to reside for any length of time in Seoul.

            l
The conf∧icting nature of the articles in the Japanese press would
indicate great reticence on the part of the Government of Japan with
reference to the appointment of Mr. Otori in a dual capacity.

                                JOSEPH R. HEROD

NO. 12   Legation of the United States
                                          Seoul Korea June 1, 1894

Secretary of State

Sir:

I have the honor to inform you that Mr. C. Waeber, Russian Chargé D'Affaires at this Capital, has been ordered to Peking, to act as Chargé D'Affaires there during the absence on leave of the Minister. Mr. Waeber leaves tomorrow. The Secretary will be in Charge of the Legation.

Also Mr. K. K. Otori, Envoy Extraordinary and Minister PleniPotentiary, to China and Korea, has left for his post in Peking, going by way of Japan, where he will stop for a short vacation. The Japanese Legation here is also in charge of the Secretary.

The departure of Mr. Otori—the ranking Diplomatic Official, leaves me in the position of Diplomatic Dean.

JOHN M. B. SILL

NO. 25   Department of State
                                          Washington, August 30, 1894

John M. B. Sill

Sir:

Your despatches Nos. 32 and 33 of the 18th and 24th ultimo respectively, have been received.

It is regretted that you should have joined with other diplomatic agents at Seoul in bringing to the attention of the representatives of their respective governments at Tokio the reported collision of the British Chargé D'Affaires with certain Japanese soldiers. Although the motive of this joint action may have been, as averred, a desire to prevent any similar incivility being shown by Japanese authorities in Korea to other members of the foreign diplomatic body there, your communication was in fact an endorsement of the truth of Mr. Gardner's statements against those of the Japanese commander.

Mr. Gardner being not only a British subject, but the accredited British agent in Korea, the question of the nature and degree of the remonstrance to be made to the Japanese Government and the remedy to be sought could properly be left to the determination of his own government.

Mr. Dun has transmitted hither copies of your letter to him of July 19th and his reply of July 27th, and he has been informed that his course in declining to make representations to the Japanese Government in regard to Mr. Gardner's complaint, meets with the Department's approval.

W. Q. GRESHAM

NO. 65   Legation of the United States
                                         Seoul, Korea, Nov. 2, 1894

Secretary of State

Sir:

I have the honor to inform you that Mr. Otori, H.I.J.M.'s Minister Plenipotentiary and Envoy Extraordinary, at this place, has been relieved by Count Inouye, who arrived on the 27th ultimo, in the same capacity. He is attended by Mr. S. Saito who has for a long time been associated with him as counsellor.

It was something of a surprise that Count Inouye should resign his cabinet portfolio to come to Korea as Minister. I find that he is disposed to be especially friendly toward this Legation, and he is apparently determined to pursue quite a different policy from that of his predecessor. Mr. Otori made the mistake of ignoring and humiliating Their Majesties and of depending too much upon the Ex-Regent—The Tai Won Khun—who at once began his old practice of intrigue and double dealing. Count Inouye is inclined to make the most of the King and Queen and thereby conciliate the people and secure the practical adoption of Japans measures.

JOHN M. B. SILL

NO. 68   Legation of the United States
                                         Seoul Korea Dec. 4, 1894

Secretary of State

Sir:

Referring to my despatch No. 65 of November 2, I have the honor to inform you that since the date of that despatch, though the political situation has grown worse by insensible degrees, there has been little to report. News of Japanese victories in the North and Northwest reach you as soon or sooner than they reach me, and it would be idle for me to report them.

In the despatch above cited, I noted the apparent friendliness of Count Inouye, the newly arrived Japanese Minister, towards this Legation, and the indications of his disposition to adopt a more humane and conciliatory policy; to put it out of the power of the Kings father—the Ex Regent—to do mischief; to make much of His Majesty instead of ignoring and humiliating him, and thus to bring a hostile people into line under the proposed reforms. All this was most encouraging, and friends of Korea here were rejoiced in the view of the better prospects of this unhappy kingdom.

I am sorry to be compelled to report that, so far, the results are not by any means commensurate with these expectations. Count Inouye seems to have grown impatient of delays, not appreciating the greatness of the task to which he has put his hand. He seems not to have won the confidence of His Majesty though both he and the Queen have been both ready and willing to trust him. He has apparently fallen off from the Koreans who could and would help him, and brought around himself as counsellors and advisers, a clique whom His Majesty has good reasons to fear and distrust. I know that he holds evidence of the bad faith and the treachery of the old Tai Won Khun—Ex Regent—and yet he still allows him and his favorites to dominate the situation and check and terrorize the King. There is in Korea a personal loyalty to His Majesty through which Count Inouye might in a great degree overcome the traditional and bitter hatred of the Korean people for the Japanese, and there is no other means in sight for the establishment of this necessary condition of reform. But he is at present doing nothing to secure the confidence of the King or to make him strong before his people.

Meanwhile the whole Kingdom is in disorder and most of it in open revolt. The insurrectionists grow stronger and bolder both here and in the provinces. The Korean factions in Seoul are at hot war with one another. One high official has been assassinated; there are attempts at more assassinations and the air is full of threats of violence. The power of Japan seems insufficient to quell the insurrection or to calm the factional warfare, possibly they may prefer it should continue as it is till they may have ample excuse for taking a more pronounced stand here, than that indicated in their previously announced intentions to establish Korean independence. Of course the revenues of the Government are almost entirely cut off by the state of revolt.

Unless Count Inouye can show himself stronger and wiser than his actions for the past fortnight show him to be, there is good prospect of serious trouble here. The situation is today more complicated and the outlook less favorable than at any time since I have been in Korea.

JOHN M. B. SILL

NO. 78 Legation of the United States
Seoul Korea Jan. 4, 1895

Secretary of State

Sir:

I have the honor to inform you that it is reported here on good authority, that the Japanese Minister here has advised this Government to discontinue its Legation in Washington and have the Japanese Minister at Washington attend to Korean affairs. As his suggestions are pretty promptly acted upon there is not much doubt that the Korean Legation property at Washington will be sold; the Representative recalled and Korean matters entrusted to the Japanese Legation.

I am privately informed from the King that this is very distasteful to him. He even wished to know if the American Government might not interfere to prevent the execution of this plan.

JOHN M. B. SILL

Telegram Seoul
Jany 9, 1895

Gresham

Washington

Japanese are insisting on the recall of the Korean Minister Washington. Korean affairs to be intrusted to Japanese Minister. King displeased—dislikes to lose this chief mark of his independence.

SILL

NO. 115   Legation of the United States
Seoul Korea May 25, 1895

Sir:

Referring to my No. 111, May 11, I now have the honor to enclose the reply of the Minister of Foreign Affairs to our joint protest against the monopoly of concessions asked for by the Japanese. It is understood that the Japanese minister aided in the drafting of this letter, which cites the precedent set by the Chinese, in enlarging their Settlement at Chemulpo, by taking in a large area adjoining the General Foreign Settlement, as well as the right to such enlargement of the Japanese Settlement accorded by Japan's treaty with Korea. The Foreign Minister agrees to consult with the Foreign Representatives regarding railroad and similar concessions.

The Japanese do not seem to be very anxious at present to embark upon any large schemes involving the expenditure of a great amount of capital here. They have surveyed a railroad between Seoul and Chemulpo, but seem to be taking no steps towards building the road.

All foreigners would like to see such a road built, and I believe no one opposes the Japanese in this scheme. We do not however, wish them to obtain a concession for all railroads in Korea for a period of 50 years as their intention was reported.

The course pursued by Count Inouye has not improved the sentiment of the Koreans toward the Japanese. He has alienated the very men placed in power by his influence. Pak, the ex-refugee, for instance, owes his position as acting Prime Minister; Minister of the Interior, and practical Dictator, to Count Inouye who forced him upon this Government. Pak, however, has drawn to himself a strong party consisting of the progressive young officials who now occupy the Chief Governmental offices. This party seems to have the best interests of Korea at heart, and is now openly opposing the encroachments of the Japanese, who have in turn formed an alliance with the conservative party headed by the Prime Minister now under suspension —he having in a hasty moment presented his resignation to His Majesty, thinking in this way to coerce the Government into favoring himself and his party.

The Japanese Minister, three months ago, was anxious to get rid of this Prime Minister and his associates and to that end he had at one time arranged that the whole cabinet should resign, see my No. 94, Mch 1. Now, however, Count Inouye is doing all he can to have this party retained in power. All along the Japanese have been constantly changing from one party to another, as though desirous of encouraging intrigue by pitting one party against another.

A very surprising feature of the present case is that the Russian Representative is privately reported, on good authority, as using his influence to have this same party retained in power. It is the only instance I know of here, where the Russian and Japanese interests have united.

JOHN M. B. SILL

NO. 120   Legation of the United States
                                  Seoul Korea June 7, 1895

Secretary of State

Sir:

Referring to my No. 115, May 25, pages 5 & 6, I now have the honor to inform you that the resignation of Prime Minister Kim Honk Gip, was accepted and the place was given to Pak Chung Yang, former Minister to the United States, and late Minister of Education, Ye Wan Yong, at one time Chargé d'Affaires at Washington and lately Vice Minister of Foreign Affairs was made Minister of Education.

This progressive party induced the King to proclaim yesterday a National Holiday, and hereafter this date the 14th of the 5th moon, will be kept as a holiday. The day was proclaimed in celebration of Korean Independence—an idea suggested, it is understood, by the Japanese. The Russian Representative at once declared that he could not in any way admit that Korea had not been independent up to this date, as his Government had made treaties with this Government as an Independent State, and he had been here for years, under that declaration. We were also privately informed that this position was the one His Majesty wished us to assume.

It was arranged that a great banquet should be held at an unoccupied Palace on yesterday and we were invited "to celebrate Korean Independence." I united with my colleagues in representing to the Korean Government that we could not accept the invitations worded in that manner, giving our reasons as above. Thereupon our invitations were changed, at our suggestion, to read, "To celebrate the establishment of peace, and the renunciation by China of any claims making against the Sovereignty of Korea."

The Foreign Representatives were all present as well as the majority of the foreign residents. Before partaking of the banquet a message from the King was read, see enclosed copy.

Pak Yong Hyo, the ex-refugee, who really controls Korean affairs, had arranged a state dinner to be held the day before the banquet in honor of Count Inouye, the Japanese minister, who was on that day to take his leave of the King, as he had been recalled by telegraph, by his Emperor. This dinner was also suggested by the Japanese, and as Pak has not been in harmony with Count Inouye of late, he induced the King to consent to sit down at dinner with his cabinet and, Count Inouye,—a thing that has never been done by a Korean ruler before.

When Pak however learned that the other ministers would take offense at being asked to the general banquet and not to the state dinner, he arranged that instead of a dinner the King should sit down at a table with himself and Count Inouye only, and simply have some wine and cake. This Inouye declined and at his audience he denounced Pak to the King as a dangerous man.

This incident is of value in showing that Pak, who was enabled to become practically the ruler of Korea, by Japanese insistance [sic], is a Korean at heart and has really broken with his late supporters —the Japanese.

JOHN M. B. SILL

NO. 123   Legation of the United States
                                            Seoul, Korea, July 9, 1895

Secretary of State

Sir:

I have the honor to inform you that I have telegraphed you today as per reading herewith, enclosure.

The "Dictator Pak" referred to in this message you will recognize, from reading my despatches, as the Ex refugee, and assassin of the *emeute* of 1884, who was brought here last year by the Japanese and forced into one of the highest Governmental positions. So that with the backing of the victorious Japanese he became practically dictator of Korean political affairs. Please see my despatches numbers, 74, Dec. 18, and 94 incls. 1.

By reference to my despatches numbered 107, April 17; 115, May 25, and 120, June 7, you will see how Pak began to break from the

Japanese until the rupture was so complete that Count Inouye denounced him to the King.

Of course Pak had no following in the country at large. He had drawn about him a party of bright young men, many of whom had been abroad, and through them he tried to make himself agreeable to the Foreign Representatives. Recently however, Mr. Waeber, the Russian Representative, denounced him at the Japanese Legation in my presence. He had gone there to call upon another matter entirely, and I did not expect Pak's name to be mentioned and resented it, stating that I had not come there to discuss Pak's affairs. This incident however was made much use of by the Japanese, who, having lost control over Pak, were anxious, at any cost, to get rid of him.

When they made known, with their own version, Mr. Waeber's action in my presence, it alarmed Pak greatly. Indeed I am informed by his friends that he was intensely disturbed. He probably then decided that he had made a grievous mistake in breaking from the Japanese, and I was soon after informed (on the 5th instant) from the Palace, that he (Pak) had gone secretly to Mr. Sugimura, the Japanese Chargé d'Affaires, and endeavored to make his peace with his former friends, offering or suggesting to assassinate the Queen, whom the Japanese dislike intensely.

This supposed plot was laid bare to the former Prime Minister and his followers, by an irresponsible Japanese who is said to have the confidence of Mr. Sugimura. This ex Prime Minister and his followers are the so-called Japanese Party, and have mostly been deprived of office by Pak. They of course conveyed this news at once to His Majesty and great excitement ensued.

After some days delay and consideration, on the 6th or the morning of the 7th, the King issued a decree (see copy enclosed) denouncing Pak as a traitor and ordering his arrest.

Pak was privately informed of this action and went direct to the Japanese Legation.

Japan is greatly divided as to public opinion on Korean matters, and Pak has a large following among influential Japanese. Moreover he was undoubtedly promised protection when brought here by the Japanese. Much as they desire to get rid of him therefore they could not allow him to suffer bodily harm. He was sent to the river under an escort of 8 Japanese armed soldiers, who were met by a large body of Korean policemen, sent unarmed, to the city gate to arrest Pak as he passed through. The native policemen did not dare attack the Japanese and Pak with three unimportant followers reached the river in safety, where a Japanese steam launch was waiting for them and took them direct to Chemulpo.

The sudden arrival at Chemulpo from Japan, of the Japanese Gunboat Masashi-Kan at 7 A.M. Monday is reported, and it is supposed that these refugees went on board this vessel which was doubtless acting under orders from home, since, at once upon their arrival an armed guard had been landed, showing that they expected some disturbance.

Naturally great excitement was caused in this city by these occurrences. The members of Pak's party, —often called the "American party" because a number of them had been in America, feared for their lives.

His Majesty however stated in his decree that these other people would not be molested, and all through this trying ordeal he has shown a magnanimous spirit. I am informed by one of his intimate friends that he is glad Pak got away, as there will now be no necessity of killing him; while the country is effectually rid of him since the Japanese will hardly venture to bring him back again.

I understand that Pak had taken care to place a large sum of money to his credit in the bank. He had great opportunities to make money as he had the Government patronage at his disposal. I also hear that the King does not wish him prevented from drawing this deposit, wishing to be well rid of him and his belongings.

I enclose a copy of the official statement regarding Pak's crime. It does not enter into details.

I at once communicated with Captain Craig of the U.S.S. "Concord" at Chemulpo. I do not as yet deem it necessary to summon a guard, as all seems fairly quiet at present.

JOHN M. B. SILL

NO. 83　　　　　　　　　　　　　　　　　Department of State
　　　　　　　　　　　　　　　　　　Washington, June 21, 1895

John M. B. Sill

Sir:

I have received your despatch No. 111 of May 11, 1895 diplomatic series, wherewith you enclose a copy of a joint note addressed by your European colleagues to the Korean Minister for Foreign Affairs, protesting against the attempts of the Japanese to secure a monopoly on all concessions from the Korean Government contrary to the spirit of the "most favored nation clause" of existing treaties. You add that this step was taken largely for the sake of affording that Government a necessary backing and to enable it the better to resist the precipitate action which was being forced upon it, with all possible vigor, by the Japanese Minister and the advisers placed by him in the Korean Government. It is intimated by you that the note and the subsequent call on the Russian representative and yourself upon the Minister of Foreign Affairs, who with the other Korean officials greatly appreciated your action, produced the desired result, "since it gave them," you say "a means of answering in the negative the onerous demands of their oppressors."

It would have been manifestly at variance with your enjoined attitude of absolute neutrality had your representations been understood by the Koreans or been permitted by you to be understood as backing them up in resisting what you are pleased to call "the onerous demands of their oppressors." In all its dealings with this Government in connection with the late war, Japan has frankly and freely disclaimed all imputation of actual or ulterior designs of conquest over Korea, and declared as its purpose the independence of Korea and the furtherance of reforms in the Korean domestic administration. Furthermore, Article I of the Treaty of July 25, 1894, between Japan and Korea, declared that instrument to be an agreement "to strongly establish the independence of Korea, as well as to fulfill the privileges and immunities which are enjoyed by both countries."

The external relations of Korea, as determined by treaties could not be effected thereby and it is not to be assumed that the responsible agency of Japan in Korea were being used or about to be used to invade the conventional favored nation rights of the powers having treaties with Korea. It is an established principle that even successful war does not annul existing treaties unless actual conquest be followed by territorial absorption.

Thus understood, your representations against Korea's granting any exclusive monopoly to the impairment of American rights of trade and intercourse may have been timely.

RICHARD OLNEY

NO. 87   Department of State
                                            Washington, July 9, 1895

John M. B. Sill

Sir:

I have to acknowledge the receipt of your No. 120, Diplomatic
Series, of the 7th ultimo, in regard to recent political changes in
Korea.

Your action in refusing to recognize that Korean independence
dates from the 6th of June, 1895, is approved. The position assumed
by this Government towards Korea since contracting a treaty with
it in 1882 has in no wise been affected by the recent events.
       treaty
Korea's∧independence since then has been for us an established and
accepted fact.

                                            ALVEY A. ADEE

NO. 92   Department of State
                                            Washington, July 17, 1895

John M. B. Sill

Sir:

I have to acknowledge the receipt of your No. 155, Diplomatic
series, the 25th May last, enclosing the reply of the Korean Minister
for Foreign Affairs to the joint protest of the foreign representatives
at Seoul against the monopoly of concessions asked for by Japan.

This reply (as translated) is not very explicit as to the policy the
Korean Government contemplates following in dealing with the concessions for carrying out the proposed internal improvements, but it
would appear to convey the idea that the various powers to whose
                                                              nation
representatives it was addressed will enjoy the most favored∧treat-
ment. It is hoped the Minister's note will be followed up by a more
explicit statement.

The Department's No. 83, of the 21st ultimo, will have sufficiently
instructed you on this subject of Japanese monopolies in Korea; it is
not necessary to add anything at this time.

To the enlargement of the present Japanese settlement by a further
grant of land by Korea there would not appear any objection. As the

Department understands the question, the opposition was to granting ground in a locality situated at some distance from the present treaty port, and thus placing foreign merchants already established at Chemulpo at very great inconvenience as regards shipping and possibly customs facilities with their Japanese competitors, in whose hands are the steamships plying to China and Japan.

Your cable of the 10th instant announcing the flight of Pak completes the information contained in your despatch on the recent political events in Korea.

ALVEY A. ADEE

Telegram Seoul
October 26, 1895

Olney

Washington

Japanese officials deeply implicated in murder of the Queen. Japanese Minister and officers of his legation and army have been sent to Japan. Count Inoye is coming to Seoul as special Ambassador. The King is under strict duress; his life in peril. I do not recognize decrees forced from him. Allen's conduct of affairs excellent.

SILL

Telegram Seoul, November 9, 1895

Olney

Washington

Japanese are not moving to restore status upset by themselves. The King is still in grievous peril and under duress of conspirators. The representatives of England, Russia, France and myself are urging Japanese to protect the King and restore status by necessary temporary force.

SILL

NO. 125   Department of State
                                        Washington, November 21, 1895

John M. B. Sill

Sir:

I have received Mr. Allen's despatches No. 156, 157, 158, 159, 160, and 161, of October 10, 11, 13, 14, 17, and 19, respectively in which he relates incidents of the revolt of October 8th which resulted in the murder of the Queen of Korea, and reports his action during and after the revolt.

Mr. Allen states, in his No. 157, that the new cabinet Ministers now in power are the facile tools of the Japanese, consulting the Japanese Minister in all matters of importance, while further on he says that "the Government is in the hands of five men of notoriously bad character, who were brought to the fore by Mr. Otori a year ago last July and dropped by Count Inouye when he put aside the Tai Wen Khun."

In view of this knowledge, and other evidence collected by Mr. Allen and his colleagues which seem to prove Japanese complicity in the matter of the murder of the Queen, Mr. Allen, in company with the representatives of Russia, Great Britain, Germany and France, declined to recognize the royal decree transmitted to him by a member of the Korean Cabinet at a meeting of the diplomatic corps to which the Japanese Minister had not been invited. In his note to the Korean Foreign Office of October 12, declining to recognize the Royal Decree, he takes occasion to give his version of the outbreak of October 8th and the murder of the Queen, and requests that a thorough and formal investigation of these occurrences be made and that the instigators as well as the perpetrators of the foul crime be traced and brought to justice.

While commending Mr. Allen's desire to serve the interest of His Majesty the King of Korea, for whose person this Government entertains sincere friendship and his welfare and happiness we shall always be willing and desirous to promote, I feel constrained to call your earnest attention to the very serious misunderstanding to which the steps taken by Mr. Allen, in conjunction with some of the other foreign representatives at Seoul, might give rise. His action, in calling on the Japanese Minister, Viscount Miura, in common with the representatives of Russia, Great Britain, Germany and France, and urging upon him the necessity of taking steps for the maintenance of order in the city (as he alone had at his command a sufficient number of Japanese troops to enforce it) was quite proper and in the line of his duty, but it is a matter of regret that Viscount Miura should have been completely ignored at the subsequent meetings of the diplomatic corps to determine upon a line of action to follow towards the new Ministry.

Regret is also felt at Mr. Allen's stand in his note to the Foreign Office, for it was no part of his duty, as representative of a friendly and absolutely neutral power whose citizens residing in Korea were not by this revolt imperiled in life or property, to in any way interfere in the internal affairs of the country. While our representative in Korea may, and should whenever opportunity arises, but always acting independently of other Powers, give to the Government to which he is accredited, when his advice is sought, such friendly counsel as he, in his judgment deems most conducive to the welfare and prosperity of the sovereign and his people, it is in no wise his function, unless acting under instructions from this Department, to take action with the representatives of other treaty powers in calling the Government to account or in any way mixing himself up with the internal affairs of the country.

In view of this undoubted Japanese tendency of the present Cabinet and the exclusion of the Japanese Minister, Viscount Miura, from the meetings of the diplomatic representatives at Seoul and the evident hostile feeling toward the cabinet shown by Mr. Allen and his colleagues in not recognizing the decree emanating from it, the Department is not surprised that "the Japanese adviser to this Cabinet had telegraphed his Government that the Russian, British, and American representatives here were interfering with the execution of Japanese plans." (Mr. Allen's No. 160, of October 19th.)

The Department attaches so much importance to your strict compliance with the views laid down in the past instruction that, although their general tenor must be well known by you by former instructions either to yourself or your predecessors, a cablegram was sent to you on the 20th instant, which I confirm herewith:

Allen's despatches Nos. 156 and following received. Confine yourself strictly protection American citizens and interests. You have no concern in internal affairs. Your actions to be taken independently of other representatives unless otherwise instructed.

RICHARD OLNEY

NO. 173   Legation of the United States
                                             Seoul, Korea, Nov. 20, 1895

Secretary of State

Sir:

I have the honor to inform you that Count Inouye, Special Ambassador of the Emperor of Japan to the King of Korea, left Seoul for Tokio on the 16th instant. He gave as his reason for returning so soon, that he came here on a mission of condolence only, that he had no power to reorganize or restore this Government and that his presence in Tokio was imperatively needed in order that he might explain to the Japanese Cabinet the exact condition of affairs here. He expressed a hope that his explanations would cause a change in the attitude of his Government towards the present Korean Cabinet and lead them to consent to the temporary use of troops to protect the life, and secure the liberty, of the King. Matters here are at a standstill. His Majesty is still under strict and active duress, and the usurping Cabinet apparently very confident of Japanese support.

Three days after my return from Japan, at the request of my Western colleagues, I convened a meeting of the entire Diplomatic Body to consider the situation. At this meeting, Mr. Komura, the Japanese Minister Resident was urged especially by Messrs. Hillier, Waeber & myself to take measures for the protection of the life of the King, and for restoring order here, even if a temporary manifestation of force should be required for the accomplishment of this result. He expressed himself as in full sympathy with our views but said the Japanese Government had recently withdrawn from their Representative in Seoul all authority over the troops in the peninsula and that he thought he saw a way to accomplish the desired results peaceably and without use of force, and that, in any event, he must obtain the consent of his Government before he could move any part of the Japanese troops for this or any other purpose. He would consider all suggestions and notify his colleagues for the purpose of another conference when he had decided upon a plan of action. No such notice has been received by us.

Count Inouye, Special Ambassador, arrived on Oct. 31st. He seemed to come with the disposition and the power to act efficiently. Hearing from him that he was to have audience with His Majesty on the 5th November, for the purpose of presenting formally a letter of condolence and certain gifts from his Emperor, and that immediately after this ceremony he intended to have a frank and full conference with His Majesty, the King of Korea, and also learning from the King that he was compelled, under threats of sharing the fate of his Queen, and by the proposed unseen presence of the conspirators to make false statements concerning the responsibility for the tragedy of 8th October, Messrs. Waeber, Hillier and myself drafted a paper and on the same day, November 5, called on Count Inouye and Mr. Komura and presented it to them at the Japanese Legation. I enclose a copy of the paper and also notes of the conversation which followed. These last were written by Mr. Hillier and have been viséd by Count Inouye. It contains among other matters, Count Inouye's allusion to a proposed interview between His Excellency and Kim Hong Gip, the Korean Prime Minister, who was holding over from the Cabinet as constituted by Count Inouye's advice and insistence before his departure in September. The substance of this interview held on November 6th, Count Inouye communicated to the Foreign Representatives through Dr. Allen. Dr. Allen's notes have been viséd, corrected, and approved by Count Inouye. These I enclose.

From this interview it seemed probable that the Japanese authorities would soon take action to secure the safety and liberty of the King, but on the morning of the 8th instant, Mr. Komura came to inform me that his Gov'mt were unwilling to take any steps that might lead to even temporary occupation of the Palace without the direct approval given in advance by the Treaty Powers. He asked me to convene a meeting of my Western colleagues in order that such direct approval in advance might if possible be obtained by telegraph. I did so, but my colleagues thought they had already done enough in this matter. Messrs. Waeber, Hillier, Lefevre and myself prepared a note expressing our views, which I was instructed to present to Mr. Komura. This was done by myself, accompanied by Dr. Allen on the evening of the same day. See enclosure 3.

In view however of the urgency of the situation several of us— certainly Messrs. Waeber, Hillier and myself—telegraphed again to our respective Governments.

On the 12th Mr. Waeber, having already received a further definite answer from his Government, Mr. Hillier and myself accompanied him to the Japanese Legation, where an interview was had with Mr. Komura. See enclosure 4.

Count Inouye takes copies of all these papers to lay before the Japanese Cabinet. I wish also to enclose copies of the correspondence between the implicated Japanese Minister Viscount Miura and the Korean Foreign Office, as completing this series of papers.

It is impossible that the events which culminated on the 8th October could have been brought about without assistance coming from the Japanese Legation, but from the sudden and most unusual reluctance of the Japanese Government to put their troops in motion for the reparation of a wrong impossible of perpetration without their aid, and from the tone of the Japanese Press, notably of the "Japan Daily Mail" (see enclosure), which we have, from experience, found to be an unfailingly correct reflector of the views of the Japanese Government, we are compelled to believe that, while that Government regrets the manner in which the Queen was taken off, they are glad she is out of the way, and intend to support the usurping Cabinet.

In regard to your telegraphic instructions to me against any "intervention in the political concerns of Korea", I can only say that, guided by the mutual promise of the exercise of friendly offices, set forth in our treaty with Korea, and by the instructions I received by telegraph on June 23, 1894, "to use every possible effort for the preservation of peaceful conditions," I have been diligent in doing what I could to bring about the amelioration of a condition of affairs which to this day endangers the life of His Majesty; takes from him all semblance of freedom in speech or action, and holds the peace of this Kingdom, especially of its Capital, in imminent and constant peril. In view of the fact that the violent capture of the Palace in July, 1894, and other arbitrary acts of the Japanese in Korea have, so far as I am aware, elicited no expression of disapproval from my Govm't, I felt safe in saying to Count Inouye and Mr. Komura, that in my judgment, the proposed temporary use of force to secure safety and liberty to His Majesty would not be objected to by my Government.

I submit this full statement of my part in the present crisis and with it this expression of my desire to be checked if I have gone wrong, and with the further assurance that I shall carefully guide my conduct by the spirit of your latest instructions.

JOHN M. B. SILL

DEPARTMENT OF STATE
WASHINGTON

November 23, 1895

Mr. Horace N. Allen

My Dear Allen:

I received day before yesterday your letter of the 15th October. Please accept my sincere thanks for your kindness in securing for me the ethnological specimens therein mentioned. You can draw on me for the amount whenever you want.

The Secretary has deemed it necessary to cable twice to Mr. Sill within the last few days as he greatly feared that any action you or he might take in conjunction with the other foreign representatives at Seoul, looking towards strengthening the authority of the King or otherwise taking part in matters which do not immediately concern the interests of the United States, might be open to serious objection on account of our consistent policy, which we carry out in Asia as well as Europe and elsewhere, of abstaining from cooperating with other powers in any intervention of whatever nature. We think, and I have not the least doubt of the accuracy of the belief, that our strength lies in our independence and the knowledge all countries possess that we never seek anything beyond what our treaties clearly entitle us to, and only do what disinterested friendship naturally suggests. You know, as well as I do, that many of the other European treaty powers have not the same amount of disinterestedness and that, however innocent their actions may appear, there may be ulterior motives which they desire to forward and with which we have no concern or liking. In the present case you must see that however much or little the Japanese were concerned in the riot of October 8th, any action on your part, tending to lessen the authority of Japan in Korea, would be open to serious objection, and that the complaint which you told us had been made at Tokio against the interference of Russia, Great Britain and the United States, had some foundation in fact.

We appreciate the difficulty of your position but we must be consistent with our own traditional policy. We do not propose to "sit on you" but we do propose having the views of this Government on record in cases such as this where cooperation with two of the great European powers was not authorized by the Department. Do not take it too much to heart, however, and believe always in my affectionate regards.

W. W. ROCKHILL

NO. 81   Department of State
                                              Washington, December 17, 1895

John M. B. Sill

Sir:

I have received your despatch No. 108, Diplomatic Series, of April 29, 1895, with accompanying correspondence in relation to the arrest for alleged treason of His Highness Yee-Chen-Yon, a nephew of the Korean King.

The Department regrets that you should have addressed your note of April 20th last, to the Japanese Minister at Seoul, as Dean of the Diplomatic Body, inquiring "whether he deemed it necessary to take any steps to allay Korean excitement to secure safety to foreign lives and property."

If, in your judgment, such a communication were thought advisable in view of the threatened condition of affairs at Seoul, arising from Mr. Yee's arrest, it should have been addressed directly to the Korean Foreign Office and not reach there as it did, in the present instance, through the medium of the Japanese Minister at Seoul, who subsequently acquainted you with the views of the Korean Government.

For these reasons the Department disapproves of your course and directs in future to transact whatever business you may have to conduct with the Korean Government to which you are accredited, directly with it.

RICHARD OLNEY

Legation of the United States
Söul, March 5th, 1887

Secretary of State

Sir:

Referring again to the question of the removal of foreign trades-people from Söul to Yong-san treated of in my despatch No. 34 of December 17th last I have the honor to inform you that a good deal of feeling has been shown of late by the Korean merchant-guilds of this city at the opening within the city of new shops for retail business by Japanese subjects. The discontent of the Koreans culminated on the 25th ultimo, when all places of business within the city were closed by order of the eight guilds which rule the trade of this place. A large body of tradespeople went the same day to the foreign office and asked the President to forbid the Japanese opening new shops within the city, and to order the removal to Yong san (some three miles outside the city) of all foreign traders. The President informed the people that this question was under discussion, and that within two or three months it would be settled. In the meanwhile, nothing could be done.

The King having also heard of the excitement, called some of the principal men to the palace and told them that they must have the shops opened, for that would not prevent them discussing the affair they wanted to have settled.

Towards evening the city had assumed its usual appearance, and the greater part of the shops had been reopened.

The Japanese authorities here felt much apprehension at this sudden manifestation of ill feeling, many of the Japanese women were sent away from town and none of their nationals were allowed for some days to go out after dark.

It is worthy of note as suggestive of the continual state of alarm in which the people live, that this slight occurrence caused the price of rice to rise considerably.

The President of the Foreign Office is waiting, I hear, for the reply of Great Britain and Germany to his despatch enclosed in my No. 34, these two powers being the only ones which have express stipulations in their treaties concerning this question of residence of tradespeople in Söul.

It is also to be noted that throughout this agitation the encroachments of the Japanese on the local retail trades appear to have alone caused the dissatisfaction, although the number of Japanese traders here is much smaller than that of the Chinese.

W. W. ROCKHILL

NO. 209

Legation of the United States
Seoul, Korea, Oct 8, 1891

Secretary of State

Sir:

I have the honor to inform you that Gen. C. N. le Gendre has been appointed by the King High Commissioner to Japan, and leaves by this steamer to assist in negotiations for the revision of the Treaty.

The native press of Japan has of late been occupying itself with Korea. There are several questions open between the two governments which have been productive of some excitement, though not likely to lead to any serious results. Among them the most prominent are the prohibition of the Export of Beans from Gensan in Oct. 1889, and a quarrel between fishermen on the Coast of Quelpaert.

The meaning of the clause of the Treaty with regard to Fishery rights has been in dispute for the last ten years. By it the Koreans are empowered to fish in a certain part of the Coast of Japan, and reciprocally the Japanese on the Southern and Eastern Coasts of Korea. The Japanese contend that as the island of Quelpaert lies off the province of Chulla Do, and, as they have the right to fish on the Coast of that province, they have equally the right, if Quelpaert be a part of Korea, to fish on the coast of Quelpaert. If the Koreans deny them this right, it can only be that Quelpaert does not belong to Korea, & of course in that event She can have no power to object. In either case, they assert their right to fish.

The Koreans contend that Quelpaert is an integral part of their country, but in giving the privilege to Japanese by treaty to fish on the coast of certain Provinces, which were named, they especially excluded other parts of the Kingdom from this right. If it had been intended that it should be included, it would have been specified.

But this dispute is a dispute of words and has no practical bearing. Any foundation there may have ever been for this idea has been done away with by years of prescriptive use. The real difficulty is in the difficulty which the Central Government finds to control the

Islanders, who are a turbulent and unruly race. They frequently maltreat the Officials who are sent from Seoul, and lately they assaulted, broke his chair, and drove away a newly arrived Governor. On the other hand, the Japanese who come are chiefly natives of Tsusima, and are hardy independent, energetic men, who come determined to insist on their rights, and, if need be, defend them by arms. It has been the custom year after year for them to provide themselves at Fusan with fishing licenses, for which they pay a moderate sum, but conflicts often take place, & recently one of more than usual virulence occurred, in which it is said that several men were Seriously injured on both sides, & one or more killed. The Japanese Consul at Chemulpo, accompanied by a high Korean Official went down a few days ago in a gunboat to hold an investigation. They have not yet returned.

Beans are an important article of the trade with Japan, and Gensan is a leading place of Export. The season of 1889 promised to be a good one, & the Japanese made their arrangements to profit by it by advances to the farmers, and by sending money into the Country in the hands of Koreans for purchase. The Governor, however, in the month of October proclaimed that a scarcity was threatened, and prohibited the Export. Some attempts having been made to evade the interdict he seized all the money & all the beans belonging to the Japanese, which he could lay his hands on, amounting to nearly $200,000. The embargo was raised by the Central Government in February 1890, but the Governor still persisted in preventing the Export by quietly intimating to the natives that they must not furnish means of transportation, so that the trade was stopped for many months and much money was lost. The Governor was recalled to Seoul to explain his conduct, was at first disgraced, but having succeeded in justifying himself in the eyes of his superiors, was given the government of this city. Meanwhile, much clamour has arisen over the dispute.

But a much more important subject has been engaging the attention of the press. It has been asserted that Korea has made a secret treaty placing herself under the protection of Russia; and the question whether she has or has not, and the probable or possible consequences of such an act had been warmly debated. Japan looks upon the Seizure or the possession of Korea by Russia as a direct menace to herself, and she cannot contemplate such a possibility without excitement.

The report does not appear to me as likely to be worthy of credence As I have stated in previous despatches—No. 2 July 10 & No. 89 Nov. 19, 1890—I think it probable that Russia may at some time move down on the peninsula, but at present such a step would be premature. She is not ready to incur the enmity of China & Japan, and she would now find both resolute to prevent her advance. She is more likely to await the completion of her Railway lines of Communication before initiating any such negotiations. It is, however, of course possible that Corea may have herself taken the initiative, and requested the protection of Russia, but in view of many circumstances,—especially the exceeding interest with which She has been watching recent events in China, and her assured desire to create among Foreign Powers a league to guarantee her neutrality—I regard it as improbable.

                                                    AUGUSTINE HEARD

NO. 481   Legation of the United States
                                             Seoul, Korea, Nov. 7, 1893

Secretary of State

Sir:

I have the honor to inform you that on yesterday I received a notice from the Korean Superintendent of Trade at Chemulpo, to the effect that the prohibition of exports, mentioned in my No. 472, Oct. 18, which was to become operative after Nov. 21st, has been postponed to Dec. 6th, one month from date.

As I informed you in my No. 477, Nov. 1, the crop prospects are much better than they were a month ago. The Customs officers have had agents in the country investigating the crops as have also the various Japanese Chambers of Commerce at the ports, and the Japanese officials. These people all report that the crop will be fair.

The Japanese are chiefly interested, since this prohibition gives advance to the country officials to squeeze in such a manner as to practically stop all exports. The result will be the failure of the Japanese Banks and merchants here, and the withdrawal of the Steamship lines, unless the Koreans act reasonably.

                                                        H. N. ALLEN

NO. 345   *Confidential*   Legation of the United States
                                       Seoul, Korea, Dec. 18, 1892

Secretary of State

Sir:

I have the honor to inform you that on the 21st ultimo I had a visit from Mr. Greathouse, Vice President of the Home Office, who wished to consult me with regard to the negotiations with Japan, now being carried on by General Le Gendre. He showed & left with me copies of a telegram to His Majesty, just received from Gen. Le Gendre, and of a letter explanatory to the President of the Foreign Office, received at about the same time, and showed me also part of a letter in which he was instructed to communicate them to me in order that I might ask the Russian, French and German Representatives here to unite with me in representing to the King the advisability of accepting the detailed proposals.

These are, you will see by the enclosed papers, substantially, that in exchange for the privilege to fish on the Coast of Quelpaert, the Korean Government should concede to the Japanese the right to dry fish at places on three [South Coast] islands, which are named, and at one port in the Province of Chulla; should also concede a small portion of Deer Island, in order to extend the Japanese settlement at Fusan—such places to be selected by a joint commission of the two countries. Chilto (Ping Yang) not to be opened.

I promised at once to Mr. Greathouse that I could not approve of the part of Deer Island nearest Fusan being given to the Japanese, unless a similar concession were made to all Foreigners. I said that this might take the shape of a General Foreign Settlement, in which the Japanese should be included; or, if a separate concession were desired by them, then an equally good site should be granted to other Foreign Nations. That I had always looked on Deer Island as the ultimate place for a Foreign Settlement when the trade of the port had become sufficiently developed, and I could not consent to the Exclusion of Americans by the Japanese.

I also said that I could not recommend consulting other Foreign powers with regard to pressing the acceptance of this agreement upon the King, as I thought their action very doubtful, and asked how it was that the English representative had not also been named.

He could give no explanation of the omission of Mr. Hillier further than that he thought it possible that the colleagues of those specified had been consulted and their support secured in Tokyo. He was himself averse to consulting them, but had been told by the officer, who brought him the despatch, that His Majesty might Very likely Send to him for their opinion, and that it was unwise not to prepare their minds for such an inquiry.

As the information had been apparently given to me expressly in order that I should communicate it to them, I went at once to see Mr. Dmitriosky. I found that he knew nothing of the proposals, but said almost immediately after taking cognizance of them, that he could not agree to them. He thought the Japanese would stretch the permission to dry fish into actual possession of the Islands and, if not of the Islands, to the exclusive possession of the trade to the great detriment of the Koreans; and furthermore that he would never consent to the alienation of Deer Island to the Japanese, which had been refused to the Russians—as was related in my report of a trip to Korean ports on Oct.–Nov. 1891.

I told him that I was entirely at one with him with regard to Deer Island, and it was out of the question that we should consent to that clause without sufficient protection of our interests, but that I did not look on the concession of drying places for fish in the same light as he did. The Japanese already used them without authority and it was better to put the trade on a regular footing, which would give the Koreans some supervision and revenue. If the Japanese extended the privileges given them so as to make them cover general trade, this would enure eventually to the benefit of all foreigners, and I did not believe the Extension of general trade would be an injury to Korea. If she desired to preserve amicable relations with Japan, it was advisable to close this open sore, which would be sure sooner or later to lead to serious trouble. The alternative was to refuse all fishing privileges to Japan at the expiration of the present convention on the ground of the outrages committed at Quelpaert. This latter was the policy approved by Mr. Dmitriosky, who thought without doubt this was the policy Korea ought to take, and was fully justified in taking.

Our conversation lasted a long time, and he finally said he would think further of it, and see me again next day. Meanwhile he would do nothing one way or the other. He would neither recommend nor discourage acceptance.

On the next day he came to see me and said that reflection only confirmed him in the attitude he had chosen. He was convinced that acceptance would be a great injury to Korea.

Two or three days later I saw Mr. Frandin. He had received a memo of the proposed Convention from Monsieur Collin de Planey, the French Chargé d'Affaires at Tokyo, who was in favor of it; but Mr. Frandin expressed himself in the same sense as Mr. Dmitrevsky. Indeed his arguments and language were so similar as to suggest the thought that he was simply repeating what he had already heard.

Mr. Krein took my view of the case.

On the 29th instant I received a telegram from Mr. Coombs, U. S. Minister at Tokyo, dated the 25th, as follows:— "Japanese Korean negotiations have been very successful. Everything now will depend upon the reply of Korea to the proposals of their Special Commissioner, telegraphed 17th instant, which are Very favorable to Korea. If not accepted international complications [word unintelligible] this is authoritatively communicated. It is very advisable you see as soon as possible the King urging upon him the necessity of immediate acceptance."

I replied to him by letter of the 2nd Instant that it was always a very delicate matter to give advice unasked, and especially to an Eastern Nation who would immediately be suspicious of the motives of a person, so intruding it. For me to ask for an audience for this purpose would be very likely to defeat its own end; if, however, the King were to seek my advice, I would support the convention, provided proper reservations were made regarding Deer Island in the sense indicated above.

I may say that the King has not sought my advice, and I have no direct knowledge of the intentions of the Government, though I presume them to be unfavorable. Mr. Dmitrevsky informed me a few days ago that Mr. Yuan had told him the Chinese were opposed to the proposed convention and that the Koreans would not grant it. I have reason to believe that Mr. Dmitrevsky sought Mr. Yuan shortly after our interview for the purpose of inducing him to agree to support the same policy as himself. Neither of them is desirous that Japan should increase her influence or power in Korea, and they are well content there should be open question between the two Governments which may lead to conflict.

Mr. Greathouse told me yesterday he did not know what decision had been arrived at by the Korean Government, if any. He added that Genl. Le Gendre would shortly return to Korea, unless ordered to remain by His Majesty, as he was anxious personally to explain the situation, which had of late completely changed.

In a recent despatch I alluded to the aggressive policy towards Korea, advocated by a large portion of the native Japanese press. There have always been two parties in Japan, one in favor of peace with China, as represented by the Li-Ito convention, which has been the policy hitherto pursued by the Government, and one opposed to it, & in favor of an independent, pushing policy. The latter has been gaining ground, and it is said that the newly-appointed Minister, Mr. Oishi is sent to represent it in Seoul. He is believed by the Koreans to be a friend of Kim Ok Kuin, the Korean rebel, who found refuge in Japan after the troubles of 1884, and his coming is feared. There has been a report that he is to be accompanied or preceeded by So Shi, who are prepared to use dynamite & the dagger, and Kim Ok Kuin himself will be at hand with his associates to take advantage of the first opportunity to raise the Standard of revolt. The King has sent two or three times to this Legation for information. Mr. Oishi himself probably belongs to the Conservative Section of the progressive party, but on the outskirts of it there are no doubt hangers-on who would stop at no measures which they thought would conduce to the success of their Schemes.

It has been a matter of frequent remark by foreigners during the past year or two that the attitude of Japanese toward Koreans when-
                                    with them
ever they come in contact ∧ in the ordinary avocations of life, has become more & more insolent and aggressive. They treat them with great contempt, and do not hesitate to strike or beat them on the slightest occasion. Naturally they are hated, and in Chemulpo a few months ago, Korean Coolies who were maltreated, were prevented with difficulty—from Setting the Japanese Settlement on fire. Chinese, on the contrary, though entertaining much the same opinion of the Koreans, treat them very differently—with good humor, if with condescension, playing the role of elder brother. Consequently they are better liked, and the Koreans look up to them with something of the confiding affection of a younger brother. There is, however, in him no recognition of vassalage, as understood by us. All Koreans say they believe in the independence of their country in its national administration and in its relations with Foreigners while accepting unreservedly the claim of China to be treated with ceremonial deference due to a family Superior. But China means more.

This feeling among the people will play its part, if ever Japan forces a rupture, and it will probably occur to you that if She designed to do so, She would not act otherwise than She is doing now.

Her army is in an efficient State, and She is rapidly increasing her navy with the avowed intention to make it equal or Superior to that of China. When She has her instruments complete, it is possible that she may be tempted to use them; and She might not be indisposed to do so in Korea, if she could find means to neutralize China & Russia or Set one against the other.

AUGUSTINE HEARD

P.S. I may add in connection with Mr. Coombs' telegram that having been called on to write him in reply to a request for a passport for an American who wished to travel from Fusan to Seoul overland, I said "If you find it in your way to aid Gen. Le Gendre in his negotiations I should be glad to have you do so. He is an American, & many people here are trying to oust him from his position. Besides, so far as I know his plans he deserves Success." At that time he was negotiating on the basis of the Cession by Korea of one or two fish drying places on Islands, and the opening of Ping Yang.

Dec. 22nd

Since writing the foregoing Mr. Dmitriosky has informed me that he had received a telegram from the Russian Minister at Tokyo, stating that he had been assured by the Japanese Government that it was not intended to make any change in its policy towards Korea, and that the new Minister would follow in the steps of his predecessor. He added his impression that Mr. Oishi was Sent away lest he Should make trouble at home.

A. H.

NO. 376   *Confidential*   Legation of the United States
                                         Seoul, Korea, March 27, 1893

Secretary of State

Sir:

I have occasionally alluded in my despatches, and particularly in my No. 345, Dec. 18, to the overbearing and oppressive demeanor of the Japanese towards Koreans. In that despatch I spoke also of the fears that were entertained at the Foreign Office of the coming of Mr. Oishi, as successor of Mr. Kajiyama, the retiring minister, and

I may now add that those fears were not apparently without foundation.

In the autumn of 1889 the Japanese merchants at Wonsan made large contracts for beans, but the Governor of the Province, alleging a scarcity, requested the Government at Seoul under the provision of the Treaty allowing that action, to prohibit the export. This was done, but so much outcry was raised in consequence that the prohibition was shortly withdrawn after having been in force only a little more than two months.

A claim for damages was presented by the Japanese, but not, as alleged by the Koreans, till some two years after the event when investigation of the facts was difficult, and after prolonged negotiation the President of the Foreign Office offered $60000 in settlement, the amount demanded being in the neighborhood of $140,000. This offer was refused, and Mr. Kajiyama was recalled, it was supposed for want of energy in pushing this claim. Mr. Oishi was named and found a new President in charge of Foreign Affairs. His demand is for $176,000 (in round numbers) made up by the addition of interest and consequential damages arising from the failure of some of the merchants interested; and he has urged it with great pertinacity.

In his last despatch the President offered $47,000 (about) principal & interest in complete satisfaction, basing the reduction from the amount previously offered upon the fact, or the assertion, that that offer had been made without investigation, in order to settle the matter amicably, but that inquiry had demonstrated that this sum was greatly exaggerated.

I enclose Summaries of the two late interviews at the Foreign Office, in one of which Mr. Oishi refused to receive this despatch, and I am told that though correct in main, the language has been much softened.

Without undertaking to offer an opinion upon the point at issue, as I have not heard the Japanese case, I may say that the largest quantity of beans ever shipped from Wonsan in one year was, as appears by the Customs Statistics, peculs 136,382 valued at $169,472 (in 1890), and the interruption of the exports on this occasion exceeded but a little two months.

Affairs are now at a deadlock. It is supposed that the Korean Government will endeavor to transfer the negotiations to Tokio, or to Secure the recall of Mr. Oishi.

AUGUSTINE HEARD

NO. 385   *Confidential*   Legation of the United States
                                          Seoul, Korea, April 6, 1893

Secretary of State

Sir:

Referring to my No. 376, March 27th, I have the honor to enclose
for your information copy of the despatch of the President of the
Foreign Office which Mr. Oishi refused to receive in the conversation of the 10th of March. It presents of course the Korean case,
but shows the exorbitance of the Japanese demands. All the papers
are now in the hands of His Majesty's Foreign adviser Genl. Le
Gendre and Mr. Greathouse, and I suspect the amount ultimately
fixed on will be much less than that offered by the President in the
above despatch.

I have recently seen the complete residue of the interview of
March 10th at the Foreign Office which was prepared for His Majesty, and it substantially agrees with the summary forwarded you
in my No. 376, March 27th.

I do not hear that any further step has been taken.

                                          AUGUSTINE HEARD

NO. 396   *Confidential*   Legation of the United States
                                          Seoul, Korea, May 6, 1893

Secretary of State

Sir:

Referring to my No. 385, April 6th, in which I handed you copy
of the despatch addressed by the President of the Foreign Office to
Mr. Oishi, regarding the Japanese claim for indemnity, and which
Mr. Oishi refused to receive, I have now the honor to inform you
that after a month of substantial non-intercourse between Mr. Oishi
and the President, the Japanese minister sought an audience of the
King in order to present some Japanese generals who are here en
route for China. They were received by His Majesty on the 4th
instant, and after the presentation and the generals had retired, Mr.
Oishi pulled out of his pocket some papers and began to discuss
the bean question. The King told him that he could not listen to
him. He had not received him for that purpose; this matter was in

the hands of his Minister for Foreign Affairs. Mr. Oishi, however, persisted, and it was only after repeated warnings that he withdrew. He said he could get no satisfaction from the President, and was instructed by his Government to present the matter directly to His Majesty.

The King was very much irritated and immediately pronounced sentence of death upon the interpreter who had dared to intrude such matter upon him, which sentence was, however, afterward commuted to banishment with imprisonment. His irritation was increased by the fact that Mr. Oishi and the generals had presented themselves in plain clothes, instead of in uniform, and, considering this as a want of respect, the King was disinclined to receive them at all, but was finally induced to do so.

Mr. Oishi on the same day sent to the Foreign Office an ultimatum, said to be by instructions from his Government—that the claim of Japan for indemnity for the prohibition of the Export of beans must be paid in full within 14 days. I have not heard that an alternative was given.

Yesterday morning, early, Mr. Dmitrevsky and Mr. Frandin called upon me, and asked if I would be willing to send for an American fleet to join with them in supporting Foreign interests. The King would immediately, they inferred, send to Mr. Oishi his passports and Japan would probably declare war or would take such forcible steps to maintain its claims as would be tantamount to such a declaration. Under these circumstances it behooved other Powers to be on the alert, or their interests would suffer. Mr. Frandin said the French fleet was at his orders, and he was quite prepared to take this step. I did not think Mr. Dmitrevsky was equally decided.

I replied in effect that, in the first place, I did not believe the King would send Mr. Oishi his passports; and in the next, I should certainly not make any public demonstration in common without referring the matter to my Government. It was the policy of America as a rule, to act independently in such matters, and I did not think it prudent with no present knowledge of what had taken place to commit myself to any line of action. If His Majesty were to appeal to me for an opinion or advice, and it were necessary to act at once, I should not hesitate to give it; and I might say, informally, now, that so far as I understood them I did not approve of the Japanese claims or the manner in which they had been pressed.

Finding that I was not disposed to go any further, Mr. Frandin declared himself perfectly satisfied and left with Mr. Dmitrevsky.

The latter gentleman called upon me again this morning, and gave me to understand that his companion had been much more emphatic than he himself desired; and this may be simply the result of 24 hours reflection. (Mr. Oishi has not received his passports.) He informed me that he had sent a long despatch to the Russian minister at Tokyo with the request that it might be answered here and to St. Petersburg. Hearing that he had seen Mr. Yuan yesterday, I asked him what China was going to do about it. "Nothing," he replied:—"and if Japan declares war or employs force—oh, nothing. She does not interfere with Foreign Relations." "Then," I said, "is she going back to her old position before the Treaties at the time of the French and American difficulties? She will not like to do that now. If she permits Japan to employ force in Korea without a word, how can she continue to maintain in her sight the role of protector and sovereign, which she affects? How delighted Russia would be to see China and Japan at arms over Korea!" "Not at all," he replied. "All we care about is to keep the status quo—peace."

AUGUSTINE HEARD

NO. 399   *Confidential*   Legation of the United States
                                          Seoul, Korea, May 20, 1893

Secretary of State

Sir:

I have the honor to inform you that on the 18th instant I received from Mr. Coombs, U. S. Minister to Japan, the following telegram.

Confidentially I am informed that minister of Japan has been ordered withdraw quite assured that your good offices would be acceptable [word unintelligible] if you think advisable to tender have telegraphed Department strictly private.

When this despatch arrived, the dispute had already been arranged, and I replied on the next day—

"Japan affair has been settled." On the 17th instant, the day before the termination of the ultimatum mentioned in my No. 396, May 6, Mr. Oishi passed a long time at the Foreign Office, but was unable to get any satisfaction from the President, and it is possible that, left to themselves, the Koreans would have held firm to the end. But a new pressure was now introduced which it was beyond their power

to withstand. I am privately informed that the Minister of Foreign
Affairs∧sent a telegraph of such a nature to Li Hung Chang, that
  in Japan
His Excellency the Viceroy deemed it expedient to yield, and dictated
the terms of settlement. Whether his action was in deference to a
request, based on the condition of parties in Japan, or whether it
was because he desired to avoid complications at present may become evident later. Whatever may have been the cause, he sent such
instructions to the Chinese Representative here for communication
to the Korean Government that the President went early on the
morning of the 18th to the Japanese Legation, and concluded a settlement on the following terms. Korea agrees to pay an indemnity
for the prohibition of the Export of beans and other grains in 1889,
$60000 in six months, $30000 more within three years, and $20000
more within six years, in all $110,000. The amount is generally re-
garded as excessive but it is not likely that Japan will derive any
permanent benefit from her apparent triumph. The Koreans look
upon the settlement with great bitterness.

AUGUSTINE HEARD

<table>
<tr><td>NO. 400</td><td style="text-align:right">Legation of the United States
Seoul, Korea, May 22, 1893</td></tr>
</table>

Secretary of State

Sir:

I had the honor this morning to receive your telegraphic despatch—
without advancing opinion on merits of controversy the Government of
the United States would gladly see amicable adjustment of dispute with
Japan and would lend friendly offices towards arbitration of amount of
indemnity by a mutual power if proposed by either party. Proposal might
appropriately come from Korea.

Immediately replied: "Dispute has been settled. Korea has agreed
to pay hundred ten thousand dollars."

For particulars of the settlement I would refer you to my confidential despatch No. 399, May 20.

AUGUSTINE HEARD

NO. 466 Legation of the United States
Seoul, Korea, Oct. 6, 1893

Secretary of State

Sir:

I have the honor to inform you that Mr. K. Otori has this day taken charge of Japanese affairs here as "His Imperial Japanese Majesty's Envoy Extraordinary and Minister Plenipotentiary in Korea".

Mr. Otori says he will remain here a few months and then proceed to Peking, where he is also accredited as Envoy Extraordinary Minister Plenipotentiary from Japan.

He was kept waiting here six days for an audience with the King. This delay is said to be due to the fact that Mr Kim Sa Chull, recently raised to the rank of Minister Resident for Korea in Japan, was not received by the Emperor for two weeks after he had notified the Foreign Office of his promotion from Chargé d'Affaires to the rank of Minister Resident.

HORACE N. ALLEN

NO. 483 *Confidential* Legation of the United States
Seoul Korea Nov. 20, 1893

Secretary of State

Sir:

I learn that 1600 Japanese Merchants in Korea have signed a petition to be presented to their Parliament asking for the removal of their minister to Korea—Mr. Otori—and I have the honor to wait upon you with a somewhat detailed account of the present status of the Japanese and Chinese in Korea.

The Japanese have of late pursued a very short sighted policy in Korea. The Koreans had lately become impressed with a regard for Japan and seemed inclined to turn to her for aid and instruction. They had previously depended Chiefly on America, but finding our Government unwilling to take the energetic interest in their affairs that they desired, and the majority of the experiments tried under the auspices of Americans having proved utter failures or only partial successes, they were pursuaded that as Japan more nearly resembled Korea, and had herself just past through the stage of development in Western methods, *she* could best aid Korea. Mr. Kim Ka Chin, Korean Chargé d'Affaires in Tokio in 1888–90, was largely responsible for this change of sentiment.

The Japanese met the new idea by raising the rank of their representative here from Chargé d'Affairs to Minister Resident, and Japanese merchants began to get contracts on all sides. With their usual lack of business fore-sight however, instead of building up a lasting regard for Japanese goods, they seized the opportunity to palm off alot of old material–, unsaleable in other markets. They sold them useless ships which required extensive repairs; they persuaded them to buy alot of discarded paper making machinery, which was erected in expensive and pretentious houses near Seoul, but never used; they induced them also to re imbark on the Minting Scheme, wherein German influences had caused them to sink some $500,000. The mint was moved to Chemulpo—nearly 30 miles—"to save freight on copper." A handsome brick mint was erected, and much additional machinery purchased—all for the sole purpose of stamping an impression on metal disks purchased at the mint in Japan,—a process which I am told was offered at one time to be done *gratis* if the disks were so purchased. This mint was operated for a short time but no coin was placed on the market, and very few have seen even a sample. The Japanese Superintendent has recently left in anger, making scandalous charges against certain Korean officials for which it is said suit is to be brought.

These are only samples of the manner in which the Japanese improved their opportunities. Friends in Japan regretted the course they were pursuing, but it was the general opinion that the Government desired to have a heavy claim against Korea to offset the many claims of China. Last spring the Japanese enforced outrageous indemnity for a supposed stoppage of the export of beans from the Eastern port—Wonsan. I was assured by the Commissioner of Customs that during the few days that the embargo was in force, there was no steamer in port, by which exports could have been made. Yet the sum of $110,000 was exacted, for this loss to Japans merchants, and is being collected. This was the climax of the series of unwise moves on the part of Japan. You know from Mr. Herod's *resumé* No. 428, July 29, and Mr. Heard's despatches at the time, Nos. 376, Mch 27; 385, Apl 6; 396, May 6; 399, May 20, that as the then Japanese Minister had been entirely too precipitate, his Government had to secure the intercession of the Chinese to extricate themselves from the unfortunate predicament, the only other alternative being to back down or use force.

For this service China undoubtedly received some compensation from Japan; something more, probably, than appointing their minister to China, to represent them in Korea as well. At any rate, the conduct of the Chinese here is more openly arrogant than formerly. The Foreign Office has been placed in the hands of a pronounced pro-Chinese official, who is said to have once been attached to Mr. Yuan's office, and I am told by Koreans that all despatches go at once to Mr. Yuan. The King, while he is compelled to bow before this increased influence, does not trust the Chinese, and while he sees his country being slowly absorbed, he resents as much as possible China's claim to Suzerainty.

The prohibition of exports mentioned in my Nos. 472, Oct. 18, & 481, Nov. 7, is now known to be the work of Mr. Yuan, and he admitted as much to Mr. Frandin. When this decree was announced the conditions were such that the Government had a perfect right to make the prohibition—according to treaty. Since then the fine weather has removed the necessity, but, while the date of enforcement of the decree has been advanced 17 days, and other articles have been exempted from the prohibition, the country officials use the opportunity to squeeze in such an outrageous manner that trade is utterly stagnated, and an artificial scarcity is produced in this and other regions, which keeps up the price.

Mr. Otori, the Japanese minister expresses himself as satisfied with the present condition, while the Banks of his countrymen here are on the point of failure, and hundreds of Japanese merchants are desperate with the fear of ruin. This is the cause of the petition above referred to.

Mr. Otori seems to be an excellent man, but he acts as though hampered by some instructions that will not allow of his interfering with Chinese wishes & interests. His countrymen voice this opinion freely, and say that the present interference with trade is an attempt on the part of China to drive Korean Commerce out of their hands into the hands of the Chinese.

The foolish mistakes above referred to have, however, caused the Koreans to distrust them, and the Japanese may reap the reward of their "penny wise" policy in seeing the Koreans turn to the Chinese,— who certainly treat them more kindly and justly, even though they do interfere in the politics of the country.

I may add in this connection that the Korean Minister to Japan, Mr. Kim Sa Chul, has returned to Korea, leaving a Chargé d'Affairs in Tokio. It is said that this was at the command of China, who has said that Korea must not be represented abroad by an officer of higher rank than Chargé d'Affaires.

Meantime England seems to be aiding China in her plans in Korea and *vice versa.* The English Admiral has made two visits to Korea within a year, and Mr. O'Conner has taken a lively interest in matters here since his visit to this Court last spring. An English Bishop and many missionaries are said to be here to imitate the early success of American Missionaries. The English officers conduct the Customs under Chinese management, and always get their pay, while Americans are left unpaid. Korea recognizes America as her best friend but seems to think that the mere recognition is all sufficient. Her domestic condition grows worse and worse. The people are oppressed to the last extent, and seem willing to welcome any change in hope of obtaining relief. Talk of revolution is less public than it was last year, but while the officials improve every opportunity to squeeze, the people stagger under their burdens, both awaiting, and the former preparing for—the "General Smash Up". And, in the midst of the general distress, the Court continues its expensive festivities; hundreds of dancing girls and musicians being daily employed at an enormous expense, while the very soldiers and attendants at the Palace are months in arrears for pay, and only live by the exertions of their relatives.

France and Russia are desirous of seeing America come to the front here as an offset to England, but the time is past for mere representation to be of much avail. Asside [sic] from our own firm —Morse Townsend & Co., who deal mostly with the Chinese & Japanese, as the Koreans are too unreliable, our interests are mostly of a missionary and benevolent character.

H. N. ALLEN

NO. 146   Legation of the United States
                                              Seoul Korea Sept. 18, 1895

Secretary of State

Sir:

Referring to this series No 142, Sept. 4, I now have the honor to inform you that Count Inouye took his final departure from Korea on yesterday, and I take the liberty of writing you somewhat at length upon his course while Japanese Representative in Korea.

Mr. Otori, who represented Japan in Korea at the beginning of the late war between Japan and China, made many mistakes, he humiliated the King, allowed Japanese troops to occupy the Palace by force (see No 33, July 24)—and it was pretty effectually sacked with his full cognizance. In fact this plundering was so complete that not enough arms and ammunition remained to equip the Kings bodyguard. He also called the Tai Won Khun—the dreaded father of the King—from retirement and made him practically the dictator of public affairs. The old man repaid this favor by intriguing against the Japanese with whom he consequently soon fell out. Also the Japanese forced the Queen aside and placed her life in great danger. They also forced upon the King, the Ex-rebel Pak Yong Hyo, though this man was not actually placed in office till after the arrival of Count Inouye.

Mr. Otori had thus arrayed against his country—the King and Queen; the Tai Won Khun; the aristocracy of Korea of all factions as well as the common people, who were loyal to their King and hated the Japanese for the indignities they had heaped upon him.

To counterbalance all this opposition the Japanese then had only the sympathy of Pak Yong Hyo, whom they had brought here from a ten-year exile in Japan, and a few of the younger dissatisfied officials who had no following or influence, and who had everything to gain and nothing to lose by affiliating with the Japanese. Consequently the power of the then Government did not extend beyond Seoul and the few localities imbued by the presence of Japanese troops.

Recognizing the mistakes of Mr. Otori, the Japanese Government recalled him last October (No 65, inc. 2) and sent Count Inouye to fill his place. The sending of such a great man to represent Japan in Korea evidently meant a considerable change in policy, and as the Count was known to be a great and broadminded statesman, much good was expected to result from his mission. At first he was very friendly with this Legation and seemed to appreciate the advice he here received, which was always to make most of the King, to strengthen him and to work through him upon his loyal subjects. This was explained to Their Majesties, and it was through the assistance of this Legation that Count Inouye obtained an interview with the Queen herself.

It was not long however before the younger of the officials headed by Pak Yong Hyo, persuaded the Count to a different course. True it is that he promptly removed from the Tai Won Khun the power secured for him by Mr. Otori, but the cabinet formed by himself continued to humiliate the King, who being mortified and hurt by the complete cutting off of all his powers—which were delegated to this cabinet—began to distrust Inouye and this distrust led to a great estrangement between them. The King held aloof from Government affairs which were practically conducted by Count Inouye through the cabinet he had formed, (No. 74, Dec. 18). This cabinet moreover was not harmonious and soon factions grew up within itself, the chief ones being the pro-Japanese set led by Pak Yong Hyo and that of the Tai Won Khun, led by the Prime Minister Kim Hong Gip, while a socalled American party began to spring up composed of men who had been in America, and their friends; these were supposed to be especially loyal to the King and before Pak's final fall he joined this faction.

Finally the cabinet fell to pieces (No. 94, Mch 1), then Count Inouye, strange to say, began to be especially friendly with the Prime Minister's party, which favored the Tai Won Khun, who had been put aside by Inouye himself.

These changes resulted in great demoralization: everything was in a chaotic stage, and about this time the Japanese began to demand all sorts of concessions in the form of monopolies (No. 111, May 11, & 115, May 25), but at this period the Russians came to the fore; their ships cleared for action at Chafoo, and the Japanese were compelled to give up Lau Tung and use more caution. No more was heard of concessions here and Count Inouye left for Japan on a leave of absence, after arranging for a great banquet to celebrate the independence given to Korea by the Japanese. By reference to No. 120, June 1, it will be seen that this banquet was not a success,—His Majesty was not present, as he was on the occasion of the celebration of the 504th anniversary of his Dynasty, see 143, Sept. 5,—and on the same day Count Inouye denounced his own tool Pak Yong Hyo to the King, much to the latter's amusement. Before leaving for Japan the Count had also tried urgently, but in vain, to have the Prime Minister retained in his office. The post was given to Pak Chong Yang former Korean Minister at Washington.

Thus through many bewildering changes, having gone against the Tai Won Khun and forced Pak Yong Hyo into supreme power, Count Inouye was before his departure favoring the Tai Won Khun's party and denouncing Pak.

The Japanese Government upon discussing the situation with Count Inouye upon his return, evidently decided that his course had been a wrong one. Probably the fear of Russian action aided them in coming to this decision, and they doubtless decided to reverse their policy over here and make much of the King. Thinking perhaps that Count Inouye could best attend himself to the inauguration of this new policy, and doubtless wishing to spare him the mortification of having his work undone by a new man, he was allowed to return to Korea for a few months, though before his arrival we were aware that his present successor Viscount Miura had been appointed.

Almost at once upon his return we knew that Count Inouye had come over to conciliate their Majesty's and the noble families, and the extract I now enclose from the Japan Mail of Sept. 4, shows that we were not wrong in this.

Pak Yong Hyo had in the meantime been gotten out of the way to the pretty general satisfaction see No. 123, July 9.

Among the early evidences of this policy of conciliation and the winning of friends, I may mention that Count Inouye soon had advised the reinstatement in power of some of the Queen's family, the powerful Mins, who had been banished and hunted about during the reign of the Inouye cabinet. The Count has at many times since his return shown his desire to favor the Queen and has openly spoken of her as the best politician and strongest person in the Korean Government. He has taken steps to place the Tai Won Khun where he cannot meddle in public affairs and he has spent hours with the cabinet impressing upon them the supremacy of the King, and that they must not attempt to act against him—completely undoing his work of last winter, when he had the cabinet assume these very powers. At one point he has been very consistent—probably for consistency's sake alone—he has insisted upon having the ex-Prime Minister Kim Hong Gip reinstated, and after many concessions, much to the King's advantage, this appointment was finally made.

Since his return the Count has consulted chiefly with the officials who are known to be loyal to the King and Queen. He has tried to undo the wrongs of last summer—the looting of the Palace—by many presents, among these I may mention the gift of $10,000 worth of cartridges, and twice he has offered very privately to His Majesty from the Japanese Government, an indemnity of 3,000,000 yen, for the devastations of the late war. This indemnity was offered in such a matter, however, that up to the present date has not been accepted. In the first place His Majesty considered the amount too small, but in the second place, and chiefly, the private terms on which it is offered are very obnoxious: they are these, 1,500,000 yen shall be given to the Treasury and the same to the Household Department, then His Majesty is to cause $1,000 yen to be withdrawn from each of these Departments and handed over to Count Inouye, at the same time commissioning him to use this sum in building a railroad from Chemulpo to Seoul.

His Majesty is not averse to having the railroad, in fact he wants it and in 1892 he tried to make a contract with James R. Morse, an American, to build such road but was prevented, see No. 135, Aug. 15. He does not see why he should not let Mr. Morse have the contract at present. All foreigners here would like to see such a road built, whoever the builder.

As I stated before, when Count Inouye came here last fall, he seemed very much inclined to profit by the friendly advice of this Legation. Certainly we were willing to use our influence at the Palace in his behalf in the interest of peace, but he soon became distant and reserved doing his numerous changes, and we were well aware that he tried to prevent the King from consulting with the Legations, especially our own. On his return from Japan however he has been very communicative and desirous of assistance. He explained recently to me at great length why he had been placed in the strange position he occupied during the past year. He blamed Pak Yung Hyo greatly and decided he had not tried to force him upon this Government.

Having now quite reversed his former policy himself and won a certain degree of confidence from the Koreans, he has left Viscount Miura a clear field for the cultivation of friendly relations with Korea.

This Government *should* be grateful to Japan for what the latter has done in shaking off the galling yoke of Chinese suzerainty, and had Count Inouye pursued a wiser course during the past year he could have won the esteem and regard of Their Majesties and the people here, instead of the doubt and suspicion that exists and must exist until future events show unmistakeably that the Japanese mean good rather than ill to Korea.

H. N. ALLEN

NO. 147   Legation of the United States
                                           Seoul Korea Sept. 18, 1895

Secretary of State

Sir:

Referring to my No. 146 of this date, I have the honor to hand you enclosed an extract from the Japan Mail of Sept. 5, in regard to Count

Miura the successor of Count Inouye as Japanese Representative at Seoul.

It is known to the Korean friends of Pak Yong Hyo here, that Pak and Viscount Miura have long been fast friends; but Pak frequently expressed a great desire to have his friend here as Minister from Japan, and that the two had pregnant conversations together while Pak was in Japan, and prior to his recent starting for America.

Possibly it may be the result of these conversations that has led the Viscount to express such public disapproval of his countrys diplomacy and such a disinclination to be taught by his predecessor, Count Inouye.

H. N. ALLEN

NO. 149   Legation of the United States
                                          Seoul Korea Sept. 20, 1895

Secretary of State

Sir:

Referring to my No. 147, Sept. 18th, I now have the honor to inform you that the new Japanese Minister—Viscount Miura, endeavored on yesterday to put into practice some of the peculiar ideas of diplomacy alluded to in the newspaper extract enclosed in the above cited number.

Yesterday was the anniversary of the Queen's return from captivity after the *emeute* of 1882. It has ever since, been kept as a holiday, with the exception of last year. As has been the custom, His Majesty accorded the Foreign Representatives an audience last evening followed by an elaborate dinner. Viscount Miura appeared at the audience without his uniform, being dressed in simple morning dress. The King upon learning this fact, declined to receive him with the other representatives. I believe he was allowed to enter and bow to the King later on, but he was absent from the dinner.

H. N. ALLEN

NO. 220   *Confidential*   Legation of the United States
                                             Seoul, Korea, Dec. 3, 1891

Secretary of State

Sir:

It was not to be supposed that the end of the year, and the end of the last year of the dynasty, if ancient prophecy be believed, was to pass without a plentiful supply of reports of conspiracy and threatenings of trouble, and I was not surprised on my return to Seoul to find the tranquillity of the Court disturbed. The present agitation appears to be more pointedly directed against the Queen, though the King partakes in some measure of the hostility felt towards her, inasmuch as he is thought to have the reins of government in her hands, and, indifferent to what passes, to allow her full sway.

She is believed to care nothing for the grave interests of the Country, but to be absorbed, when not occupied with the Consideration of her health which is precarious and which makes her the Victim & Dupe of quacks and Sorceresses—in pushing the fortunes of her family—The present Sey Do, or Royal Favorite, Min-Yung-Chun, is now an especial object of hate. That he should sell the offices of the Government, great & small, to the highest bidder is too much a matter of course to provoke remark, but that he should, after having received the price, discharge those who have paid in order to make room for others, who should pay again, is thought to be going too far. His rapacity and the Vast Sum Squandered by the Queen, together with the animosity which has been steadily growing against the family of the Mins, who have gradually seized upon most of the lucrative offices of the State, have consolidated a strong body of opposition which will soon make itself felt. At its head is said to be the Tai Wan Kun, Known at home and abroad for his Keen intelligence and firm character. He is a strong man, and notwithstanding his age (excessive for Korea) 73 years, he is looked on as a man capable of dominating a difficult situation, clear in his judgments, and of sufficient courage and determination to enforce his decisions. Commenting on the situation not long since he is said to have remarked—"A good many heads must fall." Above all he is looked upon as a true Korean, loving his Country & putting her interests first, incapable of surrendering them to any foreign—Chinese or other—influence. What his feeling is towards Europeans, probably no one, not in his intimacy, Knows. He was thought formerly to be hostile to them, and as you are aware, was regent of the Kingdom at the time of the bloody persecution of the Catholics a few years ago.

The noted rebel, Kim-ok-Kiun, for many years a refugee in Japan, is believed to be on the point of returning to Korea, and his arrival is expected to be the Signal for revolt. In connection with this rumor, Mr. Dmitrevsky, successor of Mr. Waeber, Russian Chargé d'affaires, tells me that shortly before my return, Genl. Han came to see him, ostensibly on the part of the King, to say that Kim Ok Kiun was organizing a band of Japanese for a descent upon Korea, and wished to know if the Foreign Ministers could do anything to prevent it. Mr. D. replied that the Foreign Ministers could do nothing, and the proper course for the Korean Government to pursue was to invoke the offices of the Japanese Government as a friendly power, to put a stop to this action either through their representative in Japan or the Japanese Minister here. He recommended that the President of the Foreign Office should call on Mr. Kajiyama, to explain the circumstances, & leave with him a polite note, repeating his request. Mr. D. advised him, however, to come & consult me. *He* was a Russian & anything he might say would be open to Suspicion. Before my action I presumed Genl Han had received all the information he required as he did not act on this suggestion. His visit, however, to Mr. D. had the effect of producing a new version of the old Story that the King in despair at the existing condition of things had made through Gen. Han a secret treaty with the Russian minister for the protection of Korea.

Apart from and above these particular Causes of trouble, great discontent is said to exist throughout the country in consequence of the increase of the cost of the necessaries of life, without any increase in the revenues of that large class of the lesser nobility, who cannot work to augment their resources forbidden by Social prejudice, & who are in great distress.

There is, moreover, the chronic discontent of the peasant who under the harsh rule of the noble has no property which he can call his own, and whose aspirations for a freer life are unduly repressed. His energies are crushed by the Knowledge that all his earnings beyond what is barely Sufficient to Support life may at any moment be seized by his Legal Superior.

In this city the Soldiery, upon whom the Government must rely against any rising of the people are themselves the object of grave Suspicion. So far from preserving order, they are a potent element of Disorder. Instead of suppressing crime, they are the first to commit it. Robbery is not infrequent. Nobles living in isolated situations are attacked & stripped of all they possess. Soldiers sent as police to patrol the streets seize upon the wayfarer and despoil him. This is the common talk. My impression is that these statements are exaggerated, but that the Soldiers are wanting in discipline and in respect for their officers is undoubted. From being constantly in the Palace and seeing the King every day, they have lost that Awe of his presence which is So Salutary; and the fact that they are irregularly and ill-paid they unquestionably commit many excesses.

In this condition of things it only needs a match put to the magazine to cause an explosion—a leader to combine all these elements of discord to cause a serious revolution.

How much of all these representations is true, it is difficult to say. That there is great discontent is natural. That there is a real combination to overturn the existing order is not impossible. Reasoning as we Should do in Europe and America we should say that if any outbreak were intended, the intention would not be spoken of or Known; and the mere fact of it being of public notoriety would lead to the inference that it had no serious foundation. But things are arranged differently in the East; and because an event is not probable—has no raison d'être—in the West, is no reason why it Should not be possible, or probable, here. In 1884 much of the same state of things existed. The revolution was talked of; the leaders were named and the victims designated. Mr. Foulk, Secretary of Legation, was informed of what was to take place & in his turn communicated the intelligence to Genl. Foote, the minister; but thinking if there was any real intention to revolt, the secret would be kept, they paid little attention to the warnings given. At the appointed time, however, the rising took place, and the attack on the Palace was made.

So, without placing undue confidence in these reports, but giving some heed to what I hear, as it has come to me from many sources, and from what may be considered as the highest authority, and believing that there may be some fire where there is so much smoke, I have thought it prudent to advise Admiral Belknap of the existing condition of affairs, and to suggest for the remainder of this year at any rate a vessel of his squadron should be stationed at Chemulpo. I enclose copy of my despatch to him.

AUGUSTINE HEARD

NO. 294   Legation of the United States
                                           Seoul, Korea, Aug 12, 1892

Secretary of State

Sir:

I have the honor to hand you enclosed a translation of a remarkable memorial, from the Minister of the Right to the King, in which the minister deplores the present ill condition of public affairs in Korea; the lack of proper counsel to the throne; the failure of justice, and the many abuses that oppress the people.

It is the duty of the Prime Minister and his Associates—the Ministers of the Left and Right—to counsel the King and carefully guard against wrong action. The advice has been neglected of late years, and Minister Cho has recently been continually resigning; as he could not obtain an acceptance of his resignation he delivered himself of this memorial, after which he and the Prime Minister were allowed to resign. As the Left was already vacant, an entire new Ministry had to be appointed; but the new ones are daily declining the honor and quite a little crisis is the result.

Cho is regarded as a patriot by the people, his action being without precedent in recent times. He will be a leader if there is trouble, and a historical character.

H. N. Allen

Not For Publication

5th day, 6th moon, 28 July 1892

Cho, Minister of the Right, thus expressed himself, in Audience to His Majesty.

1. Public Affairs are in such a deplorable condition that our country scarcely deserves the name of a country.

2. On all sides those who should counsel His Majesty, simply assent to everything, never advising him even against a grievous wrong. His Majesty cannot learn the truth when he tries to inquire into the conditions of his country.

3. Punishment is in the power of the King and must correspond with the crime; it cannot be made heavy or light by favoritism. Yet here we see offenders who merit death, going free. How can the law be so travestied?

4. At present the magistrates live by oppressing the people. This should be remedied. The people of the eight provinces cannot have any peace, because their Magistrates attend not to their business, and the Official Inspector does not carefully examine affairs as he should.

At present, the Inspector reports that the Magistrates in the three southern provinces are doing well, but it is to be noticed that he has found fault with, and dismissed, only those of the smallest, poorest districts. However as we have the reports and complaints of the people, the abuse of official position cannot be thus screened. We know that the dismissed officers are not the ones that most merit dismissal. Why is the country thus punished?

5. If there is a Government, then there should be an adequate arrangement of salaries. The officers should be properly paid for their services.

Why is it that of late all monthly payments have been discontinued? The official in charge of this duty does not even make an attempt to pay. This is not only unjust to those who live by their salaries, but it ruins the reputation of the Country. For instance—if a master compels his servants to labor hard and then refuses to pay them their due, can they be expected not to murmur?

6. The worst present evil, and the greatest direct cause of injury to the people, is the condition of the money. One cash pieces are forced upon the market as five cash, and five cash must be exchanged for one. Prices fluctuate daily and keep constantly rising. Everything is very dear. The people are disquieted here at the Capital and all through the country; the excitement cannot be kept down.

Such a kind of government is shameful in the eyes of our neighboring countries. The only remedy is a complete change of the existing system, rectify the abuses, and enlighten His Majesty's mind on political matters. It must be attended to at once, if time is lost it will soon be too late. I beg His Majesty to consider this carefully.

7. Regarding official methods, small matters should be settled in their proper departments. At present everything, small and great, is carried direct to His Majesty, and the Royal order conflicts with the provincial, working great confusion in the interior.

7½. The law of appointments requires that a name must be selected from a list of those elligible [sic], but now any office is in the reach of those who have money. Ought not Your Majesty to stop this traffic in rank, and know a man's qualifications before giving him an appointment?

8. As the virtue of our country's King is illustrious, and he is of such an excellence that in a thousand years we cannot hope to have his equal, how does the Country and the people become so demoralized during such a reign. It is due to the lack of proper support and counsel to the King, and this condition is worse today than ever before. If this continues what will the country come to.

7½. was not in the original copy obtained by this Legation, but was in the copy of another, and included in this.

NO. 327   *Confidential*   Legation of the United States
                                          Seoul, Korea, Nov. 10, 1892

Secretary of State

Sir:

In No. 294, Aug. 12, Mr. Allen handed you copy of a memorial to the throne, prepared by H. E. Cho, Minister of the Right, in which he dwelt on the disorganization of the Government and the deplorable state of the Country. The picture he gave was by no means overdrawn.

It is a matter of notoriety that the treasury is empty, and officials, being unpaid, are obliged to resort to every expedient to meet their own necessities; once entered upon an evil course they do not stop when their necessities are met; people are oppressed; offices are sold to the highest bidder, who is soon turned out to make way for a new purchaser. Irregularity or extortion in high places is unpunished.

While there is no money in the hands of the Government to pay its just debts and the salaries of its officers, it squanders large amounts on Court ceremonies and useless fantasies. Discontent is rife, and there is an uneasy feeling that an outbreak of some sort cannot long be delayed. The Min family, at the head of which is the Queen, which
                              positions of
has seized and holds nearly all the ∧ power and wealth in the Kingdom, is hated, and, if a leader of real ability were to offer himself, the elements for revolution would speedily group themselves about him. At present no one seems indicated for that rôle except the Tai Wan Kun, who has the will and the mental strength, but his great age and physical feebleness weigh him down. He is, however, a strong character, and the recent attempt upon his life, which, though often & strenuously denied, did in my own opinion really take place, would have the effect of stimulating still further his hostility to the Queen & her party whom he may naturally have suspected of being the authors of it. What his feelings now are towards foreigners, it is impossible to say. It will be recollected that he was Regent at the period of the last persecutions of the Christians, when so many were slaughtered, but times have changed. Korea is now open, and has made treaties with many foreign Powers. He may be intelligent enough to perceive that he can no longer hope to exterminate all strangers, as then he attempted to do, & may think it the better part to be friendly wih them, & get all the good out of them he can. This is probable. But then he is looked upon as a typical Korean, patriotic and obstinately devoted

to his country, and he may have learned nothing. He lives in retirement.

The admiral has written me—"in case of any real trouble breaking out, you could wire me and I would send a vessel to Chemulpo as soon as possible", but he has neglected to inform me where he may be found, and, under any circumstances it would be some time, even if I were able to send him a telegram, which, "in case of real trouble", would be exceedingly doubtful, before assistance could be rendered. Meanwhile we should be left to our own resources. These with some addition would probably be sufficient to cover the gap.

I have had long experience of the East, and I am confident that a few men, well armed, could keep at bay any mob by which we are likely to be assailed, but we have no arms, and the object of the present despatch is to request you will send me, if you approve, a dozen Winchister, or other, rifles with ammunition by an early opportunity. The English and German Legations are so provided. We have nothing.

The Registers which I shall shortly send you will show that there are in Seoul 60 Americans, including many women and children, and at the first alarm they will flock to this Legation for protection.

I do not wish to be understood as saying that I consider danger as imminent. I simply think it possible. Some weeks ago my French colleague wished me to unite with him in representing the situation to the King, and insisting for our proper safety upon certain reforms. It is a very delicate matter, and I am very reluctant, to give advice when it is not asked for;—and the course suggested did not seem to me advisable for many reasons. In the first place, so far from His Majesty being ignorant of the existing state of things, I believe him to be as well informed of it, at the least, as we are, and in an Eastern Country it is impossible to say what the real views or intentions of the Sovereign are. Discontent is more or less chronic in Korea, and the crisis may now pass by as it has done before.

I again am not sure that a revolution would not put better men in control. It could hardly bring about a worse regime than the present. The King is a Kindly, well-intentioned man, but he lacks the ability and courage and force of character to carry through himself the necessary reforms. He is personally liked, and it is possible that he might still be kept as the Head though the Mins were swept away. He is the son, as you are aware, of the Taiwunkun.

Mr. Frandin was much excited, and read me a despatch on the subject to his Government, in which he requested that the fleet might be placed under his orders.

Mr. Dmitriosky is Strongly opposed to taking any official notice of the existing causes of complaint. Possibly he may look upon confusion here, as more consonant with the policy of Russia. If she entertains designs upon Korea, the present state of things is favorable to them.

It has been powerful in making and keeping Korea subservient to China.

Augustine Heard

no. 381 Legation of the United States
Seoul, Korea, 4 April 1893

Secretary of State

Sir:

We have been witnessing within the past few days a curious phase of Eastern life, which has not been devoid of a personal interest for ourselves. A body, numbering about 40 men, have been kneeling before the Palace Gate, waiting for an officer of the Court to come and take from them a petition to be laid before the King. These men were representatives of a new religious Sect, which sprung into being in 1859, and whose founder, Ch'é Cheay Woo, was put to death as a heretic and as a Sorcerer by the Governor of Chulla Do in 1864. Every effort has been made to stamp it out. But, notwithstanding the persecution, or perhaps because of the persecution, the Sect has flourished, and, growing rapidly, now numbers many thousands of adherents, chiefly in the Southern provinces.

A report reached me some three months ago that they were collecting at a central point with the intention of marching on Seoul, but it died away, to be renewed again a Fortnight ago. On the 18th inst., all the Foreign Representatives were informed by their Chousas or native interpreters, that the Tong Hâk were coming many tens of thousands strong, and that one article of their creed was the expulsion of foreigners. Inquiry failed, however, to find any authority for the statement. The Chousas, when questioned had been told the report by friends, they did not know, they had heard it talked about, & in two or three days they began to doubt whether there were anything in the story. The high officials denied that there was any truth in it, and on the 28th the President of the Foreign Office assured me that it was only a rumor among the people, unworthy of attention.

Unquestionably, however, there was a sense of uneasiness in high places. The English gunboat "Peacock", and the German gunboat "Iltis" were at Chemulpo at the time, and both Mr. Hillier and Mr. Krien were approached with the view of inducing them to retain them here. Neither of the gentlemen was able; however, to get any statement that there really danger [sic] to foreigners, and they were unwilling to act on vague rumors. The gunboats went away.

on the subject
A well Known official of high rank spoke first to Mr. Hillier∧ and called upon him again on the 30th, when much of the same conversation took place. He felt there might possibly be danger, but refused to say that there was danger. The malcontents were in any event unarmed, and the soldiers could easily deal with them. Apparently he would have been pleased to have danger inferred, & precautions against it taken by foreigners, without in any way committing himself. This was the impression made upon Mr. Hillier. From the past fornight the Tong Hâk, or men of the Eastern Religion, have formed the subject of all conversation and interest in Seoul, and on the 29th about 40 of them appeared and knelt before the Palace Gate, where they remained several days. Upon a table covered with a red cloth was placed the petition which they wished to lay before the King. It bore the inscription:

The Petition of Subjects of different provinces, Scholars, of whom the chief is Pak Suing Ho, humbly Submits:—the religion of the late Ché Cheay Woo was condemned as heresy & sorcery, though in reality its teachings were to revere Heaven, to purify the heart, to protect the nation and to tranquilize this people. Now this is a grievance to be redressed.

Its contents are unknown, but its first object is said to be to procure a reversal of the sentence which condemned the founder Ch'é Cheay Woo to an ignominious death as a heretic & a sorcerer, and permission to practise their religion; and it is supposed to contain a protest against foreigners and Christianity, with the request that His Majesty should intervene.

The strength of the organization, or the strength of its backing in Seoul, may be inferred from the fact that not long ago to be suspected of having affiliations with the Tong Hâk was to insure persecution & death, & today they declare themselves broadly at the Gate of the Palace, asking, almost demanding recognition. Only 40 appeared there, but it is supposed there are many hundreds, perhaps thousands in the city; and these 40 were renewed from time to time as they became fatigued. The birthday of the Crown Prince occurred on the 24th

Mch, and the quaggas, or Examinations, then were held in honor of the event have been the pretext under which great numbers from the country have entered the city, a certain proportion of them no doubt belonging to this sect.

Their present leader is Pak Suing Ho, and he made the following statement to a Korean Christian, who went to him for information a few days ago without saying who he was:

The religion, which is the only true religion and contains all that is good in Confucianism, Buddhism & Taoism was founded by Ch'é Cheay Woo in 1859. Being inspired by God he went up into the mountains, and after praying for 1000 days, God appeared to him, & told him to search under certain rocks. He sought & found four books, which are the sacred books, known only to adepts, and containing the doctrines of the faith. Many teach the worship of one God, the creator of Heaven & earth, & sacrifice to ancestors; mutual respect between father & child, the subjection of the wife to her husband, the submission of nobles to the King, and faithfulness between friends. In sum, reverence for God, & love for man (It might be thought that the faith of the hearer had tinctured what he heard).

Pak denied that they had any hostility to foreigners, and that they practiced the acrobatic and conjuring feats ascribed to them by the common people. All their disciples are scholars & all are received who will obey the precepts inculcated.

To these principles no objection can be made, but to the sincere believer must be added many who believe in the success of the movement, who wish to be on the winning side, and by many (it is reported) who are hostile to the Roman Catholics. These are thought, either rightly or wrongly, to be protected by the priests from the exaction of the Magistrates, to which all others are liable; and if there is anything to call forth bitter hostility from the mandarin, it is to see what he considers as his lawful prey withdrawn from his clutches, and all those who *must* pay hate without measure those who are exempt. Many it is said of bad character enroll themselves under the priests to escape the payment of their just debts. I am now only repeating remarks which are not unusual among Koreans in which no doubt there is much exaggeration.

So much for the Sect as a Sect proper. But we must also look upon it as an organized body, which may be used by a political party for political purposes, and there are many who regard the present movement as only a demonstration of political intrigue.

What the government fears—if it fears anything—is not so much what may take place in Seoul, where they have a body of disciplined troups, who are probably free from the contamination, as of an outbreak in the Southern Provinces, where there is a certain feeling against foreigners, or against Catholics, & where alone apparently it exists. It was in Kuing Sang Do that the attacks were made on Pére Robert near Taiku, & recently on another priest at Kamsan. Chung Cho'ng Do, Kuing San Do, & Chulla Do are said to be full of these people & it is impossible to say how far their tenets may have gained even the officials.

The government was brought to face this dilemma. If they received the petition, & antagonized foreigners, they would have an ugly task before them. If they received and disregarded it they might bring about a revolution; and, curiously enough, the Headquarters of the Sect in Kong Chiu in Chiung Chang Do, the appointed new capital of the Kingdom after the present dynasty has been removed, which you are aware was predicted would take place after its 500th year. This is the 502nd, and these fanatics may look upon themselves as the appointed agents of Heaven to bring it about.

On Friday, the 31st, the King came to a decision. He sent out an officer to order these people to leave their station before his Gates on pain of arrest, and they did so. Many of them left the city the next day. The reason given for not receiving the petition was that it had not been forwarded through the proper channel. It should first have been presented to the Chong-Wan, a Board which enregisters the King's decrees. On the next day a decree appeared in the Gazette, in which His Majesty admonished the Tong Hâk in a fatherly way to abandon their false doctrines, and study the true Confucian Wisdom. If they did not heed his admonitions he would be compelled to chastise them even unto death.

On the night of the 31st a placard of which I enclose a translation was affixed to the School of the Presbyterian Mission, and another, identical on the gate of the residence of Mr. Jones—a member of the Methodist Mission. No other placards that I am aware of were posted on any other property in Seoul. If it were done by the Tong Hâk, it may be that the leader, Pak, knew or suspected who his interlocuter was the day before. Mr. Gifford and Mr. Jones called on me with them late Saturday afternoon, the 1st, & I at once had an interview with the President of the Foreign Office. I told him I did not wish to attach too much importance to them as being the work of irresponsible persons, but I deemed it proper in the interest of good order to bring them to his notice. He remarked that it was singular that it should have been attached to the Protestant and not to the Roman Catholic Mission. He said the Tong Hâk were now driven away, and unless they kept quiet, they would be severely dealt with. A petition to this effect to His Majesty was being prepared by the Confucian Scholars of the city. He added, there will be no trouble.

It is very difficult to estimate the importance of a movement of this Kind in a country like Korea, where all evidence accessible to foreigners is vague & untrustworthy. In no country more than Korea does what one see depend so essentially on the point of view; & although it is easy to exaggerate, one must always bear in mind that it is dangerous to despise trifling indications. Early in this affair, Mr. Hillier called to consult with me with regard to requesting naval assistance and arranging that a ship of some nationality should always remain at Chemulpo —one relieving another. I told him that under the circumstances I did not feel disposed for various reasons to telegraph for a man of war, and before we could write there might be further developments to guide us.

There is no doubt a good deal of excitement in the city, and I shall inform the Admiral of the circumstances by this mail. I do not think they warrant a telegraph. I see by the newspapers that he was at Hong Kong on the 8th Mch.

AUGUSTINE HEARD

P.S. As I was closing this despatch Mr. Jones brought me another placard which he found on his gate this morning. It is indeed more scurrilous than the others, & I doubt whether it came from the same hand. It orders him to leave the country in twenty days. I have sent a copy to the President, and told him, that, though I was not inclined to give much importance to the first, the repetition of the offense made it necessary for me to insist on his putting an immediate stop to it. He must discover the culprit and punish him severely.

[Copy of Tonghak placard of 31st March]

Alas! Alas! My little children. Receive the words of this notice with reverential fear.

Surely our Eastern Land has been a Kingdom of propriety and rectitude for several thousand years. The growth of this Kingdom of propriety and rectitude, and the practice thereof—Even this have hardly been achieved. How much less that of other creeds?

An inspection of the books of these creeds and an examination of the doctrines they inculcate disclose the fact that in their so-called teaching what is styled reverence of Heaven is really rebellion against Heaven;

what is called love towards manKind is a delusive mockery and a stealing of men's hearts.

Heaven and hell! what talk is this? Although our people talk of spirits and genii, who ever saw one?

Although these people talk about heaven, who ever saw heaven?

But upon you, you fools and foolish strangers who delude and bewilder with empty nothings; who believe in chaotic incoherence who forsake sound and great principles and follow after "universal love"; who cast aside ancestral sacrifice and practice these extravagant teachings. This is what the sages and worthies meant when they said "without father," "without sovereign."

In ancient days the illustrious Ministers and advisers of our glorious and sacred Rulers founded seminaries and established schools of thought for the gradual development of the principles of charity and patriotism and the covering as it were with a cloak of civilisation the regions of the East and West. There was universal good government brought about. Now, strange doctrines are spread abroad like a network; delusion and falsehood have sprung up like weeds. Thus is Misrule and disorder universally prevalent.

You are the descendents of these able Ministers and advisers, and you bring dishonor upon your illustrious ancestry. Is it not pitiful? Is it not a detestable state of things?

The greatness of our doctrines proceed from that Heavenly brightness, Heavenly effulgence. Dare you, then, plunge from these into profligacy and bring shame and dishonor on this teaching? The principles of universal good government are to be found in the proximity of our Ruler, who dwells in the midst of perfect refinement. Can you but be afraid of what you are doing? Can you but beware?

Alas! Alas! My little children. Follow the great doctrine; make men of your men; burn these books. So shall you live in an infinitesimal degree as you ought to live.

(Here follow four lines of unintelligible verse.)

An anonymous notice issued by Mr. Kung-i of Pai-ling Shan [verbatim] 'twixt night and day in the second moon of the cyclical year Kuei Ssŭ.

Translation Placard of April 4th

To the head of the religion addressed: You Crowd, listen with your ears. Fortune is decreasing & the doctrine of the world is being lost. The Royal Ancestral Temple has been befouled by interrelation with barbarians. There is no promise in the treaties permitting the establishment of schools and the propagation of religion. You, heads of religions, have one by one come in saying "we come to worship God"—which you do by prayer only; you say you believe in Jesus but show it only by hymns. Among you there is neither sincerity nor sense; you never perform what you preach. You say "Honor thy parents" yet during their life you neither care for nor obey them, and after their death (you have) neither tears nor (funeral) ceremony. Is this human nature? When you marry, you first mate (like beasts) and without shame even enter upon marriage a second time. Upon the least evidence of incompatibility you break the marriage tie. Your crowd, originally beggars, sold themselves for the wages offered by the Church. Your hearts are full of covetousness for good houses and an easy life. At first you deceived the children of (native) aristocrats by promises of instruction in English and Chinese, but finally you force them into your religion, and out of the money intended for Scholars food and clothing you have to get your squeeze. Is not that vile? You know that your trips for preaching are only causes for sight-seeing and the sale of books. You call this preaching! If there is an eternal hell, you shall first enter it. Do you not fear this? Why then discuss with you? We, religious scholars, how could we hold converse with a miserly crowd? To speak clearly, you Crowd, gather together your possessions and depart quickly. If you don't, with the armor & shields of patriots and crying out your sins, we will come & attack you on the 7th of the 3rd moon.

Know the same.

Legation of the United States
Seoul, Korea, April 6th, 1893

NO. 382

Secretary of State

Sir:

Continuing my despatch No. 381, April 4th, I have now the honor to inform you that the followers of Confucius in Seoul, addressed a memorial to His Majesty on that day setting forth that the Tông Hâk professed false doctrines which were corrupting the people, and asKing if they might be compelled to return to the right path or utterly exterminated. It was Known that such a petition was in preparation, and some anxiety was felt lest the opportunity might be taken, while attacking the Eastern religion, to include in their denunciations the people of the Western religion. But this does not appear to have been the case. His Majesty replied that the Government had charge of the affair and would attend to its duty, admonishing the petitioners at the same time to devote themselves to the study of the principles they professed.

This seems to end the matter for the moment.

I enclose copy of the letter I addressed to-day to the Admiral.

AUGUSTINE HEARD

Seoul, Korea, April 6th 1893

NO. 383   *(Confidential)*   Legation of the United States

Secretary of State

Sir:

I have the honor to inform you that since the affair of the Tong-Hak began, I have been in frequent communication with Mr. Hillier on the subject, and yesterday he came to give me an account of a conversation he had just had with Mr. Yuan, the Chinese representative, whom he knows very well. Mr. Yuan began by pooh-poohing the whole affair, and said it was only of the slightest consequence. The decree that was issued by the King was not nearly strong enough. He ought to cut off a few of their heads, and then the Tong-Hak would behave themselves. The numbers make no difference, they were poor people and all cowards. As soon as a man said he was a Tong-Hak, off with his head. The first two men might say "Yes" to the question, but the third would hesitate. They counted on the timidity of the King, and the Mins were just as bad. "Show them that you were not afraid of them and they would disappear. There will be no trouble. *I* will take care of the city. I have a 1000 men here and there is no Korean mob which could stand an instant."

"Yes", replied Mr. Hillier, "that is very well but you have not taken the Japanese into account. The Koreans hate them and will attack them first. What will you do if they set Ching-go-kai (the Japanese settlement) on fire? What did you send your ships away for? (Part of the southern Chinese fleet, 3 heavy ships from Nagasaki touched at Chemulpo between the 28th and 2nd and went on to Wei-Hai-Wei). Yuan: "To tell the truth I did not keep them because I know that if I did, it would make a great deal of talk. It would look as if I regarded the situation as critical, and perhaps it would be thought that I had something to do with it; and so I let them go; but I can easily get them back." Hillier: "You know Oishi would be delighted to have a
                                                                    then
row. He would get over half a dozen ships and if you got yours ∧ it would look as if you came to interfere with them." Yuan: "I had not thought of that."

Mr. Hillier then said if Yuan wanted to keep up the idea of Chinese sovereignty he must act and make the King act. Yuan understood that and said the Koreans must be made to believe the treaties would be respected and foreigners protected. "*I* will guarantee the city. I do not think there is any danger now, but there was last winter. Then I thought we should have trouble. In addition to other causes the soldiers had not been paid." (This was the time when I suggested to the Admiral that it would be prudent to have a ship here.)

Mr. Hillier asked if he had seen the placard on the missionaries' houses, "Yes," the President had shown it to him. "But," said Mr. Hillier, "you have not seen this one," and showed him the last which I had given him in the morning. Yuan shook his head at this and said the anonymous placards made a great deal of mischief in China, and it must be put a stop to at once. He would see to it.

Mr. Hillier left him under the impression that he would send for one or more of his ships.

You will notice the point made regarding Chinese Supremacy. This is too large a subject to be entered upon here, especially as I do not know that you would care to have it discussed, and I will only add that the complete withdrawal of American naval forces from these waters of late has of course been in its degree favorable to Chinese claims.

AUGUSTINE HEARD

NO. 391   Legation of the United States
                                          Seoul, Korea, April 20th, 1893

Secretary of State

Sir:

Since my despatches with regard to the Tong-Hak, No. 381, April 4, No. 382, April 6 and No. 386, April 7 no serious incident has taken place, but considerable agitation has prevailed among the national community. The officials and higher classes persist in denying that any danger is to be apprehended, though the streets are strongly patrolled at night, and it is said that several arrests have been made. Many petitions have been presented to the King by bodies of Scholars and officials, asking that the Tong Hak should be severely punished, and His Majesty replied on the 13th instant by a decree in the Royal Gazette, of which a translation is enclosed. The sensation of the fortnight, however, has been the receipt of a manifesto of the Tong-Hak a few days ago, which was affixed to the Gate of the Yamên of the Governor of Chulla-Do, and said to have been posted in every district in the Province. It is reported to have been telegraphed to the King accompanied by alarming statements of the strength and determination of the signers. It is very violent and calls for the extermination of foreigners. I hand a translation.

On the 13th instant the Japanese Consul issued a notification privately to his countrymen, warning them that, in consequence of the approach of the Tong Hak, it was necessary to prepare the women and children for immediate removal to Chemulpo. The Korean authorities would no doubt do their best to protect them, *but* this protection was not to be relied on, and all strong and able-bodied men were ordered to report themselves at the Police Station or the Consulate for instructions.

This notification was brought me on the afternoon of the 14th instant, and I at once wrote to Mr. Sugimura to ask if it were true that he had issued it, and added that, if he had, I presumed he had in his possession authentic intelligence of danger.

He replied that he had issued *a* notice, but that his information was derived only from rumor. He had, however, sent trustworthy men to Chulla-Do to investigate, and on their return he would communicate any facts they might bring. The immediate occasion of this notification was the posting on his gates of an insulting placard, ordering the Japanese to leave the country forthwith. Many families of Japanese have betaken themselves, I am told, already to Chemulpo for security.

On casting one's eyes over the summary of events, one can hardly help feeling that something serious is preparing, but yet the confidence one has in the peaceful nature of the Coreans and the long absence of any demonstration of hostility, have contributed to produce an almost total lack of alarm among foreigners, although of course there are exceptions. So much is this the case that H.M.S. "Severn," 6000 tons, a large cruiser, arrived at Chemulpo on the 15th instant and left again yesterday for Shanghai. Capt. Henderson told Mr. Hillier that he would respond to any telegraph and be here in case of necessity in less than 48 hours. I asked Mr. Hillier when he mentioned this to me, if he felt certain he would be able in the event of a serious attack on foreigners to use the telegraph. He confessed he had not thought of this.

Apart from the danger of wilful interference there is danger of accidental break, which occurs frequently. The line to Fusan is now interrupted.

Although there is a very general disinclination to regard the situation as serious, there are a very few persons who think it possible, that behind the screen of the Tong Hâk there may be preparing a return blow of the Tai WanKun for the attempt on his life last year. If this be the case, the situation is very grave indeed. Commander Dayton's statement that the State Department had telegraphed Admiral Harmony to send a ship here leads me to suspect that the King had made the request that this should be done through his Legation in Washington, as he did at the time of the death of the Queen Dowager in 1890. I think there is no question that he is much alarmed at the present state of things.

On the morning of Sunday the 16th instant, I received a telegram from Admiral Harmony dated at Nagasaki asking "Is there any trouble in Korea?" I replied immediately—"Wrote you sixth. Some alarm. Doubt if real danger. Sending ship would be prudent." On the afternoon of Tuesday the 19th instant the U.S.S. "Petrel" arrived in Chemulpo, and her commander, J. H. Dayton, with four of his officers came to Seoul the next day. They are now here. Commander Dayton informed me that he was on his way from Yokohama to Shanghai, and touching at Nagasaki on Sunday found the Admiral preparing to leave for Korea in consequence of orders from the State Department. The "Petrel" was sent instead, immediately. The Admiral had telegraphed me but had received no reply.

Commander Dayton had seen Capt. Henderson of the "Severn", and was disposed to return to his ship and leave at once. As Capt. Henderson had made up his mind to go away, he naturally did not give Commander Dayton the impression that it was necessary to remain; but I told him that under the circumstances I thought it was his duty to remain, at any rate for a few days, and then be governed by circumstances—which he very willingly consented to do.

A day or two after the date of my No. 386, Apr. 7, two Chinese ironclads arrived in Chemulpo, and since then two Japanese men-of-war. They still remain there. No ammunition having been received for the rifles, of which I had the honor to advise the receipt last mail, I have requested Commander Dayton to supply me with 50 rounds per rifle or 600 cartridges.

AUGUSTINE HEARD

Translation of manifesto issued by the members of the Tong-Hak Society

Men have three tasks which confront them in the fulfillment of the duties of life.

1.—The task of laying down rules or limitations of conduct under which they shall carry out the requirements of loyalty to their fullest extent and, if needs be, to sacrifice their lives as servants of their country;

2.–To put forth all their efforts in the direction of loyalty and filial piety and to die, if needs be, for the sake of their personal belongings;
3.–To maintain widowed chastity and to die, if needs be, in the fulfillment of conjugal obligations.

Life and death are the appointed lot of all mankind; this is the unfailing law whatever may betide. Those who are born in times of freedom from trouble and in periods of peace and happiness should pursue the path of patriotism and filial piety with a joyous heart, while, on the other hand, those who live in seasons of danger and difficulty should sacrifice their lives in the cause of patriotism and of filial piety. This is the task of all true servants of the State and is a task that may devolve upon them in the course of the permutations of things. Those who love their lives are opposed by the difficulty of sacrificing their lives in the service of their King and their parents. Those who are ready to sacrifice their lives will willingly accept the task of giving them up for their King or their parents; and no one who clings to life can be a true subject or son. Those who are ready to part joyfully with life are the men who are capable of building principles of loyalty and filial piety upon a sure foundation.

Japanese and foreign rebels and thieves are now introduced into the very bowels of our land and anarchy has reached its zenith. Just look round on the capital under present conditions. It is the lair and den of barbarians. Think of the oath of *Yen Ch'en* [the year 1592, the date of the Hideyoshi invasion], of the disgrace of *Ping tzu* [1876, date of the treaty of Kanghwa with Japan]!! Can you bear to forget it? Can you bear to talk of it? Our three thousand millions of people in the Eastern Kingdom are now all in the grasp of wild beasts, and our ancestral homes of 500 years duration will shortly witness the disaster of dispersion and dismemberments. Alas for charity! patriotism, prosperity, prudence, filial piety, brotherly love loyalty, and good faith! What has become of them all at the present time?

Let it, moreover, be remembered that most of the Japanese rebels cherish feelings of hatred towards us, and nurture within them the germs of disaster for our land, which they will bring forth to our hurt. The danger threatens us at any moment, and can we regard the situation with tranquility? It might truly be said of the present condition of affairs that it is in proximity of brushwood.

We who issue this notice are simple ignorant people but for all that we are inheritors of the laws laid down by previous Rulers and we till the ground of our king to maintain our fathers and mothers. Although officials and people differ as honourables and commons, where is there any difference between them in the obligations of loyalty and filial piety?

We desire to display our humble loyalty to the State and to secure to her loyal and upright servants their state emoluments to which they are entitled, but we are perplexed as to what to do, and it is not for us to institute comparisons as to the sincerity of our love for the king and loyalty to our country. There is an old saying,—

"When a great house is about to fall one piece of wood will not support it; when a great wave is about to roll in a single net will not keep it back."

We who number several millions have sworn to the death that we will unite in one common effort to sweep out the Japanese and foreigners and bring them to ruin in our sage desire to render to our country the fidelity which even a dog will show to his master, and we humbly hope that every one, within one common resolution, will combine their efforts and will select loyal and patriotic gentry to assist them in supporting the wish of the country. This is the earnest prayer of millions of people.

Transcribed by the Tong-hak men.

NO. 398   Legation of the United States
Seoul, Korea, May 16, 1893

Secretary of State

Sir:

Soon after the date of my No. 395, May 1, it was reported that many thousands of the Tong Hâk were collected at the town of Po-eun in the Eastern part of Chung-Chang Do, and that their numbers were daily increasing. Every day brought fresh rumors of their strength, and amongst the Koreans there was much alarm. Although almost without arms they were said to be drilling regularly, and professed their intention of marching on Seoul. They had erected a wall about their encampment, in the center of which was a large flag with the inscription "Down with the Japanese and foreigners. May the right flourish!"—and grouped about it were other flags inscribed with the names of the various districts from which the different parties came. They declared that they had no fear of the soldiers who might be sent against them as the soldiers, instead of attacking, would join them.

Many Koreans who had entirely disregarded the previous manifestations seemed to look upon this as serious, and sent their families into the country.

An officer of the Government who went down a few days ago to remonstrate with them, and induce them to disperse, reported that they refused to listen to him and asked for troops. On Saturday the 15th,
in
800 men, drilled ∧ European-style, with three Gatling guns, were sent to Suwen, about 100 li, or 30 miles from Seoul, to bar the road, but it is understood they will push on to Chong-ju, distant about 100 miles.

From the fact that their flag bears a hostile inscription many foreigners believe themselves to be in danger, but I should doubt whether
there were any real active hostility felt, and that if this body succeeded
in reaching the city we have less to fear, I think, from it than from
the mob of the idle and vicious who always abound in the streets of
cities, and who might try to burn and loot our dwellings. Of this, however, the chance is remote, although, of course, it is possible.

U.S.S. "Alert" is at Chemulpo since the 7th instant. Admiral Harmony
telegraphed me on the 14th: "Infer no need Alert Chemulpo. Will order
away." As I thought it more prudent she should not leave immediately,
I replied: "Unless important elsewhere suggest waiting few days." The
Tong Hâk in themselves, I believe, are not dangerous. They seem to be
quiet and peaceful, and would be content with little besides the re-
habilitation of their Founder and permission to practice their tenets;
but they have no doubt collected to themselves hordes of discontented
and poverty-stricken people. The whole may be, and probably is, under
the control of a political party, bent on making trouble for the Government, but who this party is, and what its strength, we have as yet no
Knowledge.

AUGUSTINE HEARD

NO. 457   Legation of the United States
                                           Seoul Korea Sept. 28, 1893
Secretary of State

Sir:

I have the honor to inform you that, owing to the fact that during
the past month we have had almost continuous and most unseasonable
rains, the crops are likely to be a failure. The rice crop is already given
up, and the crops that need less moisture are in a worse condition, if
possible. The rice plant looks fairly well in places, but there has been
no sun to mature the grain.

The price of rice has doubled in consequence and much distress
results. This distress is being improved by the Tong Haks, who created
the disturbance of last year. And Foreigners—owing to the export of
rice—are blamed for the distress.

Trouble will doubtless result during the winter, but we have guns
and ammunition here, and can arm and protect the Americans at the
Legation against mobs. I have written to Admiral Lerwin [?] on the
subject.

H. N. ALLEN

Secretary of State

Sir:

I have the honor to inform you that the Korean Government is in great anxiety over the disturbed condition of affairs in three Southern Provinces, Viz., in Chulla Do, Chung Chung Do, and Kying Sang Do. The people have risen against the bitter and Merciless oppression of the governors and other officials. While the agitation is at present confined to the three provinces named above, Chulla Do being the most turbulent, the same conditions prevail Elsewhere in the Kingdom, and a few successes on the part of the people such as are now reported from Chulla Do, will stimulate them to like disorder and blood-shed elsewhere and to a general uprising against all officials.

I have acquainted Admiral Skerrett with the situation and forwarded to him a request from the King that he send a ship from his squadron to the Port of Chemulpoo, at the same time suggesting that I would telegraph him in case the need should become more urgent.

At the earnest request of the Government, I have also called in the American Missionaries from the interior, as the Government informs me that they might not be able to protect them outside of the Treaty Ports.

So far the movement seems to be directed wholly against the oppressive officials, some of whom with their families had been put to death. Others have had houses and property destroyed and after being beaten have been driven from their districts. The Government has sent a considerable body of troops to the scene of the disorder but they seem to have neither scared nor hurt anyone, and no one here Expects them to be of any use. I believe that more frequent visits by our ships would have a salutary Moral Effect both upon the people and the Government. An occasional demonstration is needed to Keep Koreans and others in Mind of the continued existence of the United States of America. No American ship has visited Korean ports for many months. Mr. Ye Cha Yun, formerly Chargé d'Affaires at Washington, has just now left this legation, after Earnestly asking that our ships visit Korean waters more frequently.

I have also the honor to report to you the facts concerning an affair of recent occurrence at Ping Yang. The persons mentioned herein by name, and chiefly concerned are as follows: W. J. Hall, M. D., W. B.

Scranton, M.D., and Rev. S. A. Moffett. Dr. Scranton and Mr. Moffett
are American Citizens, and Dr. Hall is ∧ British subject. Dr. Scranton
                                          a
is the Chief of the American Mission and Dr. Hall is his employè in
said Mission. Dr. Hall and Mr. Moffett have recently been staying at
Ping Yang pursuing their work. Dr. Hall was at the last under notice,
in that city with his wife, an American Lady, and one young child.
Mr. Moffett had, a few days before, come down to Seoul and was
                                                     h
staying here. They had both furnished money, whic ∧ came originally
from their respective Boards of Missions, to native Koreans, with which
these Koreans had purchased two houses in Ping Yang, really for the
use and convenience of the Missions, though the Koreans were the
ostensible purchasers. This plain contravention of the letter of the
treaty had, it appears, either incensed the local authorities or given
them an opportunity to Exact money from someone. Such opportunities
are not likely to escape the notice of a provincial Korean official. But
up to the tenth instant, Dr. Hall and his family were in peaceable
possession of the house so purchased and held under cover of Korean
ownership, and, in Mr. Moffett's absence, his Korean servant was also
holding undisputed possession of his house.

On the morning of the 10th instant, Mr Christopher Gardner, Acting
British Consul General and Myself were shown a telegram from Dr.
Hall in Ping Yang dated 8 o'clock A.M. This telegram announced that
Mr. Moffett's servant, Han Syek Chin, and Dr. Hall's Korean servant
had been thrown into prison and put into stocks, as were also the
men who sold the houses to the agents of Mr. Moffett and Dr. Hall.
In the same despatch Dr. Hall asked that protection be granted to
himself and his family.

As the person conspicuously concerned, Dr. Hall, was a British
subject, Mr. Gardner took hold of the matter vigorously. Unwilling to
wait for the slow process of the interpretation into Korean of an English
despatch at the Foreign Office, he at once sent a trusty Chusa to that
office to insist on his behalf that the President send, without delay, a
telegram to Ping Yang ordering the release of the servant of Dr. Hall
and that the Dr. and his family be protected. At the same time and
after counsel with me, he telegraphed to Dr. Hall informing him what
had been done by him.

Not doubting that the telegram would be sent forthwith and that
it would be effective, I waited for further news. However, in the afternoon, Dr. Scranton brought to us another telegram from Dr. Hall more

urgent than the first. He informed us that the two servants were in the death cell and being beaten; that the payment of fifty dollars would buy off those beating them; that the men who had sold the houses to Messrs. Hall and Moffett were also in the death cell; and that unless relief should come speedily, all were likely to be Killed.

Upon this I also sent a Chusa, Mr. Hong, to the Foreign Office, instructed to insist upon the immediate release of Mr. Moffett's servant and that the cause of complaint, if any be laid before me. I also telegraphed to the servant, Han Syek Chin, what Mr. Gardner and myself had done at the Foreign Office. My Chusa was gone for more than two hours and then returned with words that the President of the Foreign Office had not yet wired the Governor; that he wanted more time to consider; that the Governor of Ping Yang had telegraphed him that the persons punished were guilty of selling houses to foreigners; that he must go at once to night counsil with His Majesty, and that he would soon determine the matter, etc. etc. By the time this word reached me, it was almost impossible to get further word to him, as he had already gone to the Palace. But at eleven P.M. the Message from him to the Governor of Ping Yang was at last despatched. It ordered that the men be released at once. "If you do it slowly a very bad business will probably arise. Release them."

But, nevertheless, at Eight A.M. of Friday, the Eleventh instant, Dr. Hall again telegraphed to Dr. Scranton that the servants were not yet released; but his own servants had been beaten in his presence; that his house had been stoned; that great excitement prevailed. Further telegrams, all of the same general tenor but Each more urgent than the last, came in at Ten-thirty A.M., and Three-twenty, and Six twenty-five P.M. No protection had been granted to Dr. Hall, the water-man had been forbidden to bring them water. The report that the governor had ordered the ∧ prisoner servants seemed to be confirmed. They had
death of the
already been cruelly beaten.

At seven P.M. came the last telegram for the day, which announced that all had been released and that the trouble seemed to be over, one of the servants having been seriously injured.

This ended immediate danger to Mr. Moffett's servant, and I have not thought it necessary to do more at present, especially as Mr. Gardner, whose national, Dr. Hall, was by far most deeply concerned, has asked for an Explanation of the delay in releasing the prisoners and in giving protection to the persons who properly looked to him for it.

On the twelfth instant, after all the immediate danger was passed, Mr. Gardner submitted to me a letter setting forth some of the relations of the Missionaries to the Koreans, the treaty, and to their general Legations. Inasmuch as the letter expressed with great clearness what I understand the views of my own government to be and as it would serve as a basis for an understanding of these views by the English speaking Missionaries, I willingly subscribed my concurrence over my own signature. I enclose a copy.

Dr. Scranton and Mr. Moffett have as a kind of justification for their virtual purchase of houses outside of treaty ports, referred to the alleged Example of the French Missionaries and the toleration of their action by the Korean Government. I have replied that I could not allow Americans to violate the treaty in this respect, Except upon previous notice to the Korean Government that their toleration of such practices on the past of other nationalities makes it proper for us to claim, under Article XIV of the treaty, the same privileges that are granted to others, but I would at any time present the facts to the Department of State and ask for its decision.

John M. B. Sill

NO. 11   Legation of the United States
Seoul, Korea, June 1, 1894

Secretary of State

Sir:

to inform
Referring to my No. 5, May 17, I have now the honor∧you that I am in receipt of advices this morning, from the Palace, to the effect that a considerable Gov'mt force marching from Chun Chu, the capital of Chulla Do, was met by a part of the rebel forces at Yung Whan, a town forty or fifty miles to the south of Chun Chu, and defeated, the rebels capturing the guns of the soldiers. Meanwhile the other portion of the rebel forces, made a detour and captured the Capital which the Kings forces had left unprotected.

I had received a reply from Admiral Skerrett, to my communication mentioned in my No. 5, in which he informs me that the greater part of the squadron under his command has been detailed for duty in the Bering Sea, and that he is unable at present to act on my suggestion to send a ship to Chemulpo. He adds, "Disturbances are continually arising among the people of Korea, but it has generally been found that the authorities have been able to afford immediate protection, and I trust such may also be the case in this instance. As soon as it is possible a vessel will be sent to Chemulpo."

I have written again to Admiral Skerrett, see my enclosure herewith, informing him that the rebellion is daily gaining strength, and that the Government is helpless to compel order, and that there might at any time be urgent need of a ship at Chemulpo to protect American interests and to make residence in Korea safe, since if the insurgents should approach Seoul they would meet with little effectual resistance. I may add that within the past few days, the British, French, Chinese and Japanese, have sent vessels to Chemulpo.

I further informed Admiral Skerrett that I would telegraph him for a ship only in case of such pressing need that a favorable response would be necessary to the safety of Americans.

JOHN M. B. SILL

NO. 551
Legation of the United States
Seoul, Korea, Apl 6, 1894

Secretary of State

Sir:

I have the honor to inform you that on the morning of the 30th ultimo, an official came to me very early from the King, announcing that the rebel—Kim Ok Kiun, who led the revolution of 1884, and has since been a refugee in Japan, had been assasinated in the American settlement at Shanghai, by a Korean—Hong Chong Oo, who had lived in Paris for some years. It seems that Hong persuaded Kim, with whom he was quite friendly, to accompany him to Shanghai.

His Majesty wished very much to have the murderer sent here for trial, —or rather to be honored—and requested me to telegraph to our Consul General at Shanghai to use his good offices in having the man given up. I did so, Mr. Hunter replying that he must decline to interfere.

Now, however, the man Hong has been turned over to the Chinese authorities for trial, and they will send him to Korea shortly by gunboat.

In Tokio something similar was taking place at about the same time.

A man Ye, who claimed to have a written order bearing the King's seal, authorizing him to kill another rebel refugee Pak Yong Ho, was arrested by the Japanese police upon advice given them by Pak. This man Ye then gave evidence of another conspirator Hung; the latter went for refuge to the Korean Legation; the Japanese Government requested the Chargé d'Affaires to give up Hung for a legal examination, but the Chargé declined to do so, unless he could sit as a Judge on the court. The Japanese declined to accede to his stipulation, and Mr. Otori their Minister here was requested by telegraph to lay the matter before the Korean Foreign Office; and this was done and another refusal was met with. It seems then that by order of the Japanese Foreign Office the Police entered the Korean Legation by force and took Hung to prison.

I have given you the facts as they came to me in many messages from the Palace. Mr. Dun being on the spot, will doubtless give you the facts far more clearly than I can.

Great excitement prevails here. His Majesty thought of withdrawing his Legation from Japan.

My advice, as well as that of others, was not to do so, as that would doubtless make little impression upon the Japanese, or if it did it might make more serious trouble, while the Chinese would be delighted with such a course. I suggested instead that they submit the matter to the Foreign Representatives in Japan, —Tokio, who would easily see who was in the wrong.

The presence of these traitors in Japan has been a constant source of anxiety to the King, and his advisers. They have tried in vain to get them back to Korea for punishment, and whether these assasins were instigated by the Government or not, they knew that their act would be appreciated at Court and well rewarded.

H. N. ALLEN

NO. 554

Legation of the United States
Seoul, Korea, April 17, 1894

Secretary of State

Sir:

Referring to my No. 551, Apl 6, I have now the honor to inform you that the body of the murdered rebel, Kim Ok Kiun, and the murdered Hong, were brought to Chemulpo on a Chinese gun-boat on the 12th inst., and handed over to the Korean authorities.

The body was brought at once to Seoul, where it was mutilated and parts of it sent around the country.

The mutilation took place on the evening of the 14th and on that morning, Mr. Otori, the Doyen, called the Representatives together and explained that he was under telegraphic orders from his Foreign Office, to remonstrate with this Government against the proposed mutilation. He asked us all to join him, but did not urge it.

It was the sentiment of all that, asside [sic] from a personal, unofficial explanation to the Koreans of the manner in which such acts are regarded abroad, we had better not meddle in this native custom.

The next morning, the Chinese Consul came to the German Consul to know if it were true that the Foreign Representatives were going to "support the Japanese in their demands for the body." The King also sent two officers to me to know if it were true that we were acting with the Japanese in this matter, showing that the Diplomatic meeting placed us in an equivocal position—a result that might have been contemplated when the meeting was called.

H. N. ALLEN

NO. 10

Department of State
Washington, May 31, 1894

Secretary of State

Sir:

I have received Mr. Allen's dispatch, of the 6th ultimo, in regard to Korean political murders.

In the case of Kim Ok-kiun, who led the revolution in Seoul in 1884, and who was murdered in Shanghai by a Korean, Mr. Allen states that at the instance of the King of Korea he telegraphed to the Consul-General of the United States at Shanghai, asking him to use his good offices in having the murderer of Kim Ok-kiun given up to Korean justice.

The Department regrets this action on the part of Mr. Allen. Kim was murdered by a Korean in the American settlement at Shanghai; but this gave our Consul-General no ground for intervention, for his power of protection and jurisdiction extended no further than over citizens of the United States residing in his purview. On this ground alone, omitting reference to any other, the Department disapproves of his action.

EDWIN F. UHL

NO. 428   *Confidential*   Legation of the United States
                                            Seoul, Korea, July 29, 1893

Secretary of State

Sir:

I have the honor to inform you that the news has reached here from Tokyo, that Mr. Otori, late Minister of Japan to China, has been designated by his Government, Envoy Extraordinary and Minister Plenipotentiary to China and Korea, and that Mr. Oishi, the former Minister to this country, has resigned from the Diplomatic Service.

This action seems to indicate a marked change in the policy of Japan toward this country; that she has put aside her hereditary jealousy and hatred of China, and has agreed to a combination of the two great Asiatic powers to prevent, together with the growth of American and European influence in Korea, the further advance of Russia southward, along the shores of the Pacific.

                                   is generally attributed
The cause of this change in attitude∧to the late "Bean Indemnity" question, referred to in Mr. Heard's Nos. 385, Apl 6, 396 May 6, and 399 May 20, 1893, in the negociations concerning which, Japan, having entangled herself in various complications, discovered that it was China who in reality held the whip hand over the Korean Government, and that the instructions of Mr. Yuan, the so called Chinese Resident at this Court, were obeyed as explicitly as though they were the orders of a Governor to provincial authorities. Desirous of extricating herself from the self incurred difficulties, it is said that Japan appealed to the Chinese Viceroy, Li Hung Chang, for his interference in her behalf, and that this is obtained by the concession on the part of the Japanese that they would thereafter acknowledge China's suzerainty over Korea. That China did urge the settlement is acknowledged by all (in fact, Mr. Yuan has said repeatedly that it was by his Government that the affair had been amicably arranged), and it is not to be supposed that China would extend any favor to her Japanese rival without some stipulation that she would be fully repaid.

Though Japan had always striven for Korean independence in hostility to China, and though she had hoped that, at some time in the future, this peninsular Kingdom might be made a part of her own empire, now, however, realizing that the diplomatic (?) actions of her last representative had destroyed every vestige of influence which she once may have had, and that perpetual altercations with the Chinese for control of the country would leave an open field for Russia to gradually encroach upon the territory from the north, she concluded that, for the present, it would be better to consent to an alliance with China against what is a menace to the desires of each Power. This was to be the more easily done by the present Japanese Government, as Mr. Oishi, late Minister to this Court, who is a strong political factor in the opposition party at home, has always advocated this step.

The first indication that something of this nature had been done was the appointment of Mr. Otori in the dual capacity of Minister to China and Korea, with a residence in Peking; it being understood, so the Chinese say, that all Korean business of importance will be transacted with Chinese officials at their own capital, and that while Korea is to be ostensibly recognized by Japan as an independent power, she will, in reality, be treated as subject to China. On the other hand, it is supposed that the Japanese official resident in Seoul will have the rank of Consul-General or Chargé d'Affaires.

A brief summary of the popular explanation of the matter is that the great fear of Russian encroachment and the conclusion that, since she cannot obtain the whole of the benefits arising from the control of Korea, it is better to share them equally with one power to the exclusion of all Americans and Europeans, have induced Japan into an alliance with her former rival.

This is, as I have said, the general opinion, but I cannot believe that Japan would consent to further the interests of China unless the inducement were greater than the one which is popularly supposed to have influenced her. To my mind, if she has in any way acknowledged China's suzerainty here, she has done so with some ulterior purpose of turning such an acknowledgement to her own advantage in eventually securing mastery of the country. Her own influence here is gone; she has nothing to lose; she joins forces with China and *perhaps* by their combined efforts they may be able to compel the Korean King to acknowledge that this country is a dependency of the Chinese Emperor. In that case, she concludes that all foreign powers must necessarily recognize Korea as such. Then in the event of a war with China, a war which seems inevitable, should Japan be successful, she would appropriate Korea as her own without any interference on the part of the western world.

Naturally, the Representatives of the European powers are anxiously awaiting some move that will display the true state of affairs, conscious that the existence of this rumored combination would necessitate, on their part, a strong policy to maintain Korean integrity and to prevent the loss of all their influence in Commerce and in the direction of the Country's growth.

The Russian Chargé d'Affaires, Mr. Dmitriosky, has told me that he is of the opinion that England may have urged this alliance, but that it was immaterial to his Government, as he was confident that it would be short-lived, and that, at any rate, Russia was desirous of peace in this quarter of the world for two years to come. The meaning of this is, that the Russian trans-Siberian railway to Vladivostock will not be completed before the expiration of that time, and, until it is constructed, Russia will postpone all active operations.

If England has interested herself in the matter, and I think she has not, it shows that she is as fearful of any Russian advance along the north Pacific coast as of a nearer advance toward India.

In order to ascertain the truth in regard this reported alliance, I have written to Mr. Edwin Dun, United States Minister to Japan, for any information he can obtain throwing light on Japan's position, and, on its receipt, I shall communicate the same to the Department.

                                                        JOSEPH R. HEROD

NO. 504   *Confidential*   Legation of the United States
                                            Seoul, Korea, Dec. 20, 1893

Secretary of State

Sir:

A very interesting contest is going on here between the Chinese and Japanese Representatives, regarding the export of rice, and as it has a distinct bearing on the present and future status of these two countries here, as well as upon the political condition of Korea itself, I have the honor to acquaint you with the facts in the case.

As I informed you in my No. 472, Oct. 18, the condition of the crops was so threatening at that time, that none of the Foreign Representatives could object to the Government prohibition of the export of rice; and as a matter of fact none did object but the Japanese.

When we found later on that the fair weather had improved the prospects, we got the date of prohibition advanced, see my No. 481, Nov. 7. Still later on, at a Diplomatic meeting called by the Doyen—the Japanese minister, we agreed—with two exceptions, the French and Russians—to ask the Government to remove the prohibition entirely, owing to the low price and plentiful supply of rice; see my Consular Report No. 53, Dec. 7.

The President of the Foreign Office assured several of us that the request would be complied with, but later he came to each of us personally, in a great state of agitation, asking us to recall our letters to him in which we had asked for the repeal of the prohibition. It was evident that some great influence had been brought to bear upon him, in consequence of which he had completely changed front. As none of us would agree to recall our letters, he finally wrote to us stating that rice was so scarce that the export would not be allowed till the next spring's barley crop was harvested.

Personally I think they are doing wisely. The prohibition has doubtless prevented a revolution. Rice is now very cheap for the reason that the people have so fought against this export of their food, which gave the dealers an ever ready excuse for raising the price, that now, with no such fear on the part of the people, or pretext for extortion on the part of dealers, things have assumed a natural healthy condition.

Nevertheless, I think it just as well to remind the Foreign Office occasionally that they cannot go too far in this line. And, considering the present easy condition, and the fact that our American Firm is interested in the rice business, I think it wise to unite with the Japanese—to a certain extent—in working for the reapeal [sic] of the prohibition.

This is especially the case as the Korean Government is very slow in discharging its obligations to Americans, and they might as well see that these courtesies should be reciprocal.

To Japanese trade the export question is one of life or death, see my No. 483, No. 20, pages 6, 7 & 8. And, while they are contesting the matter strongly, it has long been known that the Chinese used the prospective famine to get in a master stroke against Japanese trade, for, while it was soon known that Mr. Yuan proposed the prohibition, any further evidence as to his action in the matter that might be needed, is furnished by the fact that the Korean people are about to erect a memorial tablet to him in the market space; on which will be inscribed characters praising him for "prohibiting the export of rice and saving the country." I hear that the Foreign Office is very anxious to prevent the erection of this stone, lest the Foreign Representatives resent it, but it will probably be erected.

Chinese policy here is well illustrated in this incident, showing as it does that while China rules here with a rod of iron when necessary, she yet manages to make the people kiss the hand that smites them.

The Japanese on the contrary make themselves positively hated. They will in all probability push this rice export question to an ugly end, but of course if such a termination is probable, the other Foreign Representatives will not be with them.

H. N. Allen

NO. 225   Department of State
                                          Washington, February 5, 1894

H. N. Allen

Sir:

I have to acknowledge receipt of your confidential despatch No. 504, of the 20th of December last, in relation to the contest between the Chinese and Japanese representatives for supremacy in Korea, and to the success of the Chinese in causing the defeat of the effort recently made to bring about the removal of the prohibition on the export of rice.

The Department infers from your despatch, and approves, a disposition on your part not to permit the legation to favor, even in appearance, the unfortunate intrigues which are engendered at Seoul by rival interests, and to take no part in remonstrance against proposed economic measures except so far as may be needful for the expressed protection of any legitimate American interest thereby injured.

W. Q. Gresham

NO. 14   Legation of the United States
                                            Seoul, Korea, June 18, 1894

Secretary of State

Sir:

Referring to my No. 11 of June 1st, I now have the honor to inform you that the Korean Government discouraged by the success of the rebellion in the South, and upon the urgent request, which to them have the value of commands, of the Chinese representative here, asked Chinese aid, and 2000 Chinese troops were at once dispatched to Asani—a port in the South. Before they could arrive however the Korean troops succeeded in capturing the Chief rebels, and a few days later they recaptured Chun Chu—the capital of Chul La Do, taken by the rebels. The Chinese troops have not as yet actively helped in the suppression of the rebellion. Meantime it became known that the Japanese were also sending troops to Korea, and the Korean Government fearing trouble, asked the Chinese to leave. This they promised to do, but as 5000 Japanese marines landed at Chemulpo and came to Seoul on June 10th, the Chinese held their troops where they were.

On June 13th, 800 Japanese soldiers came to Seoul and relieved the Marines. These soldiers had arrived at Chemulpo on transports the day before. They also left some 200 troops at Chemulpo and along the road to Seoul, at certain points of which they threw up earth works, while they left a guard at the ferry near Seoul and at other important places along the Seoul road.

Mr. Otori, the Japanese Minister to Korea and China, who went away on leave June 1st, returned with the troops. On being interogated [sic] Mr. Otori replied that he brought over his troops for the protection of Japanese subjects and his Legation, which seemed quite plausible considering the fact that there are 1000 Japanese in this city, 4000 at Chemulpo and about 10000 at Fusan and Wonsan, while the necessity of protection was shown them in the loss of about 60 people in the rebellion of 1884 and 40 more in that of 1882.

After the rebellion in 1884, China and Japan by the Tientsin Convention of 1885 each agreed not to land troops in Korea without first informing the other. The Chinese complied with the terms of this convention and it is supposed that the Japanese did likewise.

Later on the 16th instant, 3000 Japanese troops landed at Chemulpo, and now I am informed that they are encamped with batteries upon the General Foreign Settlement at Chemulpo, without the consent of the other powers, thus wholly ignoring the treaty rights, of each nation represented here. I have joined my European Colleagues today in an earnest protest against this action.

The Koreans are terribly alarmed. The King has begged the Chinese to leave, but they refuse to do so as long as the Japanese remain, and the latter positively refuse to leave till the Chinese go. Meantime the Chinese citizens here are so greatly alarmed that 1000 of them are said to be leaving for China tomorrow, as they fear a general butchery by the Japanese.

If the Chinese troops come to Seoul from the South, or if other Chinese troups come to Chemulpo from China, bloodshed will doubtless result. England is said to be occupying Port Hamilton with her fleet. There are 28 men-of-war and transports at Chemulpo, representing 6 nationalities, as follows, Japan, China, America, England,

France & Russia. We do not know what France & particularly Russia will do in the event of a clash of arms, but the Koreans fear them very greatly.

Admiral Skerrett arrived at Chemulpo on his Flag ship "Baltimore", June 5th, in response to advices from Washington. He sent his Flag Lieutenant to confer with me, as he was thought to be too ill to come to Seoul himself. I went to the Flag ship the next day, the 8th, with the Lieutenant, and on the 12th the Admiral came to Seoul with two officers. On the 13th, the King received us in Audience and expressed his gratitude for the presence of an American ship. The Admiral returned to his ship on the 15th. He has now promised to remain till things assume a less threatening aspect.

It is pretty evident that the fault in the present difficulties is due to the action of the Chinese in forcing their troops upon Korea. Had they not done so, probably a much smaller force of Japanese, or none at all, would have been sent.

As it now stands the Japanese are here and they probably believe they cannot leave without "losing face"; they might possibly like an opportunity to assert their fast fading influence in Korea. As the two powers are jealous of each other, some irresponsible outrage committed upon a Chinaman by a Japanese, or vice versa, might be the beginning of a deplorable contest on Korean ground. Also it is not improbable that disaffected Korean officials may, upon Japanese encouragement, endeavor to repeat the political assasinations of 1884. This contingency is much feared at the Palace.

Of course this Government is primarily at fault for prostituting the competitive examinations by selling rank openly, and for such high prices, that the officials are not only encouraged, but compelled to grind the last cash, or its equivalent, from the people.

It is impossible at present to forecast the intent of Japan. It would seem that they must have some ulterior purpose. I have wired by cipher to Mr. Dun at Tokio, informing him of the situation and asking for any information within his reach.

There is a report not yet fully authenticated that Japan is sending large numbers of troops to Fusan and Wonsan.

The matter of asylum has already been mentioned. I am giving it my careful and deliberate consideration and if it becomes necessary to act, I shall endeavor to conform to established usage.

JOHN M. B. SILL

Legation of the United States
                                    Seoul, Korea, June 25, 1894

Secretary of State

Sir:

On Saturday evening the 23rd inst., I received the following despatch signed "Uhl, Acting." "In view of the friendly interest of the United States in the welfare of Korea and its people, you are instructed by direction of the President to use every possible effort for the preservation of peaceful conditions."

On yesterday I telegraphed you as follows, "Uhl, Washington. Have received telegram. I have already done and will do as much as possible for the interest of peace. Korean rebellion suppressed by themselves. Thousands of Chinese and Japanese troops occupying Korea. Neither of them will withdraw first. In their presence there is much danger. Chinese are in favor of simultaneous departure. Japanese stubborn. Ulterior purpose suspected. She seems to desire war. Korean integrity menaced. The King asks your intercession with the Government of Japan. Sill"

I wish to explain that in pursuance of the Departments instructions to my predecessor Mr. Heard, see No. 20, June 7, 1890, and in view of the fact that your message to me was in figures, I put my telegram in figures. In this shape it made 93 words, whereas, had I put it in words by the code, it would have made but 48. Hereafter I shall use words instead of figures unless otherwise instructed.

In reference to my telegram as quoted, I may say that I had it all ready when your message was received, as I was aware that for several days His Majesty and his advisers were busy in preparing a despatch asking for your intercession. It was intended at first to ask only the aid of America in this matter, but lest offence might be taken, the despatch was sent to each of the Caucasian Representatives here, (see copy) asking the kindly offices of each. At once upon the receipt of this despatch I sent off my telegram to you as quoted.

In the meantime I joined with my colleagues the Representatives of England Russia and France, here, in a request to the Japanese and Chinese authorities here for a simultaneous withdrawal of their troops, (see copy.)

The German representative did not wish to join in this request before informing his Government.

I may add that the situation grows daily more strained. The Japanese troops numbering some 5000, are encamped with batteries about

Seoul. And Mr. Otori is to have an audience with His Majesty tomorrow, when it is said he will ask certain questions which will doubtless bring matters to a crisis.

Last night I was shown a telegram to the Palace, from the Korean Minister at Tokio stating that China and Japan with 5000 soldiers each, would fight soon on Korean soil.

Admiral Skerrett is very desirous of leaving for Japan, and had publicly announced the 23rd inst, as the date of his departure. In view of the alarming aspect of the situation I succeeded in persuading him to delay his departure. It would be exceedingly unfortunate if I should be left at this time with our 80 Americans here unprotected, as the greatest personal danger would doubtless be from mob force over which the authorities would have no control.

John M. B. Sill

Foreign Office
Seoul, Korea, June 24, 1894

J. M. B. Sill

Your Excellency:

I have the honor to state that I am directed by His Majesty to bring to the notice of the Foreign Representatives a certain condition of things now Existent in this Kingdom, with a view of its being communicated to the several Governments having treaty relations with Korea.

At this moment the troops of two nations, namely China and Japan, are in occupation of Korean soil. The first by invitation, to aid in quelling a rebellion; the other without invitation and against the protest of the Korean Government, but, as represented to me, on account of solicitude for the safety of her own subjects resident here.

The necessity for the presence of both of these has now ceased. The Chinese authorities under these circumstances, are now willing to remove their troops from Korean soil, provided Japan will remove hers. But Japan refuses to remove her troops until the Chinese have been removed, and neglects to entertain any proposition for the simultaneous removal of both.

The presence of a large army in time of peace, the landing of cavalry and artillery, the placing of batteries and Keeping a guard at strategic points after internal quiet is assured, is a dangerous precedent for other nations and a menace to the peace and integrity of His Majesty's realm.

I respectfully submit to the Foreign Representatives and their Governments, that at a time when Japan and Korea are at peace the presence and holding of Japanese armed troops in Korean territory, in Extraordinary numbers, is not in accordance with the law of nations.

I am directed by His Majesty to ask that the Foreign Representatives, being fully acquainted with the facts of the situation, will use their friendly offices as profered [sic] by treaty, in affecting an amicable solution of the present situation.

[Signed] CHO PIONG CHIK

NO. 16   Legation of the United States
                                              Seoul, June 29, 1894

Secretary of State

Sir:

Referring to my No. 15, June 25, I have now the honor to inform you that, in response to the Joint note of the Caucasion [sic] Foreign Representatives here, addressed to the Representatives of China and Japan at this place, and suggesting to them the advisability of a simultaneous withdrawal of their respective military forces, a copy of which note I enclosed with my No. 15, we received on the next day, June 25, a reply, as per enclosed copy, from Mt. Otori, stating that he would communicate our suggestion to his Government. The same day we also received a reply in the same sense from Mr. Yuan, —see enclosed copy. The following day, the 26th, Mr. Yuan sent us another letter, see copy enclosed, stating that at 3 A.M. that day, the Grand Council of his Government, which includes the Emperor, had considered our communication, but were compelled to say that as Japan had refused to withdraw her troops from Korea, the troops of China must remain.

I have heard since on good authority that the Emperor of China had decided to set aside the 60,000,000 Taels, collected for his 61st birthday anniversary celebration, to be used in putting down this trouble, and that no celebration should take place until this matter is settled.

The Japanese troops have occupied the hills and all other strategic points about Seoul. They also have complete control of the river from Seoul to Chemulpo, and the roads leading to and from these points, so that the Chinese will meet with very effectual opposition when they arrive.

I have now to state also that at the urgent request of His Majesty, I have agreed to grant asylum to the Royal Family and other high officials, if it becomes necessary, at the same time deprecating any such change of location by the heads of the Government unless it becomes absolutely necessary.

In view of this event, I have finally persuaded Admiral Skerrett to increase the guard promised me from 12 to 120 men, as the former number would be quite inadequate for the protection of the legation alone.

A conflict may be expected at any time. More Japanese troops are arriving almost daily, and the Chinese Government is reported to be actively engaged in massing and equipping an adequate force.

On the 26th instant, Mr. Otori had an audience with His Majesty, in which he presented a paper, by order of his Sovereign, stating that Japan found it necessary, for the mutual welfare of the two countries, to ask that certain radical changes be made in the Government and policy of Korea, such changes to be made upon consultation with the Japanese authorities, and that until these changes are made in a manner satisfactory to Japan, the Japanese troops would not be withdrawn. See copy enclosed.

I may add that Japan seems to be very kindly disposed toward Korea. She seems only to desire, once for all, to throw off the yoke of Chinese Suzerainty and then to assist her weak neighbor in strengthening her position as an Independent State, by aiding her in such reforms as shall bring peace, prosperity and enlightenment to her people, —a motive which pleases many Korean officials of the more intelligent sort, and one which, I imagine, will not meet with disapproval in America.

JOHN M. B. SILL

NO. 23   Legation of the United States
                                              Seoul, Korea, July 2, 1894

Secretary of State

Sir:

Continuing the subject of military operations in Korea, see my Nos. 15, 16 & 17, I have now to inform you that on the 28th instant, Mr. Otori demanded a declaration to be given the next day, by the Korean Foreign Office, as to whether Korea is tributary to China or not.

This caused great consternation, as, if they answered in the negative they would offend China, while an affirmative answer, might bring down the wrath of Japan, after many consultations, and several reminders to be prompt from the Japanese, an answer was given in this sense, "Korea being an independent State enjoys the same Sovereign rights as does Japan" (See treaty of Kang Hoa 1876) and that in "both internal administration and foreign intercourse Korea enjoys complete independence" (See letter of the King to the President of the United States). They suppose that by thus granting the treaties which China allowed them to make, she cannot take offense, while Japan should be content with such answer. I hear in fact that the Japanese are quite pleased with her reply.

JOHN M. B. SILL

Telegram   Department of State
                                         Washington, July 9, 1894

Sill, Minister, Seoul.

Your telegram yesterday received. I told Korean Minister here this Government could not intervene forcibly. I did not advise him that Korea should protest and notify foreign powers. Two days ago I sent, by cable, to our Minister to Japan, the following instruction:

"The Government of the United States has heard with sincere regret that, although the insurrection has been suppressed and peace prevails in Korea, Japan refuses to withdraw her troups and demands that radical changes be made in the domestic administration of Korea. This demand is the more remarkable in view of the fact that China favors the simultaneous withdrawal of both the Japanese and Chinese troops. Cherishing sincere friendship for both Japan and Korea, the United States indulge the hope that Korea's independence and sovereignty will be respected. You are instructed to say to the Government at Tokyo that the President will be painfully disappointed should Japan visit upon her feeble and defenceless neighbor the horrors of an unjust war."

GRESHAM

Telegram   Seoul, July 8, 1894

Gresham

Washington

Admiral left on the second against my judgement. Received his notice the day after his departure; he said that, according to instructions from the Department, he has ordered "Monocacy" to relieve him and said that she is expected hourly. I am not yet advised of their sailing. I have promised the King asylum, in case of emergency. Admiral's departure places me in a humiliating and most perilous position. The Minister at Washington communicated by telegraph to this Government that you have advised them to protest against the demand of the Japanese Government made under duress and to notify the foreign ministers.

                                                                    SILL

NO. 33   Legation of the United States
                                            Seoul, Korea, July 24, 1894

Secretary of State

Sir:

Referring to my Numbers 15, 16, 23 & 32 of recent dates regarding military operations in Korea, I now have to inform you that at 4 A.M. on yesterday, the Japanese forces broke into and took possession of the Royal Palace, a number of soldiers on both sides being killed. The King was very courageous and stood his ground quieting all by his dignified bearing.

The Japanese then compelled the presence of the Ex-Regent, father of the King, and bitter enemy of the Queen's party—thus seeming to wish to pit one faction against another. We fear that assasinations will result.

In his distress, the King asked the Foreign Representatives to come to see him. We decided to do so, and, later in the day we went in a body to the Palace, the Japanese minister having arranged for us to pass his strong guard. As a result of this meeting we decided to do the only thing we could, that is, to cable the facts to our respective governments and ask their good offices. This will be the subject of another despatch.

The city was in a great turmoil. Our Legation began to fill up with refugees, and having no American guard, our Koreans were unable to protect the gates. Soon, we had 40 or more on the place and were unable to exclude others.

The telegraph to Chemulpo was cut, but the Japanese Minister kindly agreed to forward a message for me to Capt. Day of the Baltimore over his military line. I also sent a fast courier with a letter, having been furnished a Japanese military pass for him to go through the lines. The courier returned in 24 hours, bearing a letter from my agent in Chemulpo, stating that both messages had been received and delivered on board the "Baltimore". I have had no intimation from Capt. Day however as to his intentions. I may say that he has stated publicly at Chemulpo that—"Americans need no protection. If they would attend to their business and not mix in politics there would be no trouble." This has given great dissatisfaction and is very unjust. Our people are very quiet hardworking and have nothing to do with the politics here.

Capt. Impey of the Monocacy happened fortunately to come up here yesterday with his Paymaster, and from him I learn that our Navy sympathizes quite warmly with the Japanese. Many Americans here have a leaning in that direction, as we all wish to see Korea progress. Yet, as one gentleman very aptly stated, "this would be all very well were there no tomorrow."

China must resent this insult, and once her hordes begin to press accross [sic] the northern border, no force here will be able to stay the tide. The Chinese merchants have all left here, fearing the looting by their own troops that they say will surely follow their first success.

Capt. Impey seems to think that we need no guard as the Japanese will protect us. I am quite aware that the Japanese will do this. I have had only courtesy from them and have been courteous in return. At the same time I feel that I would be violating my instructions and laying myself open to severe and merited disapproval from my Government if I should ask for a Japanese guard when I may just as well apply to my own Government forces for protection. I could not do a thing more offensive to the Government to which I am accredited, while I would render our own position very precarious by doing so, since the Chinese when they come would certainly resent our having made the Japanese position so much stronger by such action.

I have 80 American men women and children, of high standing in their own country, under my care here, and I feel that I must use the greatest caution in preserving a strict neutrality in all these troubles. If I do not hear from Capt. Day very soon I shall cable you for assistance.

Also referring to this series Number 32, July 18, page 2, I may say that at a meeting of the Foreign Representatives, it was decided that we should refer the matter of the Japanese assault upon H. B. M.'s Acting Consul General, C. T. Gardner, C. M. E. to our representatives in Japan. I therefore sent to Mr. Dun a letter of which the enclosed is a copy. The enclosures called for in this copy are to be found with the above Number 32, 1/23/.

The English Naval Captain in charge of the guard at the British Consulate, called upon the Japanese General and received an apology for this insult to the British Representative, but I do not think it was entirely satisfactory.

JOHN M. B. SILL

Seoul, Korea, July 25, 1894

[Yuan Shi Kai]

[K. Otori]

Your Excellency:

We have the honor to inform you that the Korean government has asked our friendly offices in the present situation in Korea, and has suggested as a solution of the present difficulties, the simultaneous withdrawal of Chinese and Japanese troops from the Korean territory.

We the under-signed representatives solemnly submit this proposal for Your favorable consideration as a course consistent with the honor and dignity of two great nations with which all our governments are in friendly relations.

We feel confident that Your Excellency will fully understand that the interests of our governments are deeply affected as the continued presence of foreign troops on Korean soil may easily lead to complications disadvantageous to the security of our nationals.

We should esteem it a favor if Your Excellency would be pleased to present this communication to Your government at Your earliest convenience.

We will of course at the same time communicate immediately the request of the Korean government to our respective governments.

JNO. M. B. SILL FOR THE UNITED STATES
PAUL DE KEHRBERG FOR RUSSIA
I. LEFEVRE FOR FRANCE
C. T. GARDNER FOR ENGLAND

Legation of the United States
Seoul, Korea, August 3, 1894

Secretary of State

Sir:

Referring to the Naval Engagement between Japan and China mentioned in my No. 35, July 26, page 3, I have now the honor to inform you that the Japanese report of the same, unofficial, is as follows, "On July 23rd, three Japanese men-of-war, coming to Chemulpo with an Admiral on board, on passing Prince Jerome Gulf met two Chinese men-of-war who passed by without saluting the Japanese Admiral and acted in a suspicious manner.

"Japanese men-of-war followed them some distance and firing took place between the two fleets.

"At the same time the Japanese fleet noticed a Chinese gunboat and a transport steamer with a large number of soldiers.

"They were stopped and boarded by a ships boat and captain told he could not land these troops, but must follow the Japanese fleet.

"This the Captain agreed to and he lowered a boat to go to the Japanese man-of-war, but was prevented from doing so by the Chinese soldiers on board.

"The transport then began to move and opened firing with rifles. Thereupon the Japanese ship fired into her and sunk her.

"Three Europeans jumped overboard and were rescued by a boat which was lowered by the Japanese ship.

"The Chinese gunboat after exchanging some shots surrendered.

"The two Chinese cruisers above said also exchanged shots for some time with the Japanese fleet, when smoke and fog enveloped the whole fleet, and the Chinese disappeared but one of the Chinese of the Canton fleet was found afterward, burning on the beach at the entrance of Prince Jerome Gulf, at which place her crew probably landed.

"Two of the Japanese men-of-war received one shot each. One was struck on the boom and the other in a tank, but no men were wounded."

I also enclose a copy of the sworn statement of Major von Hanniken, a German officer in the employ of the Chinese Government, who was on the British transport Kow Shing above referred to. His report is of great interest. He is the only one of ten European officers on board who escaped with life and liberty. He was several hours in the water before being picked up by a Korean junk.

His report in the main confirms the Japanese report, but shows further that the transport, (which by the way was the property of the British Firm, Jardine Matheson) was flying British colors at the time, and that she was at anchor when fired into. He also shows that the men struggling in the water were fired upon by their own people on the sinking transport as well as by the Japanese soldiers.

An extensive land battle has been fought near An San some forty miles south. As all telegraph communication is interrupted our reports of this are rather vague.

The Japanese report that the battle took place on the 28th & 29th, between 3000 Japanese and 4500 Chinese, of which the Japanese loss was 70 killed and wounded while the Chinese loss 1200 and all their artillery and stores.

The English gave the figures as Japanese loss 200, Chinese 800.

The British representative here has charge of Chinese interests as all Chinese officials have fled.

JOHN M. B. SILL

H.I.J.M.'s Legation
Seoul 6, August 1894

[John M. B. Sill, *et al.*]

The undersigned has the honor to inform his colleagues that the following notice has been given by Japanese Government to all Foreign Representatives in Tokio on the 31st of July, and that war has been formally declared against China by the Imperial Rescript of August 1st.

Japanese Government having exhausted every honourable means to bring about a just lasting settlement of differences existing between China and Japan, and those efforts having proved wholly unavailing, the undersigned has the honour in fulfillment of duty devolving upon him to announce to you that state of war exists between China and Japan.

MUTSU MUNEMUTSU

The undersigned avails himself of this occasion to renew to his colleagues the assurance of his highest consideration.

(signed) K. OTORI

6 August 1894

Dear Mr. Sill:

I have the honor to acquaint you that I have received your telegram from H.I.J.M.'s Minister for Foreign Affairs that our Legation and Consulates, their archives, as well as Japanese subjects in China, have been placed under the protection of the United States, those legations and consulates having been withdrawn in consequence of the cessation of peaceful relations between our country and China.

K. OTORI

TREATY OF ALLIANCE BETWEEN JAPAN AND KOREA

Signed at Seoul, August 26, 1894

In view of the fact that on the 25th day of July, 1894, the Korean Government entrusted His Imperial Majesty's Envoy Extraordinary and Minister Plenipotentiary at Söul, Korea, with the expulsion, on their behalf, of Chinese soldiers from Korean territory, the Governments of Japan and Korea have been placed in a situation to give mutual assistance both offensive and defensive. Consequently the undersigned Plenipotentiaries, duly authorized by their respective Governments, have, with a view of defining the fact and of securing in the promises concerted action on the part of the two countries, agreed to the following Articles:—

ARTICLE I. The object of the alliance is to maintain the Independence of Korea on a firm footing and to promote the respective interests of both Japan and Korea by expelling Chinese soldiers from Korean territory.

ARTICLE II. Japan will undertake all warlike operations against China, both offensive and defensive, while Korea will undertake to give every possible facility to Japanese soldiers regarding their movements and supply of provisions.

ARTICLE III. This treaty shall cease and determine at the conclusion of a Treaty of Peace with China.

In witness whereof, the Plenipotentiaries of the two countries, have signed the treaty and hereunto affixed their seals.

> KEISUKE OTORI, H.I.J.M's Envoy Extraordinary
> and Minister Plenipotentiary
> KIM IN SHIOUKU, H.K.M's Minister for
> Foreign Affairs.

Secretary of State

Sir:

I have the honor to inform you that, hearing reports of a Japanese victory in the north, I at once wrote to the Japanese minister Mr. Otori for information on the subject and promptly received a reply from which I quote as follows:—"I can give you the following official information despatched from Ping Yang by General Nasse, Commander of the Division which had actually taken part in the battle of Ping Yang. We began attack on the Chinese at Ping Yang on the fifteenth and at the dawn of the sixteenth Ping Yang fell into the hands of our troops. The attack was made from all sides. No retreat was possible for the Chinese. The Chinese killed and captured are numberless!"

I then asked Mr. Otori to send the enclosed message in Japanese over his military line to Mr. Dun, to be translated and forwarded to you. He kindly agreed to do so.

This is the first news of any importance that I have had for the past six weeks. The telegraph lines are entirely in the hands of the Japanese who have not cared to give out information. We have been aware of the constant movement of troops but estimates of numbers were not reliable.

The Chinese force at Ping Yang has been variously estimated at from 20 to 108 thousand, probably 40,000 is near the correct number. The Japanese force engaged is said to have been one division, or 35,000 all told. The total Japanese force in Korea is estimated to be as great as 80,000. The actual figures are not given officially however and until a few days past we have known of but one army division 35,000.

JOHN M. B. SILL

NO. 51   Legation of the United States
                                            Seoul, Korea, September 20, 1894

Secretary of State

Sir:

I have the honor to inform you that last evening I received from the Japanese Legation the following official information.

"According to report brought by Moyami Gawa Maru from Tatong

River our fleet met eleven Chinese men-of-war and six torpedo boats— 35 miles off Hai Yang Island, at one oclock the 16th instant. The naval engagement took place in which four Chinese men-of-war were sunk down and seven burnt themselves. No damage to our fleet."

At once I asked Mr. Otori to forward the following telegram to Mr. Dun in Japanese to be translated and forwarded to you.

"Dun. American Minister, Tokio. Please cable Department of State. Japanese fleet destroyed eleven out of seventeen Chinese war vessels at mouth of Ping Yang river. Sixteenth instant. Japanese fleet unharmed."

This message was sent at once.

JOHN M. B. SILL

NO. 75   Legation of the United States
                                          Seoul, Korea, Dec. 20, 1894

Secretary of State

Sir:

I have the honor to hand you enclosed a translation of a Royal Decree, that appeared in the Official Gazette of this Court on the 17th instant.

This Decree restricts the residence of Chinese Subjects in Korea to the Open Ports, and forbids them to travel in the Interior, except upon the road, or river, between Seoul and Chemulpo. It requires them to report their arrival in Korea to the Korean Local Authorities within 24 hours after landing, and to give notice and get permission when they desire to change their residence. Exteritorial [sic] rights are removed and Chinese Subjects are placed under the jurisdiction of the Korean Courts.

JOHN M. B. SILL

NO. 155   Legation of the United States
                                          Seoul Korea Oct. 7, 1895

Secretary of State

Sir:

We usually expect disturbances here among the people in the interior in the Autumn. I now have the honor to inform you that they are of

a rather more serious nature than usual this year. The defeated
Chinese soldiers in fleeing from the Japanese at Peng Yang last year,
threw away their guns, belts, etc., and these have been collected, and
retained by the people who have in some instances joined bands of
robbers. These armed bands are especially bad in the provinces of
Whang Hai.

Soldiers cannot be sent after them lest they also join the robbers.
The soldiers have been very poorly paid of late and have made several
demonstrations against the Government. On the night of the 3rd
instant they attacked the Seoul police, who are better paid, killing one
man and demolishing all the police stations along the main street. It
is expected that we will witness great disorder here during the winter.

H. N. ALLEN

NO. 43   Legation of the United States
                                              Seoul, Korea, August 17, 1894

Secretary of State

Sir:

I have the honor to hand you enclosed a copy of the translation of a
despatch received by me on yesterday from the Korean Foreign Office,
announcing that, at the instance of Japan, Korea has abolished or
abrogated, all the treaty regulations made with her by China.

I have also received a despatch from the same office announcing that
the coinage of the mint erected some two years ago by Japanese for
this Government, will now be used in the transaction of all business
in Korea.

The great council mentioned in my No. 32, July 18, is still sitting
and is daily adopting reforms in accordance with the suggestions of
Japan. I will send you a copy of these when they are officially agreed
upon.

Since writing my No. 87, Aug 7, there has been nothing of a decisive
nature to write you about.

JOHN M. B. SILL

Legation of the United States
Seoul, Korea, Sept. 24, 1894

Secretary of State

Sir:

Referring to my No. 32, July 18, it will be recalled that previous to the capture of the Palace by the Japanese, His Majesty had appointed a large influential council to consider and propose reforms in the details of Korean Government. This council, consisting of seventeen members, had the date of the despatch mentioned above already proposed several sweeping reforms. This council is also referred to as engaged in their work under suggestions from Japan, in my No. 43, August 16. As their deliberations are likely to continue a long time. I have thought it best to enclose a copy of the report of their proceedings to and including August 28—the date of last adjournment.

We have no official knowledge that all of these recommendations have received the endorsement or approval of His Majesty, though I am informed by a prominent member of the council that he has, generally willingly, but sometimes quite unwillingly, approved them all; and we know that many of them have already gone into effect, at least here in Seoul, where Japanese authority is able to look to their enforcement. Outside of Seoul and its vicinity, there seems to be no efficient government. The governors and magistrates disregard the orders of the King, saying that His Majesty is a helpless prisoner and that orders coming from him are really from their traditional enemy the Japanese, and that they best serve their King by refusing obedience to commands so obtained from him.

There is little of what we would call true patriotism in Korea, but there is almost universal hatred of the Japanese and a good degree of loyal love of the King. It would seem good Japanese policy to work through His Majesty who could easily be brought to favor Japanese views and whose subjects would generally fall into line if they saw him kindly and respectfully treated and believed him to have some freedom of choice. But the forcible entry of the Japanese into the Palace and the cramping limitations under which it is notorious that His Majesty is held, tend, on the contrary, to break down his authority and belittle him in the eyes of his subjects, and so render him powerless to help in establishing the forms set forth in the accompanying enclosure.

JOHN M. B. SILL

NO. 325   Legation of the United States
                                       Seoul, Korea, Nov. 5, 1892

Secretary of State

Sir:

In my No. 222, Dec. 17, 1891, I gave some details of the situation
and working of the Royal Korean School in charge of an American
Instructor, Mr. D. A. Bunker.

Since that time a school has been established by His Majesty in
Seoul under much the same conditions for the purpose of teaching the
Japanese language to Korean youths, and has been reasonably successful. The pupils number about 30, and are drawn chiefly from the
middle classes, from whom interpreters are generally taken. They
acquire Japanese with great facility, owing to its resemblance in
character and idiom to the Korean language, and—as a measure of
comparison—the principal is of opinion that they would learn as much
Japanese in one year as of English in five years.

This school affords another means of diffusing Japanese influence,
of which I spoke in my No. 301, Sept 12.

                                                 AUGUSTINE HEARD

NO. 74   Legation of the United States
                                       Seoul, Korea, Dec. 18, 1894

Secretary of State

Sir:

I have the honor to inform you that the Official Gazette of this Court,
on yesterday, had the announcement of the appointment of the new
Korean Cabinet, a translation of which I enclose herewith.

The cabinet is quite a representative one. The two political exiles
who are largely concerned in the *emeute* of 1884 have been made
Chiefs of Departments. Pak Yong Ho, who has sojourned in Japan
for the past ten years being made Minister of the Department of
(Interior) Home Affairs, and Soh Kwan Pon—lately returned from
America—being given the Department of Law (Justice). One other
political suspect who has been in hiding in Korea during these ten
years, Yuhn Hoong Yul, is the newly appointed Inspector of Police.

This man's son, who will soon return from a ten years absence, was the first interpreter to this Legation.

The so-called "American Party" is represented by Pak Chung Yang, late Korean Minister at Washington, who retains his position as Minister of Education. Ye Wan Yong, Vice Minister of Foreign Affairs, and Ye Cha Yun, Vice Minister of Agriculture and Commerce, each served for some time in Washington as Korean Chargé d'Affaires, while Chung Kyung Won, Vice Minister of the Department of Justice (Law) was Korean Commissioner to the Worlds Fair at Chicago.

Kim Ka Chin, Kwan Chai Hyun, and An Kyung Soo, Vice Ministers of Construction; the Army, and Finance, have each served as Korean Representative in Japan, and they have been the close friends and supporters of the Japanese in the recent movement for reform in Korea. They were given subordinate positions it is supposed with a view to arouse as little possible, at this stage, the class prejudice of this people, for these men are all illegitimate or concubines sons, and heretofore have been unable to associate on terms of equality with the true nobility. They are bright men however, as is often the case with men of their class, and they will probably continue to exert an increasing influence over Korean affairs.

Even the "Chinese Party" is represented by, notably, Ye Choong Ha, Vice Minister of the Department of Home Affairs, who accompanied the 2000 Chinese soldiers who went to An San in June and thus opened the present war.

The Tai Won Khuns (Ex-regents) party is represented by the old man's son, brother of the King, who as Minister of the Household will exert a considerable influence in the Palace.

On the 22nd of December, The Winter Solstice, according to the Korean calendar, His Majesty will go to his ancestral halls and swear before the tablets of his Ancestors, and before the Gods of Nature, to faithfully support the new constitution.

The Council which has for months past been drawing up reform measures, is now abolished.

With the sincere support of the Japanese this new cabinet should be able to do something to relieve the distress of their country.

JOHN M. B. SILL

NO. 84   Legation of the United States
                                        Seoul, Korea, Jan. 17, 1895

Secretary of State

Sir:

I have the honor to hand you enclosed a translation of the Oath
taken by the King of Korea, to support the new order of Government.
It was intended that this Oath should be taken on Dec. 22nd, but it
was not taken till Jan. 7th because of the King's illness.

                                        JOHN M. B. SILL

The Oath sworn (taken) at the Royal Temple by His Majesty the
King of Korea, while he worshipped (bowed) on the 12th, day of the
12th moon of the 503rd year of the foundation of Tah Chosen (Korea)

                                                    January 7th 1895

I

To give up all idea of any subjection to China and agree to labor
to firmly establish the Independence of Korea.

II

To arrange the Royal Succession in such a manner as to distinguish
clearly between the Heir and the next of kin.

III

To (His Majesty will) decide all political affairs in council with
his Cabinet in the Hall of Audience.

IV

Her Majesty the Queen, the Royal Secondary Wife (concubine)
and the Royal relations shall not interfere with such decisions.

V

Affairs of State and those of the Royal Household shall be sepa-
rated so as not to produce confusion.

VI

The duties and functions of the Ministry and Departments shall be
defined in a clear and intelligible manner.

VII

No taxes shall be collected from the subjects of the Kingdom, except in regular order and by just and legal enactments.

VIII

The Department of Finance shall have charge of the collection of taxes and the disbursement of moneys for the expenses of State.

IX

The expenses of the Royal Household shall be reduced and arranged first, as an example for the different Departments and the lesser officials.

X

All the expenses of the Royal Household and of all offices and Departments shall be computed for one year in advance, and a budget made of the total expenses of State.

XI

The most intelligent of the young men shall be sent to foreign countries to be educated in art, literature and science.

XII

All the Officers of the Army must be educated in the school for Military Officers.

XIII

The laws governing subjects and criminals shall be clearly defined, and prisoners shall not be punished without being regularly tried. Good laws for the protection of persons and property shall be made.

XIV

All officers must be selected, from the various parts of the country, for their ability and regardless of family.

Secretary of State

Sir:

Referring to my No. 74, Dec. 18, in which I informed you of the appointment of a cabinet; the organization of the new government, and my subsequent letters, notably Nos. 84, 85 & 91, I have now the honor to wait upon you further with an account of the general political dead-lock now in force at this Court.

This Cabinet, above mentioned was inharmonious from start. Pak Yong Ho, Minister for Home Affairs, seemed unable to bear moderately the honors suddenly thrust upon him. He has been a destitute refugee in Japan for the past ten years and was forced upon this Government by the Japanese. He for a time intrigued with the Tai Won Khun, but the Queen who is very clever, soon won him over to her side till be became quite her tool. She soon began pitting him against his friends and his friends against him, so that now I hear he has refused to accede to certain great concessions for railroads recently proposed by Count Inouye. In fact this Pak has assumed a position almost of a dictator but has not foresight enough to avoid the mistakes that a weak man in such a position would be likely to make. He has angered the staunch loyalists and the anti-Japanese people. He fell out with the other members of the Cabinet, and now he is in danger of being deserted by the Japanese who raised him, less than three months ago, from the position of an assassin, hated and feared by His Majesty and the Government, for his past crimes, to the high position he now occupies.

The Minister of Finance—Uh Yung Chun; of Foreign Affairs, —Kim Yun Sik; the Prime Minister, —Kim Hong Jip, and the Secretary of the Cabinet, —Yon Kill Chun, who was educated in Boston, are of the Tai Won Khun's party. There are other factions in the Cabinet, but the above combination is the strongest and they have been plotting serious mischief. Letters were intercepted from the Tai Won Khun to the insurrectionists in the country, wherein he was found to be arranging for a general assassination of the officials opposed to him.

These people cannot differ politically and be good friends at the same time, and two weeks ago the various factions were not on speaking terms one with the other.

On the 5th February Count Inouye assembled the Cabinet and

lectured them soundly, whereupon they all handed in their resignations. I am privately informed that this was what Inouye desired, hoping in that way to get rid of the objectionable members and make Pak Yung Ho Prime Minister. He changed his mind, however, doubtless because of the marked disaffection of Pak, and sent a letter to the King telling him not to accept these resignations. The King complied naturally, but was much puzzled by Count Inouye's change of front.

While all this was going on the Departments were closed and no business was transacted for ten days. In the meantime however, the letter from the King's father to the insurrectionists mentioned above, was discovered, and arrests began to be made on all sides, two of the would-be assassins, caught all but red handed, in order to avoid giving testimony inflicted severe injuries upon themselves; one bit his tongue off, and the other cut his throat badly in an attempt at suicide.

The rumors of these disturbances at the capital increase the disorder in the interior. Soldiers sent to suppress the Tong Haks, or rebels, have wantonly killed women and children, burned villages, stolen the last remaining effects of the people and arrested the defenseless ones who remained in the village when the real offenders fled. These have been brought to Seoul as "chiefs of the Tong Haks," here to undergo indescribable torture by way of examination, for the old methods are still followed and, with Japan in full power here, we have, during the past month, had heads of supposed Tong Haks erected on poles on the principal streets, while their bodies lay outside the gate where they were thrown to the dogs. All these acts of arrest and punishment have been countenanced by Japan and in the presence of her police and soldiery with the Korean police and soldiers.

Meantime the King insists confidentially that he has been given good reason to believe that Russia intends soon to come to his assistance, and since seeing the telegraphic news of joint action on the part of Russia, England and France, for the restoration of peace, I am inclined to believe that the King has been rightly informed.

Hatred toward the Japanese, always intense and hereditary, has grown more and more bitter, and the people are in a condition to welcome a conqueror of some other than this detested nation whose historic connection with Korea is written in blood. The placing in supreme power of the ex-assassins of 1884 only aggravates the trouble. The Koreans cannot believe the Japanese to be sincere in their professions of good will.

In conclusion I should perhaps mention an unfortunate incident that, while not of a political nature, may affect the situation of foreigners in this troubled city. I refer to the ravishing of an honest but poor Korean woman by drunken Russian soldiers. These men caught the poor woman in the street, pushed her into a shop and outraged her. Much excitement prevailed for a time and an American lady was insulted on the street, soon after, for the first time.

The Russian authorities are giving the matter their full attention and justice will doubtless be meted out.

JOHN M. B. SILL

NO. 107   *Confidential*   Legation of the United States
Seoul, Korea, April 17, 1895

Secretary of State

Sir:

I have the honor to hand you enclosed a translation of the appropriations laid down by the new Government under the direction of the Japanese, as suitable for the Royal Household.

I am fortunate in being able to secure a copy of this, and as it came to me in a private manner I must ask that it be not made public. I hope in the same manner to secure copies of the budgets and regulations for the other Departments of the new Government.

These appropriations and regulations for the Royal Household are very distasteful to His Majesty and it is the opinion of my European Colleagues that the Japanese would have done better had they given the King a large lump sum from which he would have to pay the expenses of his household rather than to order for him a salary of $5,000 silver, even though $500,000 is given for the whole expense of conducting the Royal Household. Formerly the Palace was supplied very generously by special tribute in kind, from each province, and in addition, His Majesty had the revenue from the sale of the red ginseng, which amounted to over $200,000 per annum. This sum he has of late placed in bank in Hong Kong, where I am told he now has nearly $1,000,000 in silver at interest.

The Japanese have not been particularly generous in their recent proposals here. In my No. 103, Apl 3, I mentioned the subject of the recent loan which I reported on more fully in my Consular Series No. 15, Apl 6. Some time ago Count Inouye demanded a franchise for all rail-roads in Korea for a period of 50 years; of telegraph lines for

25 years, and of posts for 5 years, with certain one sided mining franchises. A rail-road was surveyed between Chemulpo and Seoul, and work was to have been begun early in the Spring, but nothing has as yet been done upon this line. The Koreans unexpectedly developed a quiet but stubborn determination not to swear away all these rights and priviledges [sic], and in view of the peace negotiations and the avowed intention of certain powers, notably Russia and England, to insist on the privileges accorded by the "most favored nation clause", the Japanese have evidently felt the risk of probable complications and seem not to care to invest any great amount of actual capital here just now.

The Ex-refugee Pak, now Minister of Home Affairs and virtual dictator, is giving the Japanese a great deal of trouble. He seems to have a sincere regard for his own country and resents Japan's attempts to take everything to herself.

Meantime the Japanese have placed advisers and assistants of their own nationality in every department of the Government, and they have tried, and are still trying, earnestly to expel all other foreign employees, especially the few Americans now employed by Korea. The King however is doing all he can to retain these Americans and will doubtless succeed.

As I mentioned to you once before, the Russian Minister is reported as holding out certain inducements to Korea, promising relief of an indeffinite [sic] nature within a short time. The Koreans certainly expect practical intervention soon by Russia England and France.

JOHN M. B. SILL

NO. 110

Legation of the United States
Seoul, Korea, May 10, 1895

Secretary of State

Sir:

In connection with the subject of Korean Reforms, I now enclose a copy of a translation of an official order to the provincial magistrates, issued by the Minister of the Home Department, correcting certain abuses and relieving the condition of the people.

Through the influence of this same Minister, 130 selected young men have just been sent to Japan to be educated.

I may also mention in this connection that the law forbidding Buddhist Priests from entering the gates of the city has been abolished and priests may, and now do enjoy the liberties of the city.

JOHN M. B. SILL

NO. 121   Legation of the United States
                                              Seoul, Korea, June 25, 1895

Secretary of State

Sir:

I have the honor to hand you enclosed the Budget of the Korean Government for the current year.

While this is the work of the Japanese, it is interesting in being the first real budget arranged for this Government.

JOHN M. B. SILL

NO. 128   Legation of the United States
                                              Seoul, Korea, July 27, 1895

Secretary of State

Sir:

I have the honor to advise you of the return to Seoul of the Japanese Minister Count Inouye, who was accorded an audience on the 25th instant. The audience lasted from 1:30 P.M. till 9 P.M. and was characterized by a great desire on the part of Count Inouye to please and concilliate their Majesties. In fact it would seem that Japan has discovered that her harsh measures were forcing the Koreans into friendly alliance with other powers, and that they desire now to win the confidence and regard of the Koreans. From Count Inouye's reported utterances it is evident they are glad to be rid of Pak Yong Hyo, and that he will not figure again in Korean Politics.

JOHN M. B. SILL

NO. 151   Legation of the United States
                                            Seoul, Korea, Sept. 25, 1895

Secretary of State

Sir:

I have the honor to report the return to Korea on yesterday of Min Yung Chün, commonly known as "the Great Min".

Of late years this man became the leader of the powerful Min family of which the Queen is a member. Under his sway the country fell into such a state because of official corruption, that a cause was furnished for the late war between China and Japan. When the troops of the latter country occupied Seoul this man fled. He was searched for but made his escape to China where he has lived for the past year at Hong Kong.

When Count Inouye changed his policy, see my No. 146, Sept. 18, he advised Her Majesty to call this man back to Korea. This advice seems to have been quickly followed.

                                                            H. N. ALLEN

NO. 156   Legation of the United States
                                            Seoul, Korea, Oct. 10, 1895

Secretary of State

Sir:

On yesterday I telegraphed you the news of the overturn of this Government, the murder of the Queen, and kindred topics, (Enclosure 1.) I have delayed this despatch as long as possible that I might be able to give you the facts as clearly as possible, which I now have the honor to do.

In my No. 155, Oct. 7, I mentioned the disturbances between the soldiers and the police. On the morning of the 8th instant, these soldiers escorted the Tai Won Khun and his eldest son from their suburban house to the Palace, a distance of 3 miles. It is said an escort of Japanese regular soldiers attended them, but as no foreigner saw this it may possibly be a mistake. On arrival at the Palace some of the soldiers scaled the walls and opened the gates. The guards fired at them and the fire was returned, 6 or 8 being killed, chiefly if not altogether on the side of the guards. These attacking soldiers then took possession of the Palace. They were led by Japanese, heavily armed with swords and pistols, but in civilians dress. Reliable testimony now comes in play as these men were seen by General Wm. McDye, an American of excellent reputation, as well as by Mr. A. J. S. Sabatin a Russian employed with Gen'l Dye in the military service of Korea. These gentlemen were in charge of the Palace guard, and did what they could to keep out the intruders. Mr. Sabatin was swept to one side by the frightened guard who fled when the invaders began pouring in. He was roughly handled by some of these evil looking Japanese and feared for his life, but hearing one of them, who acted as leader, speak English, he asked and obtained protection. He was placed near a post in a court off the womens quarters of the Palace and a sentry stationed near him. He says the Korean soldiers were drawn up in three lines and remained there while the Japanese went about looking into windows and enquiring where the Queen was. A Korean man being so accosted referred the Japanese to him (Sabatin) and the leader then asked him in English to point out the Queen. He could not do so and said as much. While he was stationed here however he saw these Japanese drag three ladies through a window by the hair, but he did not see them killed.

General Dye was in another enclosure and did not see this but he did see squads of regular Japanese soldiers arriving in bodies of about 12 each. They did not take part in this lawlessness but they neither stopped it or arrested the perpetrators.

For what took place inside the Queen's apartments I am indebted for my information to the Second Prince, who got the story from one of the Court Ladies who was an eye witness.

This lady says that hearing the disturbance she and her companions assembled in the Queen's room, where they were joined by the Minister of the Household—Ye Kyung Chik. Some Japanese forced their way into this room and the Minister tried to shield the Queen but was cut down and killed by a Japanese, with a sword. The Queen fearing for her life called out that she was simply a visitor there, but as the others all said the same a Japanese threw the Queen down, jumped upon her breast with his shoes three times and then stabbed her. Three other ladies were killed at the same time. This lady further says that the Japanese then took the body of the Queen to a little grove near by where it was afterwards seen being burned, by a runner of the Palace.

A Korean Colonel named Hyun In Tak, who alone kept on his uniform and fought while his brother officers tore off their uniforms and fled, broke away from his Japanese captors and rushed into the

Queen's apartments to rescue her. (He saved her life in 1882) but he was knocked down, bound and badly beaten. He saw the Queen run into another room but did not see her killed. This man is now a refugee at this Legation and comparing his accounts with the others I am forced to believe that the Queen was murdered by these Japanese ruffians and that her body was burned by prearranged plan to conceal the crime. I shall hold to this belief until I am convinced of my error by seeing the Queen alive.

The three ladies killed at the same time doubtless owe their fate to a fancied resemblance to the Queen, by the assassins who intended to make a complete job of it.

I was awakened by the firing at 5 o'clock and at the same time Hon. Ye Pum Chin, late Acting Minister of the Household and then Minister of Public Works, came to me in a very excited state, having been sent to me by the King at the first alarm to beg me to come to the Palace. I learned afterwards that a messenger was also sent to the Japanese Minister at the same time. No other representatives being so appealed to, I at once got ready and started but stopped on the way to consult with the Russian Representative Mr. Waeber, and got him to accompany me.

I thought we would accomplish more by going first to the Japanese Minister and getting him to accompany us, feeling sure that he would not countenance such acts on the part of his people. We only knew at the time that Japanese civilians and Korean soldiers were attacking the Palace and did not know that the Japanese Minister had been called.

We found that Viscount Miura had just left for the Palace, so we followed him. Near the Palace and also inside its walls we met more than 30 very evil looking Japanese with disordered clothes, long swords and sword canes, coming away. While near the King's quarters we met a well-dressed portly Japanese who answered well the description given us by Mr. Sabatin of the leader of the invading party. I should here mention that we met Mr. Sabatin at the Russian Legation before starting. He had escaped and hastened to report to his Minister.

Colonel Hong who saved the Queen's life once before, and who was thoroughly loyal to her though in charge of the insurgent soldiers, was cut down and killed because he halted his soldiers and refused to attack the Palace. It is said he was cut down by a Japanese officer. This was only seen by Koreans but it is generally believed to be true.

While we were in the Palace the eldest son of the Tai Won Khun,

and elder brother of the King, was appointed Minister of the Household in place of the murdered Ye Kyung Chik.

We were kept from seeing the King on one silly pretext after another
for two hours, while we sat with General Dye and other foreign employees and gained information. We finally went boldly into the King's
apartments to the great relief of the latter. We found him in the most
abject terror, uncertain as to the fate of the Queen, and surrounded
by his enemies—the bitterest of all being his own father.

We gave him such consolation as we could and then saw Viscount
Miura who agreed to call a Diplomatic meeting in the afternoon to
inquire into the events of the morning.

I enclose a copy of my notes of this meeting, also a copy of the
despatch received from the Foreign Office giving an account of the
same events. I should add that the Minister for Foreign Affairs is a
loyal follower of the Tai Won Khun.

Before attempting to account for these occurrences I must call your
attention to the fact that Viscount Miura says he did not send his
soldiers to the relief of the King until he was awakened by the messenger from the Palace announcing the disturbance and calling for
help. While General Dye states that he saw these regular troops
arriving in good order just after the invaders had entered and all of
the lawlessness was in full swing, I must also go ahead a little and
state that on the 8th instant, the day of the outbreak, a number of
Cabinet officers were removed and their places filled by men of very
strong Tai Won Khun and Japanese sympathies, most of whom had
been denounced by Count Inouye as thoroughly bad men with whom
he would have no more dealings.

The presence of the regular Japanese troops at the Palace before
Viscount Miura could have had time to send them seems to indicate
a fore knowledge on the part of the Japanese military officers of what
was to take place. The appointment of these men to office would
indicate that the Japanese had again taken up the Tai Won Khun party,
contrary to the avowed policy of Count Inouye. Though I must call
your attention to the insistence with which Count Inouye urged, and
finally obtained, the appointment of Kim Hong Gip, the chief tool of
the Tai Won Khun, as Prime Minister, see my despatch No. 146, Sept.
18, page 13.

I cannot believe that Count Inouye was simply acting a farce during
his last two months here, or that these terrible acts were planned by
Viscount Miura. An explanation may be that the Tai Won Khun party
angered and alarmed by the return of the Mins to power, see my

despatches No. 151, Sept. 25, and No. 152, Oct. 3, and taking advantage of the disaffection of the Japanese-drilled Korean soldiers, made this plan with the Tai Won Khun and hired a lot of lawless Japanese, such as are only too plenty [sic] in Seoul, to assist them by leading these mutinous troups and by killing the Queen.

At first the Japanese Minister would not admit that there could have been any such Japanese so engaged, but after hearing the overwhelming testimony at the Diplomatic meeting, of their presence, the Japanese Consul on yesterday stated to the British and German Consuls that there were a few lawless Japanese who joined the Tai Won Khun's procession and entered the Palace to see the fight. He further stated that the murders were committed by Koreans dressed as Japanese in European clothes—a statement too absurd to need contradiction.

The Japanese do not admit that the Queen is dead, neither do the followers of the Tai Won Khun, but the evidence is all against them and they can only prove the truth of their statements by showing her alive.

The officers of known loyalty to the Queen have been hunted down and imprisoned, with the exception of a few refugees most of whom are at this Legation. I found them in my bedroom on my return from the Palace on the morning of the 8th instant. We have no guard and they could not be kept out. I cannot drive them out to their death now.

I have kept Capt. Folger of the U.S.S. Yorktown at Chemulpo, fully posted, and he has a guard ready to send me when necessity shall demand. I am not disposed to send for the guard as long as the populace remains quiet. Though His Majesty in a whisper urged me to get a guard, when I saw him again on yesterday, he knows a guard here at this Legation can be of no assistance to him, but he doubtless thinks that the coming of American Marines to Seoul might cause his enemies to pause. I shall ask for the guard when I think that safety of the Legation demands it.

The Tai Won Khun hates foreigners. He may act with the Japanese for a time but such a union cannot be permanent. It is doubtful if the small Japanese force now present in Seoul will be able to preserve order.

The Tai Won Khun is virtually the ruler now, and there is no one strong enough now to cope with him. The Queen has been much maligned. We have long appreciated her as a strong character the chief supporter of the King. Count Inouye came around to this view also and it was his apparent intention to work through her as the only sure means of bringing about a better state of things in Korea. The

American Community here feel deeply grieved and feel that the surest support to progressive ideas has been removed. This plot is much the same as the one Pak Yung Hyo was accused of (see No. 123, July 9) this succeeded through greater secrecy.

H. N. ALLEN

NO. 158   Legation of the United States
Seoul Korea Oct. 13, 1895

Secretary of State

Sir:

I have telegraphed you today and now have the honor to hand you the confirmation of the same.

In my No. 157 of yesterday, I enclosed a copy of a letter from the Korean Foreign Office containing a decree said to have been issued by the King, deposing and degrading the Queen. At a meeting of the Diplomatic Body, exclusive of the Japanese Representative, it was decided that this was not the Act of the King, the official publication not having the King's seal or signature. Furthermore we had evidence enough to warrant our belief that the Royal Seal could be put to anything. We therefore agreed to reply to this letter as well as to the one, a copy of which I enclosed in my No. 156, Oct. 10, Enclosure 3, which purported to be an explanation of the events of the 8th inst. I now enclose a copy of the reply we agreed upon sending in. I may add here that I have been asked by a member of the Korean Government if the Representatives generally believed the statements made in these letters to be true. We do not and we say as much in our reply.

In explanation of my telegram I must say that the Japanese Minister here is in control of all the Japanese troops in this city. They could not have been up the most of the night under their officers preparing for and executing the coup d'état of the 8th inst. without his knowing it. Yet at 3 P.M. in that day he stated in a diplomatic meeting that the soldiers only went after he had been asked to send them by the King after the disturbance arose. As I have told you, Gen'l Dye, whose testimony is absolutely unquestionable, saw Japanese Regular troops leading the way into the Palace for the assassins and insurgents. And those troops witnessed the atrocities without making any attempt to prevent it. As this was at 3 oclock and Viscount Miura was called at 5 oclock, there is a great discrepancy between the facts and his statements. He also stated positively that Japanese troops did not accompany the Tai Won Khun to the Palace. The latter's eldest son assured me in an unguarded moment that they did. While General Dye asserts that he saw them entering the Palace, escorting the Tai Won Khun, at about 5:10 A.M.—they had travelled 3 English miles from the Tai Won Khun's suburban house previous to that. Again at this same meeting Viscount Miura denied that there were any such Japanese in civillians [sic] clothes at the Palace, as were described to him. Mr. Waeber and myself having called at his Legation a few minutes, not more than a half hour, after he had started for the Palace, followed him, and saw at least 30 of these men with long swords and disordered clothes returning from the Palace. He could not have missed them. Further a Secretary of the Foreign Office informed me that Viscount Miura had compelled the Minister for Foreign Affairs to write him a letter stating that the assassins of the 8th were Koreans in Japanese dress. Today however, under pressure from Tokio I am informed that the Japanese authorities now admit that irresponsible Japanese were implicated in the feat and they have therefore arrested 15 of them.

The Government is in the hands of five men of notoriously bad character who were brought to the fore by Mr. Otori a year ago last July and dropped by Count Inouye when he put aside the Tai Won Khun. The worst and most powerful of these men, next to the Tai Won Khun, is Cho He Yun, Minister of War and Inspector of Police, to which posts he was appointed on the morning of the 8th in place of the former incumbents who were dismissed and ordered to be arrested. This man 18 months ago was the most ordinary man of low position. I knew him well and never trusted him. He spoke Japanese and cultivated Mr. Otori, who put him in office.

This man has taken a very great dislike to General Dye. The latter was recommended to the Korean Government by Gen'l Sheridan, under instructions of the Dept. of State, in 1888. He is a graduate of West Point, has served the Khedive and was in charge of the Washington Police at one time. He is a brave man and a staunch gentleman. His word is most reliable. He was asked by His Majesty under arrangements made by Mr. Sill, last summer, to stay in the Palace all the time in charge of the Palace Guard. He was given assistants. He and one of these assistants, Mr. Sabatin, a Russian, witnessed many of the acts of the 8th as I have already told you. Their presence there is no longer desired by the new party. They have tried bribery and threats to get him out, he would not go unless the King ordered him to do so in the presence of his Representative. On yesterday it was arranged that His

Majesty should ask him in my presence to leave. I was privately informed by His Majesty in a whisper that he did not want him to go but was compelled to ask it. He asked me not to consent. The interview was held at 5 P.M. yesterday. Mr. Waeber was present, also General Dye, and Lieut. Knepper in charge of our guard, and Col. Cockerell of the N.Y. Herald. The King asked me to arrange for Gen'l Dye to leave the Palace now, as all was quiet and he was needed more at the War Office. I replied that Gen'l Dye was here by arrangements made by Mr. Sill, and that under the present circumstances I could not consent to his leaving the Palace without instruction from my Government. The Minister of War asked me to telegraph for instructions. I told him I would not do so. I would write and would not expect an answer for four months. He said he would consult with the Cabinet about it. I told him it was not necessary as my decision was final and anything he might say further would make no difference.

This has already had a good effect. This morning the Inspector of Police and the Minister of Education, friends of the Queen, and now refugees at this Legation have been officially pardoned. The Inspector of Police is the son-in-law of the Tai Won Khun, but they are bitter enemies. The Minister of Education is his brother.

In my telegram I asked you if I should recognize this Government. A part of the Cabinet are good men enough and were not in the recent plot, but they are now under the control of the five traitors mentioned above, who being backed by Japan and the Japanese officered Korean troops, are all powerful. In the interview cited above I think I declined to recognize the Minister of War, and I further declined to recognize the Cabinet as a whole in my reply to the Foreign Office, Enclosure 2.

I hear the Japanese Government is highly incensed at the recent occurrences here and are about to conduct a searching investigation into the facts. If they are fair and just, they will remove these men who can only be classed as murderers. If they do not remove them it is possible Russia may interfere. I mentioned in my telegram that Mr. Waeber had sent for a fleet. He now tells me that His Admiral telegraphed him that he is coming.

The people are taking up the cause of their murdered Queen. They look to the Foreign Powers whom they expect to put Japan out of Korea. But they are already rising to do the work themselves. We hear of two bands of 2000 each marching on Seoul, while every day the Japanese are receiving reinforcements from Chemulpo for their Legation.

H. N. ALLEN

Legation of the United States
                                          Seoul, Korea, Oct. 17, 1895

Secretary of State

Sir:

Continuing the subject of my despatches Nos 156, 157, 158 & 159, on the Tai Won Khun Revolution, I have now the honor to inform you that yesterdays Official Gazette announced that a new Queen was to be at once selected, and we also learned that the Cabinet was about to raise the Kings title to that of Emperor. As usual I made my regular daily visit to His Majesty, being accompanied by Mr. Waeber, Russian Representative with the officer and his guard. Mr. Lefevre, French, with the Captain and Lieutenant of the French cruiser "Isle," the French Bishop and two U.S. Naval Officers attached to our own guard. According to private suggestions of His Majesty and by pre-arrangement, we stated what we had heard regarding the proposed new title of emperor and stated that while we would be glad to see any action taken that might increase His Majesty's honors we must urge him not to consent to any such change at this present time of trouble. We then referred the matter of the selection of a new Queen. We stated that we had been accredited to this court with the Queen by His Majestys side. Where she might be now was a matter of deepest interest to ourselves and to our Governments and we must protest any such present action as that announced in the Official Gazette, that the decree deposing the Queen we had declined to recognize and we could not quietly witness the heaping of further indignities upon her. This was most satisfactory to His Majesty and we hope it may have as good an effect as our previous firm stand on other questions. Already we see a weakening of the opposition. I referred to the resignation of the Minister of the Interior, Pak Chung Yang. Other conservative members of the Cabinet have shown an unmistakeable dislike to the action of the five traitors who now rule, and we may expect further resignations, while Kim Ka Chin, one of the leading conspirators has gotten himself appointed Minister to Japan, to get out of the country. He declined this position some months ago.

Another decree has been issued raising the missing Queen from the position of a common woman to that of a Royal Concubine, out of regard for the filial piety of the Crown Prince. This however is strange reward since it is believed that, according to Korean law, the

Crown Prince cannot remain in his position now that he is the son of a concubine unless the Cabinet make him a legitimate son.

The Japanese Commissioner of Investigation arrived here night before last. The chief official called on Mr. Waeber yesterday, and the latter gave him unquestionable evidence that the Tai Won Khun was escorted to and into the Palace by regular Japanese soldiers; that such soldiers preceded the assassins and the insurgent Korean troops into the Palace, and witnessed the atrocities committed by civilian Japanese. We hear today that some of the latter have been arrested and that the military officers will be court-martialed.

We also know that a Japanese ship entered Chemulpo suddenly on the morning of the 8th and took away a lot of the civilians.

H. N. ALLEN

Telegram   Seoul, Korea
                                                         October 26, 1895

Olney

Washington

Japanese officials deeply implicated in murder of the Queen. Japanese Minister and officers of his legation and army have been sent to Japan. Count Inouye is coming to Seoul as special Ambassador. The King is under strict duress; his life in peril. I do not recognize decrees forced from him. Allen's conduct of affairs excellent.

SILL

Telegram   Seoul, Korea
                                                         November 9, 1895

Olney

Washington

Japanese are not moving to restore status upset by themselves. The King is still in grievous peril and under duress of conspirators. The representatives of England, Russia, France and myself are urging Japanese to protect the King and restore status by necessary temporary force.

SILL

Legation of the United States
Seoul, Korea, Nov. 10, 1895

Secretary of State

Sir:

I have the honor to confirm my telegram of last night as per reading appended.

My reason for asking your approval in this matter is as follows.

The Japanese Minister has informed us that since the events of the
8th October, when Japanese troops were put in motion by the Japanese Minister for a lawless purpose, the control of Japanese troops
at Seoul has been taken away from the Minister and their troops
stationed here can only be moved by the consent of the Japanese
Cabinet. That the Cabinet refuses to allow the Japanese guard to
enter the Palace except on the direct approval of the Foreign Powers
represented here. I gave my consent to this necessary measure but
found they would only accept such consent upon my receiving the
instructions I have asked for, from you.

JOHN M. B. SILL

Reading of telegram of November 9, 1895

Japan will restore status, using temporary force if approved by foreign
powers Russian Government have telegraphed approval. Answer is expected from others. I hope you will approve. Answer by telegraph.

Telegram   Washington
November 11, 1895

John M. B. Sill

Intervention in the political
concerns of Korea is not
among your functions, and
is forbidden by diplomatic
instruction 64.

RICHARD OLNEY

Appendixes

AMERICAN DIPLOMATIC PERSONNEL TO 1895[*]

REPRESENTATIVE IN KOREA	SECRETARY OF STATE	PRESIDENT
George F. Seward[1] N.Y., Jly 27, '68	William H. Seward N.Y., Mar 6, '61– Mar 3, '69	Abraham Lincoln Andrew Johnson
Frederick F. Low[1] Cal., 1870	Hamilton Fish N.Y., Mar 17, '69– Mar 12, '77	Ulysses S. Grant
None	Wm. M. Evarts N.Y., Mar 12, '77– Mar 7, '81	Rutherford B. Hayes
R. W. Shufeldt[1] Cal., Nov 14, '81	James G. Blaine Me., Mar 7, '81– Dec 19, '81	James A. Garfield
Lucius H. Foote[2] Cal., May 13, '83– June 12, '86	Frederick T. Freling-huysen, N.J., Dec 19, '81–Mar 6, '85	Garfield Chester A. Arthur
George C. Foulk[3] Penn., Jan 12, '85– June 12, '86	Frelinghuysen	Arthur
William H. Parker[4] D.C., June 12, '86– Sept 1, '86	Thomas F. Bayard Del., Mar 7, '85– Mar 6, '89	Grover Cleveland

---

[*] Adapted from Tyler Dennett, *Americans in Eastern Asia* (New York, 1922). Inclusive dates of the Ministers in Korea refer to the period in which they actually assumed responsibility, not the dates of their official appointment.

[1,2,3] See page 372.

REPRESENTATIVE IN KOREA	SECRETARY OF STATE	PRESIDENT
George C. Foulk[5] Sept 1, '86– Dec 11, '86	Bayard	Cleveland
W. W. Rockhill[3] Penn., Dec 11, '86– April 1, '87	Bayard	Cleveland
Hugh A. Dinsmore[4] Ark., Apl 1, '87– May 26, '90	Bayard	Cleveland
William O. Bradley[4] Ky., Apl 1, '89– Declined	James G. Blaine Me., Mar 7, '89– June 4, '92	Benjamin Harrison
Augustine Heard[4] Mass., May 26, '90– Jly 1, '93	Blaine	Harrison
	John W. Foster Ind., June 29, '92– Feb 23, '93	Harrison
Joseph R. Herod[3] July 1, '93– Aug 31, '93	Walter Q. Gresham Ill., Mar 6, '93– May 28, '95	Grover Cleveland
Horace N. Allen[3] Ohio, Aug 31, '93 Apl 30, '94	Gresham	Cleveland
John M. B. Sill[4] Mich., Apl 30, '94– through 1895	Gresham Richard Olney	Cleveland Cleveland

---

[1] Commissioned to make a treaty.

[2] Envoy Extraordinary and Minister Plenipotentiary.

[3] Charge d'Affaires ad interim. Only those Charge d'Affaires are indicated here who served in the event of there not being a higher responsible officer available. Periods when the Minister was on vacation or other temporary leaves are not cited.

[4] Minister Resident and Consul General.

[5] Charge d'Affaires.

APPENDIX B

KOREAN DIPLOMATIC PERSONNEL TO 1895[*]

MINISTER PLENIPOTEN- TIARY TO THE U. S.	FOREIGN OFFICE PRESIDENT	KING
Min Yŏng-ik[1] 閔泳翊 July 14, '83	Min Yŏng-mok 閔泳穆 Feb 19, '83 (Date of appointment)	Kojong 高宗
	Kim Pyŏng-si 金炳始 Apl 8, '84	
	Kim Hong-jip 金弘集 Oct 23, '84	
	Sŏ Kwang-bŏm[2] 徐光範 Dec 4, '84	
	Cho Pyŏng-ho 趙秉鎬 Dec 10, '84	
	Kim Yun-sik 金允植 Jan 22, '85	

[*] These data have been derived from a comparison of the diplomatic correspondence with:

Chōsen-shi 朝鮮史 (History of Korea).
Keijō: Chōsen Sōtokufu, 1938. Series No. 6, Vol. 4.
Yi Sŏn-gŭn 朝鮮穆督府 (ed.), *Hanguk sa* [Modern Period] 韓国史 (History of Korea). Seoul: Ŭlyu Munhwasa, 1961.

[1,2] See page 375.

MINISTER PLENIPOTEN- TIARY TO THE U. S.	FOREIGN OFFICE PRESIDENT	KING
		高宗
	Sǒ Sang-u[2] 徐相雨 May 19, '86	
	Sǒ Sang-u 徐相雨 July 20, '87	
Pak Chǒng-yang[3] 朴定陽 Nov 9, '87	Cho Pyǒng-sik 趙秉式 Sept 20, '87	
	Yi Chung-ch'il[2] 李重七 Sept 5, '88	
	Cho Pyǒng-jik[2] 趙秉櫻 Oct 16, '88	
	Min Chong-muk 閔種默 August, 1889	
	Yi Yong-jik[2] 李容植 Oct 26, '92	
	Cho Pyǒng-jik 趙秉櫻 Nov 11, '92	
Pak Chǒng-yang 朴定陽	Nam Chǒng-ch'ǒl 南廷哲 May 13, '93	
(returns from U.S., March 16, 1893)	Kim Hak-chin[2] 金鶴鎭 Dec 2, '93	

---

[2], [3] See page 375.

MINISTER PLENIPOTEN- TIARY TO THE U. S.	FOREIGN OFFICE PRESIDENT	KING
		高宗
Yi Sŭng-su[4] 李承壽 Yi Sŭng-su 李承壽 Dec 30, '93	Cho Pyŏng-jik 趙秉稷 Jan 2, '94	
	Kim Hak-chin[2] 金鶴鎮 Apl 23, '94	
	Kim Ka-jin[2] 金嘉鎮 July 26, '94	
	Kim Yun-sik 金允植 Jan 12, '95	

---

[1] Min Yŏng-ik headed an initial good-will and treaty ratification mission to the United States in 1883. This represented a significant development in Korean-American intercourse, but Min was not empowered to establish diplomatic offices in the United States.

[2] Vice-president acting as President.

[3] Established the first Korean diplomatic office in the United States, serving as Envoy Extraordinary and Minister Plenipotentiary.

[4] Charge d'Affaires ad interim.

Index to Documents

1. THE EQUIVOCAL SINO-KOREAN RELATIONSHIP

2. YÜAN SHIH-K'AI'S PROTESTATIONS OF A PRIVILEGED POSITION

3. RECALL OF GEORGE C. FOULK

4. OCCUPATION OF HSIM HSIN CHANG

7. ". . . THE SUBJECT OF KOREAN INDEPENDENCE"

8. U. S. MILITARY INSTRUCTORS

10. TRADE AND COMMERCE

11. CHRISTIAN MISSIONARIES

12. BRITISH INTERESTS

13. RUSSIAN CONCESSIONS

14. AMERICAN POLICY VIS-À-VIS JAPAN

15. KOREAN-JAPANESE PROBLEMS

16. TONGHAK REBELLION

17. ASSASSINATION OF KIM OK-KYUN

18. SINO-JAPANESE CONFRONTATION

20. MURDER OF QUEEN MIN